German-English
English-German
Dictionary

GEDDES &
GROSSET

© 1998 Geddes & Grosset Ltd, David Dale House,
New Lanark, ML11 9DJ

ISBN 1 85534 325 8

Printed and bound in France by Maury Eurolivres

2 4 6 8 10 9 8 7 5 3 1

Abbreviations/Abkürzung

acc	accusative	Akkusativ
adj	adjective	Adjektiv
adv	adverb	Adverb
art	article	Artikel
auto	automobile	Automobil
aux	auxiliary	Hilfs-
bot	botany	Botanik
chem	chemistry	Chemie
col	colloquial term	umgangssprachlich
com	commerce	Handel
compd	in compounds	Kompositum
comput	computers	Informatik
conj	conjunction	Konjunktion
dat	dative	Dativ
etw	something	etwas
excl	exclamation	Ausruf
f	feminine noun	Femininum
fam	colloquial term	umgangssprachlich
fig	figurative use	übertragen
gr	grammar	Grammatik
jdm	somebody (*dat*)	jemandem
jdn	somebody	jemanden
imp	impersonal	unpersönlich
inform	computers	Informatik
interj	interjection	Ausruf
invar	invariable	unveränderlich
irr	irregular	unregelmäßig
jur	law term	Rechtswesen
law	law term	Rechtswesen
ling	linguistics	Sprachwissenschaft
m	masculine noun	Maskulinum
mar	marine term	Marine
mat, math	mathematics	Mathematik
med	medicine	Medizin
mil	military term	militärisch
mus	music	Musik
n	noun	Substantiv
n	neuter	Neutrum

nom	nominative	Nominativ
pej	pejorative	abschätzig
pl	plural	Plural
pn	pronoun	Pronomen
prep	preposition	Präposition
rad	radio	radio
rail	railway	Eisenbahn
rel	relative	Relativ-
relig	religion	Religion
sl	slang	Slang
teat	theatre	Theater
tec	technology	Technik
TV	television	Fernsehen
vb	verb	Verb
vi	intransitive verb	intransitives Verb
vr	reflexive verb	reflexives Verb
vt	transitive verb	transitives Verb
zo, zool	zoology	Zoologie

German-English

A

ab *prep* from:—*adv* away; down; off.
abändern *vt* to alter.
Abänderung *f* alteration.
abbrechen *vt vi* to break off; to stop.
abbringen *vt* to divert; to dissuade.
Abbruch *m* breaking off; demolition.
abdanken *vi* to resign.
Abdankung *f* resignation.
abdecken *vt* to uncover; to clear (table).
abdrehen *vt vi* to turn off.
Abdrift *f* drift.
Abend *m* evening:—**guten ~** good evening.
Abendblatt *n* evening paper.
Abendessen *n* dinner.
Abendmahl *n* Holy Communion.
abends *adv* in the evening(s).
Abenteuer *n* adventure.
abenteuerlich *adj* adventurous.
aber *conj* but, however.
Aberglaube *m* superstition.
abergläubisch *adj* superstitious.
abermals *adv* again.
abfahren *vi* to leave; to cover (distance):—*vt* to remove.
Abfahrt *f* departure; descent.
Abfall *m* waste; slope; decline.
Abfalleimer *m* rubbish bin.
Abfalleisen *n* scrap iron.
abfallend *adj* sloping.
abfertigen *vt* to dispatch; to clear (customs); to serve (customer).
Abfertigung *f* dispatch, clearance.
abfliegen *vi* to take off, fly off.
abfließen *vi* to flow away.
Abflug *m* departure, takeoff.
Abfluß *m* outflow.
Abfuhr *m* removal; defeat.

abfüllen *vt* to fill.
Abgabe *f* delivery; pass (ball); tax.
abgabenfrei *adj* duty-free.
Abgang *m* departure.
Abgas *n* exhaust (gas).
abgeben *vt* to hand over; to pass (ball).
abgehen *vi* to leave.
abgelegen *adj* isolated.
Abgelegenheit *f* remoteness.
Abgeordnete(r) *f(m)* deputy, member of parliament.
abgesehen von apart from.
abgesondert *adj* separate.
Abgott *m* idol.
Abgötterei *f* idolatry.
abgöttisch *adj* idolatrous.
abgrenzen *vt* to demarcate.
Abgrund *m* abyss.
abgründig *adj* abysmal.
Abhang *m* slope.
abhängen *vt* to take down; to detach:— *vi* to hang up (telephone):—**~ von** depend on.
abhängig *adj* dependent; sloping.
Abhängigkeit *f* dependence.
abholen *vt* to collect; to meet.
Abitur *n* German school-leaving examination.
Abkehr *f* turning away; departure.
abkehren *vt vr* turn away.
Abkommen *n* agreement.
Abkömmling *m* descendant.
abkürzen *vt* to abbreviate.
Abkürzung *f* abbreviation.
abladen *vt* to unload.
Ablage *f* storeroom.
ablagern *vt* to store.
Ablauf *m* drain; course; expiry.

ablaufen *vi* to drain away; to happen; to expire.

ablehnen *vt vi* to refuse.

ablehnend *adj* critical.

Ablehnung *f* refusal.

Abnahme *f* removal; purchase; decrease.

abnehmbar *adj* removable.

abnehmen *vt* to remove; to purchase: —*vi* to decrease.

Abnehmer *m* purchaser, customer.

Abneigung *f* reluctance, dislike.

abnutzen *vt* to wear out.

Abnutzung *f* wear.

Abonnement *n* subscription.

Abonnent(in) *m(f)* subscriber.

abonnieren *vt* to subscribe.

Abordnung *f* delegation.

Abort *m* lavatory.

abräumen *vt* to clear up.

abrechnen *vt* to deduct:—*vi* to settle.

Abrechnung *f* settlement; account.

Abreise *f* departure.

abreisen *vi* to leave.

abrüsten *vi* to disarm.

Abrüstung *f* disarmament.

Absage *f* refusal; cancellation.

absagen *vi vt* to call off.

Absatz *m* sales; paragraph; ledge, landing; heel.

abschaffen *vt* to abolish.

Abschaffung *f* abolition.

abschalten *vt vi* to switch off.

Abscheu *m* loathing.

abscheulich *adj* horrible.

Abschied *m* departure:—~ **nehmen** take one's leave.

Abschlag *m* reduction.

abschlagen *vt* to knock off; to take down; to refuse.

abschlägig *adj* negative.

abschließen *vt* to lock; to conclude.

abschließend *adj adv* final(ly).

Abschluß *m* conclusion.

Abschnitt *m* section.

abschreiben *vt* to copy; to write off; to write down, deduct.

Abschreibung *f* depreciation, write-off.

Abschrift *f* copy.

abseits *adv* aside, apart, offside.

Absicht *f* intention.

absichtlich *adj adv* deliberate(ly), intentional(ly).

absolut *adj* absolute.

Abstand *m* distance.

Abstinenz *f* abstinence.

Abstinenzler(in) *m(f)* teetotaller.

abstoßend *adj* repellent.

abstrakt *adj adv* abstract(ly).

Abstrich *m* cut, deduction; (*med*) smear.

abstufen *vt* to grade.

absurd *adj* absurd.

Abszeß *m* abscess.

Abt *m* abbot.

Abtei *f* abbey.

Abteil *n* compartment.

abteilen *vt* to divide.

Abteilung *f* department, section.

Abtreibung *f* abortion.

abtreten *vt* to wear out; to hand over:— *vi* to resign.

Abtritt *m* resignation.

abwandeln *vt* to adapt.

abwandern *vi* to migrate.

Abwanderung *f* migration.

abwärts *adv* down(wards).

Abwasch *m* washing-up.

abwaschen *vt* to wash off, wash up.

Abwasser *n* sewage.

Abweg *m* detour, wrong way.

Abwehr *f* defence.

abwehren *vt* to fend off.

abweichen *vi* to deviate; to differ.

abwesend *adj* absent.

Abwesenheit *f* absence.

abwischen *vt* to wipe (off).

abzahlen *vt* to pay off.

Abzahlung f repayment, hire purchase.
ach excl oh:—— **ja!** oh, yes!:—— **nein?** you don't say?:—— **so!** I see.
Achse f axis, axle.
Achsel f shoulder.
Achselhöhle f armpit.
acht num eight.
Acht f ban; attention.
achtbar adj respectable.
achte(r, s) adj eighth.
achten vt to respect:—vi to pay attention.
achtlos adj careless.
achtsam adj careful.
Achtung f attention, respect.
achtzehn num eighteen.
achtzig num eighty.
ächzen vi to groan.
Acker m field.
Ackerbohne f broad bean.
Adel m aristocracy.
ad(e)lig adj noble.
Ader f vein.
Adler m eagle.
Admiral m admiral.
adoptieren vt to adopt.
Adoption f adoption.
Adrenalin n adrenaline.
Adresse f address.
adressieren vt to address.
Affäre f affair.
Affe m monkey.
affektiert adj affected.
Afrika n Africa.
Afrikaner(in) m(f) African.
afrikanisch adj African.
Agent m agent.
Aggression f aggression.
aggressiv adj aggressive.
Ägypten n Egypt.
Ägypter(in) m(f) Egyptian.
ägyptisch adj Egyptian.
ahnen vt to suspect.
ähnlich adj similar.

Ähnlichkeit f similarity.
Ahnung f suspicion.
Ahorn m maple.
Ähre f ear (corn, etc).
Aids n Aids.
Akademie f academy.
Akademiker(in) m(f) graduate.
akademisch adj academic.
Akkord m chord.
Akrobat(in) m(f) acrobat.
Akt m act.
Akte f document, file.
Aktenschrank m filing cabinet.
Aktentasche f briefcase.
Aktie f share.
Aktiengesellschaft f joint-stock company.
Aktion f campaign, action.
Aktionär(in) m(f) shareholder.
aktiv adj active.
Aktiva pl assets.
aktivieren vt to activate.
Aktivität f activity.
aktuell adj topical, up-to-date.
Akustik f acoustics.
akut adj acute.
Akzent m accent, stress.
akzeptieren vt to accept.
Alarm m alarm.
Albanien n Albania.
albern adj absurd.
Album n album.
Algebra f algebra.
Alibi n alibi.
Alimente pl alimony.
Alkohol m alcohol.
Alkoholiker(in) m(f) alcoholic.
alkoholisch adj alcoholic.
All n universe.
all (aller, alles) pn all:—adj all, every, any.
Allee f avenue.
allein adj alone:—conj only.

allerdings *adv* certainly.
Allergie *f* allergy.
allergisch *adj* allergic.
alles *pn* everything.
allgemein *adj* general.
Allianz *f* alliance.
allmählich *adj* gradual.
Alltag *m* everyday life.
alltäglich *adj adv* everyday.
Alpen *pl* (the) Alps.
Alphabet *n* alphabet.
alphabetisch *adj* alphabetical.
Alptraum *m* nightmare.
als *conj* when; as; than:—~ **ob** as if.
also *conj* therefore.
alt *adj* old.
Alt *m* alto.
Alter *n* age.
altern *vi* to age.
Alternative *f* alternative.
altmodisch *adj* old-fashioned.
Aluminium *n* aluminium.
am = **an dem**.
Ameise *f* ant.
Amerika *n* America.
Amerikaner(in) *m(f)* American.
amerikanisch *adj* American.
Ampel *f* traffic light.
Amsel *f* blackbird.
Amt *n* office; post.
amtlich *adj* official.
amüsant *adj* amusing.
amüsieren *vt* to amuse:—*vi* to enjoy oneself.
an *prep* at, on, near, to.
Analyse *f* analysis.
analysieren *vt* to analyse.
Ananas *f* pineapple.
Anarchie *f* anarchy.
Anatomie *f* anatomy.
Anbetracht *m*:—**in** ~ (+*gen*) in view of.
anbieten *vt* to offer.
Anblick *m* sight.

anblicken *vt* to look at.
anbrechen *vt* to break into:—*vi* to begin (night, day).
Anbruch *m* beginning.
Andacht *f* attention.
andächtig *adj* devout.
andauern *vi* to continue.
andauernd *adj* continual.
Anden *pl* (the) Andes.
andere(r, s) *adj* other; different.
ändern *vt vr* to change.
andernfalls *adv* otherwise.
anders *adv* differently; else.
anderswo *adv* somewhere else.
anderthalb *adj* one and a half.
Änderung *f* change.
andeuten *vt* to indicate.
Andeutung *f* indication.
andrehen *vt* to turn on.
androhen *vt* to threaten.
aneignen *vt* sich (*dat*) **etwas** ~ to acquire.
Anemone *f* anemone.
anerkannt *adj* recognized.
anerkennen *vt* to recognize.
Anerkennung *f* recognition.
Anfall *m* attack, fit.
anfallen *vt* to attack:—*vi* to occur; to accrue.
Anfang *m* beginning.
anfangen *vt* to begin.
Anfänger(in) *m(f)* beginner.
anfänglich *adj* initial.
anfangs *adv* at first.
anfassen *vt* to touch; *vr* to help.
anfechten *vt* to dispute; to trouble.
anfordern *vt* to demand, call on; to requisition.
Anfrage *f* inquiry.
anfragen *vi* to inquire.
anfügen *vt* to attach; to add.
Anführungszeichen *pl* quotation marks *pl*.
Angabe *f* statement; specification.
angeben *vt* to give; to specify.

angeblich *adj* alleged.
Angebot *n* offer, tender; supply:—~ **und Nachfrage** supply and demand.
angebracht *adj* appropriate.
angehören *vi* to belong.
Angelegenheit *f* matter, issue.
angeln *vi* to fish.
Angeln *n* fishing.
angemessen *adj* appropriate.
angenehm *adj* pleasant.
angenommen *adj* assumed, assuming.
angesichts *prep* in view of.
angespannt *adj* tense.
Angestellte(r) *f(m)* employee.
Angewohnheit *f* habit.
angreifen *vt* to attack; to touch.
Angriff *m* attack.
Angst *f* fear, anxiety.
ängstigen *vt* to frighten:—*vr* to worry.
ängstlich *adj* nervous.
Anhalt *m* support.
anhalten *vt vi* to stop.
Anhaltspunkt *m* clue, criterion.
anhand *prep* with.
Anhang *m* appendix.
anhangen *vt* to hang up, add on.
Anker *m* anchor.
Anklage *f* accusation.
anklagen *vt* to accuse.
Ankläger *m* plaintiff.
ankommen *vi* to arrive.
ankündigen *vt* to announce.
Ankündigung *f* announcement.
Ankunft *f* arrival.
Anlage *f* layout, structure; installation.
Anlaß *m* occasion; reason.
anläßlich *prep* on the occasion of.
anlegen *vt* to lay, design; to invest; to aim.
Anleihe *f* loan.
anmaßend *adj* arrogant.
Anmaßung *f* arrogance.
anmelden *vt* to announce.
Anmeldung *f* announcement.

anmerken *vt* to note (down).
Anmerkung *f* comment.
annähern *f* to approach.
annähernd *adj adv* approximate(ly).
Annäherung *f* approach.
Annahme *f* acceptance.
annehmbar *adj* acceptable.
annehmen *vt* to accept, assume.
anonym *adj* anonymous.
Anonymität *f* anonymity.
anordnen *vt* to arrange; to order.
Anordnung *f* arrangement, order.
anpassen *vt vr* to adapt.
Anpassung *f* adaptation, adjustment.
anreden *vt* to speak to.
anregen *vt* to touch; to stimulate.
Anregung *f* suggestion; stimulus.
Anruf *m* call.
anrufen *vt* to call; to invoke.
ans = **an das.**
ansässig *adj* resident, located.
Ansatz *m* beginning; extension.
Ansatzpunkt *m* starting point.
anschaffen *vt* to buy, acquire.
Anschaffung *f* purchase, acquisition.
anschalten *vt* to switch on.
anschauen *vt* to look at.
Anschauung *f* opinion, view.
Anschein *m* appearance.
anscheinend *adj adv* apparent(ly).
Anschlag *m* impact; advertisement.
anschließend *adj* adjacent; subsequent:—*adv* then.
Anschluß *m* connection; supply; annexation:—**im ~ an** further to.
Anschrift *f* address.
Anschuldigung *f* accusation.
ansehen *vt* to look at.
Ansehen *n* respect; reputation.
ansetzen *vt* to affix; to develop:—*vi* to try; to begin.
Ansicht *f* view:—**zur ~** on approval: — **meiner ~ nach** in my opinion.

Anspruch *m* claim.
anspruchslos *adj* undemanding.
anspruchsvoll *adj* demanding.
Anstalt *f* institution.
Anstand *m* decency.
anständig *adj* decent.
anstatt *prep conj* instead of.
anstecken *vt* to stick on; to infect:—*vi* to be infectious.
ansteckend *adj* infectious.
Ansteckung *f* infection.
anstellen *vt* to turn on; to recruit, employ.
Anstellung *f* employment, position.
Anstieg *m* climb, rise.
Anstrengung *f* effort.
Antarktis *f* the Antarctic.
antarktisch *adj* antarctic.
Anteil *m* share.
Antenne *f* antenna.
Antibiotikum *n* antibiotic.
antik *adj* antique.
Antike *f* antique; antiquity.
Antilope *f* antelope.
Antrag *m* application; proposal.
antreiben *vt* to propel.
Antrieb *m* drive.
Antwerpen *n* Antwerp.
Antwort *f* answer.
antworten *vi* to answer.
Anwalt *m* **Anwältin** *f* lawyer, solicitor.
anweisen *vt* to instruct.
Anweisung *f* instruction; remittance.
anwendbar *adj* applicable.
anwenden *vt* to use.
Anwendung *f* use.
anwesend *adj* present.
Anwesenheit *f* presence.
Anzahl *f* number.
Anzeige *f* advertisement.
anzeigen *vt* to advertise, announce.
anziehen *vt* to put on; to dress; to attract:—*vr* to get dressed.
Anziehung *f* attraction.

Anziehungskraft *f* attraction; magnetism; gravitation.
Anzug *m* suit.
anzünden *vt* to light, ignite.
Anzünder *m* lighter.
Apathie *f* apathy.
apathisch *adj* apathetic.
Apfel *m* apple.
Apfelsine *f* orange.
Apfelwein *m* cider.
Apostel *m* apostle.
Apostroph *m* apostrophe.
Apotheke *f* chemist's, pharmacy.
Apotheker(in) *m(f)* pharmacist.
Apparat *m* item of equipment; telephone; camera:—**am ~!** speaking!: —**am ~ bleiben** hold the line.
Appell *m* appeal.
Appetit *m* appetite:—**guten ~** enjoy your meal.
appetitlich *adj* appetising.
Applaus *m* applause.
Aprikose *f* apricot.
April *m* April.
Aquarell *n* watercolour.
Aquarium *n* aquarium.
Äquator *m* equator.
äquatorial *adj* equatorial.
Araber *m* **Arabin** *f* Arab.
Arabien *n* Arabia.
arabisch *adj* Arabian.
Arbeit *f* work.
Arbeiter(in) *m(f)* worker.
arbeiten *vt vi* to work.
arbeitslos *adj* unemployed.
Arbeitslosigkeit *f* unemployment.
Arbeitsplatz *m* job; place of work, workstation.
Arbeitszeit *f* working hours.
Archäologe *m* archaeologist.
Archäologie *f* archaeology.
Architekt(in) *m(f)* architect.
Architektur *f* architecture.

Archiv *n* archive.
arg *adj* bad, evil:—*adv* badly.
Arg *n* malice, harm.
Argentinien *n* Argentina.
Ärger *m* anger; trouble.
ärgerlich *adj* angry; annoying.
ärgern *vt* to annoy:—*vr* to get annoyed.
Ärgernis *n* annoyance.
Arglist *f* cunning, deceit.
arglistig *adj* malicious.
arglos *adj* guileless.
Arglosigkeit *f* innocence.
Argument *n* argument.
Argwohn *m* suspicion, distrust.
Arie *f* aria.
Aristokrat *m* aristocrat.
Aristokratie *f* aristocracy.
Arithmetik *f* arithmetic.
arithmetisch *adj* arithmetic(al).
Arktis *f* Arctic.
arktisch *adj* arctic.
arm *adj* poor.
Arm *m* arm.
Armband *n* bracelet.
Armbanduhr *f* wristwatch.
Armee *f* army.
Ärmel *m* sleeve.
Ärmelkanal *m* (the) English Channel.
ärmlich *adj* poor, shabby.
Ärmlichkeit *f* poverty, shabbiness.
armselig *adj* poverty-stricken.
Armut *f* poverty.
Aroma *n* aroma.
aromatisch *adj* aromatic.
Arrest *m* arrest, detention.
arrogant *adj* arrogant.
Arroganz *f* arrogance.
Arsch *m* arse, bum.
Art *f* way; sort; species.
Arterie *f* artery.
artig *adj* well-behaved.
Artikel *m* article.
Artillerie *f* artillery.

Arznei *f* medicine.
Arzt *m* **Ärztin** *f* doctor.
ärztlich *adj* medical.
As *n* ace; A flat.
Asbest *m* asbestos.
Asche *f* ash(es).
Aschenbecher *m* ashtray.
Aschermittwoch *m* Ash Wednesday.
Asien *n* Asia.
Asiat(in) *m(f)* Asian.
asiatisch *adj* Asian.
Aspekt *m* aspect.
Assistent(in) *m(f)* assistant.
Assoziation *f* association.
Ast *m* branch.
ästhetisch *adj* aesthetic.
Asthma *n* asthma.
Astrologe *m* astrologer.
Astrologie *f* astrology.
astrologisch *adj* astrological.
Astronaut *m* astronaut.
Astronom *m* astronomer.
Astronomie *f* astronomy.
Asyl *n* asylum.
Asylbewerber *m* asylum-seeker.
Atem *m* breath.
atemlos *adj* breathless.
Atheismus *m* atheism.
Atheist *m* atheist.
Athen *n* Athens.
Äther *m* ether.
Äthiopien *n* Ethiopia.
Athlet *m* athlete.
Atlantik *m* Atlantic (Ocean).
Atlas *m* atlas.
atmen *vt vi* to breathe.
Atmosphäre *f* atmosphere.
atmosphärisch *adj* atmospheric.
Atmung *f* breathing.
Atom *n* atom.
Atomkraftwerk *n* nuclear power station.
Atomkrieg *m* nuclear war.
ätzen *vt* to corrode.

Ätzdruck *m* etching.

ätzend *adj* corrosive, caustic.

auch *adv* also.

auf *prep* + *dat* on, in, at; + *acc* on, in, at, to; up:—~ **und ab** up and down.

Aufbau *m* building, structure.

aufbauen *vt* to build.

aufbewahren *vt* to keep.

Aufbewahrung *f* storage.

aufbleiben *vi* to stay open, stay up.

Aufbruch *m* departure; uprising.

aufdecken *vt* to uncover:—*vi* to lay the table.

Aufenthalt *m* stay; stop; delay.

Auferstehung *f* resurrection.

Auffahrt *f* approach; entry; driveway.

auffallen *vi* to fall, hit; to be conspicuous.

auffallend, auffällig *adj* conspicuous.

Aufgabe *f* job; homework; giving up.

Aufgang *m* ascent; stairway; germination.

aufgeben *vt* to give up; to send; to hand in.

aufgeregt *adj* excited.

aufgeweckt *adj* intelligent, alert.

aufgrund *prep* on the basis of, because of.

aufhalten *vt vr* to stay.

aufheben *vt* to lift; to cancel:—*vr* to offset, cancel out.

Aufheben(s) *n* fuss.

aufhorchen *vi* to listen closely.

aufhören *vi* to stop.

aufklären *vt* to clarify; to enlighten.

Aufklärung *f* enlightenment.

Auflage *f* edition; circulation; imposition; tax.

auflesen *vt* to pick up, gather.

auflösen *vt* to dissolve, disintegrate; to solve.

Auflösung *f* solution; break-up; termination.

aufmachen *vt* to open:—*vr* to set off for.

Aufmachung *f* format; layout; outfit.

aufmerksam *adj* alert:—**auf etw ~ machen** to point out.

Aufmerksamkeit *f* alertness.

Aufnahme *f* absorption; beginning; inclusion; photograph; recording.

aufnehmen *vt* to lift; to absorb; to begin; to photograph; to record.

aufpassen *vi* to listen, watch, pay attention.

Aufprall *m* impact.

aufräumen *vt vi* to clear away.

aufrechnen *vt* to calculate; to charge; to settle.

aufrecht *adj adv* upright.

aufregen *vt* to excite:—*vr* to get excited.

aufregend *adj* exciting.

Aufregung *f* excitement.

Aufruf *m* call, summons.

aufrufen *vt* to call up; to call out.

Aufruhr *m* uproar; revolt.

aufrühren *vt* to stir up.

aufs = auf das.

aufschließen *vt* to open, unlock:—*vr* to close ranks.

Aufschluß *m* information.

Aufschrei *m* cry.

aufschreien *vi* to cry out.

Aufschrift *f* inscription; label.

Aufschwung *n* upturn.

Aufsicht *f* supervision.

Aufstand *m* rebellion.

aufständisch *adj* rebellious.

aufstehen *vi* to be open; to stand up; to rebel.

aufstellen *vt* to put up; to display; to prepare; to set up.

Aufstellung *f* arrangement; preparation; list.

Aufstieg *m* ascent.

Auftrag *m* job; order:—**im ~ von** on behalf of.

auftreten *vi* to step; to appear; to enter; to occur.

Auftreten *n* appearance, occurrence.
Auftritt *m* entrance; appearance; scene.
auftun *vt vr* to open.
aufwachen *vi* to wake up.
Aufwand *m* expenditure; extravagance.
aufwärts *adv* upwards.
aufwecken *vt* to wake up.
aufweisen *vt* to display.
aufwenden *vt* to spend; to devote.
aufwendig *adj* expensive.
Aufzug *m* lift, elevator; procession.
Augapfel *m* eyeball; apple of one's eye.
Auge *n* eye; bud.
Augenblick *m* moment.
augenblicklich *adj* momentary; present.
Augenbraue *f* eyebrow.
Augenheilkunde *f* ophthalmology.
Augenmerk *n* attention.
Augenschein *m* appearance.
augenscheinlich *adj* obvious.
Augenstern *m* pupil.
Augentäuschung *f* optical illusion.
Augenwimper *f* eyelash.
Augenzeuge *m* eyewitness.
August *m* August.
Auktion *f* auction.
Auktionator(in) *m(f)* auctioneer.
Aula *f* hall, auditorium.
aus *prep* out of, from; made of:—*adv* finished, over.
ausarbeiten *vt* to work out.
Ausbau *m* extension.
ausbauen *vt* to extend.
Ausbeute *f* profit.
ausbeuten *vt* to exploit.
Ausbeutung *f* exploitation.
ausbezahlen *vt* to pay off.
ausbilden *vt* to train; to educate.
Ausbildung *f* education, training.
Ausblick *m* outlook.
ausbrechen *vt* to break out; to vomit: —*vi* to break out.
ausbreiten *vt* to expand.

ausbringen *vt* to bring out; to yield.
Ausbruch *m* outbreak; breakout; eruption.
Ausdauer *f* endurance.
ausdauern *vi* to endure.
ausdehnen *vt vr* to extend.
Ausdruck *m* expression; printout.
ausdrucken *vt* to print out.
ausdrücken *vt* to express; to squeeze; to stub out.
ausdrücklich *adj* express.
auseinander *adv* apart.
auseinandersetzen *vt* to put asunder; to explain; to argue; to agree.
Auseinandersetzung *f* disagreement.
auserlesen *adj* selected.
Ausfahrt *f* departure; excursion; exit.
Ausfall *m* falling out; loss; shortage; fallout.
ausfallen *vi* to fall out; to be missing; to be cancelled; to break down; to stop.
ausfertigen *vt* to draw up.
Ausfertigung *f* drawing up.
ausfließen *vi* to flow out.
Ausflucht *f* pretext.
Ausflug *m* excursion.
Ausfluß *m* outflow.
Ausfuhr *f* export(s).
ausführbar *adj* feasible.
ausführen *vt* to take out, carry out; to export.
ausführlich *adj* detailed:—*adv* in detail.
Ausführung *f* execution, implementation.
ausfüllen *vt* to fill in.
Ausgabe *f* expenditure; edition, issue.
Ausgang *m* exit.
ausgeben *vt* to spend; to distribute:— *vr* to pass oneself off.
ausgebildet *adj* qualified.
ausgefallen *adj* exceptional.
ausgeglichen *adj* balanced.
ausgehen *vi* to go out; to end:—**davon ~** to assume.

ausgenommen *prep* except.
ausgeprägt *adj* prominent.
ausgeschlossen *adj* excluded.
ausgesprochen *adj adv* distinct(ly).
ausgezeichnet *adj* excellent.
Ausgleich *m* balance; equalization.
ausgleichen *vt* to reconcile:—*vi* to equalize.
auskleiden *vr* undress.
auskommen *vi* to manage.
auskömmlich *adj* adequate.
Auskunft *f* information.
Ausland *n*:—im ~ abroad.
Ausländer(in) *m(f)* foreigner.
ausländisch *adj* foreign.
auslassen *vt* to leave out; to let out.
auslegen *vt* to lay out; to put down; to lend; to explain.
Auslegung *f* explanation, interpretation.
Auslese *f* selection.
auslesen *vt* to select.
ausliefern *vt* to hand over.
Auslieferung *f* delivery.
ausmachen *vt* to turn off; to make out, distinguish; to agree; to represent, constitute; to matter.
Ausmaß *n* size, scale.
Ausnahme *f* exception.
ausnahmslos *adv* without exception.
ausnehmen *vt* to take out; to clean out:—*vr* to look.
Auspuff *m* exhaust.
Auspuffrohr *n* exhaust pipe.
Auspufftopf *m* silencer (car).
ausräuchern *vt* to fumigate.
ausräumen *vt* to empty, clear away.
ausrechnen *vt* to calculate, work out.
Ausrede *f* excuse.
ausreden *vt* to dissuade:—*vi* to have one's say.
ausreichen *vi* to suffice.
ausreichend *adj* sufficient.
Ausreise *f* departure.

ausreißen *vt* to tear out:—*vi* to get torn; to run away.
ausrichten *vt* to arrange; to hand over; to line up.
Ausruf *m* cry; announcement.
ausrufen *vt* to call out, proclaim.
Ausrufungszeichen *n* exclamation mark.
ausrüsten *vt* to equip, fit.
Ausrüstung *f* equipment.
Aussage *f* statement.
aussagen *vt vi* to state.
ausschauen *vi* to look out.
ausscheiden *vt* to separate; to excrete; to secrete; to depart.
Ausscheidung *f* separation; excretion; secretion; departure.
ausschlafen *vi* to sleep in.
ausschlagen *vt* to knock out; to reject:—*vi* to kick out; to germinate.
ausschlaggebend *adj* decisive:—~e Stimme casting vote.
ausschließen *vt* to exclude.
ausschließlich *adj adv* exclusive(ly): —*prep* excluding.
Ausschluß *m* exclusion.
ausschneiden *vt* to cut out.
Ausschnitt *m* extract; section.
ausschöpfen *vt* to drain; to exhaust.
ausschreiben *vt* to write out; to advertise.
Ausschreibung *f* announcement; call for tenders.
Ausschuß *m* committee; waste.
aussehen *vi* to look.
Aussehen *n* appearance.
außen *adv* outside.
Außenhandel *m* foreign trade.
Außenminister *m* foreign minister.
Außenministerium *n* foreign ministry.
Außenpolitik *f* foreign policy.
Außenseite *f* outside.
Außenseiter *m* outsider.

außer *prep* out of, except:—~ **sich** beside oneself:—*conj* except.

außerdem *conj* besides, moreover.

äußere(r, s) *adj* outer.

außerehelich *adj* illegitimate; extramarital.

außergerichtlich *adj* extrajudicial.

außergewöhnlich *adj* unusual.

außerhalb *adv prep* outside.

äußerlich *adj* external, outward.

äußern *vt* to utter:—*vr* to express one's opinion.

außerordentlich *adj* unusual.

äußerst *adv* extremely:—*adj* utmost.

Äußerung *f* utterance.

Aussicht *f* view.

aussichtslos *adj* hopeless.

Aussichtspunkt *m* viewpoint.

aussichtsreich *adj* promising.

aussöhnen *vt* to reconcile:—*vr* to be reconciled.

Aussöhnung *f* reconciliation.

Aussprache *f* pronunciation; discussion.

aussprechen *vt* to pronounce:—*vr* to speak; xto discuss:—*vi* to finish speaking.

Ausspruch *m* utterance.

ausstatten *vt* to equip.

Ausstattung *f* equipment; outfit.

aussteigen *vi* to get out.

ausstellen *vt* to exhibit.

Ausstellung *f* exhibition.

Aussteuer *f* dowry.

Ausstieg *m* exit.

Austausch *m* exchange.

austauschen *vt* to exchange.

austeilen *vt* to distribute.

Auster *f* oyster.

austoben *vr* to run wild:—*vi* to calm down.

Australien *n* Australia.

Australier(in) *m(f)* Australian.

australienisch *adj* Australian.

austreiben *vt* to drive out.

austreten *vt* to wear out:—*vi* to leave.

Austritt *m* emission; withdrawal.

ausüben *vt* to exercise, perform.

Ausverkauf *m* (clearance) sale.

ausverkaufen *vt* to sell out, sell up.

ausverkauft *adj* sold out.

Auswahl *f* selection.

auswählen *vt* to select.

Auswanderer(in) *m(f)* emigrant.

auswandern *vi* to emigrate.

Auswanderung *f* emigration.

auswärtig *adj* foreign, external.

auswärts *adv* outside; outwards; away.

Ausweg *m* way out.

Ausweis *m* passport, identity card.

ausweisen *vt* to expel:—*vr* to prove one's identity.

ausweiten *vt vr* extend.

auswendig *adv* by heart.

auswirken *vt* to effect:—*vr* to have an effect.

Auswirkung *f* effect.

Auswuchs *m* outgrowth.

Auswurf *m* ejection.

Auszug *m* departure; extract.

Auto *n* car.

Autobahn *f* motorway, freeway.

Autobiographie *m* autobiography.

autobiographisch *adj* autobiographical.

Autobus *m* bus, coach.

Autofähre *f* car ferry.

Autofahrer(in) *m(f)* motorist.

Autogramm *n* autograph.

Autohändler *m* car dealer.

Autokrat *m* autocrat.

Automat *m* vending machine.

automatisch *adj* automatic.

Autor(in) *m(f)* author.

autorisieren *vt* to authorize.

Autorität *f* authority.

Axt *f* axe.

B

Baby *n* baby.
Bach *m* stream.
Backbord *n* port (ship).
backen *vt vi* to bake.
Bäcker *m* baker.
Bäckerei *f* bakery.
Backofen *m* oven.
Backstein *m* brick.
Bad *n* bath; swim.
Badeanzug *m* swimming costume.
baden *vt vi* to bathe, bath.
Badewanne *f* bathtub.
Badezimmer *n* bathroom.
Bahn *f* railway; road; track.
Bahnhof *m* station.
Bahnsteig *m* platform.
Bahre *f* barrow; stretcher.
bald *adv* soon.
Balkon *m* balcony.
Ball *m* ball.
Ballett *n* ballet.
Ballon *m* balloon.
Banane *f* banana.
Band *m* band; tape; volume.
Bandage *f* bandage.
Bande *f* band, team.
Bandit *m* bandit.
Bank *f* bench; bank.
Bankier *m* banker.
Bankkonto *n* bank account.
Banknote *f* banknote.
Bankraub *m* bank robbery.
Bankräuber *m* bank robber.
bankrott *adj* bankrupt.
Bankrott *m* bankruptcy.
Bankwesen *n* banking.
Banner *n* banner.

Bar *f* bar.
Bär *m* bear.
barbarisch *adj* barbaric.
Bargeld *n* cash.
Bariton *m* baritone.
barock *adj* **Barock** *n* baroque.
Barometer *n* barometer.
Baron(esse) *m(f)* baron(ess).
Barrikade *f* barricade.
Bart *m* beard.
Base *f* base; female cousin.
Basel *n* Basle.
basieren *vt* to base:—*vi* to be based.
Basis *f* base, basis.
Baß *m* bass (voice).
basteln *vt* to make:—*vi* to practise a hobby.
Bastler *m* hobbyist.
Batterie *f* battery.
Bau *m* building; structure.
Bauarbeiter *m* construction worker.
Bauch *m* stomach.
Bauchschmerzen *mpl* stomach ache.
bauen *vt vi* to build.
Bauer *m* farmer; peasant.
Bäuerin *f* farmer; farmer's wife.
Bauernhaus *n* farmhouse.
Bauernhof *m* farmyard.
Baum *m* tree.
Baumgarten *m* orchard.
Baumwolle *f* cotton.
Bauplatz *m* building site.
Bayern *n* Bavaria.
bayrisch *adj* Bavarian.
beabsichtigen *vt* to intend.
beachten *vt* to comply with.
beachtlich *adj* considerable.

Beachtung f notice, compliance.
Beamte(r) m **Beamtin** f official, civil servant.
beängstigen vt to worry.
beängstigend adj worrying.
beanstanden vt to complain.
Beanstandung f complaint.
bearbeiten vt to work on.
Bearbeitung f treatment.
beaufsichtigen vt to supervise.
Beaufsichtigung f supervision.
beauftragen vt to order; to entrust.
beben vi to shake.
Becher m mug.
bedanken vr to thank.
Bedarf m need, demand:—**bei ~** if necessary.
bedauerlich adj regrettable.
bedauern vt to regret.
Bedauern n regret.
bedenken vt to consider.
Bedenken n consideration; doubt.
bedenklich adj dubious.
bedeuten vt to mean.
bedeutend adj important.
Bedeutung f meaning.
bedeutungslos adj insignificant.
bedeutungsvoll adj significant.
bedienen vt to serve; to operate:—vr to help oneself:—~ **Sie sich!** help yourself.
Bedienung f service.
Bedingung f condition.
bedrohen vt to threaten.
bedrohlich adj threatening.
Bedrohung f threat.
bedürfen vi to need.
Bedürfnis n need.
beehren vt to honour.
beeilen vr to hurry.
beendigen vt to end.
beerben vt to inherit.
Beere f berry.

Beet n bed (in garden).
befassen vr to handle, deal with.
Befehl m order.
befehlen vt to order:—vi to give orders.
befestigen vt to fasten; to strengthen.
Befestigung f fastening; strengthening.
befinden vr to be (located); to feel.
befreien vt to release.
Befreiung f liberation.
befreunden vr to make friends.
befriedigen vt to satisfy.
befriedigend adj satisfactory.
Befriedigung f satisfaction.
befristet adj time-limited.
befruchten vt to fertilize.
Befruchtung f fertilization.
befugen vt to authorize.
Befugnis f authority.
befugt adj authorized.
begabt adj gifted.
Begabung adj talent.
begegnen vi to meet.
Begegnung f meeting.
begehen vt to go along; to commit; to celebrate.
begehren vt to covet.
begehrlich adj covetous.
begeistern vt to excite.
begeisternd adj exciting.
Begeisterung f enthusiasm.
Beginn m beginning.
beginnen vt vi to begin.
beglaubigen vt to certify.
beglaubigt adj certified.
Beglaubigung f certification.
begleiten vt to accompany.
Begleiter m companion.
Begleitung f accompaniment.
begraben vt to bury.
Begräbnis n burial, funeral.
begreifen vt to understand.
begreiflich adj understandable.
begrenzen vt to limit.

begrenzt *adj* limited.

Begrenzung *f* limitation.

Begriff *m* concept:—**im ~ sein** be about to.

begründen *vt* to justify.

begründet *adj* justified.

begrüßen *vt* to greet.

Begrüßung *f* greeting.

begünstigen *vt* to favour; to promote.

Begünstigung *f* promotion; favour.

behagen *vi* to please.

behaglich *adj* comfortable.

Behaglichkeit *f* comfort.

behalten *vt* to keep.

Behälter *m* container.

behandeln *vt* to handle.

Behandlung *f* handling.

behaupten *vt* to assert:—*vr* to assert oneself.

Behauptung *f* claim.

beheben *vt* to remove.

Behebung *f* removal.

beherrschen *vt* to control; to master.

Beherrschung *f* control.

beherzt *adj* courageous.

Beherztheit *f* courage.

behindern *vt* to hinder.

Behinderte(r) *f(m)* handicapped person.

Behinderung *f* hindrance; handicap.

Behörde *f* official body:—**die Behörden** *pl* the authorities.

behördlich *adj* official.

behüten *vt* to protect:—**Gott behüte!** God forbid.

behutsam *adj* careful.

bei *prep* near; by; at; at the home of; among; in; during.

beibehalten *vt* to keep.

Beibehaltung *f* retention.

beibringen *vt* to bring forward; to provide.

Beichte *f* confession.

beichten *vt vi* to confess.

beide(r, s) *adj* both.

beiderseitig *adj* mutual.

beiderseits *adv* mutually:—*prep* on both sides of.

beidhändig *adj* ambidextrous.

Beifahrer *m* passenger.

Beifall *m* applause.

beifügen *vt* to enclose.

Beifügung *f* enclosure.

Beihilfe *f* assistance; subsidy.

Beil *n* axe.

Beilage *f* enclosure; vegetables; garnish.

beiläufig *adj adv* incidental(ly).

beiliegend *adj* enclosed.

Bein *n* leg; bone.

beinah(e) *adv* nearly.

beinhalten *vt* to contain.

Beirat *m* adviser; supervisory board.

Beispiel *n* example:—**zum ~** for example.

beispielhaft *adj* exemplary.

beispielsweise *adv* for example.

beißen *vt vi* to bite.

Beistand *m* support.

beistehen *vi* to assist.

beistimmen *vi* to agree with.

Beitrag *m* contribution.

beitragen *vt* to contribute.

Beize *f* corrosion.

bejahen *vt* to say yes to.

bejahrt *adj* elderly.

Bejahung *f* affirmation.

bekannt *adj* (well-)known; acquainted.

Bekannte(r) *f(m)* acquaintance.

bekanntgeben *vt* to announce.

bekanntmachen *vt* to announce.

Bekanntmachung *f* announcement.

Bekanntschaft *f* acquaintance.

bekehren *vt vi* to convert.

bekennen *vt* to admit.

Bekenntnis *n* admission; confession.

beklagen *vt* to lament:—*vr* to complain.

Beklagte(r) *f(m)* defendant; respondent.

bekleiden *vt* to clothe.

Bekleidung f clothing.
bekommen vt to receive.
Belag m covering, coating.
belagern vt to besiege.
Belagerung f siege.
belasten vt to burden; to charge.
Belastung f load; charge.
beleben vt to enliven.
belebend adj invigorating.
belebt adj busy.
Belebung f animation.
Beleg m receipt; proof.
belegen vt to cover; to prove.
beleidigen vt to insult.
Beleidigung f insult; libel; slander.
beleuchten vt to illuminate.
Beleuchtung f illumination.
Belgien n Belgium.
Belgier(in) m(f) Belgian.
belgisch adj Belgian.
Belgrad n Belgrade.
belichten vt to expose (film).
Belichtung f exposure.
Belieben n:—**nach ~** as you wish.
beliebt adj popular.
Beliebtheit f popularity.
beliefern vt to supply.
bellen vi to bark.
belohnen vt to reward.
Belohnung f reward.
belüften vt to ventilate.
Belüftung f ventilation.
bemannen vt to staff.
bemerkbar adj noticeable.
bemerken vt to notice; to remark.
bemerkenswert adj remarkable.
Bemerkung f remark.
bemessen vt to measure; to assess.
bemühen vr to endeavour.
Bemühung f effort.
benachbart adj neighbouring.
benachrichtigen vt to notify.
Benachrichtigung f notification.

benehmen vr to take away; to behave.
Benehmen n behaviour.
beneiden vt to envy.
beneidenswert adj enviable.
benennen vt to name.
Benennung f naming.
benötigen vt to need.
benutzen, benützen vt to use.
Benutzer m user.
Benutzung f use.
Benzin n petrol.
beobachten vt to watch.
Beobachter m observer.
Beobachtung f observation.
bequem adj comfortable.
Bequemlichkeit f convenience, comfort.
beraten vt to advise.
Berater m adviser.
Beratung f advice; consultation.
berechnen vt to calculate; to charge.
Berechnung f calculation; charge.
berechtigen vt to entitle.
berechtigt adj justified.
Berechtigung f entitlement.
Bereich m area.
bereit adj ready.
bereiten vt to prepare.
Berg m mountain, hill.
bergab adv downhill.
bergauf adv uphill.
Bergbau m mining.
bergen vt to shelter; to save; to hide.
bergig adj mountainous.
Bergmann m miner.
Bergsteigen n mountaineering.
Bergsteiger(in) m(f) mountaineer.
Bergwerk n mine.
Bericht m report.
berichten vt vi to report.
Berichterstatter m reporter.
berichtigen vt to correct.
Berichtigung f correction.
bersten vi to burst.

berücksichtigen vt to consider.
Berücksichtigung f consideration.
Beruf m occupation.
berufen vt to appoint:—vr to appeal.
beruflich adj professional.
Berufung f calling.
beruhen vi to be based.
beruhigen vt to calm:—vr to calm down.
Beruhigung f calming.
berühmt adj famous.
Berühmtheit f fame.
berühren vt to touch; to affect:—vr to come into contact.
Berührung f contact.
besagen vt to mean.
besagt adj in question.
Besatzung f garrison; crew; occupation.
beschädigen vt to damage.
Beschädigung f damage.
beschaffen vt to obtain.
Bechaffenheit f nature.
Beschaffung f acquisition.
beschäftigen vt to occupy.
beschäftigt adj occupied.
Beschäftigung f occupation; concern.
beschämen vt to shame.
beschämend adj shameful, shaming.
beschämt adj ashamed.
Bescheid m information; directions: — ~ **wissen** be well aware.
bescheiden vr to make do:—adj modest, shy.
bescheinigen vt to confirm.
Bescheinigung f certificate, confirmation.
beschießen vt to fire at.
beschimpfen vt to insult.
Beschimpfung f abuse.
beschleunigen vt vi to accelerate.
Beschleunigung f acceleration.
beschränken vt to confine.
beschränkt adj confined.
Beschränkung f limitation.

beschreiben vt to describe.
Beschreibung f description.
beschuldigen vt to accuse.
Beschuldigung f accusation.
Beschwerde f complaint.
beseitigen vt to remove.
Beseitigung f removal.
Besen m broom.
besetzen vt to occupy; to fill.
besetzt adj occupied.
Besetzung f occupation.
besichtigen vt to inspect.
Besichtigung f inspection.
Besitz m possession.
besitzen vt to possess.
Besitzer(in) m(f) owner.
besoffen adj drunk.
besondere(r, s) adj particular, special.
Besonderheit f peculiarity.
besonders adv particularly.
besonnen adj sensible.
besonnt adj sunny.
besorgen vt to provide, acquire.
Besorgnis f concern.
besorgt adj concerned.
Besorgtheit f concern.
Besorgung f acquisition.
besprechen vt vr to discuss.
Besprechung f discussion, meeting.
besser adj adv better.
bessern vt to improve.
Besserung f improvement.
Bestand m durability; stock, supply.
Bestandteil m component.
bestärken vt to strengthen.
bestätigen vt to confirm.
Bestätigung f confirmation.
bestatten vt to bury, cremate.
Bestatter m undertaker.
Bestattung f funeral.
beste(r, s) adj best.
bestechen vt to bribe.
Bestechung f bribery.

Besteck n cutlery.
bestehen vi to exist:—vt to pass (exam, etc):—~ **auf** insist on:—~ **aus** consist of.
bestellen vt to order; to appoint.
Bestellung f order.
bestenfalls adv at best.
bestens adv very well, best.
bestimmen vt to determine; to specify.
bestimmt adj adv definite(ly).
Bestimmung f determination; destination.
bestrahlen vt to shine on; to irradiate.
Bestrahlung f irradiation; radiotherapy.
Besuch m visit.
besuchen vt to visit, attend.
Besucher(in) m(f) visitor.
betätigen vt to operate, control.
Betätigung f activity.
betäuben vt to deafen; to stun.
Betäubungsmittel n anaesthetic.
Bete f beetroot.
beteiligen vt to involve:—vr to participate.
Beteiligung f participation.
beten vt vi to pray.
Beton m concrete.
betonen vt to emphasize.
Betonung f emphasis.
Betracht m consideration.
betrachten vt to consider.
beträchtlich adj considerable.
Betrag m amount.
betragen vt to amount to:—vr to behave.
betreffen vt to relate, affect.
betreffend adj relevant.
betreten vt to enter:—~ **verboten** no entry:—adj confused, embarrassed.
Betrieb m company; factory; operation:—**außer** ~ out of order.
Betriebsrat m works council.
betrinken vr to get drunk.

betroffen adj affected; shocked.
betrüben vt vr to grieve.
betrübt adj grieved.
Betrug m deception; fraud.
betrügen vt to deceive.
Betrüger(in) m(f) cheat.
betrunken adj drunk.
Bett n bed.
betteln vi to beg.
betten vt to put to bed; to embed.
Bettflasche f hot water bottle.
Bettlaken n sheet.
Bettler(in) m(f) beggar.
Beuge f bend.
beugen vt to bend:—vr to bow.
Beule f bump, lump.
beurteilen vt to judge.
Beurteilung f judgment.
Beute f loot.
Beutel m bag; purse.
Bevölkerung f population.
bevollmächtigen vt to authorize.
Bevollmächtigte(r) f(m) authorized representative.
Bevollmächtigung f authorization; power of attorney.
bevor conj before.
bevorzugen vt to prefer.
Bevorzugung f preference.
bewachen vt to watch.
Bewachung f guard.
bewahren vt to keep.
bewähren vt to prove.
bewährt adj tried and tested.
Bewährung f probation.
bewaldet adj wooded.
bewältigen vt to overcome, manage.
Bewältigung f conquest.
bewässern vt to water.
Bewässerung f irrigation.
bewegen vt vr to move.
beweglich adj movable.
bewegt adj rough (sea); moved.

Bewegung f movement.
Beweis m proof.
beweisen vt to prove.
bewohnen vt to inhabit.
Bewohner(in) m(f) inhabitant.
bewölkt adj cloudy.
Bewunderer(in) m(f) admirer.
bewußt adj conscious; deliberate.
bewußtlos adj unconscious.
Bewußtsein n consciousness.
bezahlen vt vi to pay (for).
Bezahlung f payment.
bezeichnen vt to describe; to mark; to call; to label.
Bezeichnung f description; name.
beziehen vt vr to refer.
Beziehung f connection, relationship.
beziehungsweise adv or; respectively.
Bezirk m district.
Bezug m covering; purchase; income; reference:—**in ~ auf** with reference to.
bezüglich prep adj concerning.
Bezugnahme f reference.
bezweifeln vt to doubt.
Bibel f bible.
Bibliographie f bibliography.
Bibliothek f library.
Bibliothekar(in) m(f) librarian.
biblisch adj biblical.
biegen vt vr to bend; vi to turn (corner).
biegsam adj flexible.
Biegung f bend.
Biene f bee.
Bienenkorb m beehive.
Bier n beer.
bieten vt to offer, bid.
Bieter(in) m(f) bidder.
Bigamie f bigamy.
Bikini m bikini.
Bilanz f balance; balance sheet.
Bild n picture.
bilden vt to form; to educate:—vr to develop.

Bildhauer(in) m(f) sculptor.
Bildschirm m TV screen.
Bildung f formation; education.
Billard n billiards.
billig adj cheap; reasonable.
billigen vt to approve.
Billigkeit f fairness; cheapness.
Billigung f approval.
Binde f band, bandage; sanitary towel.
binden vt to tie.
Bindestrich m hyphen.
Bindfaden m string.
Bindung f connection; compound.
binnen prep within.
Biographie f biography.
Biologe m biologist.
Biologie f biology.
biologisch adj biological.
Birke f birch.
Birne f pear; lightbulb.
bis prep until; by; to, as far as; up to: — conj to; until.
Bischof m bishop.
bisexuell adj bisexual.
bisher adv hitherto.
bisherig adj previous.
bislang adv hitherto.
Biskuit n biscuit.
Biß m bite.
bißchen adj adv:—**ein ~** a bit, a little.
bissig adj biting.
bisweilen adv sometimes.
Bitte f request.
bitte excl please:—**(wie) bitte?** pardon?:—**bitte (schön)** don't mention it.
bitten vt vi to ask.
bitter adj bitter.
Bitterkeit f bitterness.
blank adj bright; bare; broke.
Blase f bubble; blister; bladder.
blasen vt vi to blow.
Blasphemie f blasphemy.

blaß *adj* pale.
Blässe *f* paleness.
Blatt *n* leaf; page; sheet; newspaper.
blättern *vi:*—~ **in** to leaf through.
blau *adj* blue; drunk.
blaumachen *vi* to play truant.
Blech *n* tin; sheet metal.
Blei *n* lead.
bleiben *vi* to remain.
bleifrei *adj* unleaded.
Bleistift *m* pencil.
Blende *f* blind.
blenden *vt* to blind.
Blick *m* look.
blicken *vt* to look.
blind *adj* blind.
Blindheit *f* blindness.
blinken *vi* to flash; to sparkle.
blinzeln *vi* to blink, wink.
Blitz *m* lightning; flash.
blitzschnell *adj adv* quick as a flash.
Block *m* block; notepad.
Blockflöte *f* recorder.
blockieren *vt* to block.
blöd *adj* stupid.
Blödsinn *m* nonsense.
blond *adj* blond(e).
bloß *adj* naked; sheer:—*adv* only.
Blöße *f* bareness.
blühen *vi* to flower; to flourish.
Blume *f* flower; bouquet (wine).
Blumenkohl *m* cauliflower.
Bluse *f* blouse.
Blut *n* blood.
Blüte *n* blossom.
bluten *vi* to bleed.
blutig *adj* bloody.
Bö *f* gust.
Bock *m* buck; ram; support.
Boden *m* ground, floor, soil.
Bogen *m* bow; arch; curve.
Bohle *f* board.
Bohne *f* bean.

bohren *vt* to drill.
Bohrer *m* drill.
Bolzen *m* bolt.
Bombe *f* bomb.
Bonbon *m* sweet.
Boot *n* boat.
Bord *n* shelf; edge:—**an** ~ on board.
Bordell *n* brothel.
borgen *vt* to borrow; to lend.
Börse *f* purse; stock exchange.
bös *adj* angry; bad.
bösartig *adj* malicious.
Bösartigkeit *f* malice.
Botanik *f* botany.
Botaniker *m* botanist.
botanisch *adj* botanical.
Bote *m* messenger.
Botschaft *f* message; embassy.
Botschafter(in) *m(f)* ambassador.
boxen *vi* to box.
Boxen *n* boxing.
Boxer *m* boxer.
Branche *f* (sector of) industry.
Brand *m* fire; gangrene.
branden *vi* to surge; to break.
Brandstifter *m* arsonist.
Branntwein *m* brandy, spirits.
braten *vt* to roast; to bake; to fry.
Bratpfanne *f* frying pan.
Bratwurst *f* grilled sausage.
brauchbar *adj* usable.
brauchen *vt* to use; to need.
Braue *f* brow.
brauen *vt* to brew.
Brauerei *f* brewery.
braun *adj* brown.
Bräune *f* brownness; tan.
braunen *vt* to brown.
Braut *f* bride, fiancée.
Brautigam *m* bridegroom, fiancé.
brechen *vt vi* to break; to vomit.
Brei *m* porridge, oatmeal; pulp.
breit *adj* wide.

Breite *f* width; latitude.
breiten *vt* to spread.
Bremse *f* brake.
bremsen *vt vi* to brake.
brennbar *adj* (in)flammable.
brennen *vr vi* to burn.
Brett *n* board.
Brief *m* letter.
Briefkasten *m* letter box.
Briefmarke *f* stamp.
Briefträger(in) *m(f)* postman.
Brille *f* glasses.
bringen *vt* to bring.
Brombeere *f* blackberry.
Bronze *f* bronze.
Broschüre *f* brochure.
Brot *n* bread; loaf.
Brötchen *n* (bread) roll.
Bruch *m* break.
Brücke *f* bridge.
Bruder *m* brother.
brüderlich *adj* brotherly.
Brunnen *m* well; spring; fountain.
Brüssel *n* Brussels.
Brust *f* breast, chest.
brüten *vi vt* to hatch, brood.
Bube *m* lad; jack (cards).
Buch *n* book.
Buche *f* beech.
buchen *vt* to book.
Buchführung *f* bookkeeping.
Büchse *f* box; can; rifle.
Büchsenöffner *m* can opener.
Buchstabe *m* letter; character.
buchstabieren *vt* to spell.
Bucht *f* bay.
Buckel *m* hump.
bücken *vt vr* to bend.
Bude *f* booth; stall.
Büffel *m* buffalo; oaf.
Bug *m* bow (ship); nose (aircraft).
Bügel *m* clothes hanger; stirrup.
Bügelbrett *n* ironing board.

Bügeleisen *n* iron.
bügeln *vt vi* to iron.
Bühne *f* stage, platform.
Bukarest *n* Bucharest.
Bulgarien *n* Bulgaria.
Bulle *m* bull.
Bummel *m* stroll.
bummeln *vi* to stroll, dawdle.
Bund *n* bundle; band:—*m* tie; alliance;
     federation.
Bündel *n* bundle.
bundeln *vt* to bundle.
Bundes- *prefix* federal, German.
Bundesrat *m* upper house of German
     parliament.
Bundesrepublik *f* Federal Republic (of
     Germany).
Bundestag *m* lower house of German
     parliament.
Bündnis *n* alliance.
bunt *adj* colourful.
Burg *f* castle.
bürgen *vt* to guarantee.
Bürger(in) *m(f)* citizen.
Bürgerkrieg *m* civil war.
bürgerlich *adj* middle-class; civil.
Bürgermeister *m* mayor.
Bürgersteig *m* pavement.
Bürgschaft *f* security, guarantee.
Büro *n* office.
Büroangestellte(r) *f(m)* office worker.
Büroklammer *f* paperclip.
Bursche *m* lad; guy; servant.
Bürste *f* brush.
bürsten *vt* to brush.
Bus *m* bus.
Busch *m* bush.
Büste *f* bust.
Büstenhalter *m* bra.
Butter *f* butter.
Butterblume *f* buttercup.
Butterbrot *n* bread and butter.
Butterbrotpapier *n* greaseproof paper.

C

Café *n* café.
Cafeteria *f* cafeteria.
Camp *n* camp.
campen *vi* to camp.
Camper *m* camper.
Caravan *m* caravan.
CD-Spieler *m* CD player.
Cellist *m* cellist.
Cello *n* cello.
Celcius *n* Celsius.
Chamäleon *n* chameleon.
Chance *f* chance, opportunity.
Chaos *n* chaos.
chaotisch *adj* chaotic.
Charakter *m* character.
charakterisieren *vt* to characterize.
charakteristisch *adj* characteristic.
charmant *adj* charming, delightful.
Charme *m* charm.
Chauffeur *m* chauffeur.
Chauvinist *m* chauvinist.
Chef(in) *m(f)* boss, head (of firm).
Chemie *f* chemistry.
Chemikalie *f* chemical.
Chemiker(in) *m(f)* chemist.
chemisch *adj* chemical.
chilenisch *adj* Chilean.
Chinese *m* Chinese.

Chinesin *f* Chinese.
chinesisch *adj* Chinese.
Chirurg *m* surgeon.
Chirurgie surgery.
chirurgisch *adj* surgical.
Chlor *n* chlorine.
Cholera *f* cholera.
cholerisch *adj* choleric.
Chor *m* choir; chorus.
Choral *m* chorale.
Choregraph *m* choreographer.
Christ(in) *m(f)* Christian.
Christbaum *m* Christmas tree.
Christenheit *f* Christianity.
christlich *adj* Christian.
Christus *m* Christ.
Chrom *n* chromium; chrome.
Chronik *f* chronicle.
chronisch *adj* chronic.
Chronologie *f* chronology.
chronologisch *adj* chronological.
Chrysantheme *f* chrysanthemum.
Cocktail *m* cocktail.
Computer *m* computer.
Container *m* container.
Creme *f* cream; polish; (tooth)paste.
cremig *adj* creamy.

D

da *adv* there; here; then; so:—*conj* as.
dabei *adv* in the process.
Dach *n* roof.

Dachs *m* badger.
dadurch *adv* through it; by it:—~ **daß** because.

dafür *adv* for it.

dagegen *adv* against it; however:—*conj* whereas.

daher *adv* from there; hence.

dahin *adv* there; then; gone.

Dahlie *f* dahlia.

damalig *adj* then:—**der ~e Präsident** the then president.

damals *adv* at that time.

Dame *f* lady; queen (cards, chess).

damit *adv* with it; by it:—*conj* so that.

dämmern *vi* to dawn; to grow dusky.

Dämmerung *f* dawn; dusk.

Dampf *m* steam; vapour.

dampfen *vi* to steam.

dämpfen *vt* to steam; to dampen.

Dampfer *m* steamer.

danach *adv* after that; accordingly.

daneben *adv* beside it; also.

Däne *m* **Dänin** *f* Dane.

Dänemark *n* Denmark.

dänisch *adj* Danish.

dank *prep* thanks to.

Dank *m* thanks.

dankbar *adj* grateful.

Dankbarkeit *f* gratitude.

danke (schön) *excl* thank you, thanks.

danken *vt* to thank.

dann *adv* then.

daran *adv* on it; of it; about it.

darauf *adv* on it; to it; afterwards.

daraufhin *adv* afterwards.

daraus *adv* from it.

darin *adv* in there; in it.

darlegen *vt* to explain.

Darlegung *f* explanation.

Darleh(e)n *n* loan.

Darm *m* intestine.

darstellen *vt* to depict.

Darstellung *f* presentation.

darüber *adv* over it; about it:—~ **hinaus** in addition, furthermore.

darum *adv* around it; therefore.

darunter *adv* under it.

das *def art* the:—*pn* that.

daß *conj* that.

dasselbe *art pn* the same.

datieren *vt* to date.

Dattel *f* date (fruit).

Datum *n* date.

Dauer *f* duration.

dauerhaft *adj* lasting.

dauern *vi* to last.

Daumen *m* thumb.

Daune *f* down.

davon *adv* of that/it; away.

davor *adv* before it, in front of it.

dazu *adv* to that, to it; also.

dazwischen *adv* between (them).

Deck *n* deck.

Decke *f* covering; blanket; ceiling.

Deckel *m* lid.

decken *vt* to cover; to lay (table):—*vr* to cover oneself; to coincide.

Deckung *f* covering.

Defekt *m* defect.

defekt *adj* defective.

definieren *vt* to define.

Definition *f* definition.

definitiv *adj* definit(iv)e.

deftig *adj* heavy; rude.

Degen *m* sword.

dehnen *vt vr* to stretch.

dein(e) *poss adj* your.

deine(r, s) *poss pn* yours.

dekorieren *vt* to decorate.

Delegation *f* delegation.

delegieren *vt* to delegate.

Delegierte(r) *f(m)* delegate.

delikat *adj* delicate; delicious.

Delikt *n* offence.

Delphin *m* dolphin.

demnach *adv* therefore.

demnächst *adv* soon.

Demokratie *f* democracy.

demokratisch *adj* democratic.

demolieren *vt* to demolish.
Demut *f* humility.
demütig *adj* humble.
demüten *vt* to humiliate.
Demütung *f* humiliation.
demzufolge *adv* accordingly.
den *art acc of* **der**.
denen *pn dat pl of* **der, die, das**.
denkbar *adj* conceivable.
denken *vt vi vr* to think.
Denkmal *n* monument.
denn *conj* as; than:—*adv* then:—**es sei ~, daß** unless.
dennoch *adv conj* however.
Depot *n* deposit; warehouse.
Depression *f* depression.
deprimieren *vt* to depress.
der *def art* the.
derb *adj* solid.
dergleichen *on* such.
derjenige *pn* he, she, it; the one (who); that (which).
derselbe *art pn* the same.
derzeitig *adj* current.
des *art gen of* **der, das**.
desgleichen *pn* the same.
deshalb *adv* therefore.
dessen *pn gen of* **der, das**.
Dessert *n* dessert.
desto *adv* all the, so much the.
deswegen *conj* therefore.
Detail *n* detail.
Detektiv *m* detective.
deuten *vt* to interpret:—*vi* to point.
deutlich *adj* clear.
Deutlichkeit *f* clarity.
deutsch *adj* German.
Deutsch *n* German (language).
Deutsche(r) *f(m)* German.
Deutschland *n* Germany.
Deutung *f* interpretation.
Devise *f* foreign currency.
Dezember *m* December.

dezent *adj* unobtrusive.
dezimal *adj* decimal.
Diagnose *f* diagnosis.
diagonal *adj* diagonal.
Diagonale *f* diagonal.
Dialekt *m* dialect.
Dialog *m* dialogue.
Diamant *m* diamond.
Diapositiv *n* slide.
Diät *f* diet.
dich *pn acc of* **du** you, yourself.
dicht *adj* tight; dense:—*adv* close.
Dichte *f* density, thickness; tightness.
dichten *vt* to seal.
Dichter(in) *m(f)* poet(ess).
Dichtung *f* poetry.
dick *adj* thick; fat.
Dicke *f* thickness; fatness.
die *def art* the.
Dieb(in) *m(f)* thief.
Diebstahl *m* theft.
dienen *vi* to serve.
Diener(in) *m(f)* servant.
Dienst *m* service; duty.
Dienstag *m* Tuesday.
dies *pn* this; these.
diesbezüglich *adj* relevant.
dieselbe *pn art* the same.
diese(r, s) *pn* this (one).
diesmal *adv* this time.
diesseits *adv prep* on this side.
Diktat *n* dictation.
Diktator *m* dictator.
Diktatur *f* dictatorship.
diktieren *vt* to dictate.
Dilemma *n* dilemma.
Dimension *f* dimension.
Ding *n* thing.
Diplom *n* diploma.
Diplomat *m* diplomat.
Diplomatie *f* diplomacy.
diplomatisch *adj* diplomatic.
dir *pn dat of* **du** (to) you.

direkt adj direct.
Direktion f management.
Direktor m director.
Dirigent m conductor.
Dirne f prostitute.
Diskette f diskette.
Diskothek f disco(thèque).
diskret adj discreet.
Diskretion f discretion.
Diskussion f discussion.
diskutieren vt vi to discuss.
Dissertation f dissertation.
Dissident(in) m(f) dissident.
Distanz f distance.
Distel f thistle.
Disziplin f discipline.
Dividende f dividend.
dividieren vt to divide.
Division f division.
doch conj however:—adv after all, yet.
Dock n dock(yard).
Doktor(in) m(f) doctor.
Dolch m dagger.
Dollar m dollar.
dolmetschen vt vi to interpret.
Dolomien pl (the) Dolomites.
Dometscher(in) m(f) interpreter.
Dom m cathedral.
dominieren vt vi to dominate.
Donau f Danube.
Donner m thunder.
donnern vi to thunder.
Donnerstag m Thursday.
doof adj dull.
Doppelbett n double bed.
doppeln vt to double.
Doppelpunkt m colon.
doppelt adj double.
Dorf n village.
Dorn m thorn.
dorren vi to dry up.
dörren vt to dry.
Dorsch m cod.

dort adv there.
dorther adv from there, hence.
dorthin adv (to) there.
dorthinaus adv out there.
dorthinein adv in there.
dortig adj there.
dösen vi to doze.
Dose f box, can.
Dosenöffner m can opener.
dosieren vt to dose, measure out.
dösig adj dozy.
Dosis f dose.
Dozent m lecturer.
Drache m dragon.
Drachen m kite.
Draht m wire.
Drahtzange f pliers.
Drall m twist, spin.
Drama n drama.
Dramatiker m dramatist.
dramatisch adj adv dramatic(ally).
Drang m pressure; impulse.
drängeln vi to jostle.
drängen vt to push:—vi to be urgent.
dränieren vt to drain.
drastisch adj adv drastic(ally).
draußen adv outside.
Dreck m filth.
dreckig adj filthy.
drehbar adj revolving.
drehen vt vi to turn.
Drehung f turn.
drei num three.
Dreibein n tripod.
Dreieck n triangle.
dreieckig adj triangular.
Dreieinigkeit f Trinity.
dreifach adj adv triple.
dreißig num thirty.
dreizehn num thirteen.
drillen vt to drill.
dringen vi to penetrate; to insist.
dringlich adj urgent.

drinnen *adv* inside.
dritte(r, s) *adj* third.
Dritte(r) *m* third (party).
Drittel *n* third.
Droge *f* drug.
Drogerie *f* drugstore.
drohen *vi* to threaten.
Drohung *f* threat.
Drossel *f* thrush; throttle.
drüben *adv* over there.
Druck *m* pressure; printing.
drücken *vt* to press; to oppress:—*vi* to press, touch:—*vr* to get out of.
Drucker *m* printer.
Dschungel *m* jungle.
du *pn nom* you.
Duell *n* duel.
Duett *n* duet.
Duft *m* scent.
duften *vi* to smell (pleasant).
duftig *adj* fragrant.
dulden *vt* to tolerate.
dumm *adj* stupid.
Dummheit *f* stupidity.
Dummkopf *m* idiot.
dunkel *adj* dark.
Dunkelheit *f* darkness.
dunkeln *vi* to darken.
dünn *adj* thin.
Dunst *m* vapour.
Dur *n* (*mus*) major.
durch *prep* through, by.
durchaus *adv* completely.
durchbrechen *vt vi* to break through.
Durchbruch *m* breakthrough.

durchdringen *vi* to penetrate.
Durchdringung *f* penetration.
durcheinander *adv* higgledy-piggledy.
Durcheinander *n* confusion.
Durchfall *m* diarrhoea.
durchfallen *vi* to fall through; to fail.
durchführbar *adj* feasible.
durchführen *vt* to carry through.
Durchführung *f* completion.
Durchgang *m* passage.
durchlässig *adj* permeable.
Durchmesser *m* diameter.
Durchschnitt *m* average.
durchschnittlich *adj* average:—*adv* on average.
durchsehen *vt vi* to look through.
durchsichtig *adj* transparent.
durchweg *adv* throughout.
dürfen *vi* to be allowed.
dürftig *adj* needy.
dürr *adj* arid.
Durst *m* thirst:—~ **haben** to be thirsty.
dürstig *adj* thirsty.
Dusche *f* shower.
duschen *vt vi* to shower.
Düse *f* nozzle; jet.
Düsenflugzeug *n* jet (aircraft).
Düsentriebwerk *n* jet engine.
düster *adj* dark.
Düsterheit, Düsterkeit *f* gloom.
Dutzend *n* dozen.
duzen *vt* to call someone *du*, be familiar.
dynamisch *adj* dynamic.
Dynamit *n* dynamite.
Dynamo *m* dynamo.

E

Ebbe *f* low tide.
eben *adj* level:—*adv* exactly.

Ebene *f* plain.
ebenfalls *adv* also.

ebenso *adv* equally.
Echo *n* echo.
echt *adj* genuine.
Ecke *f* corner; angle.
edel *adj* noble; precious.
Efeu *m* ivy.
effektiv *adj* effective.
egal *adj* equal:—**das ist mir ~** it's all the same to me.
Egoismus *m* egotism.
Egoist(in) *m(f)* egotist.
egoistisch *adj* selfish.
ehe *conj* before.
Ehe *f* marriage.
Ehebrecher(in) *m(f)* adulterer.
ehebrecherisch *adj* adulterous.
Ehebruch *m* adultery.
Ehefrau *f* wife.
ehelich *adj* matrimonial.
ehemalig *adj* former.
ehemals *adv* formerly.
Ehemann *m* husband.
Ehepaar *n* married couple.
eher *adv* sooner; rather.
Ehering *m* wedding ring.
Ehescheidung *f* divorce.
ehrbar *adj* honourable.
Ehre *f* honour.
ehren *vt* to honour.
Ehrgeiz *m* ambition.
ehrgeizig *adj* ambitious.
ehrlich *adj* honest:—*adv* honestly.
Ehrlichkeit *f* honesty.
ehrlos *adj* dishonourable.
Ei *n* egg.
Eibe *f* yew.
Eiche *f* oak.
Eichel *f* acorn.
eichen *vt* to standardize.
Eichhörnchen *n* squirrel.
Eid *m* oath.
Eidechse *f* lizard.
eidgenössisch *adj* Swiss.

Eidotter *n* egg yolk.
Eierbecher *m* eggcup.
Eierkuchen *m* omelette, pancake.
Eierschale *f* eggshell.
Eierstock *m* ovary.
Eifer *m* enthusiasm.
eifern *vi* to be eager for.
Eifersucht *f* jealousy.
eifersüchtig *adj* jealous.
eiförmig *adj* egg-shaped, oval.
eifrig *adj* eager.
Eigelb *n* egg yolk.
eigen *adj* own; particular; unusual.
Eigenart *f* peculiarity.
eigenartig *adj* peculiar.
Eigenheit *f* peculiarity.
eigens *adv* deliberately.
Eigenschaft *f* characteristic.
eigentlich *adj* actual, real:—*adv* actually, really.
Eigentor *n* own goal.
Eigentum *n* property, ownership.
Eigentümer(in) *m(f)* owner.
eigentümlich *adj* special, particular.
Eigentümlichkeit *f* peculiarity.
eignen *vr* to suit.
Eigner *m* owner.
Eignung *f* suitability.
Eilbote *m* courier.
Eilbrief *m* express letter.
Eile *f* hurry.
eilen *vi vr* to hurry.
eilig *adj* hurried.
Eimer *m* bucket.
ein(e) *num* one:—*indef art* a, an:—*pn*
eine(r, s) one.
Einblick *m* view; insight.
einbringen *vt* to bring in.
Einbruch *m* break-in; invasion; arrival (night).
eindeutig *adj* clear.
Eindruck *m* impression.
eineinhalb *num* one and a half.

einerseits *adv* on the one hand.

einfach *adj* single; simple:—*adv* simply.

Einfachheit *f* simplicity.

Einfahrt *f* entrance.

Einfall *m* idea; incursion.

einfallen *vi* to raid; to occur; to fall in.

einfließen *vi* to flow in.

Einfluß *m* influence.

Einfuhr *f* import(s).

einführen *vt* to introduce; to import.

Einführung *f* introduction.

Eingabe *f* application.

Eingang *m* entrance; arrival; receipt.

eingenommen *adj* partial, biased.

Eingenommenheit *f* bias.

Eingeweide *pl* entrails.

Einheit *f* unit; unity.

einheitlich *adj* uniform.

Einheitlichkeit *f* uniformity.

einholen *vt vi* to bring in; to catch up.

einig *adj* united; agreed.

einige(r, s) *adj pn* some.

einigen *vt* to unite:—*vr* to agree.

Einigkeit *f* unity.

Einigung *f* agreement; unification.

Einkauf *m* purchase.

einkaufen *vt* to buy:—*vi* to shop.

Einkaufszentrum *n* shopping centre.

Einklang *m* harmony.

einkommen *vi* to apply; to come in.

Einkommen *n* income.

Einkommen(s)steuer *f* income tax.

Einkünfte *fpl* income.

einladen *vt* to invite.

Einladung *f* invitation.

einleiten *vt* to introduce.

Einleitung *f* introduction.

einmal *adv* once; one day; even:—**auf ~** suddenly.

einmalig *adv* unique.

einmütig *adj* unanimous.

Einmütigkeit *f* unanimity.

Einnahme *f* capture; income.

einnehmen *vt* to take (in, up).

Einöde *f* desert.

Einreise *f* entry.

einrichten *vt* to arrange.

Einrichtung *f* furnishings; installation; institution.

eins *num* one.

Eins *f* one.

einsam *adj* lonely.

Einsamkeit *f* loneliness.

Einsatz *m* insert; use; effort.

einschlafen *vi* to fall asleep.

Einschlag *m* impact; hint.

einschlägig *adj* relevant.

einschließen *vt* to lock up; to enclose.

einschließlich *adv* inclusive:—*prep* including.

Einschluß *m* inclusion.

Einschreiben *n* recorded delivery.

Einsicht *f* inspection; insight.

Einspruch *m* objection.

einst *adv* once.

einstig *adj* former.

einstweilen *adv* meanwhile.

einstweilig *adj* temporary.

eintönig *adj* monotonous.

Eintönigkeit *f* monotony.

Eintrag *m* entry.

eintreten *vi* to enter; to join; to occur.

Eintritt *m* entrance.

Eintrittskarte *f* (entrance) ticket.

Einvernehmen *n* agreement.

einverstanden *adj* agreed.

Einverständnis *n* agreement.

Einwand *m* objection.

Einwanderer *m* immigrant.

einwandern *vi* to immigrate.

Einwanderung *f* immigration.

einwandfrei *adj* impeccable:—*adv* absolutely.

einwärts *adv* inward(s).

einwenden *vt* to object.

Einwendung *f* objection.

einwirken *vi* to affect.
Einwirkung *f* effect.
Einwohner(in) *m(f)* inhabitant.
Einwurf *m* throw-in; slot; objection.
Einzelfall *m* individual case.
Einzelhandel *m* retailing.
Einzelhändler *m* retailer.
Einzelheit *f* detail.
einzeln *adj* single:—*adv* individually.
einzig *adj* single; only.
einzigartig *adj* unique.
Einzug *m* entrance.
Eis *n* ice (cream).
Eisbahn *f* skating rink.
Eisbär *m* polar bear.
Eisberg *m* iceberg.
Eisen *n* iron.
Eisenbahn *f* railway, railroad.
eisern *adj* iron.
Eishockey *n* ice hockey.
eisig *adj* icy.
eiskalt *adj* ice-cold.
Eislauf *m* skating.
eislaufen *vi* to skate.
Eisläufer(in) *m(f)* skater.
Eisschrank *m* fridge.
eitel *adj* vain.
Eitelkeit *f* vanity.
Eiweiß *n* egg white; protein.
Ekel *m* disgust.
ekelhaft, ek(e)lig *adj* disgusting.
ekeln *vt* to disgust.
Ekstase *f* ecstasy.
ekstatisch *adj* ecstatic.
elastisch *adj* elastic.
Elefant *m* elephant.
elegant *adj* elegant.
Elektriker *m* electrician.
elektrisch *adj* electrical.
Elektrizität *f* electricity.
Elektronik *f* electronics.
elektronisch *adj* electronic.
Element *n* element.

elementar *adj* elementary.
Elend *n* misery.
elend *adj* miserable.
elf *num* eleven.
Elfenbein *n* ivory.
eliminieren *vt* to eliminate.
Elite *f* elite.
Ellenbogen *m* elbow.
Elsaß *n* Alsace.
Eltern *pl* parents.
Empfang *m* reception; receipt.
empfangen *vt* to receive.
Empfänger *m* recipient.
Empfängnis *f* conception.
Empfängnisverhütung *f* contraception.
empfehlen *vt* to recommend.
Empfehlung *f* recommendation.
empfinden *vt* to feel.
empfindlich *adj* sensitive.
Emfindlichkeit *f* sensitivity.
empfindsam *adj* sentimental.
Emfindsamkeit *f* sentimentality.
Empfindung *f* feeling.
empfindungslos *adj* insensitive.
Ende *n* end.
enden *vi* to end.
endgültig *adj* final.
endlich *adj adv* final(ly).
endlos *adj* endless.
Energie *f* energy.
energisch *adj* energetic.
eng *adj* narrow; close; tight.
Engel *m* angel.
England *n* England.
Engländer *m* Englishman.
Engländerin *f* Englishwoman.
Englisch *n* English (language).
englisch *adj* English.
Enkel *m* grandson.
Enkelin *f* granddaughter.
enorm *adj* enormous.
entarten *vi* to degenerate.
entartet *adj* degenerate.

entbinden *vt* to release.
entdecken *vt* to discover.
Entdeckung *f* discovery.
Ente *f* duck.
entfallen *vi* to fall; to escape.
entfalten *vt* to unfold.
entfernen *vt* to remove.
entfernt *adj* distant.
Entfernung *f* distance.
entführen *vt* to abduct.
Entführer *m* kidnapper.
Entführung *f* abduction.
entgegen *adv prep* against, contrary to.
entgegengesetzt *adj* opposite.
entgehen *vi* to escape.
Entgelt *n* compensation, reward.
entkommen *vi* to escape.
entladen *vt* to unload; to set off:—*vr* to discharge.
entlang *adv prep* along.
entlassen *vt* to dismiss.
Entlassung *f* dismissal.
Entnahme *f* withdrawal.
entnehmen *vt* to remove.
entschädigen *vt* to compensate.
Entschädigung *f* compensation.
entscheiden *vt vi* to decide.
entscheidend *adj* decisive.
Entscheidung *f* decision.
entschlossen *adj* determined.
Entschlossenheit *f* determination.
Entschluß *m* decision.
entschuldigen *vt* to excuse:—*vr* to apologize.
Entschuldigung *f* excuse:—~! sorry!
entsetzen *vt* to dismiss; to frighten; to appal.
Entsetzen *n* terror; dismay.
entsetzlich *adj* appalling.
Entsetzung *f* dismissal.
entspannen *vt vr* to relax.
Entspannung *f* relaxation.
entsprechen *vi* to correspond.

entsprechend *adj adv* appropriate(ly).
entstehen *vi* to come into being.
enttäuschen *vt* to disappoint.
Enttäuschung *f* disappointment.
entweder *conj*:—~... oder either... or.
entwickeln *vt vr* to develop.
Entwicklung *f* development.
Entwurf *m* design.
entzücken *vt* to delight.
entzückend *adj* delightful.
Enzyklopädie *f* encyclopedia.
Epidemie *f* epidemic.
Episode *f* episode.
Epoche *f* epoch.
er *pn nom* he.
erachten *vi* to consider.
Erachten *n* opinion.
Erbarmen *n* pity.
Erbe *m* heir.
erben *vt* to inherit.
Erbin *f* heiress.
erbitten *vt* to ask for.
erblicken *vt* to see.
erbrechen *vt vr* to vomit.
erbringen *vt* to provide.
Erbschaft *f* inheritance, estate.
Erbse *n* pea.
Erdbeben *n* earthquake.
Erdbeere *f* strawberry.
Erde *f* earth.
Erdgas *n* natural gas.
Erdgeschoß *n* ground floor.
Erdkunde *f* geography.
Erdnuß *f* peanut.
ereignen *vr* to occur.
Ereignis *n* event.
erfahren *vt* to experience:—*adj* experienced.
Erfahrung *f* experience.
erfassen *vt* to grasp; to understand.
erfinden *vt* to discover, invent.
Erfinder *m* inventor.
Erfindung *f* invention.

Erfolg *m* result; success:—**~ haben** to succeed.
erfolgen *vi* to result; to happen.
erfolglos *adj* unsuccessful.
erfolgreich *adj* successful.
erforderlich *adj* necessary.
erfordern *vt* to require.
erforschen *vt* to explore; to investigate.
Erforschung *f* exploration; investigation.
erfreuen *vt* to please:—*vr* to enjoy.
erfreulich *adj* pleasing.
Erfrischung *f* refreshment.
erfüllen *vt* to fill; to comply with:—*vr* to be fulfilled.
Erfüllung *f* fulfilment.
ergänzen *vt* to supplement.
ergänzend *adj* additional.
Ergänzung *f* supplement.
Ergebnis *n* result.
ergreifen *vt* to grasp.
erhalten *vt* to receive; to maintain.
erhältlich *adj* available.
Erhaltung *f* maintenance; preservation.
erheben *vt* to raise:—*vr* to rise.
erheblich *adj* considerable:—*adv* considerably.
erhöhen *vt* to raise.
erholen *vr* to recover.
Erholung *f* recovery.
erhören *vt* to hear; to grant.
erinnern *vt* to remind:—*vr* to remember.
Erinnerung *f* memory.
erkälten *vr* to catch cold.
Erkältung *f* cold.
erkennbar *adj* recognizable.
erkennen *vt* to recognize.
erkenntlich *adj* perceptible.
Erkenntnis *f* knowledge; acknowledgment.
Erkennung *f* recognition.
erklären *vt* to explain; to declare.
Erklärung *f* explanation.
erklettern, erklimmen *vt* to climb.

erkundigen *vr* to inquire.
Erkundigung *f* inquiry.
erlangen *vt* to reach.
Erlaß *m* exemption; decree.
erlassen *vt* to issue; to exempt.
erläßlich *adj* allowable.
erlauben *vt* to allow.
Erlaubnis *f* permission.
erlaubt *adj* allowed.
erläutern *vt* to explain.
Erläuterung *f* explanation.
erleben *vt* to experience.
Erlebnis *n* experience.
erledigen *vt* to carry out; to finish.
erledigt *adj* done.
Erledigung *f* settlement; handling.
erleichtern *vt* to relieve.
erleichtert *adj* relieved.
Erleichterung *f* relief.
erleiden *vt* to suffer.
erlernen *vt* to learn.
erlesen *vt* to select:—*adj* select.
Erlös *m* proceeds.
erlöschen *vi* to be extinguished.
ermächtigen *vt* to authorize.
Ermächtigung *f* authorization.
ermitteln *vt* to determine.
Ermitt(e)lung *f* determination.
ermöglichen *vt* to make possible.
ermorden *vt* to murder.
Ermordung *f* murder.
ermüden *vt* to tire.
ermunten, ermutigen *vt* to encourage.
ernähren *vt* to feed:—*vr* to earn a living.
Ernährung *f* nutrition.
ernennen *vt* to appoint.
erneuern *vt* to renew.
Erneuerung *f* renewal, renovation.
erneut *adj* renewed:—*adj* again.
Ernst *m* seriousness:—**im ~** in earnest.
ernst *adj* serious.
Ernstfall *m* emergency.
ernsthaft *adj* serious.

ernstlich *adj adv* serious(ly).

Ernte *f* harvest.

ernten *vt vi* to harvest.

Eroberer *m* conqueror.

erobern *vt* to conquer.

Eroberung *f* conquest.

eröffnen *vt* to open.

erörtern *vt* to discuss.

erotisch *adj* erotic.

erreichbar *adj* accessible.

erreichen *vt* to reach.

errichten *vt* to erect.

erringen *vt* to achieve.

Ersatz *m* compensation; alternative, substitute.

Ersatzreifen *m* spare tyre.

Ersatzteil *n* spare part.

erscheinen *vi* to appear.

Erscheinung *f* appearance.

erschießen *vt* to shoot (dead).

Erschießung *f* shooting, execution.

erschöpfen *vt* to exhaust.

erschöpft *adj* exhausted.

Erschöpfung *f* exhaustion.

erschrecken *vt* to frighten:—*vi vr* to be frightened.

erschrocken *adj* frightened.

erschüttern *vt* to shake; to upset.

erschütternd *adj* shocking.

Erschütterung *f* shock.

ersehen *vt* to see, note.

ersetzbar *adj* replaceable.

ersetzen *vt* to replace.

ersichtlich *adj* obvious.

ersparen *vt* to spare, save.

erst *adv* first; only; not until.

erstaunen *vt* to astonish:—*vi* to be astonished.

erstaunlich *adj* astonishing.

erste(r, s) *adj* first.

erstellen *vt* to provide; to construct.

erstens *adv* firstly.

erstklassig *adj* first-class.

erstmals *adv* for the first time.

erstrecken *vr* to extend.

ersuchen *vt* to request.

Ersuchen *n* request.

erteilen *vt* to give, grant.

Ertrag *m* yield, profit.

ertragen *vt* to endure.

erträglich *adj* bearable.

ertrinken *vi* to drown.

erwachen *vi* to awake.

erwachsen *adj* grown-up.

Erwachsene(r) *f(m)*dult.

erwägen *vt* to consider.

Erwägung *f* consideration.

erwähnen *vt* to mention.

Erwähnung *f* mention.

erwärmen *vt* to warm, heat:—*vr* to heat up.

erwarten *vt* to expect.

Erwartung *f* expectation.

erwartungsvoll *adj* expectant:—*adv* expectantly.

erwecken *vt* to wake, stir up.

erweisen *vt* to prove.

erweitern *vt vr* to widen, expand.

Erweiterung *f* expansion.

Erwerb *m* acquisition; occupation.

erwerben *vt* to acquire; to earn.

erwidern *vt* to return; to reply.

Erwiderung *f* reply.

erwünscht *adj* desired.

erwürgen *vt* to strangle.

Erz *n* ore.

erzählen *vt* to tell.

Erzählung *f* story.

Erzbischof *m* archbishop.

erzeugen *vt* to produce.

Erzeugnis *n* product.

Erzeugung *f* production.

erziehen *vt* to bring up; to educate.

Erziehung *f* bringing up; education.

erzielen *vt* to achieve.

erzwingen *vt* to force.

es *pn nom acc* it.
Esche *f* ash (tree).
Esel *m* donkey.
eßbar *adj* edible.
essen *vt vi* to eat.
Essen *n* food; meal.
Essig *m* vinegar.
Estland *n* Estonia.
etablieren *vt vr* to establish.
Etage *f* floor, storey.
ethisch *adj* ethical.
Etikett *n* label.
Etikette *f* etiquette.
etwa *adv* about, approximately; for example.
etwaig *adj* any; possible.
etwas *pn* something; anything:—*adj* some, a little.
euch *pn* (*acc dat of* **ihr**) (to) you; (to) yourselves.
euer *pn* (*gen of* **ihr**) of you:—*poss adj* your.
Eule *f* owl.
eure(r, s) *poss pn* yours.
Europa *n* Europe.
Europäer(in) *m(f)* European.
europäisch *adj* European.
eventuell *adj* possible:—*adv* possibly, if necessary.
ewig *adj* eternal.

Ewigkeit *f* eternity.
Examen *n* examination.
Exemplar *n* sample; copy (of book).
Exil *n* exile.
Existenz *f* existence.
existieren *vi* to exist.
exklusiv *adj* exclusive.
exklusive *adv* excluding.
Exkursion *f* excursion.
exotisch *adj* exotic.
Expansion *f* expansion.
Expedition *f* dispatch; expedition.
Experiment *n* experiment.
experimentell *adj* experimental.
experimentieren *vi* to experiment.
Experte *m* **Expertin** *f* expert.
explodieren *vi* to explode.
Explosion *f* explosion.
explosiv *adj* explosive.
Export *m* export.
Exporteur *m* exporter.
exportieren *vt* to export.
expreß *adv* express(ly).
extensiv *adj* extensive.
extern *adj* external.
extra *adj adv* extra.
extravagant *adj* extravagant.
extrem *adj* extreme.
exzentrisch *adj* eccentric.
Exzeß *m* excess.

F

Fabel *f* fable.
fabelhaft *adj* fabulous.
Fabrik *f* factory.
Fabrikant *m* manufacturer.
Fach *n* compartment; subject.
fächeln *vt* to fan.
Fachhochschule *f* technical university.

fachlich *adj* technical, professional.
Fachmann *m* expert.
fade *adj* dull.
Faden *m* thread.
fähig *adj* capable.
Fähigkeit *f* ability.
Fahne *f* flag.

Fähre f ferry.
fahren vt vi to travel; to drive.
Fahrer(in) m(f) driver.
Fahrgeld n fare.
Fahrkarte f ticket.
fahrlässig adj negligent.
Fahrlässigkeit f negligence.
Fahrlehrer(in) m(f) driving instructor.
Fahrplan m timetable.
Fahrprüfung f driving test.
Fahrrad n bicycle.
Fahrt f journey:—**gute** ~ have a good trip.
Fahrzeug n vehicle.
faktisch adj factual:—adv actually, de facto.
Faktor m factor.
Falke m falcon.
Fall m fall; case:—**auf jeden ~, auf alle Fälle** in any case:—**auf keinen ~** by no means.
fallen vi to fall:—~ **lassen** to drop.
fällig adj due.
falls conj in case.
falsch adj wrong; false.
fälschen vt to falsify.
Falschheit f falsity.
fälschlich adv falsely.
Fälschung f fake.
falten vt to fold.
Familie f family.
Familienname m surname.
Fanatiker m fanatic.
fanatisch adj fanatic(al).
Fang m catch.
fangen vt to catch.
Farbe f colour; dye; paint.
Farbfernsehen n colour television.
farbig adj coloured.
farblos adj colourless.
Farbstoff m dye, colouring.
Faser f fibre.
Faß n barrel.
fassen vt to grasp; to understand.

Fassung f frame, mount; version; composure.
fast adv nearly.
fasten vi to fast.
Fastzeit f Lent.
faszinieren vt to fascinate.
fatal adj fatal; awkward.
faul adj rotten; lazy.
faulen vi to rot.
Faulheit f laziness.
Fäulnis f decay.
Faust f fist.
Februar m February.
fechten vi to fence; to fight.
Feder f feather; spring; nib.
Fee f fairy.
fegen vt vi to sweep.
fehlen vi to be absent; to lack:—**Ich fehle sie** I miss her.
Fehler m mistake; fault.
fehlerfrei adj faultless.
fehlerhaft adj faulty.
Fehlschlag m miss; failure.
fehlschlagen vi to fail.
Feier f celebration.
feierlich adj festive; ceremonious.
feiern vt to celebrate.
Feiertag m holiday.
feig(e) adj cowardly.
Feige f fig.
Feigheit f cowardice.
Feigling m coward.
Feile f file.
feilen vt to file.
fein adj fine.
Feind m enemy.
feindlich adj hostile.
Feindlichkeit f hostility.
Feinheit f fineness, refinement.
Feinkost f delicatessen.
Feld n field.
Feldwebel m sergeant.
Fell n skin, hide.

Fels *m* rock.
Felsen *m* cliff.
Fenster *n* window.
Ferien *pl* holidays, vacation.
Ferkel *n* piglet.
fern *adj adv* far, distant.
Ferne *f* distance.
ferner *adj* further:—*adv* furthermore.
Fernglas *n* binoculars.
fernhalten *vt* to keep away.
Fernrohr *n* telescope.
Fernsehen *n* television.
fernsehen *vi* to watch television.
Fernseher *m* television (set).
Ferse *f* heel.
fertig *adj* ready; complete.
Fertigkeit *f* skill.
fertigmachen *vt* to complete.
Fertigung *f* production.
fesseln *vt* to bind.
fest *adj* firm; solid; fixed.
Fest *n* festival; party.
festbinden *vt* to fasten.
festhalten *vt* to hold; to arrest.
festigen *vt* to strengthen.
Festigkeit *f* strength.
festlegen *vt* to fix.
festlich *adj* festive.
festmachen *vt* to fix:—*vi* to moor.
Festnahme *f* capture.
festnehmen *vt* to capture, arrest.
feststehen *vi* to be certain.
feststellen *vt* to establish; to state.
Festung *f* fortress.
Fett *n* fat, grease.
fett *adj* fat, greasy.
fetten *vt* to grease.
feucht *adj* damp.
Feuchtigkeit *f* damp, humidity.
Feuer *n* fire:—**haben Sie ~?** have you got a light?
Feueralarm *n* fire alarm.
feuergefährlich *adj* (in)flammable.

Feuerlöscher *m* fire extinguisher.
Feuermann *m* **-frau** *f* fireman, -woman.
feuern *vt vi* to fire.
Feuerversicherung *f* fire insurance.
Feuerwehr *f* fire brigade.
Feuerwehrwagen *n* fire engine.
Feuerwerk *n* fireworks.
Feuerzeug *n* cigarette lighter.
feurig *adj* fiery.
Fichte *f* spruce, pine.
Fieber *n* fever.
fieberhaft *adj* feverish.
Figur *f* figure; chess piece.
Fiktion *f* fiction.
fiktiv *adj* fictitious.
Filiale *f* branch; subsidiary.
Film *m* film.
filmen *vt vi* to film.
Filter *m* filter.
filtern *vt* to filter.
Filz *m* felt.
Filzstift *m* felt-tip (pen).
Finanz *f* finance.
finanziell *adj* financial.
finanzieren *vt* to finance.
Finanzminister *m* finance minister.
Finanzministerium *n* finance ministry.
finden *vt* to find; to think, believe:—*vr* to be (located).
Finger *m* finger.
Fingerabdruck *m* fingerprint.
Fingerhut *m* thimble; foxglove.
Fingernagel *m* fingernail.
Finke *m* finch.
Finne *m* **Finnin** *f* Finn.
finnisch *adj* Finnish.
Finnland *n* Finland.
finster *adj* dark, gloomy.
Finsternis *f* darkness.
Firma *f* company.
Fisch *m* fish.
fischen *vt vi* to fish.
Fischermann *m* fisherman.

Fischfang *m* fishing.
Fischhändler *m* fishmonger.
fischig *adj* fishy.
fix *adj* fixed; clever.
flach *adj* flat; shallow.
Fläche *f* surface; area.
flackern *vi* to flicker; to flare.
Flagge *f* flag.
Flamme *f* flame.
flammen *vi* to blaze.
Flanke *f* flank; wing (football, etc).
Flasche *f* bottle.
Flaschenöffner *m* bottle opener.
flattern *vi* to flutter.
flau *adj* weak.
Flaute *f* calm; recession.
Fleck *m* spot; stain.
Fledermaus *f* bat.
flehen *vi* to implore.
Fleisch *n* flesh; meat.
fleißig *adj* hard-working.
Flieder *m* lilac.
Fliege *f* fly; bow tie.
fliegen *vt vi* to fly.
Fliegenpilz *m* toadstool.
Flieger *m* flier.
fliehen *vt vi* to flee.
Fliese *f* tile.
Fließband *n* conveyor belt.
fließen *vi* to flow.
fließend *adj* flowing; fluent.
flimmern *vi* to glitter.
flink *adj* quick, agile.
Flinte *f* rifle.
Flitterwochen *pl* honeymoon.
Flocke *f* flake.
Floh *m* flea.
Florenz *n* Florence.
Flöte *f* flute.
Fluch *m* curse.
fluchen *vi* to curse, swear.
Flucht *f* flight.
flüchten *vi* to flee.

flüchtig *adj* fugitive; fleeting.
Flüchtling *m* refugee.
Flug *m* flight.
Flugblatt *n* leaflet.
Flügel *m* wing; grand piano.
Fluggast *m* (air) passenger.
Fluggesellschaft *f* airline.
Flughafen *m* airport.
Flugzeug *n* aircraft.
Flugzeugträger *m* aircraft carrier.
Flur *m* hall.
Fluß *m* river; flow.
flüssig *adj* liquid.
Flüssigkeit *f* liquid, fluid.
flüstern *vi vt* to whisper.
Flut *f* flood; high tide.
fluten *vi* to flood.
Folge *f* result; series; sequence.
folgen *vi* to follow.
folglich *adv* consequently.
folgsam *adj* obedient.
Folie *f* foil, film.
Folter *f* torture.
foltern *vt* to torture.
Fön *m* hair drier.
Fonds *m* fund.
Fontäne *f* fountain.
Förderband *n* conveyor belt.
fordern *vt* to demand.
fördern *vt* to promote, encourage.
Forderung *f* demand.
Förderung *f* promotion, encouragement.
Forelle *f* trout.
Form *f* form, shape; mould.
Formalität *f* formality.
Format *n* format; importance.
formatieren *vt* to format.
Formation *f* formation.
Formel *f* formula.
formell *adj* formal.
formen *vt* to form.
förmlich *adj* formal; literal.
formlos *adj* shapeless; informal.

Formular *n* form.
formulieren *vt* to formulate.
forschen *vi* to investigate, research.
Forscher(in) *m(f)* researcher, scientist.
Forschung *f* research.
Forst *m* forest.
fort *adv* away; gone; on(wards).
fortan *adv* from now on.
Fortbestand *m* continuance.
fortbestehen *vi* to continue, survive.
fortbewegen *vt* to move on, away.
Fortbildung *f* further education.
fortdauern *vi* to continue.
fortfahren *vi* to drive on; to leave.
fortgehen *vi* to go away, continue.
fortgeschritten *adj* advanced.
fortleben *vi* to survive.
fortpflanzen *vt vr* to reproduce.
Fortschritt *m* progress.
fortsetzen *vt* to continue.
Fortsetzung *f* continuation.
Foto *n* photo(graph).
Fotoapparat *m* camera.
Fotograf(in) *m(f)* photographer.
Fotografie *f* photograph(y).
fotografieren *vt* to photograph:—*vi* to take photographs.
fotografisch *adj* photographic.
Fotokopie *f* photocopy.
fotokopieren *vt* to photocopy.
Fracht *f* freight.
Frage *f* question.
fragen *vt vi* to ask.
Fragezeichen *n* question mark.
fraglich *adj* questionable, doubtful.
frankieren *vt* to frank.
franko *adv* post-paid.
Frankreich *n* France.
Franzose *m* Frenchman.
Französin *f* Frenchwoman.
französisch *adj* French.
Frau *f* woman; wife; Mrs, Ms.
Fräulein *n* young woman; Miss, Ms.

frech *adj* cheeky.
Frechheit *f* cheek.
frei *adj* free; freelance.
freigebig *adj* generous.
Freihandel *m* free trade.
Freiheit *f* freedom.
freilassen *vt* to release.
Freilassung *f* release.
freilich *adv* certainly.
Freimaurer *m* freemason.
freisprechen *vt* to acquit.
Freispruch *m* acquittal.
freistellen *vt* to exempt.
Freitag *m* Friday.
freiwillig *adj* voluntary:—*adv* voluntarily.
Freiwillige(r) *f(m)* volunteer.
Freizeit *f* free time.
fremd *adj* strange, foreign.
Fremde(r) *f(m)* stranger, foreigner.
Frequenz *f* frequency.
fressen *vt vi* to eat, guzzle.
Freude *f* joy.
freudig *adj* joyful.
freuen *vt* to please:—*vr* to be happy; to look forward.
Freund *m* (boy)friend.
Freundin *f* (girl)friend.
freundlich *adj* friendly.
Freundschaft *f* friendship.
Frieden *m* peace.
Friedhof *m* cemetery.
friedlich *adj* peaceful.
frieren *vt vi* to freeze.
frisch *adj* fresh.
Frische *f* freshness.
Friseur *m* **Friseuse** *f* hairdresser.
Frist *f* period; time limit, deadline.
fristlos *adj* without notice.
froh, fröhlich *adj* happy.
fromm *adj* pious.
Frömmigkeit *f* piety.
Front *f* front.
Frosch *m* frog.

Frost *m* frost.
frostig *adj* frosty.
Frucht *f* fruit; corn.
fruchtbar *adj* fruitful.
fruchtlos *adj* fruitless.
Fruchtsaft *m* fruit juice.
früh *adj adv* early; in the morning.
Frühling *m* spring.
Frühstück *n* breakfast.
frühzeitig *adj* early, premature.
Frustration *f* frustration.
frustrieren *vt* to frustrate.
Fuchs *m* fox.
Füchsin *f* vixen.
fügen *vt* to place; to ordain:—*vr* to comply, adapt.
fügsam *adj* obedient.
fühlbar *adj* tangible.
fühlen *vt vi vr* to feel.
führen *vt vi* to lead; to manage:—*vr* to behave.
Führer *m* leader.
Führerschein *m* driver's licence.
Führung *f* leadership, management.
füllen *vt* to fill.
Fund *m* find.
fünf *num* five.

fünfte(r, s) *adj* fifth.
Fünftel *n* fifth.
fünfzehn *num* fifteen.
fünfzig *num* fifty.
Funk *m* radio.
Funke *m* spark.
funkeln *vi* to sparkle.
Funkgerät *n* radio (set).
Funkstation *f* radio station.
Funktion *f* function.
funktionell *adj* functional.
funktionieren *vi* to function.
für *prep* for:—**was ~** what kind of.
Furcht *f* fear.
furchtbar *adj* fearful, dreadful.
fürchten *vt* to fear:—*vr* to be afraid.
fürs = **für das**.
Fürsorge *f* care; welfare.
Fürst(in) *m(f)* prince(ss).
Fürstentum *n* principality.
Fusion *f* fusion, merger.
Fuß *m* foot.
Fußball *m* football.
Fußboden *m* floor.
Fußgänger(in) *m(f)* pedestrian.
füttern *vt* to feed.

G

Gabe *f* gift.
Gabel *f* fork.
gähnen *vi* to yawn.
Galerie *f* gallery.
Gang *m* walk; operation; corridor; gangway; aisle; gear.
Gans *f* goose.
Gänseblümchen *n* daisy.
ganz *adj* all; whole:—*adv* very; completely.

gar *adj* well cooked; *adv* absolutely: — **~ nicht** not at all:—**~ nichts** nothing at all.
Garage *f* garage.
Garantie *f* guarantee.
garantieren *vt* to guarantee.
Garderobe *f* wardrobe; cloakroom.
Gardine *f* curtain.
gären *vi* to ferment.
Garten *m* garden.

Gartenarbeit *f* gardening.
Gärtner(in) *m(f)* gardener.
Gärung *f* fermentation.
Gas *n* gas.
Gasse *f* street, alley.
Gast *f* guest.
Gastarbeiter(in) *m(f)* foreign worker.
gastfreundlich *adj* hospitable.
Gastfreundschaft *f* hospitality.
Gastgeber(in) *m(f)* host(ess).
Gaststätte *f* restaurant.
Gastwirt *m* landlord, hotelier.
Gaswerk *n* gasworks.
Gaszähler *m* gas meter.
Gatte *m* **Gattin** *f* spouse.
Gattung *f* type, genus.
gaukeln *vi* to juggle, do tricks.
Gauner *m* swindler.
Gebäck *n* pastry.
Gebärde *f* gesture.
gebärden, gebaren *vr* to behave.
gebären *vt* to give birth to.
Gebärmutter *f* womb.
Gebäude *n* building.
geben *vt* to give:—**es gibt** there is/are.
Gebet *n* prayer.
Gebiet *n* area.
Gebilde *n* object; structure.
gebildet *adj* educated.
Gebinde *n* bundle.
Gebirge *n* mountains.
Gebiß *n* teeth; dentures.
geboren *adj* born; née.
geborgen *adj* safe.
Geborgenheit *f* safety.
Gebot *n* commandment; bid.
Gebrauch *m* use; custom.
gebrauchen *vt* to use.
gebräuchlich *adj* customary.
Gebrauchsanweisung *f* instructions (for use).
gebraucht *adj* used.
gebrochen *adj* broken.

Gebühr *f* fee.
Geburt *f* birth.
Geburtsdatum *n* date of birth.
Geburtsort *m* place of birth.
Geburtstag *m* birthday.
Gedächtnis *n* memory.
Gedanke *m* thought.
gedeihen *vi* to thrive.
Gedicht *n* poem.
gedrängt *adj* crowded, compressed.
gedrückt *adj* depressed.
Geduld *f* patience.
geduldig *adj* patient.
geehrt *adj* honoured:—**sehr geehrter Herr...** Dear Mr...
geeignet *adj* suitable.
Gefahr *f* danger; risk.
gefährden *vt* to endanger.
gefährlich *adj* dangerous.
Gefallen *m* favour, kindness:—*n* pleasure.
gefallen *vi* to please:—**es gefällt mir** I like it.
gefällig *adj* pleasant.
gefangen *adj* captive.
Gefangene(r) *f(m)* prisoner.
Gefängnis *n* prison.
Gefühl *n* feeling.
gegebenenfalls *adv* if necessary.
gegen *prep* towards; against; about; in return for; versus.
Gegend *f* area.
Gegensatz *m* contrast; contrary.
gegensätzlich *adj* contrary.
gegenseitig *adj* mutual.
Gegenspieler *m* opponent.
Gegenstand *m* object.
Gegenteil *n* opposite; to the contrary.
gegenüber *adv* opposite:—*prep* opposite, towards.
Gegenwart *f* present.
gegenwärtig *adj* present.
Gegner *m* opponent.
gegnerisch *adj* opposing.

Gegnerschaft f opposition.
Gehalt m contents; salary.
geheim adj secret.
Geheimnis n secret.
gehen vt vi to go; to walk:—**wie geht's?** how are you?
Gehirn n brain.
Gehör n hearing.
gehorchen vi to obey.
gehören vi to belong to.
gehörig adj belonging to; appropriate.
gehorsam adj obedient.
Gehorsam m obedience.
Geier m vulture.
Geige f violin.
Geiger(in) m(f) violinist.
geil adj randy.
Geisel f hostage.
Geist m spirit, mind; ghost.
geistig adj intellectual.
geistlich adj spiritual.
Geistliche(r) f(m) priest.
Geistlichkeit f clergy.
Geiz m meanness.
Geizhals m miser.
geizig adj mean.
gekonnt adj clever.
Gelächter n laughter.
geladen adj loaded; live (wire).
Geländer n railings, banisters.
gelangen vi to reach.
gelassen adj calm.
Gelassenheit f calmness.
geläufig adj fluent; common.
gelaunt adj:—**gut/schlecht ~** in a good/bad mood.
gelb adj yellow.
Geld n money.
Geldstück n coin.
Gelee m or n jelly.
gelegen adj located; convenient.
Gelegenheit f opportunity; occasion.
gelegentlich adj adv occasional(ly).

gelehrt adj learned.
Geleit n escort.
geleiten vt to escort.
Gelenk n joint.
gelernt adj skilled.
gelingen vi to succeed:—**es gelang mir** I succeeded.
geloben vt to promise.
Gelöbnis n promise.
gelten vt to be worth:—vi to be valid, apply.
Geltung f validity.
gelungen adj successful.
Gemälde n painting.
gemäß prep in accordance with.
gemäßigt adj moderate.
gemein adj common.
Gemeinde f district.
gemeinsam adj joint, common.
Gemeinschaft f community.
Gemisch n mixture.
gemischt adj mixed.
Gemüse n vegetables.
Gemüt n nature, temperament.
gemütlich adj cosy, comfortable.
Gemütlichkeit f cosiness, comfort.
Gen n gene.
genau adj exact:—adv exactly.
Genauigkeit f accuracy.
genauso adv just the same.
genehm adj acceptable.
genehmigen vt to approve, allow.
Genehmigung f approval, authorization.
geneigt adj inclined.
Generation f generation.
Generator m generator.
genesen vi to recover.
Genf n Geneva.
Genick n neck.
Genie n genius.
genießen vt to enjoy; to eat.
Genosse m **Genossin** f companion.
Genossenschaft f cooperative (society).
Genua n Genoa.

genug *adj adv* enough.
genügen *vi* to suffice.
Genugtuung *f* satisfaction.
Genuß *m* pleasure; enjoyment.
genußreich *adj* enjoyable.
Geograph *m* geographer.
Geographie *f* geography.
geographisch *adj* geographical.
Geologe *m* geologist.
Geologie *f* geology.
geologisch *adj* geological.
Gepäck *n* baggage.
gepflegt *adj* smart.
Gepflogenheit *f* habit.
gerade *adj* straight:—*adv* exactly; especially; even (number); just (about).
geradeaus *adv* straight on.
geradezu *adv* almost.
Gerät *n* tool, (item of) equipment.
geraten *vi* to turn out.
geräumig *adj* spacious.
Geräusch *n* noise.
geräuschlos *adj* noiseless.
geräuschvoll *adj* noisy.
gerecht *adj* fair.
Gerechtigkeit *f* justice.
Gerede *n* talk.
geregelt *adj* regular.
gereizt *adj* irritated.
Gereiztheit *f* irritation.
Gericht *n* dish, course; court.
gerichtlich *adj* judicial.
Gerichtshof *m* court.
gering *adj* little, slight.
geringfügig *adj* minor, slight.
gern(e) *adv* willingly:—~ **haben, mögen, tun** to like:—**ich schwimme** ~ I like swimming.
Gerste *f* barley.
Geruch *m* smell.
Gerücht *n* rumour.
gesamt *adj* whole.
Geschäft *n* business; transaction; shop.

Geschäftsfrau *f* businesswoman.
Geschäftsführer *m* director.
Geschäftsführung *f* management.
Geschäftsmann *m* businessman.
geschehen *vi* to happen.
gescheit *adj* clever.
Geschenk *n* gift.
Geschichte *f* story; history.
geschichtlich *adj* historic(al):—*adv* historically.
Geschick *n* destiny; skill.
geschickt *adj* skilful.
geschieden *adj* divorced.
Geschirr *n* crockery, kitchen utensils; harness.
Geschirrtuch *n* dishcloth.
Geschlecht *n* sex, gender; species.
geschlechtlich *adj* sexual.
geschlossen *adj* closed.
Geschmack *m* taste.
Geschöpf *n* creature.
Geschoß *n* projectile; floor, storey.
Geschrei *n* shouting.
Geschütz *n* gun.
Geschwader *n* squadron.
Geschwindigkeit *f* speed.
Geschwister *pl* brother(s) and sister(s).
Geselle *m* companion.
gesellig *adj* sociable.
Geselligkeit *f* sociability.
Gesellschaft *f* company; society.
Gesetz *n* law.
Gesetzgebung *f* legislation.
gesetzlich *adj* legal, statutory.
gesetzlos *adj* lawless.
gesetzmäßig *adj* legal.
gesetzwidrig *adj* illegal.
Gesicht *n* face.
Gesichtspunkt *m* point of view.
gesinnt *adj* disposed.
Gesinnung *f* disposition.
Gespann *n* team.
gespannt *adj* tight; in suspense.

Gespenst n ghost.
gespensterhaft adj ghostly.
Gespinst n tissue, fabric.
Gespött n mockery.
Gespräch n talk, conversation.
gesprächig adj talkative.
Gesprechspartner m interlocutor.
Gestalt f shape; figure.
gestalten vt to form; to design:—vr to turn out.
Gestalter(in) m(f) designer.
Gestaltung f formation; arrangement.
Geständnis n confession.
gestatten vt to allow.
Geste f gesture.
gestehen vt vi to confess.
Gestein n rock.
Gestell n frame.
gestern adv yesterday.
Gestirn n star; constellation.
gestrichen adj painted; cancelled.
Gesuch n request.
gesucht adj sought-after.
gesund adj healthy.
Gesundheit f health.
Gesundung f recovery.
Getränk n drink.
Getreide n corn; grain, cereals.
Getriebe n gears, gearbox.
geübt adj experienced.
Geübtheit f skill, experience.
Gewächs n growth; plant.
Gewächshaus n greenhouse.
gewagt adj daring.
gewählt adj selected.
gewahren vt to perceive.
Gewähr f guarantee.
gewähren vt to grant.
gewährleisten vt to guarantee.
Gewährleistung f guarantee.
Gewahrsam m/n safekeeping; custody.
Gewalt f power; violence.
gewaltig adj huge.

gewalttätig adj violent.
gewandt adj agile, skilful.
Gewebe n fabric, tissue.
Gewehr n gun.
Gewerbe n occupation; industry.
gewerblich adj commercial, industrial.
Gewerkschaft f trade union.
Gewicht n weight.
gewichtig adj heavy.
gewiegt adj experienced.
gewillt adj willing.
Gewinn n profit.
gewinnbringend adj profitable.
gewinnen vt vi to win.
Gewinner(in) m(f) winner.
Gewinnung f winning; extraction.
gewiß adj certain:—adv certainly.
Gewissen n conscience.
gewissenhaft adj conscientious.
gewissenlos adj unscrupulous.
gewissermaßen adv as it were; to an extent.
Gewißheit f certainty.
Gewitter n (thunder)storm.
gewöhnen vt to accustom:—vr to become used to.
Gewohnheit f habit.
gewöhnlich adj usual:—adv usually.
gewohnt adj usual; used to.
gewollt adj deliberate.
Gewürz n spice.
Gezeiten pl tide.
gezielt adj deliberate; specific.
Gier f greed, eagerness.
gierig adj greedy.
gießen vt vi to pour.
Gießkanne f watering can.
Gift m poison.
giftig adj poisonous.
Gigant m giant.
Gipfel m summit.
Gips m gypsum; plaster.
gipsen vt to plaster.

Gipser *m* plasterer.
Giraffe *f* giraffe.
Giro *n* giro.
Girobank *f* clearing bank.
Girokonto *n* current account.
Gitarre *f* guitar.
Gitter *n* grille, grating.
Glanz *m* brightness; glory.
glänzen *vt* to polish:—*vi* to gleam.
glänzend *adj* brilliant.
Glas *n* glass.
Glaser *m* glazier.
gläsern *adj* glassy.
glatt *adj* smooth:—*adv* smoothly.
Glatteis *n* (black) ice.
Glatze *f* bald patch, bald head.
Glauben *m* belief.
glauben *vt vi* to believe.
glaubhaft *adj* credible.
gläubig *adj* believing.
Gläubiger(in) *m(f)* creditor.
glaublich, glaubwürdig *adj* credible.
gleich *adj* same:—*adv* equally; immediately:—*prep* like.
gleichartig *adj* similar.
gleichen *vi* to be equal to; to resemble.
gleichfalls *adv* also.
Gleichgewicht *n* balance.
Gleichheit *f* equality.
gleichkommen *vi* to equal.
gleichlautend *adj* similar.
gleichmachen *vt* to equalize.
gleichmäßig *adj* proportionate; uniform.
Gleichmäßigkeit *f* uniformity.
gleichmütig *adj* even-tempered.
gleichsam *adv* as it were.
gleichsehen *vi* to resemble.
Gleichstrom *m* direct current.
Gleichung *f* equation.
gleichwertig *adj* equivalent.
gleichzeitig *adj* simultaneous.
Gleis *n* track; platform.
gleiten *vi* to glide; to slide.

Gletscher *m* glacier.
Glied *n* member; limb.
Gliederung *f* structure; classification.
glimmen *vi* to smoulder, glimmer.
Globus *m* globe.
Glocke *f* bell.
Glück *n* luck; happiness:—~ **haben** to succeed.
glücklich *adj* fortunate; happy:—*adv* fortunately.
glücklicherweise *adv* fortunately.
glückselig *adj* ecstatic.
Glückwunsch *m* best wishes.
Glückwunschkarte *f* greetings card.
Glühbirne *f* light bulb.
glühen *vi* to glow.
glühend *adj* glowing.
Gnade *f* grace, favour; mercy.
gnädig *adj* gracious.
Gold *n* gold.
golden *adj* golden.
Goldfisch *m* goldfish.
Goldschmied *m* goldsmith.
Golf *m* gulf:—*n* golf.
gönnen *vt* to allow.
Gorilla *m* gorilla.
Gott *m* god, God.
Göttin *f* goddess.
göttlich *adj* divine.
Götze *m* idol.
Grab *n* grave.
graben *vt vi* to dig.
Graben *m* ditch.
Grabstein *m* gravestone.
Grad *m* degree.
Graf *m* count; earl.
Gräfin *f* countess.
Gram *m* grief.
grämen *vt vr* to grieve.
Gramm *n* gram.
Grammatik *f* grammar.
grammatisch *adj* grammatical.
Gran *n* grain.

Granate f grenade.
Granit m granite.
Graphik f graphics.
graphisch adj adv graphic(ally).
Gras n grass.
grasen vi to graze.
gräßlich adj horrible.
Grat m ridge.
Gräte f fishbone.
gratulieren vi to congratulate.
grau adj grey.
grausam adj cruel.
Grausamkeit f cruelty.
gravieren vt to engrave.
Gravitation f gravitation.
Gravüre f engraving.
greifbar adj tangible.
greifen vt to grip.
Greis m old man.
grell adj shrill; garish.
Gremium n body, group.
Grenze f boundary, frontier.
Greuel m horror.
greulich adj horrible.
Griecher m **Griechin** f Greek.
Griechenland n Greece.
griechisch adj Greek.
Griff m grasp, hold; lever; handle.
Grill m grill.
Grille f cricket; whim.
grillen vt to grill.
Grinsen n grin.
grinsen vi to grin.
Grippe f flu.
grob adj coarse; gross.
Groll m grudge.
grollen vi to sulk.
Gros n gross; majority.
Groschen m ten pfennig coin.
groß adj great; large; tall; adv greatly, highly.
großartig adj great.
Großbritannien n (Great) Britain.

Großbuchstabe m capital (letter).
Größe f size; quantity.
Großeltern pl grandparents.
großenteils adv largely.
Großhandel m wholesale (trade).
Großhändler m wholesaler.
Großmut f generosity.
großmütig adj generous.
Großmutter f grandmother.
Großstadt f city.
größtenteils adv mainly.
großtun vi to boast.
Großvater m grandfather.
großzügig adj large-scale; generous.
Großzügigkeit f grandness; generosity.
grotesk adj grotesque.
Grube f pit, mine.
grün adj green.
Grund m ground; reason.
Grundbesitz m property.
gründen vt to establish:—vr ~ auf to be based on.
Gründer(in) m(f) founder.
Grundgesetz n constitution.
Grundlage f basis.
grundlegend adj fundamental.
gründlich adj thorough.
grundlos adj groundless.
Grundriß m ground-plan, layout.
Grundsatz m principle.
grundsätzlich adj fundamental:—adv fundametally.
Grundschule f primary school.
Grundstück n (piece of) land.
Gründung f foundation.
grunzen vt vi to grunt.
Gruppe f group.
gruppieren vt to group.
Gruß m greeting; salute:—**mit freundlichen Grüßen** yours sincerely:—**viele Grüße** best wishes.
grüßen vt to greet, welcome.
gucken vi to look, peep.

gültig *adj* valid.
Gültigkeit *f* validity.
Gummi *m/n* rubber.
Gunst *f* favour.
günstig *adj* favourable.
Gurgel *f* throat.
gurgeln *vt vi* to gurgle, gargle.
Gurke *f* cucumber, gherkin.
Gurt, Gürtel *m* belt.
gut *adj* good:—*adv* well.
Gut *n* good(s); property.

Gutachten *n* assessment, valuation.
gutartig *adj* good-natured.
gutaussehend *adj* good-looking.
Güte *f* goodness.
gutgelaunt *adj* cheerful.
gütig *adj* kind.
gütlich *adj* amicable.
Gymnasium *n* secondary school.
Gymnastik *f* gymnastics.
Gynäkologe *m* gynaecologist.
Gynäkologie *f* gynaecology.

H

Haar *n* hair.
haarig *adj* hairy.
haben *vt v aux* to have.
hacken *vt vi* to chop.
Hafen *m* port, harbour.
Hafer *m* oats.
Haft *f* custody.
haftbar *adj* liable.
haften *vi* to stick, persist; to be liable.
Haftung *f* liability.
Hagel *m* hail.
Hahn *m* cock, rooster; tap.
Hähnchen *n* cockerel; chicken.
Hai *m* shark.
Hain *m* copse.
Haken *m* hook.
Hakenkreuz *n* swastika.
halb *adj adv* half:—~ **vier** half past three.
Halbfinale *n* semi-final.
halbieren *vt* to halve.
Halbinsel *f* peninsula.
Halbkreis *m* semicircle.
Halbkugel *f* hemisphere.
halboffen *adj* half-open, ajar.
halbrund *adj* semicircular.
Halbtagsarbeit *f* part-time work.

Halbton *m* semitone.
halbwegs *adv* halfway.
Hälfte *f* half.
Halle *f* hall.
hallen *vi* to echo.
Hals *m* neck, throat.
Halskette *f* necklace.
Halt *m* hold; stop.
haltbar *adj* lasting.
Haltbarkeit *f* durability.
halten *vt* to hold; to keep; to contain:
　—~ **für** to consider.
Haltestelle *f* stop.
Haltung *f* attitude.
Hammer *m* hammer.
hämmern *vt vi* to hammer.
Hand *f* hand.
Handbremse *f* handbrake.
Handbuch *n* manual.
Handel *m* trade, commerce; deal.
handeln *vi* to act; to trade:—*vr* **sich ~
　um** to be a matter of.
Handgelenk *n* wrist.
handhaben *vt* to handle.
Händler(in) *m(f)* dealer; shopkeeper.
handlich *adj* handy.

Handlung f action; shop.
Handschrift f handwriting.
Handschuh m glove.
Handtasche f handbag.
Handtuch n towel.
Hang m slope.
hängen vt vi to hang.
Hannover n Hanover.
Harfe f harp.
Harke f rake.
harmlos adj harmless.
Harmonie f harmony.
harmonisch adj harmonious.
Harn m urine.
harnen vi to urinate.
harren vi to wait.
hart adj hard.
Härte f hardness.
härten vt vi to harden.
hartnäckig adj obstinate.
Hase m hare.
Haß m hatred.
hassen vt to hate.
häßlich adj ugly.
Hast f haste.
hasten vi to hurry.
hastig adj adv hurried(ly).
Haube f hood; bonnet.
Hauch m breath; trace.
hauchen vi to breathe.
hauen vt to cut; to thrash.
häufeln vt vi to pile (up).
Haufen m pile.
häufen vt vr to pile (up).
häufig adj frequent:—adv frequently, often.
Häufigkeit f frequency.
Haupt n head; chief.
Haupt- in compounds chief, main.
Hauptbahnhof m main station.
Hauptmann m captain.
hauptsächlich adj main:—adv main-ly.
Hauptschule f secondary school.

Hauptstadt f capital city.
Haus n house; building:—**nach ~e** home:—**zu ~e** (at) home.
Hausarbeit f housework; homework.
Hausfrau f housewife.
Haushalt m household.
häuslich adj domestic.
Haustier n pet.
Haut f skin.
Hebel m lever.
heben vt to lift.
Hecke f hedge.
Heer n army.
Hefe f yeast.
Heft n handle; notebook; issue.
heften vt to attach.
heftig adj strong, intense.
hegen vt to tend; to harbour (grudge).
Heide f heath, heather.
heikel adj fussy; difficult.
Heil n well-being.
heil adj safe, uninjured.
heilen vt to cure:—vi to heal.
heilig adj holy.
Heilige(r) f(m)saint.
Heilung f cure.
Heim n home.
heim adv home.
Heimat f home(land).
heimisch adj home, native.
heimlos adj homeless.
heimisch adj home, native:—**sich ~ fühlen** to feel at home.
Heimweh n homesickness.
Heirat f marriage.
heiraten vt vi to marry.
heiser adj hoarse.
Heiserkeit f hoarseness.
heiß adj hot.
heißen vt to call:—vi to be called; to mean:—**das heißt** that is (to say).
heiter adj bright; cheerful; sunny.
Heiterkeit f cheerfulness.

heizen *vt* to heat.
Heizung *f* heating.
hektisch *adj* hectic.
Held(in) *m(f)* hero.
heldenhaft *adj* heroic:—*adv* heroically.
Heldentum *n* heroism.
helfen *vi* to help.
Helfer(in) *m(f)* helper.
Helium *n* helium.
hell *adj* clear; bright; light (colour).
Helle, Helligkeit *f* brightness.
hellwach *adj* wide awake.
Helm *m* helmet; rudder.
Hemd *m* shirt.
Hemisphäre *f* hemisphere.
hemmen *vt* to obstruct.
Henkel *m* handle.
henken *vt* to hand.
Henker *m* hangman.
Henne *f* hen.
her *adv* here; from; ago.
herab *adv* down(wards).
heran *adv* this way; here; near.
herauf *adv* up(wards), up here.
heraus *adv* out(wards); from.
herausfordern *vt* to challenge.
Herausforderung *f* challenge.
herb *adj* bitter.
herbei *adv* here.
Herberge *f* hostel, inn.
Herbst *m* autumn.
Herd *m* cooker.
herein *adv* in (here); into:—~! come in!
Hering *m* herring.
herkommen *vi* to approach.
herkömmlich *adj* traditional.
Herkunft *f* origin.
Herr *m* lord; Mr; gentleman.
herrlich *adj* magnificent.
Herrschaft *f* domination; rule.
herrschen *vi* to rule; to prevail.
Herrscher(in) *m(f)* ruler.
herstellen *vt* to produce.

Hersteller(in) *m(f)* manufacturer.
Herstellung *f* production.
herum *adv* around.
herunter *adv* down.
hervor *adv* forth, out.
hervorragend *adj* outstanding.
Herz *n* heart.
Herzanfall *m* heart attack.
herzlich *adj* cordial.
herzlos *adj* heartless.
Herzog *m* duke.
Herzogin *f* duchess.
hetzen *vt* to hunt:—*vi* to hurry.
Heu *n* hay.
Heuchelei *f* hypocrisy.
heucheln *vt* to pretend:—*vi* to be a hypocrite.
heulen *vi* to howl; to hoot; to cry.
heute *adv* today.
heutig *adj* present-day.
heutzutage *adv* nowadays.
Hexagon *m* hexagon.
Hexe *f* witch.
Hexerei *f* witchcraft.
Hieb *m* blow; cut.
hier *adv* here.
hierauf *adv* thereupon.
hieraus *adv* from this.
hierbei *adv* at this, herewith.
hierdurch *adv* through here.
hierfür *adv* for this.
hierher *adv* here.
hierin *adv* in this.
hiermit *adv* herewith.
hiernach *adv* after this.
hierüber *adv* over here; about this.
hierum *adv* about this.
hierunter *adv* under this.
hiervon *adv* of this.
hierzu *adv* to this; moreover.
Hilfe *f* help:—**erste** ~ first aid.
hilflos *adj* helpless.
hilfreich *adj* helpful.

Hilfskraft f assistant.
Hilfsmittel n aid, means.
Himbeere f raspberry.
Himmel m sky; heaven.
Himmelfahrt f ascension.
hin adv there; away; gone:—~ **und zurück** there and back:—~ **und her** to and fro.
hinauf adv up(wards).
hinaufsteigen vi to climb.
hinaus adv out.
Hinblick m:—**in ~ auf** in view of.
hindern vt to hinder.
Hindernis n hindrance f obstacle.
hindeuten vi to point.
hindurch adv through.
hinein adv in(to).
Hingabe f devotion.
hingeben vr to devote oneself.
hinken vi to limp.
Hinsicht f respect, regard.
hinsichtlich adv with regard to.
hinten adv behind.
hinter prep behind.
Hintergrund m background.
hinterher adv behind; afterwards.
hinterlassen vt to leave (behind).
Hintertür f back door.
hinüber adv across.
hinunter adv down.
hinweg adv away; off.
Hinweis m reference; instruction.
hinweisen vt to refer to:—vi to point at.
hinzu adv there; also.
hinzufügen vt to add.
Hirn n brain.
Hirsch m stag.
Hirt m herdsman.
hissen vt to hoist.
Historiker m historian.
historisch adj adv historic(ally).
Hitze f heat.
Hitzewelle f heatwave.
hitzig adj hot-headed.

Hobby n hobby.
Hobel m plane.
hoch adj high.
Hochachtung f respect.
hochachtungsvoll adj yours faithfully.
Hochfrequenz f high frequency.
Hochmut m pride.
hochmütig adj haughty.
Hochschule f college.
Hochsprung m high jump.
Hochspringer(in) m(f) high-jumper.
höchst adj highest:—adv highly.
höchstens adv at most.
hochwertig adj high-quality.
Hochzeit f wedding.
hochziehen vt to raise.
hocken vi to crouch.
Hocker m stool.
Höcker m hump.
Hockey n hockey.
Hoden m testicle.
Hof n court(yard); farm.
hoffen vt vi to hope.
hoffentlich adv hopefully.
Hoffnung f hope.
hoffnungslos adj hopeless.
hoffnungsvoll adj hopeful.
höflich adj polite:—adv politely.
Höflichkeit f politeness.
Höhe f height; amount.
Hoheit f Highness; sovereignty.
Höhepunkt m climax.
höher adj adv higher.
hohl adj hollow.
Höhle f cave.
Hohn m scorn.
höhnen vi to mock.
höhnisch adj scornful.
holen vt to fetch, get.
Holland n Holland; Netherlands.
Holländer(in) m(f) Dutchman(woman).
holländisch adj Dutch.
Hölle f hell.

höllisch *adj* hellish.
holp(e)rig *adj* bumpy.
holpern *vi* to stumble.
Holz *n* wood.
hölzern *adj* wooden.
Holzfäller *m* woodcutter.
holzig *adj* woody.
Holzkohle *f* charcoal.
homosexuell *adj* homosexual.
Honig *m* honey.
Hopfen *m* hop(s).
Hörapparat *m* hearing aid.
hörbar *adj* audible.
horchen *vi* to listen.
hören *vt vi* to hear; to listen.
Hörer(in) *m(f)* listener; receiver.
Horizont *m* horizon.
horizontal *adj* horizontal.
Hormon *n* hormone.
Horn *n* horn.
Horoskop *n* horoscope.
Hörsaal *m* lecture hall.
Hörspiel *n* radio play.
horten *vt* to hoard.
Hose *f* trousers.
Hoseträger *m* braces.
Hotel *n* hotel.
hübsch *adj* pretty.
Hubschrauber *m* helicopter.
Huf *m* hoof.
Hufeisen *n* horseshoe.
Hüfte *f* hip.
Hügel *m* hill.
Huhn *n* hen, chicken.
huldigen *vi* to pay homage to.

Hülle *f* covering; wrapping.
hüllen *vt* to wrap.
Hülse *f* husk.
Hummel *f* bumblebee.
Hummer *m* lobster.
Humor *m* humour.
humoristisch, humorvoll *adj* humorous.
Hund *m* dog.
hundert *num* hundred.
hundertprozentig *adj* a hundred per cent.
Hündin *f* bitch.
Hunger *m* hunger:—~ **haben** to be hungry.
hungern *vi* to starve.
hungrig *adj* hungry.
Hupe *f* horn.
hupern *vi* to hoot.
hüpfen *vi* to hop.
Hürde *f* hurdle.
Hure *f* whore.
husten *vi* to cough.
Husten *m* cough.
Hut *m* hat:—*f* care.
hüten *vt* to guard:—*vr* to take care.
Hütte *f* hut; foundry.
Hygiene *f* hygiene.
hygienisch *adj* hygienic:—*adv* hygienically.
Hymne *f* hymn; anthem.
Hypnose *f* hypnosis.
hypnotisch *adj* hypnotic.
Hypothek *f* mortgage.
Hypothese *f* hypothesis.
hypothetisch *adj* hypothetical.
Hysterie *f* hysteria.
hysterisch *adj* hysterical.

I

ich *nom pn* I.
ideal *adj* ideal.

Ideal *n* ideal.
Idee *f* idea.

identifizieren *vt vr* to identify.
Identifizierung *f* identification.
identisch *adj* identical.
Identität *f* identity.
Ideologie *f* ideology.
ideologisch *adj* ideological.
Idiot *m* idiot.
idyllisch *adj* idyllic.
Igel *m* hedgehog.
ihm *dat pn* (to) him, (to) it.
ihn *acc pn* him, it.
ihnen *dat pn* (to) them.
Ihnen *dat pn* (to) you.
ihr *nom pn* you:—*dat* (to) her, (to) it: —*poss adj* her, its, their.
illegal *adj* illegal.
Illusion *f* illusion.
Illustration *f* illustration.
illustrieren *vt* to illustrate.
Illustrierte *f* magazine.
Imbiß *m* snack.
Imitation *f* imitation.
imitieren *vt* to imitate.
immer *adv* always, ever:—**noch ~** still:—**~ wieder** repeatedly.
immerhin *adv* after all.
impfen *vt* to vaccinate.
Import *m* import.
importieren *vt* to import.
Impuls *m* impulse.
impulsiv *adj* impulsive.
in *prep* in, into.
indem *conj* as; while.
Inder(in) *m(f)* Indian.
Indianer(in) *m(f)* (Red) Indian.
indianisch *adj* (Red) Indian.
Indien *n* India.
indirekt *adj* indirect.
indisch *adj* Indian.
individuell *adj* individual.
Indonesien *n* Indonesia.
Industrie *f* industry.
industriell *adj* industrial.

Infektion *f* infection.
infizieren *vt* to infect:—*vr* to become infected.
Inflation *f* inflation.
infolge *prep* due to.
Information *f* information.
informieren *vt* to inform.
Ingenieur *m* engineer.
Inhaber(in) *m(f)* owner.
Inhalt *m* content(s).
Initiative *f* initiative.
Inland *n* home country.
innehaben *vt* to hold.
innehalten *vt* to comply with:—*vi* to pause.
innen *adv* inside.
Innenminister *m* minister of the interior.
inner *adj* inner, interior.
innerhalb *adv prep* within.
innerlich *adj* inner; mental.
innig *adj* warm; sincere.
inoffiziell *adj* unofficial.
Insasse *m* occupant.
insbesondere *adv* in particular.
Inschrift *f* inscription.
Insekt *n* insect.
Insel *f* island.
insgesamt *adv* altogether.
insofern, insoweit *adv* in so far, in this respect:—*conj* if; so.
Inspektion *f* inspection.
Inspiration *f* inspiration.
inspirieren *vt* to inspire.
instandhalten *vt* to maintain, service.
instandsetzen *vt* to repair.
Instanz *f* authority; court.
Instinkt *m* instinct.
instinktiv *adj* instinctive.
Institut *n* institution.
Instrument *n* instrument.
intellektuell *adj* intellectual.
Intellektuelle(r) *f(m)* intellectual.
intelligent *adj* intelligent.

Intelligenz *f* intelligence.
intensiv *adj* intensive.
interessant *adj* interesting.
Interesse *n* interest
interessieren *vt* to interest:—*vr* to be interested.
intern *adj* internal.
international *adj* international.
Interpretation *f* interpretation.
interpretieren *vt* to interpret.
Intervall *n* interval.
Interview *n* interview.
interviewen *vt* to interview.
intim *adj* intimate; cosy.
Intimität *f* intimacy.
Intrige *f* intrigue.
Invasion *f* invasion.
Inventar *n* inventory.
Inventur *f* stocktake.
investieren *vt* to invest.
Investition *f* investment.
inwendig *adv* inward.
inwiefern, inwieweit *adv* to what extent.
inzwischen *adv* meanwhile; since.
Irak *m* Iraq.
Iran *n* Iran.
irdisch *adj* earthly.
Ire *m* Irishman.
irgend *adv* some, any; at all; ever:—**wer** ~ whoever:—~ **etwas** something, anything.

irgendein *adj* some, any.
irgendeiner *pn* somebody.
irgendwann *adv* sometime.
irgendwie *adv* somehow.
irgendwo *adv* somewhere.
irgendwohin *adv* somewhere.
Irin *f* Irishwoman.
Iris *f* iris.
irisch *adj* Irish.
Irland *n* Ireland.
Irländer(in) *m(f)* Irishman, Irishwoman.
Ironie *f* irony.
ironisch *adj* ironic.
irre *adj* mad.
Irre(r) *f(m)* lunatic.
irreführen *vt* to mislead.
irren *vi vr* to get lost; to make a mistake.
irritieren *vt* to irritate.
Irrtum *m* error.
irrtümlich *adj* wrong.
Island *n* Iceland.
islandisch *adj* Icelandic.
Isolation *f* isolation; insulation.
isolieren *vt* to isolate; to insulate.
Israel *n* Israel.
Israeli *m* Israeli.
israelisch *adj* Israeli.
Italien *n* Italy.
Italiener(in) *m(f)* Italian.
italienisch *adj* Italian.

J

ja *adv* yes.
Jacht *f* yacht.
Jacke *f* jackct.
Jagd *f* hunt(ing).
jagen *vt vi* to hunt.
Jäger *m* hunter.

Jahr *n* year.
Jahreszeit *f* season.
Jahrhundert *n* century.
jährlich *adj adv* annual(ly).
Jahrzehnt *n* decade.
Jammer *m* misery.

jämmerlich *adj* lamentable.
jammern *vt* to arouse pity:—*vi* to lament.
Januar, Jänner *m* January.
Japaner(in) *m(f)* Japanese (person).
japanisch *adj* Japanese.
jawohl *adv* yes (certainly).
Jazz *m* jazz.
je *adv* ever, every; each:—~ **größer, desto besser** the bigger the better.
jede(r, s) *pn* each, every.
jedenfalls *adv* in any case.
jedermann *pn* everyone.
jederzeit *adv* at any time.
jedesmal *adv* every time.
jedoch *adv* however.
jemals *adv* ever.
jemand *pn* somebody, anybody.
jene(r, s) *adv* that:—*pn* that one.
jetzt *adv* now.
jeweilig *adj* respective.
jeweils *adv* respectively.

Jordanien *n* Jordan.
Journalist(in) *m(f)* journalist.
Jubiläum *n* jubilee; anniversary.
jucken *vi* to itch.
Jude *m* **Jüdin** *f* Jew, Jewess.
jüdisch *adj* Jewish.
Jugend *f* youth.
Jugendherberge *f* youth hostel.
jugendlich *adj* youthful.
Jugendliche(r) *f(m)* young person.
Jugendstil *m* art nouveau.
Juli *m* July.
jung *adj* young.
Junge *m* boy.
Jungfer *f* spinster.
Jungfrau *f* virgin.
Juni *m* June.
Jurist *m* lawyer.
Justiz *f* justice.
Juwel *n* jewel.
Juwelier *m* jeweller.

K

Kabarett *n* cabaret.
Kabel *n* cable.
Kabine *f* cabin; cubicle.
Kabinett *n* cabinet.
Kachel *f* tile.
Käfer *m* beetle.
Kaffee *m* coffee.
Käfig *m* cage.
kahl *adj* bare, bald.
Kai *m* quay.
Kaiser(in) *m(f)* emperor (empress).
Kakao *m* cocoa.
Kaktus *m* cactus.
Kalb *n* calf.
Kalbfleisch *n* veal.
Kalender *m* calendar.

Kalk *m* calcium, chalk.
kalkulieren *vt* to calculate.
kalt *adj* cold:—**mir ist** ~ I am cold.
Kälte *f* cold.
Kamel *n* camel.
Kamera *f* camera.
Kamerad(in) *m(f)* comrade.
Kameradschaft *f* comradeship.
Kamin *m* chimney; fireplace.
Kamm *m* comb; crest.
kämmen *vt vi* to comb:—*vr* to comb one's hair.
Kammer *f* chamber.
Kampf *m* fight; battle.
kämpfen *vi* to fight.
Kämpfer *m* fighter.

Kanada *n* Canada.
Kanadier(in) *m(f)* Canadian.
kanadisch *adj* Canadian.
Kanal *m* channel; canal.
Kanalisation *f* drain.
Kanarienvogel *m* canary.
Kandidat(in) *m(f)* candidate.
Känguruh *n* kangaroo.
Kaninchen *n* rabbit.
Kanne *f* can; pot.
Kanone *f* cannon.
Kante *f* edge.
Kantine *f* canteen.
Kanton *m* canton.
Kanu *n* canoe.
Kanzel *f* pulpit.
Kanzler *m* chancellor.
Kap *n* cape.
Kapazität *f* capacity.
Kapelle *f* chapel.
kapieren *vt vi* to understand.
Kapital *n* capital.
Kapitalismus *m* capitalism.
Kapitalist *m* capitalist.
kapitalistisch *adj* capitalist.
Kapitän *m* captain.
Kapitel *n* chapter.
Kappe *f* cap.
Kapsel *f* capsule.
Kapstadt *n* Cape Town.
kaputt *adj* broken.
Karawane *f* caravan.
Karfreitag *m* Good Friday.
karg, kärglich *adj* meagre.
karibisch *adj* Caribbean.
Karneval *m* carnival.
Karo *n* square; diamonds (cards).
Karotte *f* carrot.
Karriere *f* career.
Karte *f* card; chart; map; ticket; menu.
Kartell *n* cartel.
Kartoffel *f* potato.
Karton *m* cardboard.

Karussell *n* roundabout.
Käse *m* cheese.
Kaserne *f* barracks.
Kasino *n* casino.
Kaskade *f* cascade.
Kasse *f* cashbox; booking office.
Kassette *f* cassette; box.
kassieren *vt vi* to collect (money).
Kassierer(in) *m(f)* cashier.
Kastanie *f* chestnut.
Kasten *m* box.
kastrieren *vt* to castrate.
Katalog *m* catalogue.
Katapult *m* catapult.
katastrophal *adj* catastrophic.
Katastrophe *f* catastrophe.
Kategorie *f* category.
kategorisch *adj* categorical.
Kater *m* tom-cat; hangover.
Katholik(in) *m(f)* Catholic.
katholisch *adj* Catholic.
Katze *f* cat.
Katzenjammer *m* hangover.
kauen *vt vi* to chew.
Kauf *m* purchase.
kaufen *vt vi* to buy.
Käufer(in) *m(f)* buyer.
Kaufhaus *n* department store.
Kaufleute *pl* tradespeople.
käuflich *adj* for sale.
Kaufmann *m* businessman.
Kaugummi *m* chewing gum.
kaum *adv* hardly.
Kegel *m* skittle; cone.
Kegelbahn *f* bowling alley.
Kehle *f* throat.
Kehlkopf *m* larynx.
Kehre *f* turn, bend.
kehren *vt vi* to turn; to sweep.
Keil *m* wedge.
Keim *m* germ; bud.
kein(er, e, es) *adj* no, not any.
keinesfalls, keineswegs *adv* not at all.

keinmal *adv* never.
Keks *m/n* biscuit.
Keller *m* cellar.
Kellner(in) *m(f)* waiter (waitress).
kennbar *adj* recognizable.
kennen *vt* to know.
kennenlernen *vt* to get to know; to meet.
Kenner(in) *m(f)* connoisseur, expert.
Kenntnis *f* knowledge.
Kennzeichen *n* sign; characteristic.
kennzeichnen *vt* to characterize.
kennzeichnend *adj* characteristic.
Keramik *f* ceramics.
Kerl *m* chap, guy.
Kern *m* kernel; nucleus.
Kernenergie *f* nuclear energy.
Kernkraftwerk *n* nuclear power station.
Kerze *f* candle; spark plug.
Kessel *m* kettle; boiler.
Kette *f* chain.
kichern *vi* to giggle.
Kiefer *m* jaw:—*f* pine.
Kies *m* gravel.
Kiesel(stein) *m* pebble.
Kilogramm *n* kilogram.
Kilometer *m* kilometre.
Kind *n* child.
Kindergarten *m* nursery school.
Kinderwagen *m* pram.
Kindheit *f* childhood.
kindisch *adj* childish.
kindlich *adj* childlike.
Kinn *n* chin.
Kino *n* cinema.
Kiosk *m* kiosk.
Kippe *f* cigarette end.
kippen *vt vi* to tip, tilt.
Kirche *f* church.
Kirchenlied *n* hymn.
Kirchturm *m* steeple.
Kirsche *f* cherry.
Kissen *n* cushion.
Kiste *m* box, chest.

Kitsch *m* kitsch, trash.
kitschig *adj* trashy.
Kitt *m* putty.
kitzeln *vt* to tickle.
Klage *f* complaint; lawsuit.
klagen *vi* to complain.
Kläger(in) *m(f)* plaintiff.
kläglich *adj* lamentable.
Klang *m* sound.
Klappe *f* flap; valve.
klappen *vt vi* to tip:—**das klappt nicht**
it doesn't work.
klar *adj* clear.
klären *vt* to clarify.
Klarheit *f* clarity.
Klarinette *f* clarinet.
klarmachen *vt* make clear; to prepare.
Klärung *f* clarification.
Klasse *f* class.
klassifizieren *vt* to classify.
Klassifizierung *f* classification.
Klassiker *m* classic.
klassisch *adj* classical; traditional.
Klatsch *m* clap; smack; gossip.
klatschen *vi* to clap; to smack; to gossip.
Klaue *f* claw.
Klausel *f* clause.
Klavier *n* piano.
Klavierspieler(in) *m(f)* pianist.
kleben *vt vi* to stick.
klebrig *adj* sticky.
Klebestreifen *m* sticky tape.
Kleb(e)stoff *m* glue.
Kleid *n* dress; **Kleider** *pl* clothes.
kleiden *vt* to clothe:—*vr* to dress.
Kleiderschrank *m* wardrobe.
Kleidung *f* clothing.
klein *adj* small.
Kleingeld *n* change.
Kleinigkeit *f* trifle.
klettern *vi* to climb.
Klient(in) *m(f)* client.
Klima *n* climate.

Klimaanlage *f* air conditioning.
klimatisch *adj* climatic.
klimmen *vi* to climb.
Klinge *f* blade, sword.
Klingel *f* bell.
klingeln *vi* to ring.
Klinik *f* clinic.
Klinke *f* handle.
Klippe *f* cliff; reef; obstacle.
klirren *vi* to clink, clatter.
Klo *n* loo.
klopfen *vt vi* to knock.
Kloster *n* monastery; convent.
Klotz *m* log.
Klub *m* club.
Kluft *f* gap; chasm.
klug *adj* clever.
Klugheit *f* cleverness.
Klumpen *m* lump.
knabbern *vt vi* to nibble.
Knabe *m* boy.
knacken *vt vi* to crack.
Knall *m* bang.
knallen *vi* to bang.
knapp *adj* tight; scarce; brief:—*adv* just under.
Knappheit *f* tightness; scarcity; brevity.
knarren *vi* to creak.
Knauf *m* knob.
Kneipe *f* bar.
Knick *m* crack; fold.
knicken *vt vi* to crack.
Knie *n* knee.
knien *vi* to kneel.
knirschen *vi* to grind.
knistern *vi* to crackle.
Knitter *m* crease.
Knoblauch *m* garlic.
Knöchel *m* knuckle; ankle.
Knochen *m* bone.
Knochengerüst *n* skeleton.
Knödel *m* dumpling.
Knolle *f* bulb.

Knopf *m* button.
knöpfen *vt* to button.
Knopfloch *n* buttonhole.
Knospe *f* bud.
Knoten *m* knot; lump.
knüpfen *vt* to tie.
Knüppel *m* club, truncheon.
knusperig *adj* crisp.
Koalition *f* coalition.
Koch *m* (male) cook.
kochen *vt vi* to cook; to boil.
Kocher *m* cooker.
Köchin *f* (female) cook.
Kochtopf *m* saucepan.
Koffer *m* (suit)case.
Kofferraum *m* boot (of vehicle).
Kognak *m* brandy.
Kohl *m* cabbage.
Kohle *f* coal; charcoal; carbon.
Kohlendioxyd *n* **Kohlensäure** *f* carbon dioxide.
Kokosnuß *f* coconut.
Kollege *m* **Kollegin** *f* colleague.
kollektiv *adj* collective.
Köln *n* Cologne.
Kolonie *f* colony.
Kolonne *f* column.
Kolumbien *n* Colombia.
Kolumbus *m* Columbus.
Kombination *f* combination.
kombinieren *vt vi* to combine:—*vi* to deduce.
Kombi(wagen) *m* estate car, station wagon.
Komfort *m* comfort.
Komik *f* comedy.
Komiker(in) *m(f)* comedian.
komisch *adj* funny; strange.
Komma *n* comma; decimal point.
Kommandant *m* commander.
kommandieren *vt vi* to command.
Kommando *n* command; squad.
kommen *vi* to come.

Kommentar m commentary.
Kommentator m commentator.
kommentieren vt to comment upon.
kommerziell adj commercial.
Kommissar m commissioner; (police) inspector.
Kommission f commission; committee.
Kommode f chest of drawers.
Kommunikation f communication.
Kommunion f communion.
Kommunismus m communism.
Kommunist(in) m(f) communist.
kommunistisch adj communist.
kommunizieren vi to communicate.
Komödie f comedy.
Kompaß m compass.
kompensieren vt to compensate.
kompetent adj competent; responsible.
Kompetenz f competence; jurisdiction.
komplett adj complete.
Kompliment n compliment.
komplimentieren vt to compliment.
kompliziert adj complicated.
Komponente f component.
komponieren vt to compose.
Komponist m composer.
Komposition f composition.
Kompromiß m compromise.
Kondensation f condensation.
kondensieren vt to condense.
Konditorei f café; cake shop.
Kondom n condom.
Konferenz f conference.
Konfession f religion; denomination.
Konfirmation f confirmation.
konfirmieren vt to confirm.
konfiszieren vt to confiscate.
Konfiszierung f confiscation.
Konfitüre f jam.
Konflikt m conflict.
konfrontieren vt to confront.
Konfusion f confusion.
Kongreß m congress.

König m king.
Königin f queen.
königlich adj royal.
Königreich n kingdom.
Konjunktur f (state of the) economy.
konkret adj concrete.
Konkurrent(in) m(f) competitor.
Konkurrenz f competition.
konkurrieren vi to compete.
Konkurs m bankruptcy.
können v aux to be able:—**ich kann** I can:—**ich kann Deutsch** I speak German.
Können n ability.
konsequent adj consistent.
Konsequenz f consistency; consequence.
konservativ adj conservative.
Konserve(n) f tinned food.
konservieren vt to preserve.
Konservierung f preservation.
konsolidieren vt vr to consolidate.
Konsolidierung f consolidation.
Konsonant m consonant.
konstant adj constant.
konstatieren vt to state; to establish.
Konstanz n Constance.
Konstellation f constellation.
konstruieren vt to construct.
Konstruktion f construction.
Konsul m consul.
Konsulat n consulate.
konsultieren vt to consult.
Konsum m consumption.
Konsument(in) m(f) consumer.
Kontakt m contact.
kontaktarm adj unsociable.
kontaktfreudig adj sociable.
Kontaktlinsen pl contact lenses.
Kontinent m continent.
kontinental adj continental.
kontinuierlich adj continuous.
Konto n account.
Kontoauszug m statement.

Kontrabaß *m* double bass.
Kontrast *m* contrast.
Kontrolle *f* control; check.
Kontrolleur *m* inspector.
kontrollieren *vt* to check.
Kontroverse *f* controversy.
Konvention *f* convention.
konventionell *adj* conventional.
Konversation *f* conversation.
konvertieren *vt vi* to convert.
Konzentration *f* concentration.
konzentrieren *vt vr* to concentrate.
Konzept *n* draft.
Konzern *m* group (of companies).
Konzert *n* concert; concerto.
Konzertsaal *m* concert hall.
Konzession *f* concession.
Kooperation *f* cooperation.
kooperativ *adj* cooperative.
koordinieren *vt* to coordinate.
Koordinierung *f* coordination.
Kopenhagen *n* Copenhagen.
Kopf *m* head.
Kopfkissen *n* pillow.
Kopfschmerzen *mpl* headache.
Kopftuch *n* headscarf.
Kopfzeile *f* headline.
Kopie *f* copy.
kopieren *vt* to copy.
koppeln *vt* to link.
Korb *m* basket.
Korbball *m* basketball.
Kordel *f* cord.
Kork *m* cork.
Korkenzieher *m* corkscrew.
Korn *n* corn; grain; (gun)sight.
Körper *m* body.
körperlich *adj* physical.
Körperschaft *f* corporation.
korrekt *adj* correct.
Korrektur *f* correction.
Korrespondent(in) *m(f)* correspondent.
Korrespondenz *f* correspondence.

Korridor *m* corridor.
korrigieren *vt* to correct.
Korrosion *f* corrosion.
Korruption *f* corruption.
Kosmetik *f* cosmetics.
kosmetisch *adj* cosmetic.
Kosmos *m* cosmos.
Kost *f* food; accommodation.
kostbar *adj* precious; costly.
Kosten *pl* costs.
kosten *vt vi* to cost; to taste.
kostlos *adj adv* free (of charge).
köstlich *adj* precious; delicious.
Kostüm *n* costume.
Kot *m* excrement.
Kotelett *n* cutlet.
Krabbe *f* shrimp.
krabbeln *vi* to crawl.
Krach *m* crash; noise; argument.
krachen *vi* to crash:—*vr* to have a row.
krächzen *vi* to croak.
Kraft *f* strength, force, power:—**in ~ treten** to come into force.
Kraftfahrer(in) *m(f)* driver.
Kraftfahrzeug *n* motor vehicle.
kräftig *adj* strong:—*adv* strongly.
kräftigen *vt* to strengthen.
kraftlos *adj* powerless.
kraftvoll *adj* strong.
Kraftwagen *m* motor vehicle.
Kraftwerk *n* power station.
Kragen *m* collar.
Krähe *f* crow.
Kralle *f* claw.
Kram *m* stuff, odds and ends.
Krampf *m* cramp; spasm.
Kran *m* crane; tap.
krank *adj* ill.
Kranke(r) *f(m)* sick person, patient.
kranken *vi* to suffer.
kränken *vt* to hurt.
Krankenhaus *n* hospital.
Krankenschwester *f* nurse.

Krankenwagen m ambulance.
Krankheit f illness, disease.
kränklich adj sickly.
Kränkung f insult.
Kranz m wreath.
kratzen vt vi to scratch.
Kratzer m scratch.
kraus adj curly.
Kraut n cabbage; herb; plant.
Krawall m uproar.
Krawatte f tie.
Krebs m crab; cancer.
Kredit m credit.
Kreditkarte f credit card.
Kreide f chalk.
Kreis m circle; district.
kreischen vi to scream.
Kreisel m top; roundabout.
kreisen vi to rotate.
kreisförmig adj circular.
Kreislauf m circulation.
Krematorium n crematorium.
kremieren vt to cremate.
Kreuz n cross; clubs (cards).
kreuzen vt vi vr to cross.
Kreuzfahrt f cruise.
kreuzigen vt to crucify.
Kreuzigung f crucifixion.
Kreuzung f crossing.
Kreuzweg m crossroads.
Kreuzworträtsel n crossword.
Kreuzzug m crusade.
kriechen vi to creep, crawl.
Krieg m war.
kriegen vt to get, receive.
Krieger m warrior.
kriegerisch adj warlike.
Krimi m thriller.
kriminell adj criminal.
Kriminelle(r) f(m) criminal.
Krise f crisis; recession.
Kristall m crystal:—n crystal (glass).
Kritik f criticism.

Kritiker m critic.
kritisch adj critical.
kritisieren vt vi to criticize.
Krokodil n crocodile.
Krone f crown.
krönen vt to crown.
Kronjuwelen pl crown jewels.
Kronleuchter m chandelier.
Krönung f coronation.
Kröte f toad.
Krug m jug.
Krümel m crumb.
krümeln vi vr to crumble.
krumm adj crooked.
Krümmung f curve.
Krüppel m cripple.
Kruste f crust; scab.
Küche f kitchen.
Kuchen m cake.
Kuckuck m cuckoo.
Kugel f ball; sphere; bullet.
Kugellager n ball bearing.
Kugelschreiber m ballpoint pen.
Kuh f cow.
kühl adj cool.
Kühle f coolness.
kühlen vt to cool.
Kühlschrank m refrigerator.
kühn adj bold.
kultivieren vt to cultivate.
Kultur f culture.
kulturell adj cultural.
Kunde f information:—m customer.
kündigen vt to terminate, cancel:—vi
    to give notice.
Kündigung f notice.
Kundschaft f customers.
künftig adj future:—adv in future.
Kunst f art; skill.
Künstler(in) m(f) artist.
künstlich adj artificial.
kunstvoll adj artistic.
Kupfer n copper.

Kupplung f clutch (car); coupling.
Kur f cure; stay in a health resort.
Kurort m health resort.
Kurs m price; exchange rate.
Kurse, Kursus m course (of teaching).
Kurve f curve.
kurz adj adv short(ly).
kürzen vt to shorten, reduce.

kurzfristig adj short-term.
kürzlich adv recently.
kurtzsichtig adj short-sighted.
Kusine f cousin.
Kuß m kiss.
küssen vt vr to kiss.
Küste f coast.
Kutsche f coach.

L

Labor(atorium) n lab(oratory).
lächeln vi to smile.
Lächeln n smile.
lachen vi to laugh.
lächerlich adj ridiculous.
Lachs m salmon.
Lack m varnish; paint.
laden vt to load; to charge; to invite.
Laden m shop.
Ladentisch m counter.
Ladung f load; invitation.
Lage f position; layer.
Lager n camp; warehouse; bearing.
lagern vt to store:—vi to lie down; to camp.
Lagerraum m storeroom.
lahm adj lame.
lähmen vt to cripple, paralyse.
Lähmung f paralysis.
Laib m loaf.
Laibach n Ljubljana.
Laie m layman, lay person.
Laken n sheet.
lallen vt vi to babble.
Lamm n lamb.
Lampe f lamp.
Lampenschirm m lampshade.
Land n land; country; countryside; state (of Germany).

Landhaus n country house.
landen vi to land.
ländlich adj rural.
Landschaft f countryside; landscape.
Landstraße f country road.
Landtag m state parliament.
Landung f landing.
Landwirt m farmer.
Landwirtschaft f agriculture.
lang adj long; tall.
lange adv for a long time.
Länge f length; height; longitude.
Längegrad m (degree of) longitude.
länger adj adv longer.
Langeweile f boredom.
langfristig adj long-term.
längs adv prep along.
langsam adj slow.
Langsamkeit f slowness.
längst adv for a long time; long ago.
langweilen vt to bore:—vr to be bored.
langweilig adj boring.
Langwelle f long wave.
langwierig adj protracted.
Lanze f lance.
Lappen m rag; lobe.
Lärm m noise.
lärmen vi to make a noise.
Laser m laser.

lassen *vt* to let; to leave; to stop:—*v aux* to cause to be;.

Last *f* load; trouble; tax, charge.

lasten *vi* to burden.

Laster *n* vice.

lästig *adj* burdensome.

Lastkraftwagen *m* lorry.

Latein *n* Latin.

Lateinamerika *n* Latin America.

lateinisch *adj* Latin.

latent *adj* latent.

Laterne *f* lantern.

Laternenpfahl *m* lamppost.

Latte *f* lath, slat.

Lattich *m* lettuce.

Laub *n* foliage.

lauern *vi* to lurk.

Lauf *m* run; race; course.

Laufbahn *f* career.

laufen *vt vi* to run; to walk.

Laufen *n* running, walking.

laufend *adj* continuous; current.

Läufer(in) *m(f)* runner.

Laune *f* mood.

lauschen *vi* to eavesdrop.

laut *adj* loud:—*adv* loudly:—*prep* according to.

Laut *m* sound.

lauten *vi* to sound; to say.

läuten *vt vi* to ring.

lauter *adj* pure, sheer.

Lautheit *f* loudness.

Lautsprecher *m* loudspeaker.

lauwarm *adj* lukewarm.

Lawine *f* avalanche.

Leben *n* life.

leben *vt vi* to live.

lebendig *adj* alive, lively.

Lebensalter *n* age.

Lebensgefahr *f* danger (of death).

Lebenslauf *m* life; curriculum vitae.

Lebensmittel *pl* food.

Lebensraum *m* living space.

Lebenszeit *f* lifetime.

Leber *f* liver.

lebhaft *adj* lively.

leblos *adj* lifeless.

Leck *n* leak.

lecken *vt* to lick:—*vi* to leak.

lecker *adj* delicious.

Leder *n* leather.

ledig *adj* unmarried; empty.

lediglich *adv* only, merely.

leer *adj* empty.

Leere *f* emptiness.

leeren *vt vr* to empty.

legal *adj* legal.

legalisieren *vt* to legalize.

Legalität *f* legality.

legen *vt* to lay, place:—*vr* to lie down, abate.

legendar *adj* legendary.

Legende *f* legend.

legitim *adj* legitimate.

Legitimität *f* legitimacy.

Lehne *f* support; arm(rest), back(rest).

lehnen *vt vr* to lean.

Lehnstuhl *m* armchair.

Lehrbuch *n* textbook.

Lehre *f* teaching.

lehren *vt* to teach,

Lehrer(in) *m(f)* teacher.

Lehrgang *m* course.

Lehrling *m* apprentice.

Leib *m* body.

leiblich *adj* bodily.

Leibwache *f* bodyguard.

Leiche *f* corpse.

Leichenwagen *m* hearse.

Leichnam *m* corpse.

leicht *adj* light; easy.

leid *adj*:—**es tut mir ~** I am sorry.

Leid *n* pain, sorrow.

leiden *vt vi* to suffer.

Leiden *n* suffering.

Leidenschaft *f* passion.

leidenschaftlich *adj* passionate.
leider *adv* unfortunately.
leihen *vt* to lend:—*vr* to borrow.
Leim *m* glue.
Leine *f* cord; leash.
Leinen *n* linen.
Leinwand *f* canvas.
leise *adj* soft, quiet.
Leiste *f* ledge, edge.
leisten *vt* to perform:—*vr* to afford.
Leistung *f* performance; output.
leistungsfähig *adj* efficient.
Leistungsfähigkeit *f* efficiency.
leiten *vt* to lead, manage.
Leiter *m* leader:—*f* ladder.
Leitmotiv *n* leitmotiv, recurring theme.
Leitung *f* management; pipe; cable.
Lektion *f* lesson.
lenken *vt* to steer.
Lenkrad *n* steering wheel.
Leopard *m* leopard.
Lerche *f* lark.
lernen *vt vi* to learn.
lesbar *adj* legible.
Lesbarkeit *f* legibility.
Lesbierin *f* lesbian.
lesbisch *adj* lesbian.
lesen *vt vi* to read; to pick.
Leser(in) *m(f)* reader.
letzte(r,s) *adj* last; latest.
letztens *adv* recently.
letztlich *adv* recently; ultimately.
Leuchte *f* light.
leuchten *vi* to shine.
Leuchtturm *m* lighthouse.
leugnen *vt vi* to deny.
Leute *pl* people.
Leutnant *m* lieutenant.
Libanon *m* Lebanon.
liberal *adj* liberal.
Libyen *n* Libya.
Licht *n* light.
Lid *n* eyelid.

lieb *adj* dear; pleasant.
Liebe *f* love.
lieben *vt vi* to love; to like.
liebenswert *adj* lovable.
liebenswürdig *adj* kind.
lieber *adv* rather.
liebevoll *adj* loving.
liebhaben *vt* to like.
Liebhaber(in) *m(f)* lover.
lieblich *adj* lovely.
Liebling *m* darling; favourite.
Liebschaft *f* love affair.
liebste(r, s) *adj* favourite.
Lied *n* song.
liederlich *adj* careless.
Lieferant *m* supplier.
liefern *vt vi* to deliver, supply.
Lieferung *f* delivery.
liegen *vi* to lie.
Liegestuhl *m* deckchair.
Likör *m* liqueur.
Lilie *f* lily.
Limonade *f* lemonade.
Linde *f* lime (tree).
Linie *f* line.
Linke *f* left (side).
links *adv* (on/to the) left.
linkshändig *adj* left-handed.
Linse *f* lens; lentil.
Lippe *f* lip.
Lippenstift *m* lipstick.
lispeln *vi* to lisp.
Lissabon *n* Lisbon.
List *f* cunning; trick.
Liste *f* list.
listig *adj* cunning.
Litauen *n* Lithuania.
litauisch *adj* Lithuanian.
Liter *m/n* litre.
literarisch *adj* literary.
Literatur *f* literature.
Lizenz *f* licence.
Lob *n* praise.

lobenswert *adj* praiseworthy.
Loch *n* hole.
Locke *f* lock; curl.
locken *vt* to entice; to curl.
locker *adj* loose.
Löffel *m* spoon.
Logik *f* logic.
logisch *adj* logical.
Lohn *m* wages; reward.
lokal *adj* local.
Lokal *n* bar.
Lokomotive *f* locomotive.
Los *n* lot; lottery ticket.
los *adj* loose; separate:—**was ist ~?**
  what's the matter?
löschen *vt* to extinguish.
Löschpapier *n* blotting paper.
losfahren, losgehen *vi* to leave.
loskommen *vi* to come off, escape.
loslassen *vt* to release.
löslich *adj* soluble.
losmachen *vt* to undo.
Lösung *f* solution.
loswerden *vt* to get rid of.

Lothringen *n* Lorraine.
Löwe *m* lion; (*astrol*) Leo.
Löwenzahn *m* dandelion.
Lücke *f* gap.
Luft *f* air.
luftdicht *adj* airtight.
lüften *vt* to ventilate.
Luftfahrt *f* aviation.
luftig *adj* airy.
Luftkissenfahrzeug *n* hovercraft.
Luftpost *f* airmail.
Lüftung *f* ventilation.
Luftwaffe *f* air force.
Lüge *f* lie.
lügen *vi* to lie, tell lies.
Lügner(in) *m(f)* liar.
Lumpen *m* rag.
Lunge *f* lung.
Lust *f* pleasure; willingness:—~ **haben**
  to feel like.
lustig *adj* cheerful.
lustlos *adj* listless.
Luxus *m* luxury.

M

machen *vt* to make, do.
Macht *f* power.
mächtig *adj* powerful; huge.
Mädchen *n* girl.
Magazin *n* magazine.
Magen *m* stomach.
mager *adj* meagre, thin.
Magie *f* magic.
Magier *m* magician.
magisch *adj* magical.
Magnet *m* magnet.
magnetisch *adj* magnetic.
mähen *vt vi* to mow.

Mahl *n* meal.
mahlen *vt vi* to grind.
Mahlzeit *f* meal.
Mai *m* May.
Mailand *n* Milan.
Mais *m* maize; corn.
Makler(in) *m(f)* broker.
Mal *n* time, occasion:—**zum ersten ~**
  for the first time.
mal *adv* times; once.
malen *vt vi* to paint.
Maler(in) *m(f)* painter.
Malz *n* malt.

man *pn* one.
Manager *m* manager.
Management *n* management.
manche(r, s) *adj* many:—*pn* some.
manchmal *adv* sometimes.
Mangel *m* defect; shortage.
mangelhaft *adj* defective; incomplete.
mangeln *vt* to mangle; *vi* to be missing.
mangels *prep* in the absence of.
Mann *m* man; husband.
männlich *adj* male, masculine.
Mannschaft *f* team.
Manöver *n* manoeuvre.
Mantel *m* coat.
Märchen *n* fairytale.
märchenhaft *adj* fairytale.
Mark *n* marrow; boundary; (deutsch)-mark.
markant *adj* striking.
Marke *f* mark; brand(name).
Markt *m* market.
Marmelade *f* jam.
Marmor *m* marble.
Marokko *n* Morocco.
Marsch *m* march:—*f* marsh.
marschieren *vi* to march.
Marxismus *m* Marxism.
März *m* March.
Masche *f* mesh; stitch.
Maschine *f* machine.
Maschinenbau *m* mechanical engineering.
Maschinengewehr *n* machine gun.
maschineschreiben *vi* to type.
Maschineschreiber(in) *m(f)* typist.
Maske *f* mask.
maskieren *vt* to mask.
Maß *n* measure; extent:—*f* litre (of beer).
Massage *f* massage.
Masse *f* mass.
Maßgabe *f* proportion:—**nach ~** according to.
maßgebend, maßgeblich *adj* authoritative.

mäßig *adj* moderate.
Maßnahme *f* measure.
Mast *m* mast.
Material *n* material.
Materialismus *m* materialism.
materialistisch *adj* materialistic.
materiell *adj* material.
Mathematik *f* mathematics.
Matratze *f* mattress.
Matrose *m* sailor.
matt *adj* matt; dull; mate (chess).
Matte *f* mat.
Mauer *f* wall.
mauern *vt* *vi* to lay bricks.
Maul *n* mouth.
Maulwurf *m* mole.
Maurer *m* bricklayer.
Maus *f* mouse.
Maximum *n* maximum.
Mechaniker *m* mechanic.
mechanisch *adj* mechanical.
Medaille *f* medal.
Medizin *f* medicine.
Meer *n* sea.
Mehl *n* flour.
mehr *adj* *adv* more.
Mehrarbeit *f* overtime.
mehrere(r, s) *adj* several.
mehrfach *adj* multiple:—*adv* repeatedly.
Mehrheit *f* majority.
mehrmals *adv* several times.
Mehrwertsteuer *f* value added tax.
Mehrzahl *f* majority.
Meile *f* mile.
mein(e) *poss adj* my.
meine(r, s) *poss pn* mine.
meinen *vt* *vi* to think, be of the opinion.
Meinung *f* opinion.
meist *adj* most:—*adv* mostly.
meistens *adv* usually, generally.
Meister *m* master; champion.
meisterhaft *adj* masterly.

Meisterschaft *f* mastery; championship.
Meisterwerk *n* masterpiece.
Melancholie *f* melancholy.
melancholisch *adj* melancholic.
melden *vt vi* to report.
Meldung *f* report.
melken *vt vi* to milk.
Melodie *f* melody.
Menge *f* crowd; quantity.
Mensch *m* human being; person.
Menschheit *f* humanity.
menschlich *adj* human.
merkbar *adj* noticeable.
merken *vt* to notice.
merklich *adj* noticeable.
Merkmal *n* characteristic.
Merkur *f* Mercury.
merkwürdig *adj* noteworthy; remarkable.
Messe *f* mass; (trade) fair.
messen *vt* to measure, to compare:— *vr* to compete.
Messer *n* knife.
Messing *n* brass.
Metall *n* metal.
metallisch *adj* metallic.
Meter *m/n* metre.
Methode *f* method.
Metzger *m* butcher.
Metzgerei *f* butcher's.
Mexiko *n* Mexico.
mich *pn acc* me, myself.
Miete *f* rental.
mieten *vt* to rent, hire.
Mieter(in) *m(f)* tenant.
Mikrofilm *m* microfilm.
Mikrofon *n* microphone.
Mikroskop *n* microscope.
mikroskopisch *adj* microscopic.
Milch *f* milk.
mild *adj* mild, soft.
militärisch *adj* military.
Milliarde *f* billion.

Millimeter *m/n* millimetre.
Million *f* million.
Millionär(in) *m(f)* millionaire(ss).
minder *adj* inferior:—*adv* less.
Minderheit *f* minority.
minderjährig *adj* minor, under age.
mindern *vt vr* to decrease, diminish.
Minderung *f* decrease.
minderwertig *adj* inferior.
Minderwertigkeit *f* inferiority.
mindeste(r, s) *adj* least.
mindestens *adv* at least.
Mine *f* mine; lead; refill.
Mineral *n* mineral.
mineralisch *adj* mineral.
Mineralwasser *n* mineral water.
minimal *adj* minimal.
Minimum *n* minimum.
Minister *m* minister.
Ministerium *n* ministry.
minus *adj* minus.
Minute *f* minute.
Minze *f* mint.
mir *pn dat* (to) me, (to) myself.
mischen *vt vr* to mix.
Mischung *f* mixture.
Mißbrauch *m* misuse, abuse.
mißbrauchen *vt* to misuse, abuse.
missen *vt* to miss.
Mission *f* mission.
Missionar *m* missionary.
mißtrauen *vi* to distrust.
Mißtrauen *n* distrust.
mißtrauisch *adj* distrustful.
Mist *m* manure.
mit *prep* with.
Mitarbeit *f* cooperation.
mitarbeiten *vi* to cooperate.
Mitarbeiter(in) *m(f)* colleague.
Mitglied *n* member.
Mitgliedschaft *f* membership.
mithelfen *vi* to help.
Mithilfe *f* assistance.

Mitleid *n* pity.
Mittag *m* midday.
Mittagessen *n* lunch.
Mitte *f* middle.
mitteilen *vt* to inform.
Mitteilung *f* communication.
Mittel *n* means, resources; average.
Mittelamerika *n* Central America.
mittelbar *adj* direct.
Mitteleuropa *n* central Europe.
mittelfristig *adj* medium-term.
Mittelmeer *n* Mediterranean (Sea).
Mittelwelle *f* medium wave.
Mitternacht *f* midnight.
Mittwoch *m* Wednesday.
mitwirken *vi* to cooperate.
Mitwirkung *f* cooperation.
Möbel *n* (item of) furniture.
Mode *f* fashion.
Modell *n* model.
modern *adj* modern.
modernisieren *vt* to modernize.
Modernisierung *f* modernization.
mögen *v aux* to want, like.
möglich *adj* possible.
möglicherweise *adv* possibly.
Möglichkeit *f* possibility.
Mohn *m* poppy.
Moldau *f* Vltava.
Molekül *n* molecule.
Molkerei *f* dairy.
Moll *n* (*mus*) minor.
Moment *m* moment.
momentan *adj* momentary; present: — *adv* at/for the moment.
Monarchie *f* monarchy.
Monat *m* month.
monatlich *adj* monthly.
Mönch *m* monk.
Mond *m* moon.
Mondlicht *n*, **Mondschein** *m* moonlight.
Monitor *m* monitor.
monogam *adj* monogamous.

Monogamie *f* monogamy.
Monolog *m* monologue.
Monopol *n* monopoly.
monoton *adj* monotonous.
Monotonie *f* monotony.
Monsun *m* monsoon.
Montag *m* Monday.
Montage *f* assembly, installation.
Moor *n* moor(land).
Moos *n* moss.
Moral *f* moral; morality; morale.
Mord *m* murder.
morden *vt vi* to murder.
Mörder(in) *m(f)* murderer.
mörderisch *adj* murderous.
Morgen *m* morning:—**guten** ~ good morning.
morgen *adv* tomorrow:—~ **früh** tomorrow morning.
Morgenrock *m* dressing gown.
morgens *adv* in the morning(s).
Mosaik *n* mosaic.
Moschee *f* mosque.
Mosel *m* Moselle.
Moskau *n* Moscow.
Moskito *m* mosquito.
Moslem *m* Moslem.
Motel *n* motel.
Motiv *n* motif; motive.
motivieren *vt* to motivate.
Motivierung *f* motivation.
Motor *m* motor, engine.
Motte *f* moth.
Motto *n* motto.
Möwe *f* seagull.
Mücke *f* gnat, mosquito.
müde *adj* tired.
Müdigkeit *f* fatigue.
Mühe *f* trouble, effort.
mühelos *adj* easy.
mühevoll *adj* difficult.
Mühle *f* mill.
Mühlstein *m* millstone.

mühsam *adj* troublesome.
Müll *m* rubbish, refuse.
Mülleimer *m* dustbin.
Müllwagen *m* dustcart.
Mumie *f* mummy.
München *n* Munich.
Mund *m* mouth.
mündlich *adj* oral, verbal.
Mündung *f* mouth (of river).
Mundwasser *n* mouthwash.
Munition *f* ammunition.
munter *adj* lively.
Munterkeit *f* liveliness.
Münze *f* coin.
murmeln *vt vi* to murmur.
murren *vi* to grumble.
Muschel *f* mussel; shell(fish); earpiece.
Museum *n* museum.

Musik *f* music.
musikalisch *adj* musical.
Musiker *m* musician.
Muskel *m* muscle.
müssen *vi v aux* to have to.
müßig *adj* idle.
Muster *n* pattern, sample.
Mut *m* courage.
mutig *adj* courageous.
Mutter *f* mother.
mütterlich *adj* motherly, maternal.
Mutterschaft *f* maternity.
Mutti *f* mum(my).
Mütze *f* cap.
mysteriös *adj* mysterious.
Mythe *f* myth.
Mythologie *f* mythology.
mythologisch *adj* mythological.

N

nach *prep* after; to; according to:—~ und ~ little by little.
nachahmen *vt vi* to imitate.
Nachahmung *f* imitation.
Nachbar(in) *m(f)* neighbour.
Nachbarschaft *f* neighbourhood.
nachdem *adv* afterwards:—*conj* after:—je ~ it depends.
Nachdruck *m* emphasis.
nachdrücklich *adj* express:—*adv* expressly.
Nachfahr *m* descendant.
Nachfolge *f* succession; emulation.
nachfolgen *vi* to succeed; to emulate.
Nachfolger(in) *m(f)* successor.
Nachfrage *f* inquiry; demand.
nachfragen *vi* to inquire.
nachlässig *adj* negligent.
Nachlässigkeit *f* negligence.

nachmals *adv* afterwards.
Nachmittag *m* afternoon.
nachmittags *adv* in the afternoon.
nachprüfen *adj* to verify.
Nachricht *f* (item of) news, message.
Nachrichten *fpl* news.
Nachruf *m* obituary.
Nachschrift *f* postscript.
Nachsicht *f* tolerance.
nachsichtig *adj* tolerant.
Nachspeise *f* dessert.
nächst *prep* next to.
nächste(r, s) *adj* next; nearest.
nächstens *adv* soon.
Nacht *f* night.
Nachteil *m* disadvantage.
Nachtigall *f* nightingale.
Nachtklub *m* nightclub.
Nachtrag *m* supplement.

nachtragen vt to carry; to add.
nachträglich adj adv subsequent(ly).
nachts adv at night(s).
Nachweis m proof, evidence.
nachweisbar adj demonstrable.
nachweisen vt to prove.
nackt adj naked.
Nacktheit f nakedness.
Nadel f needle; pin; brooch.
Nagel m nail.
nageln vt vi to nail.
nagen vt vi to gnaw.
nah(e) adj near(by); close:—adv near(by); close; closely:—prep near (to), close to.
Nähe f nearness, proximity; vicinity: — in der ~ close by.
nahebei adv nearby.
nahekommen vi to approach.
naheliegen vi to be obvious.
naheliegend adj nearby; obvious.
nahen vi vr to approach.
nähen vt vi to sew.
näher adj nearer; more specific.
nähern vt vr to approach.
nahestehend adj close.
nahezu adv nearly.
Nähmaschine f sewing machine.
nähren vt to feed.
nahrhaft adj nutritious.
Nahrung f **Nahrungsmittel** n food.
Naht f seam; stitch.
naiv adj naive.
Naivität f naivety.
Name m name.
namens adv called:—prep on behalf of.
namentlich adj adv by name; in particular.
namhaft adj renowned.
nämlich adv namely.
Narbe f scar.
Narkose f anaesthetic.
narkotisch adj narcotic.

Narr m fool.
Narrheit f folly.
närrisch adj foolish.
Narzisse f daffodil.
naschen vt vi to nibble.
Nase f nose.
Nasenloch n nostril.
Nashorn n rhinoceros.
naß adj wet.
Nässe f wetness.
nässen vt to wet.
Nation f nation.
national adj national.
nationalisieren vt to nationalize.
Nationalisierung f nationalization.
Nationalismus m nationalism.
Nationalist m nationalist.
nationalistisch adj nationalistic.
Nationalität f nationality.
Nativität f nativity.
Natrium n sodium.
Natron n soda, sodium hydroxide.
Natur f nature.
Naturalismus m naturalism.
Naturalist m naturalist.
naturalistisch adj naturalistic.
natürlich adj natural:—adv naturally, of course.
Naturschutz m conservation.
Naturwissenschaftler(in) m(f) (natural) scientist.
Nazi m Nazi.
Nazismus m Nazism.
Neapel n Naples.
Nebel m mist, fog.
neb(e)lig adj misty, foggy.
neben prep beside.
Nebenprodukt n by-product.
nebensächlich adj secondary, incidental.
nebst prep in addition to.
necken vt to tease.
nee adv no.

Neffe *m* nephew.
negativ *adj* negative.
Negative *n* negative.
Neger(in) *m(f)* negro.
nehmen *vt* to take.
Neid *m* envy, jealousy.
neidisch *adj* envious, jealous.
neigen *vt* to incline; to bow:—*vi* to tend.
Neigung *f* inclination, tendency; like.
nein *adv* no.
Nektar *m* nectar.
Nelke *f* pink, carnation; clove.
nennen *vt* to name, call.
Nenner *m* denominator.
Neon *n* neon.
Nerv *m* nerve.
nervenkrank *adj* mentally ill.
Nervensystem *n* nervous system.
Nervenzusammenbruch *m* nervous breakdown.
nervös *adj* nervous.
Nessel *f* nettle.
Nest *n* nest.
nett *adj* nice.
netto *adv* net.
Netz *n* net; network.
Netzhaut *f* retina.
neu *adj* new.
Neufundland *n* Newfoundland.
Neugier(de) *f* curiosity.
neugierig *adj* curious.
Neuheit *f* newness.
Neuigkeit *f* news.
Neujahr *n* New Year.
neulich *adv* recently.
Neumond *m* new moon.
neun *num* nine.
neunzehn *num* nineteen.
neunzig *num* ninety.
Neurose *f* neurosis.
neurotisch *adj* neurotic.
Neuseeland *n* New Zealand.
neutral *adj* neutral.

Neutrum *n* neuter.
nicht *adv* not.
Nichte *f* niece.
nichts *pn* nothing.
Nickel *n* nickel.
nicken *vi* to nod.
nie *adv* never.
nieder *adj* low; inferior:—*adv* down.
niederfallen *vi* to fall down.
Niedergang *m* descent, decline.
niedergehen *vi* to go down, descend.
niedergeschlagen *adj* downcast.
Niederlage *f* defeat.
Niederlande *pl* the Netherlands.
Niederländer(in) *m(f)* Dutchman (-woman).
niederländisch *adj* Dutch.
niederlassen *vr* to settle.
Niederlassung *f* settlement; branch (bank, etc).
niederlegen *vt* to put down; to resign.
Niedersachsen *n* Lower Saxony.
niemals *adv* never.
niemand *pn* no one.
Niere *f* kidney.
nieseln *vi* to drizzle.
niesen *vi* to sneeze.
Nikotin *n* nicotine.
nimmer *adv* never.
nirgendwo(hin) *adv* nowhere.
Niveau *n* level.
nivellieren *vt* to level.
noch *adv* yet; still; also; even; else:— **immer** ~ still:—~ **nicht** not yet:—~ **besser** even better:—~ **einmal** once again.
nochmals *adv* once again.
Nominativ *m* (*gr*) nominative.
nominieren *vt* to nominate.
Nonne *f* nun.
Nord(en) *m* north.
Nordamerika *n* North America.
Nordeuropa *n* northern Europe.

Nordirland *n* Northern Ireland.
nordisch *adj* northern.
nördlich *adj* northern, northerly.
Nordlicht *n* northern lights, aurora borealis.
Nordost(en) *m* mortheast.
Nordpol *m* North Pole.
Nordrhein-Westfalen *n* North Rhine-Westphalia.
Nordsee *f* North Sea.
nordwärts *adv* northwards.
Nordwest(en) *m* northwest.
nörgeln *vt* to nag, carp.
Nörgler *m* faultfinder.
Norm *f* standard, norm.
normal *adj* normal.
normalerweise *adv* normally.
Normandie *f* Normandy.
Norwegen *n* Norway.
Norweger(in) *m(f)* Norwegian.
norwegisch *adj* Norwegian.
Not *f* need; emergency; poverty.
Notar *m* notary.
Notausgang *m* emergency exit.
Note *f* note; mark.
Notfall *m* emergency.
notfalls, nötigenfalls *adv* if necessary.
notieren *vt* to note; to quote:—*vi* to be quoted.
Notierung *f* quotation, price.
nötig *adj* necessary:—~ **haben** to need.
Notiz *f* note, notice.

Notlandung *f* emergency landing.
notleidend *adj* needy.
Notlüge *f* white lie.
notorisch *adj* notorious.
Notstand *m* state of emergency.
Notwehr *f* self-defence.
notwendig *adj* necessary.
Notwendigkeit *f* necessity.
Notzucht *f* rape.
Novelle *f* short novel; amendment.
November *m* November.
nüchtern *adj* sober, sensible.
Nüchternheit *f* sobriety.
Nudel *f* noodle.
Null *f* zero, nought.
null *adj:*—~ **und nichtig** null and void.
numerisch *adj* numerical.
Nummer *f* number.
Nummernschild *n* number plate.
nun *adv* now:—*excl* well.
nur *adv* only.
Nürnberg *n* Nuremberg.
Nuß *f* nut.
Nußbaum *m* walnut tree.
Nußknacker *m* nutcracker.
nutzbar *adj* useful, usable.
Nutzen *m* use; benefit.
nutzen, nützen *vt* to use:—*vi* to be useful.
nützlich *adj* useful.
nutzlos *adj* useless.
Nylon *n* nylon.

O

ob *conj* if, whether.
oben *adv* above; upstairs.
obenerwähnt, obengenannt *adj* above mentioned.
Ober *m* waiter.

Oberarm *m* upper arm.
Oberfläche *f* surface.
oberflächlich *adj* superficial.
oberhalb *adv prep* above.
Oberkellner *m* head waiter.

Oberlicht *n* skylight.
Oberst *m* colonel.
oberste(r, s) *adj* very top, topmost.
obgleich *conj* although.
Objekt *n* objective.
Objektiv *n* lens.
objektiv *adj* objective.
Objektivität *f* objectivity.
obligatorisch *adj* obligatory, mandatory.
Oboe *f* oboe.
obschon *conj* although.
Observatorium *n* observatory.
obskur *adj* obscure; dubious.
Obst *n* fruit.
Obstbaum *m* fruit tree.
Obstgarten *m* orchard.
obszön *adj* obscene.
Obszönität *f* obscenity.
obwohl *conj* although.
Ochse *m* ox.
öd(e) *adj* waste, barren; chill.
Öde *f* desert, waste(land); tedium.
oder *conj* or.
Ofen *m* stove; oven; cooker.
offen *adj* open; frank; vacant.
offenbar *adj* obvious.
offenbleiben *vi* to stay open; to remain open.
offenhalten *vi* to keep open.
Offenheit *f* candour, frankness.
offensichtlich *adj* obvious, evident.
offenstehen *vi* to be open; to be unpaid.
öffentlich *adj* public.
Öffentlichkeit *f npl* the general public.
offiziell *adj* official.
Offizier *m* officer.
öffnen *vt vr* to open.
Öffnung *f* opening.
oft *adv* often.
ohne *prep conj* without:—~ **weiteres** without a second thought.
Ohnmacht *f* faint; impotence:—**in ~ fallen** to faint.

Ohr *n* ear; hearing.
Ohrring *m* earring.
Ökologe *m* **Ökologin** *f* ecologist.
Ökologie *f* ecology.
ökologisch *adj* ecological.
ökonomisch *adj* economical.
Oktan *n* octane.
Oktave *f* octave.
Oktober *m* October.
Öl *n* oil.
ölen *vt* to fuel, lubricate.
Ölfeld *n* oilfield.
ölig *adj* oily.
Ölindustrie *f* oil industry.
Olive *f* olive.
Öltanker *m* oil tanker.
Ölung *f* lubrication; oiling; anointment.
olympisch *adj* Olympic.
Oma *f* granny.
Omelett *n* omelette.
onanieren *vi* to masturbate.
Onkel *m* uncle.
Opa *m* grandpa.
Oper *f* opera; opera house.
Operation *f* operation.
operieren *vt* to operate on:—*vi* to operate.
Opernsänger(in) *m(f)* opera singer.
Opfer *n* sacrifice; victim.
opfern *vt* to sacrifice.
Opposition *f* opposition.
Optik *f* optics.
Optiker *m* optician.
optimal *adj* optimal, optimum.
Optimismus *m* optimism.
Optimist *m* optimist.
optimistisch *adj* optimistic.
Optimum *n* optimum.
optisch *adj* optical.
oral *adj* oral.
Orange *f* orange.
orange *adj* orange.
Orangenmarmelade *f* marmalade.

Orchester *n* orchestra.
ordentlich *adj* decent, respectable; proper:—*adv* properly.
ordinär *adj* common, vulgar.
ordnen *vt* to order, put in order.
Ordner *m* steward; file.
Ordnung *f* order; ordering; tidiness: — in ~! okay!
ordnungsgemäß *adj* proper, according to the rules.
Organ *n* organ; voice.
Organisation *f* organization.
organisieren *vt vr* to organize.
Organismus *m* organism.
Organist *m* organist.
Orgel *f* organ.
Orientierung *f* orientation.
original *adj* original.
Original *n* original.
Originalität *f* originality.

originell *adj* original.
Orkan *m* hurricane.
Ornament *n* decoration, ornament.
Ort *m* place:—**an ~ und Stelle** on the spot.
orthodox *adj* orthodox.
örtlich *adj* local.
Osten *m* east.
Osterei *n* Easter egg.
Osterglocke *f* daffodil.
Osterhase *m* Easter bunny.
Ostern *n* Easter.
Österreich *n* Austria,
Österreicher(in) *m(f)* Austrian.
österreichisch *adj* Austrian.
östlich *adj* eastern, easterly.
Ostsee *f* Baltic Sea.
Otter *m* otter:—*f* adder.
Ouvertüre *f* overture.
oval *adj* oval.
Ozean *m* ocean.

P

Paar *n* pair; couple:—**ein paar** a few.
Pacht *f* lease.
Pack *m* pack, bundle:—*n* mob, rabble.
packen *vt* to pack; to grasp, seize; to grip.
Packung *f* packet.
Paket *n* parcel; packet.
Pakt *m* pact.
Palast *m* palace.
Palme *f* palm (tree).
Pampelmuse *f* grapefruit.
Panik *f* panic.
panisch *adj* panic-stricken.
Panne *f* breakdown.
Panther *m* panther.
Pantoffel *m* slipper.
Pantomime *f* mime.
Panzer *m* tank; armour.

Papagei *m* parrot.
Papier *n* paper.
Pappel *f* poplar.
Papst *m* pope.
päpstlich *adj* papal.
Paradox *n* paradox.
Paragraph *m* paragraph; section.
parallel *adj* parallel.
Parasit *m* parasite.
Parfüm *n* perfume, scent.
Paris *n* Paris.
Park *m* park, public garden.
parken *vt vi* to park.
Parkplatz *m* car park; parking space.
Parkuhr *f* parking meter.
Parlament *n* parliament.
Parodie *f* parody.

Partei f (political) party.
Partie f part; game; outing.
Partizip n participle.
Partner(in) m(f) partner.
Partnerschaft f partnership.
Party f party.
Paß m pass; passport.
Passagier m passenger.
passen vi to fit; to suit, be convenient.
passieren vt to pass; to strain:—vi to happen.
Passion f passion.
passioniert adj passionate, enthusiastic.
passiv adj passive.
Passivität f passiveness.
Paste f paste.
Pastell n pastel.
Pastete f pie, pastry.
Pate m godfather.
Patenkind n godchild.
Patent n patent.
Patentante f godmother.
patentieren vt to patent.
Pathologe m pathologist.
pathologisch adj pathological.
Patient(in) m(f) patient.
Patin f godmother.
Patina f patina.
Patriot m patriot.
patriotisch adj patriotic.
Patriotismus m patriotism.
Pauke f kettledrum.
pauschal adj inclusive; sweeping.
Pauschalsumme f lump sum.
Pause f interval; break; pause.
pausen vt to trace.
Pavian m baboon.
Pazifik m Pacific (Ocean).
Pedal n pedal.
Pedant m pedant.
pedantisch adj pedantic.
Pein f pain, agony.
peinigen vi to torture; to torment.

peinlich adj awkward, painful; painstaking.
Peitsche f whip.
peitschen vt to whip.
Pelikan m pelican.
Pelle f skin.
pellen vi to skin, peel.
Pelz m fur.
Pendel n pendulum.
Pendler m commuter.
Penis m penis.
Penner m tramp.
Pension f pension; retirement; guesthouse.
Pensionär(in) m(f) pensioner.
pensionieren vt to pension off.
pensioniert adj retired.
Pensionierung f retirement.
per prep by, per.
perfekt adj perfect.
perforieren vt to perforate.
Periode f period.
periodisch adj periodic; recurring.
Perle f pearl.
perlen vi to sparkle; to trickle.
Perlmutt n mother-of-pearl.
Person f person.
Personal n personnel, staff.
Personalausweis m identity card.
Personenaufzug m lift, elevator.
persönlich adj personal:—adv personally; in person.
Persönlichkeit f personality.
Perspektive f perspective.
Perücke f wig.
Pessimismus m pessimism.
Pessimist m pessimist.
pessimistisch adj pessimistic.
Pest f plague.
Petersilie f parsley.
Pfad m path.
Pfadfinder(in) m(f) boy scout (girl guide).
Pfahl m post, stake.

Pfand n pledge, security.
pfänden vt to seize, distrain.
Pfändung f seizure, distraint.
Pfanne f frying pan.
Pfannkuchen m pancake.
Pfarrer m vicar; priest.
Pfarrhaus n vicarage.
Pfau m peacock.
Pfeffer m pepper.
Pfefferminz n peppermint.
pfeffern vt to pepper.
Pfeife f whistle.
pfeifen vi vt to whistle.
Pfeiler m pillar.
Pferd n horse.
Pferdestall m stable.
Pfirsich m peach.
pflanzen vt to plant.
Pflanzenwuchs m vegetation.
Pflaume f plum; prune.
pflegen vt to nurse, look after.
Pfleger(in) m(f) nurse.
Pflicht f duty.
pflücken vt to pick, pluck, gather.
Pflug m plough.
pflügen vt to plough.
Pfote f paw.
Pfund n pound.
Pfütze f puddle.
Phänomen n phenomenal.
phänomenal adj phenomenal.
Phantasie f fancy, imagination.
phantasieren vi to fantasize.
phantasievoll adj imaginative.
phantastisch adj fantastic.
Philippinen pl (the) Philippines.
Philologe m philologist.
Philologie f philology.
Philosoph m philosopher.
Philosophie f philosophy.
philosophisch adj philosophical.
Phonetik f phonetics.
phonetisch adj phonetic.

Phosphor m phosphorus.
Phrase f phrase.
Physik f physics.
physikalisch adj of physics.
Physiker(in) m(f) physicist.
Physiologie f physiology.
physisch adj physical.
Pianist(in) m(f) pianist.
picken vi to pick, peck.
Picknick n picnic.
piepen vi to chirp.
piepsen vi to chirp.
Pigment n pigment.
Pilger(in) m(f) pilgrim.
Pilgerfahrt f pilgrimage.
Pille f pill.
Pilot m pilot.
Pilz m fungus; mushroom; toadstool.
Pinguin m penguin.
Pinie f pine.
pinkeln vi to pee.
Pinsel m paintbrush.
Pirat m pirate.
Pistole f pistol.
Pizza f pizza.
Plage f plague; nuisance.
plagen vt to torment:—vr to toil, slave.
Plakat n placard; poster.
Plan m plan; map.
planen vt to plan; plot.
Planer m planner.
Planet m planet.
planieren vt to plane, level.
Planke f plank.
Plankton n plankton.
planmäßig adj systematic; according to plan.
planschen vi to splash.
Plantage f plantation.
Planung f planning.
Plasma n plasma.
Plastik f sculpture:—n plastic.
Plastiktüte f plastic bag.

plastisch *adj* plastic.
Platane *f* plane (tree).
Platin *n* platinum.
platonisch *adj* platonic.
platschen *vi* to splash.
plätschern *vi* to babble.
platschnaß *adj* drenched.
platt *adj* flat.
Platte *f* plate; flag; record; tile.
Plattenspieler *m* record-player.
Platz *m* place; seat; space, room; square:—~ **nehmen** to take a seat.
platzen *vi* to burst; to explode.
Platzkarte *f* seat reservation.
Platzmangel *m* lack of space.
Plauderei *f* chat, conversation.
plaudern *vi* to chat, talk.
plausibel *adj* plausible.
plazieren *vt* to place:—*vr* to be placed.
Pleite *f* bankruptcy.
Plombe *f* lead seal; (tooth) filling.
plombieren *vt* to seal; to fill (tooth).
plötzlich *adj adv* sudden(ly).
plump *adj* clumsy; heavy-looking.
Plunder *m* rubbish.
plündern *vt* to plunder; to sack:—*vi* to plunder.
Plural *m* plural.
Plus *n* plus; advantage; profit.
Plutonium *n* plutonium.
Poesie *f* poetry.
Poet *m* poet.
poetisch *adj* poetic.
Pol *m* pole.
polar *adj* polar.
Polarkreis *m* Arctic circle.
Pole *m* Pole.
Polen *n* Poland.
Police *f* insurance policy.
polieren *vt* to polish.
Polin *f* Pole.
Politik *f* politics; policy.
Politiker(in) *m(f)* politician.

politisch *adj* political.
Politur *f* polish.
Polizei *f* police.
Polizeibeamte(r) *m* police officer.
Polizeiwache *f* police station.
Polizist(in) *m(f)* policeman (-woman).
polnisch *adj* Polish.
poltern *vi* to crash; to rant.
populär *adj* popular.
Popularität *f* popularity.
Pore *f* pore.
Porree *f* leek.
Portefeuille *n* portfolio.
Portemonnaie *n* purse.
Portugal *n* Portugal.
Portugiese *m* **Portugiesin** *f* Portuguese.
portugiesisch *adj* Portuguese.
Posaune *f* trombone.
Pose *f* pose.
Position *f* position.
positiv *adj* positive.
possessiv *adj* possessive.
Post *f* post (office); mail.
Postamt *n* post office.
Poster *n* poster.
Postfach *n* PO box.
Postkarte *f* postcard.
Postleitzahl *f* post code.
Poststempel *m* postmark.
potent *adj* potent.
Potential *n* potential.
potentiell *adj* potential.
Potenz *f* power; potency.
Pracht *f* splendour, magnificence.
prächtig *adj* splendid.
prachtvoll *adj* splendid, magnificent.
Prag *n* Prague.
prägen *vt* to stamp; to mint; to coin; to form.
Prägung *f* minting; forming.
prahlen *vi* to boast, brag.
Prahlerei *f* boasting.
Praktik *f* practice.

praktikabel *adj* practicable.
Praktikant(in) *m(f)* trainee.
praktisch *adj* practical, handy.
praktizieren *vt vi* to practise.
Praline *f* chocolate.
prall *adj* taut; firmly rounded; plump.
prallen *vi* to bounce, rebound; to blaze.
Prämie *f* premium; prize, award.
prämieren *vt* to give an award to.
Präparat *n* preparation; medicine.
Präposition *f* preposition.
Prärie *f* prairie.
Präsens *n* present tense.
präsentieren *vt* to present.
Präsident(in) *m(f)* president.
Präsidentschaft *f* presidency.
Präsidium *n* presidency, chairmanship.
prasseln *vi* to crackle; to drum.
Praxis *f* practice; surgery; office.
präzis *adj* precise.
Präzision *f* precision.
predigen *vt vi* to preach.
Predigt *f* sermon.
Preis *m* prize; price.
preisbewußt *adj* price-conscious.
Preiselbeere *f* cranberry.
preisen *vi* to praise.
preisgeben *vt* to abandon; to sacrifice; to expose.
Preisklasse *f* price range.
Preisliste *f* price list.
prekär *adj* precarious.
prellen *vt* to bump; to cheat, swindle.
Prellung *f* bruise.
Premiere *f* premiere.
Premierminister *m* prime minister.
Presse *f* press, newspapers.
Pressekonferenz *f* press conference.
pressen *vt* to press.
pressieren *vi* to (be in a) hurry.
Preßburg *n* Bratislava.
Preßluft *f* compressed air.
Prestige *n* prestige.

Preuße *m* Prussian.
Preußen *n* Prussia.
preußisch *adj* Prussian.
prickeln *vt vi* to tingle; to tickle.
Priester *m* priest.
prima *adj* excellent, first-class.
primär *adj* primary.
Primel *f* primrose.
primitiv *adj* primitive.
Prinz *m* prince.
Prinzessin *f* princess.
Prinzip *n* principle.
Priorität *f* priority.
Prisma *n* prism.
privat *adj* private.
privatisieren *vt* to privatize.
Privatisierung *f* privatization.
pro *prep* per.
Probe *f* test; sample; rehearsal.
proben *vt* to try; to rehearse.
probieren *vt vi* to try; to taste.
Problem *n* problem.
problematisch *adj* problematical.
Produkt *n* product; produce.
Produktion *f* production; output.
produktiv *adj* productive.
Produktivität *f* productivity.
Produzent(in) *m(f)* manufacturer; producer.
produzieren *vt* to produce.
Professor *m* professor.
Profil *n* profile; image.
Profit *m* profit.
profitieren *vi* to profit.
Prognose *f* prognosis, prediction.
Programm *n* program(me).
Projekt *m* project.
progressiv *adj* progressive.
Projektion *f* projection.
Projektor *m* projector.
proklamieren *vt* to proclaim.
Promenade *f* promenade.
Promotion *f* doctorate.

prompt *adj* prompt.
Pronomen *n* pronoun.
Propaganda *f* propaganda.
Prophet *m* prophet.
prophezieren *vt* to prophesy.
Prophezierung *f* prophecy.
Proportion *f* proportion.
Prosa *f* prose.
prosaisch *adj* prosaic.
Prospekt *m* prospectus; brochure, leaflet.
prost *excl* cheers.
Prostituierte *f* prostitute.
Prostitution *f* prostitution.
Protein *n* protein.
Protest *m* protest.
Protestant(in) *m(f)* Protestant.
protestantisch *adj* Protestant.
protestieren *vi* to protest.
Provinz *f* province.
provinziell *adj* provincial.
Provision *f* commission; bank charges.
provisorisch *adj* provisional.
Provokation *f* provocation.
provozieren *vt* to provoke.
Prozent *n* per cent, percentage.
Prozeß *m* lawsuit, action, trial.
Prozession *f* procession.
prüde *adj* prudish.
Prüderie *f* prudery.
prüfen *vt* to examine, test; to check.
Prüfer *m* examiner.
Prüfung *f* test, examination; checking.
prügeln *vt* to beat:—*vr* to fight.
Psalm *m* psalm.
Psychiater *m* psychiatrist.

psychiatrisch *adj* psychiatric.
psychisch *adj* mental.
Psychoanalyse *f* psychoanalysis.
Psychologe *m* psychologist.
Psychologie *f* psychology.
psychologisch *adj* psychological.
Pubertät *f* puberty.
Publikum *n* crowd; audience.
publizieren *vt* to publish, publicize.
Pudel *m* poodle.
Puder *m* powder.
Puderdose *f* powder compact.
pudern *vt* to powder.
Puffer *m* buffer.
Puls *m* pulse.
Pulsader *f* artery.
pulsieren *vi* to throb, pulsate.
Pult *n* desk.
Pulver *n* powder.
pulverig *adj* powdery.
Pumpe *f* pump.
pumpen *vt* to pump.
Punkt *m* point; dot; full stop.
pünktlich *adj* punctual.
Pünktlichkeit *f* punctuality.
Punktzahl *f* score.
Pupille *f* pupil.
Puppe *f* doll; puppet; chrysalis.
pur *adj* pure; sheer; neat.
purpurn *adj* purple, crimson.
Pute *f* turkey-hen; **Puter** *m* turkey-cock.
Putz *m* plaster, roughcast.
putzen *vt* to clean:—*vr* to clean oneself.
Pyramide *f* pyramid.
Pyrenäen *pl* (the) Pyrenees.

Q

quadratisch *adj* square.
quaken *vi* to croak; to quack.

Qual *f* pain, agony; anguish.
quälen *vt* to torment.

Qualifikation *f* qualification.
qualifizieren *vt vr* to qualify.
Qualität *f* quality.
Qualle *f* jellyfish.
qualvoll *adj* agonising, excruciating.
Quantität *f* quantity.
quantitativ *adj* quantitative.
Quantum *n* quantity, amount.
Quarantäne *f* quarantine.
Quartal *n* quarter (year).
Quartett *n* quartet.
Quatsch *m* nonsense, rubbish.
quatschen *vi* to chat, natter.
Quecksilber *n* mercury.
Quelle *f* spring; source.
quellen *vi* to well up; to stream.

Quellwasser *n* spring water.
quengling *adj* whining *f*.
quer *adv* crosswise; at right angles.
Querschnitt *m* cross-section.
Querstraße *f* intersecting road.
quetschen *vt* to squash, crush; to bruise.
Quetschung *f* bruise.
quietschen *vt* to screech.
Quintett *n* quintet.
quitt *adj* quits, even.
Quitte *f* quince.
quittieren *vt* to give a receipt for.
Quittung *f* receipt.
Quiz *n* quiz.
Quote *f* rate, number.
Quotient *m* quotient.

R

Rabe *f* raven.
Rache *f* revenge.
rächen *vt* to avenge:—*vr* to take (one's) revenge.
Rad *n* wheel; bike.
Radar *m/n* radar.
radfahren *vi* to cycle.
Radfahrer(in) *m(f)* cyclist.
radieren *vt* to rub out, erase; to etch.
Radiergummi *m* rubber, eraser.
Radierung *f* etching.
Radieschen *n* radish.
radikal *adj* radical.
Radio *n* radio.
radioaktiv *adj* radioactive.
Radioaktivität *f* radioactivity.
Radius *m* radius.
Radkappe *f* hub cap.
Radrennen *n* cycling race.
Rahm *m* cream.
Rahmkase *m* cream cheese.

Rahmen *m* frame(work):—**im ~ von** within the framework of.
rahmen *vt* to frame.
Rakete *f* rocket.
Rand *m* edge; rim; margin.
Rang *m* rank; standing; quality.
rar *adj* rare.
Rarität *f* rarity; curio.
rasch *adj* quick, swift.
rascheln *vi* to rustle.
Rasen *m* lawn; grass.
rasen *vi* to rave; to race.
rasend *adj* furious.
rasieren *vt vr* to shave.
Rasse *f* race; breed.
Rast *f* rest.
rasten *vi* to rest.
rastlos *adj* tireless; restless.
Rasur *f* shaving.
Rat *m* councillor; counsellor; counsel, advice.

Rate *f* instalment.
raten *vt vi* to guess:—**jdm ~** to advise somebody.
Rathaus *n* town hall.
Ration *f* ration.
rational *adj* rational.
ratsam *adj* advisable.
Ratschlag *m* piece of advice.
Rätsel *n* puzzle; riddle.
rätselhaft *adj* mysterious.
Ratte *f* rat.
Rattenfänger *m* ratcatcher.
Raub *m* robbery.
rauben *vt* to rob; to kidnap, abduct.
Räuber *m* robber.
raubgierig *adj* rapacious.
Raubtier *n* predator.
Raubvogel *m* bird of prey.
Rauch *m* smoke.
rauchen *vt vi* to smoke.
Raucher(in) *m(f)* smoker.
räuchern *vt* to smoke, cure.
rauchig *adj* smoky.
raufen *vt* to pull out (hair):—*vi vr* to fight.
Rauferei *f* brawl.
rauh *adj* rough, coarse; harsh.
Raum *m* room; space.
räumen *vt* to clear; to vacate; to put away.
Raumfähre *f* space shuttle.
Raumfahrt *f* space travel.
räumlich *adj* spatial.
Räumlichkeiten *fpl* premises.
Räumung *f* evacuation; clearing away, vacating.
raunen *vi* to whisper, murmur.
Raupe *f* caterpillar.
Rausch *m* intoxication.
rauschen *vi* to rush; to rustle; to hiss.
rauschend *adj* thunderous; sumptuous.
Rauschgift *n* drug.
Razzia *f* raid.
reagieren *vi* to react.

Reaktion *f* reaction.
Reaktor *m* reactor.
real *adj* real, material.
realisieren *vi* to carry out.
Realismus *m* realism.
realistisch *adj* realistic.
Rebe *f* vine.
rebellieren *vi* to rebel.
Rebellion *f* rebellion.
rebellisch *adj* rebellious.
Rebhuhn *n* partridge.
rebooten *vt* to reboot.
Rechen *m* rake.
rechen *vt vi* to rake.
Rechenfehler *m* miscalculation.
rechnen *vt vi* to calculate.
Rechnen *n* arithmetic.
Rechner *m* calculator; computer.
Rechnung *f* calculation(s); bill, invoice.
Rechnungsprüfer *m* auditor.
Rechnungswesen *n* accountancy.
Recht *n* right, law:—**das ~ verletzen** to break the law.
recht *adj* right:—*adv* really, quite:—**~ haben** to be right.
Rechte *f* right (hand); (*pol*) right.
rechte(r, s) *adj* right; right-wing.
Rechteck *n* right angle.
rechten *vi* to argue, dispute.
rechtfertigen *vt* to justify:—*vr* to justify oneself.
Rechtfertigung *f* justification.
rechtlich *adj* legal.
rechtmäßig *adj* legal, lawful.
rechts *adv* on/to the right.
Rechtsanwalt *m* **Rechtsanwältin** *f* lawyer.
rechtzeitig *adj* timely:—*adv* on time.
Redakteur *m* editor.
Redaktion *f* editing; editorial staff.
Rede *f* talk; speech.
redegewandt *adj* eloquent.
reden *vt vi* to say; to talk.

redlich adj honest.
Redner(in) m(f) orator, speaker.
reduzieren vt to reduce.
Reeder m shipowner.
Reederei f shipping company.
referieren vi:—~ über +acc to speak/ talk on.
reflektieren vt to reflect.
Reflex m reflex.
reflexiv adj (gr) reflexive.
Reform f reform.
Reformation f reformation.
reformieren vt to reform.
Regal n shelves, bookcase; stand, rack.
rege adj lively; keen.
Regel f rule; (med) period:—**in der ~** as a rule.
regelmäßig adj regular.
Regelmäßigkeit f regularity.
regeln vt to regulate, control; settle: — vr **sich von selbst ~** to take care of itself.
Regelung f regulation; settlement; ruling.
regelwidrig adj irregular, against the rules.
regen vt vr to move, stir.
Regen m rain.
Regenbogen m rainbow.
Regenguß m shower.
Regenmantel m raincoat.
Regenschirm m umbrella.
Regenwald m rainforest.
Regenwurm m earthworm.
Regenzeit f rainy season.
regieren vt to govern, rule.
Regierung f government.
Regiment n regiment.
Region f region.
Regisseur m producer; film director.
Register n register; table of contents, index.
registrieren vt to register.

Regler m regulator, governor.
reglos adj motionless.
regnen vi to rain.
regnerisch adj rainy.
regulär adj regular.
regulieren vt to regulate; to settle; to adjust.
Regung f motion; feeling, impulse.
Reh n roe, deer.
Rehbock m roebuck.
Rehkitz n fawn.
Reibe f grater.
reiben vt to rub; grate.
Reibung f friction.
Reich n realm; kingdom, empire:—**das Dritte ~** the Third Reich.
reich adj rich.
reichen vi to reach; to be enough:—vt to hold out; to pass, hand out.
Reichtum m wealth, riches.
reif adj ripe; mature.
Reif m ring, hoop.
Reife f ripeness; maturity.
reifen vi to ripen; to mature.
Reifen m ring, hoop; tyre.
Reihe f row; series.
Reihenfolge f sequence.
Reiher m heron.
Reim m rhyme.
reimen vt to rhyme.
rein adj clean; pure:—adv purely.
Reinfall m let-down.
Reingewinn m net profit.
Reinheit f purity; cleanness.
reinigen vt to clean, purify.
Reinigung f cleaning.
Reinigungsmittel n detergent.
Reis m rice.
Reise f journey; voyage.
Reisebüro n travel agency.
Reisebus m coach.
Reiseführer m guide; guidebook.
Reiseindustrie f travel industry.

Reiseleiter m courier.
reisen vi to travel.
Reisende m traveller.
Reisepaß m passport.
reißen vt to tear; to pull, drag:—vi to tear; to pull, drag.
reißend adj raging.
Reißnagel m drawing pin.
Reißverschluß m zip, zip fastener.
reiten vt vi to ride (horse).
Reiter(in) m(f) rider.
Reiz m charm; attraction; stimulus.
reizbar adj irritating.
Reizbarkeit f irritability.
reizen vt to stimulate; to irritate; to appeal to, attract.
reizend adj charming.
reizevoll adj attractive.
rekeln vr to stretch out; to lounge about.
Reklamation f complaint.
Reklame f advertisement; advertising.
reklamieren vt to demand back; to put in a claim.
rekonstruieren vt to reconstruct.
Rekord m record.
Rektor m rector; headteacher.
Rektorat n rectorate; headship.
Rekrut m recruit, conscript.
Relais n relay.
relativ adj relative.
Relativität f relativity.
relevant adj relevant.
Religion f religion.
religiös adj religious.
Rendezvous n rendezvous.
Rendite f rate of return.
Rennbahn f racecourse; race track.
rennen vi to run, race.
Rennen n race; running.
Rennfahrer m racing driver.
Rennpferd n racing horse.
Rennwagen m racing car.
renommiert adj renowned.

renovieren vt to renovate, refurbish.
Renovierung f renovation, refurbishment.
rentabel adj profitable, lucrative.
Rentabilität f profitability.
Rente f pension.
Rentier n reindeer.
rentieren vr to pay, be profitable.
Rentner(in) m(f) pensioner.
Reparatur f repair; repairing.
reparieren vt to repair.
Reportage f report; live coverage.
Reporter m reporter, commentator.
repräsentativ adj representative; impressive.
repräsentieren vt to represent; to constitute:—vi to perform official duties.
reprivatisieren vt to denationalize.
Repravitisierung f denationalization.
Reproduktion f reproduction.
reproduzieren vt to reproduce.
Reptil n reptile.
Republik f republic.
Republikaner m Republican.
republikanisch adj republican.
Reservat n reservation.
Reserve f reserve.
Reserverad n spare wheel.
reservieren vt to reserve.
Reservoir n reservoir.
Reservierung f reservation.
Residenz f residence, seat.
resignieren vi to resign.
resolut adj resolute.
Resonanz f resonance; response.
Respekt m respect.
respektieren vt to respect.
respektlos adj disrespectful.
respektvoll adj respectful.
Ressort n departure.
Rest m rest, remainder; remains.
Restaurant n restaurant.
restaurieren vt to restore.

restlich *adj* remaining.
Resultat *n* result.
retten *vt* to save, rescue.
Retter(in) *m(f)* rescuer.
Rettich *m* radish.
Reue *f* remorse; regret.
reuig *adj* penitent.
Revanche *f* revenge.
Revier *n* district; police station; beat.
Revolte *f* revolt.
revoltieren *vi* to rebel.
Revolution *f* revolution.
Revolutionär *m* revolutionary.
revolutionieren *vt* to revolutionize.
Revolver *m* revolver.
rezensieren *vt* to review.
Rezension *f* review.
Rezept *n* recipe; (*med*) prescription.
Rezeption *f* reception.
Rezession *f* recession.
rezitieren *vt* to recite.
Rhabarber *m* rhubarb.
Rhein *m* Rhine.
rhetorisch *adj* rhetorical.
Rheuma *n* rheumatism.
rheumatisch *adj* rheumatic.
Rheumatismus *m* rheumatism.
Rhinozeros *n* rhinoceros.
rhythmisch *adj* rhythmical.
Rhythmus *m* rhythm.
richten *vt* to adjust; to direct; to aim:
　—*vr* **sich ~ an** +*acc* to direct at.
Richter(in) *m(f)* judge, magistrate.
richterlich *adj* judicial.
Richtlinie *f* guideline.
Richtung *f* direction; tendency.
riechen *vt vi* to smell.
Riese *m* giant.
rieseln *vt* to trickle; to fall gently.
Riesenrad *n* big wheel.
riesig *adj* gigantic.
Riesenschlange *f* boa constrictor.
Riff *n* reef.

Rind *n* ox; cow; cattle; beef.
Rinde *f* bark; crust; rind.
Rindfleisch *n* beef.
Ring *m* ring.
Ringelnatter *f* grass snake.
ringen *vi* to wrestle; to struggle.
Ringen *n* wrestling.
Ringfinger *m* ring finger.
Ringkämpfer *m* wrestler.
ringsherum *adv* round about.
Ringstraße *f* ring road.
Rinne *f* gutter, drain.
rinnen *vi* to run, trickle.
Rippe *f* rib.
Risiko *n* risk; venture.
riskant *adj* risky, hazardous.
riskieren *vt* to risk.
Riß *m* tear; crack; scratch.
rissig *adj* torn; cracked; scratched.
Ritt *m* ride.
Ritter *m* knight.
ritterlich *adj* chivalrous.
Rivale *m* rival.
Rivalität *f* rivalry.
Robbe *f* seal.
Roboter *m* robot.
robust *adj* robust.
Rock *m* skirt; jacket; tunic.
Rodel *m* toboggan.
Rodelbahn *f* toboggan run.
rodeln *vi* to toboggan.
roden *vi* to clear.
Rogen *m* roe, spawn.
Roggen *m* rye.
Roggenbrot *n* rye bread.
roh *adj* raw; coarse, crude.
Rohmaterial *n* raw material.
Rohöl *n* crude oil.
Rohr *n* pipe, tube; cane; reed; barrel.
Röhre *f* tube, pipe; valve; oven.
Rohrleitung *f* pipeline.
Rohrzucker *m* cane sugar.
Rohstoff *m* raw material.

Rokoko n rococo.
Rolladen m shutter.
Rollbahn f runway.
Rolle f roll; role; spool:—**keine ~ spielen** not to matter.
rollen vt vi to roll; to taxi.
Rollschuh m roller skate.
Rollstuhl m wheelchair.
Rolltreppe f escalator.
Rom n Rome.
Roman m novel.
Romantik f romanticism.
romantisch adj romantic.
Romanze f romance.
Römer m Roman.
römisch adj Roman.
römisch-katholisch adj Roman Catholic.
röntgen vt to X-ray.
Röntgenstrahlen pl X-rays.
rosa adj pink.
Rose f rose.
Rosenholz n rosewood.
Rosenkohl m Brussels sprouts.
Rosenkranz m rosary.
Rosenstock m rosebush.
rosig adj rosy.
Rosine f raisin, currant.
Roß n horse, steed.
Roßkastanie f horse chestnut.
Rost m rust; grill.
rosten vi to rust.
rösten vt to roast; to toast; to grill.
rostfrei adj rust-free; rustproof; stainless.
rostig adj rusty.
rot adj red.
Rotkehlchen n robin.
rötlich adj reddish.
Rotwein m red wine.
Route f route.
Routine f experience; routine.
Rube f turnip.
Rubin m ruby.
Ruck m jerk, jolt.

rücken vt to move.
Rücken m back; ridge.
Rückfahrt f return journey.
Rückfall m relapse.
rückfällig adj relapsing.
Rückgabe f return.
Rückgang m decline, fall.
Rückhalt m backing, support.
Rückkehr f return.
rücklings adv from behind; backwards.
Rucksack m rucksack.
Rücktritt m resignation.
rückversichern vt to reinsure.
Rückversicherung f reinsurance.
rückwärtig adj rear.
rückwärts adv back, backwards.
Rückweg m return journey, way back.
rückwirkend adj retroactive.
Rückwirkung f retroactive effect.
Rückzahlung f repayment.
Rudel n pack; herd.
Ruder n oar; rudder.
Ruderboot n rowing boat.
rudern vt vi to row.
Rudersport m rowing.
Ruf m shout, call; reputation.
rufen vi vt to call, cry.
rügen vt to rebuke.
Ruhe f rest; peace, quiet; calm; silence.
ruhelos adj restless.
ruhen vi to rest.
Ruhestand m retirement:—**in den ~ treten** to retire.
ruhig adj quiet; still; steady.
Ruhm m glory, fame.
rühmen vt to praise:—vr to boast.
Ruhr f dysentery.
Rührei n scrambled eggs.
rühren vt vr to stir:—vr ~ **von** to come from.
rührend adj moving, touching.
Rührung f emotion.
Ruin m ruin.

Ruine f ruin.
ruinieren vt to ruin.
rülpsen vi to burp, belch.
Rumäne m Romanian.
Rumänien n Romania.
Rumänin f Romanian.
rumänisch adj Romanian.
Rummel m hubbub; fair.
Rummelplatz m fair, fairground.
Rumpf m trunk, torso; fuselage; hull.
rund adj round:—adv around.
Rundbrief m circular.
Runde f round; lap; circle.
Rundfahrt f round trip.
Rundfunk m broadcasting.
Rundfunkgerät n wireless set.
Rundfunksender m transmitter.
Rundfunksendung f broadcast, radio programme.
rundheraus adv straight out, bluntly.
rundherum adv round about; all round.
rundlich adj plump, rounded.

Rundreise f round trop.
Rundschreiben n circular.
Runzel f wrinkle.
runzeln vt to wrinkle.
rupfen vt to pluck.
Ruß m spot.
Russe m Russian.
Rüssel m snout; (elephant's) trunk.
rußig adj sooty.
Russin f Russian.
russisch adj Russian.
Rußland n Russia.
rüsten vt to prepare:—vi to prepare; to arm:—vr to prepare oneself; to arm oneself.
Rüstung f preparation; arming; armour; armaments.
Rute f rod.
Rutsch m slide; landslide.
rutschen vi to slide; to slip.
rutschig adj slippery.
rütteln vt vi to shake, jolt.

S

Saal m hall; room.
Saat f seed; crop.
Sabotage f sabotage.
Sache f thing, object; affair, business; matter.
sächlich adj neuter.
Sachse m Saxon.
Sachsen n Saxony.
sächsisch adj Saxon.
Sachverständige(r) f(m) expert, specialist.
Sack m sack.
säen vt vi to sow.
Saft m juice.
saftig adj juicy.

Sage f saga.
Säge f saw.
Sägemehl n sawdust.
sagen vt vi to say, tell.
sägen vt vi to saw.
Sahne f cream.
Saison f season.
Saite f string, chord.
Saiteninstrument n string instrument.
Salat m salad; lettuce.
Salz n salt.
salzen vt to salt.
salzig adj salty.
Salzsäure f hydrochloric acid.
Salzwasser n salt water.

Samen *m* seed; sperm.
sammeln *vt* to collect:—*vr* to assemble, gather.
Sammlung *f* collection; assembly, gathering.
Samstag *m* Saturday.
Samt *m* velvet.
samt *prep* (along) with, together with.
Sand *m* sand.
sanft *adj* gentle, soft.
Sänger(in) *m(f)* singer.
Saphir *m* sapphire.
Sardelle *f* anchovy.
Sardine *f* sardine.
Sardinien *n* Sardinia.
Sarg *m* coffin.
Sarkasmus *m* sarcasm.
Satan *m* Satan, devil.
Satellit *m* satellite.
Satire *f* satire.
satirisch *adj* satirical.
satt *adj* full; rich, deep.
Sattel *m* saddle.
satteln *vt* to saddle.
Satz *m* sentence; clause; (*mus*) movement; set; jump.
Satzlehre *f* syntax.
Satzung *f* by-law, statute.
Satzzeichen *n* punctuation mark.
Sau *f* sow.
sauber *adj* clean.
säubern *vt* to clean.
Säuberung *f* cleaning.
sauer *adj* sour; acid.
Sauerkraut *n* sauerkraut.
Sauerstoff *m* oxygen.
saufen *vt vi* to drink, booze.
saugen *vt vi* to suck; to vacuum.
säugen *vi* to suckle.
Sauger *m* dummy; teat.
Säugetier *n* mammal.
Säugling *m* infant.
Säule *f* pillar, column.

Saum *m* hem; seam.
säumen *vt* to hem; to seam:—*vi* to hesitate, delay.
Sauna *f* sauna.
Saxophon *n* saxophone.
schäbig *adj* shabby.
Schablone *f* stencil; pattern.
Schach *n* chess; check.
schachmatt *adj* checkmate.
Schachspiel *n* game of chess.
Schacht *m* shaft.
Schachtel *f* box.
schade *adj* a pity/shame:—*excl* **(wie)** ~! (what a) pity/shame.
Schädel *m* skull.
Schaden *m* harm, damage; injury.
schaden *vi* +*dat* to hurt.
Schadenersatz *m* damages.
Schadenfreude *f* malicious glee.
schädigen *vt* to damage, harm.
Schaf *n* sheep.
Schafbock *m* ram.
Schäfer(in) *m(f)* shepherd(ess).
Schäferhund *m* sheepdog.
schaffen *vt* to create; to manage.
Schakal *m* jackal.
Schal *m* scarf.
Schale *f* shell, peel, skin, pod, husk.
schälen *vt* to peel; to shell:—*vr* to peel.
Schall *m* sound.
Schalldämpfer *m* silencer.
schalldicht *adj* soundproof.
Schallmauer *f* sound barrier.
Schallplatte *f* record player.
schalten *vt* to switch:—*vi* to change gear.
Schalter *m* ticket office; (bank, etc) counter; switch.
Schaltjahr *n* leap year.
Scham *f* shame; modesty.
schämen *vr* to be ashamed.
schamlos *adj* shameless.
Schande *f* shame, disgrace.

schändlich *adj* shameful, disgraceful.

scharf *adj* sharp.

Schärfe *f* sharpness.

schärfen *vt* to sharpen.

Schatten *m* shadow, shade.

schattig *adj* shady.

Schatz *m* treasure.

schätzen *vt* to estimate; to value.

schauen *vi* to look.

Schaufel *f* shovel; scoop.

Schaukel *f* swing.

Schaum *m* foam; froth.

schäumen *vi* to foam.

schaumig *adj* frothy, foamy.

Schauspiel *n* spectacle; play.

Schauspieler(in) *m(f)* actor (actress).

Schauspielhaus *n* theatre.

Scheck *m* cheque.

Scheckheft *m* chequebook.

Scheckkarte *f* cheque (guarantee) card.

Scheibe *f* pane; disc; slice; target.

Scheibenwischer *m* windscreen wiper.

Scheide *f* sheath; boundary; vagina.

scheiden *vt* to separate; to dissolve:— *vi* to depart; to part.

Scheidung *f* divorce.

Schein *m* light; appearance; bank-note; certificate.

scheinbar *adj* apparent.

scheinen *vi* to shine; to look, seem, appear.

Scheitel *m* top; (hair) parting.

scheiteln *vt* to part.

scheitern *vi* to fail.

Schellfisch *m* haddock.

Schelte *f* scolding.

schelten *vt* to scold.

Schema *n* scheme, plan.

schematisch *adj* schematic.

Schenkel *m* thigh.

schenken *vt* to give.

Schere *f* scissors.

scheren *vt* to cut; to shear.

Scherz *m* joke.

scherzen *vi* to joke.

Scheu *f* shyness.

Scheune *f* barn.

Schicht *f* layer; shift.

schichten *vt* to heap, layer.

schicken *vt* to send.

Schicksal *n* fate, destiny.

schieben *vt vi* to push.

schief *adj* crooked; sloping; leaning.

Schiene *f* rail.

schießen *vt vi* to shoot.

Schiff *m* vessel, boat, ship; nave.

Schikane *f* dirty trick; harassment.

schikanieren *vt* to harass, torment.

Schild *m* shield; sign, nameplate.

schildern *vt* to depict, portray.

Schildkröte *f* tortoise; turtle.

Schilling *m* schilling.

Schimmel *m* mould; white horse.

Schimmer *m* shimmer; glimmer.

schimmern *vi* to shimmer, glimmer.

Schimpanse *f* chimpanzee.

schimpfen *vt* to scold:—*vi* to curse, complain.

Schinken *m* ham.

Schirm *m* umbrella; parasol; screen.

schizophren *adj* schizophrenic.

Schlacht *f* battle.

schlachten *vt* to slaughter, kill.

Schlachter *m* butcher.

Schlachtfeld *n* battlefield.

Schlachthof *m* slaughterhouse, abattoir.

Schlaf *m* sleep, doze.

schlafen *vi* to sleep:—~ **gehen** to go to bed.

schlaflos *adj* sleepless.

Schlaflosigkeit *f* sleeplessness, insomnia.

schläfrig *adj* sleepy.

Schlafwagen *m* sleeping car, sleeper.

schlafwandeln *vi* to sleepwalk.

Schlafzimmer *n* bedroom.

Schlag *m* blow; stroke; beat:—**mit einem ~** all at once:—**~ auf ~** in rapid succession.

Schlagader *f* artery.

schlagen *vt vi* to beat; to strike, hit:—*vr* to fight.

Schlager *m* hit.

Schlagsahne *f* whipped cream.

Schlamm *m* mud.

schlammig *adj* muddy.

Schlange *f* snake, serpent; queue.

Schlangengift *n* snake venom.

schlank *adj* slim, slender.

Schlankheit *f* slimness, slenderness.

Schlankheitskur *f* diet.

schlapp *adj* limp.

schlau *adj* sly, cunning.

Schlauheit *f* cunning.

schlecht *adj adv* bad(ly).

Schlechtigkeit *f* badness, wickedness.

schlecken *vt vi* to lick.

schleichen *vi* to crawl, creep.

schleichend *adj* gradual; creeping.

Schleier *m* veil.

Schleim *m* slime.

schleimig *adj* slimy.

schlendern *vi* to stroll.

Schleppe *f* train.

schleppen *vt* to tow; drag; haul.

Schlepper *m* tug; tractor.

Schlesien *n* Silesia.

Schleuse *f* lock; sluice.

schlicht *adj* simple, plain.

schließen *vt vi vr* to close, shut.

schließlich *adv* finally.

schlimm *adj* bad.

schlimmer *adj* worse.

schlimmste(r, s) *adj* worst.

Schlips *m* tie.

Schlitten *m* sledge.

Schlittenfahren *n* tobogganing.

schlittern *vi* to slide.

Schlitz *m* slit; slot.

schlitzen *vt* to slit.

Schloß *n* lock; castle.

Schlott *m* chimney; funnel.

schlottern *vi* to shake, tremble.

Schlucht *f* ravine, gorge.

schluchzen *vi* to sob.

Schluck *m* swallow.

Schluckauf *m* hiccups.

schlucken *vt vi* to swallow.

Schluß *m* end, conclusion.

Schlüssel *m* key.

Schlüsselblume *f* cowslip, primrose.

schmal *adj* narrow.

Schmalz *n* dripping, lard.

schmecken *vt vi* to taste.

schmelzen *vi* to melt.

Schmerz *m* pain, grief.

schmerzen *vi* to hurt, be painful, to grieve.

schmerzhaft *adj* painful, sore.

schmerzlich *adj* painful; grievous.

schmerzlos *adj* painless.

Schmetterling *m* butterfly.

Schmied *m* (black)smith.

schmieren *vt* to smear.

Schmuck *m* jewellery; adornment.

schmücken *vt* to decorate.

Schmuggel *m* smuggling.

schmuggeln *vt vi* to smuggle.

Schmuggler *m* smuggler.

Schmutz *m* filth, dirt.

schmutzig *adj* dirty.

Schnabel *m* bill, beak.

Schnake *f* cranefly; gnat.

Schnaps *m* spirits; schnaps.

Schnauze *f* snout, muzzle; spout.

Schnecke *f* snail.

Schnee *m* snow.

Schneeball *m* snowball.

Schneeflocke *f* snowflake.

Schneeglöckchen *n* snowdrop.

Schneemann *n* snowman.

Schneepflug *m* snowplough.

schneiden *vt* to cut.

Schneider(in) *m(f)* tailor.

Schneiderei *f* tailor's.

schneien *vi* to snow.

schnell *adj* quick, rapid, fast:—*adv* quickly, fast.

Schnelligkeit *f* speed.

Schnellimbiß *m* snack bar.

schnellstens *adv* as quickly as possible.

Schnellzug *m* express train.

schneuzen *vr* to blow one's nose.

Schnitt *m* cut(ting); (inter)section.

Schnitte *f* slice.

Schnitzel *n* chip; escalope.

schnitzen *vt* to carve.

Schnitzer *m* carver.

schnüffeln *vt* to sniff.

Schnupfen *m* cold.

schnuppern *vt* to sniff.

Schnur *f* string, cord.

schnüren *vt* to tie.

schnurgerade *adj* straight (as a die).

Schnurrbart *m* moustache.

schnurren *vi* to purr; to hum.

Schnursenkel *m* shoelace.

Schock *m* shock.

schockieren *vt* to shock, outrage.

Schokolade *f* chocolate.

schon *adv* already; all right; just.

schön *adj* beautiful; nice.

Schönheit *f* beauty.

schöpfen *vt* to scoop, ladle; to breathe in.

Schöpfer *m* creator; founder.

schöpferisch *adj* creative.

Schöpfung *f* creation; genesis.

Schornstein *m* chimney; funnel.

Schornsteinfeger *m* chimney sweep.

Schotte *m* Scot(sman).

Schottin *f* Scot(swoman).

schottish *adj* Scottish.

Schottland *n* Scotland.

schräg *adj* slanting.

Schrank *m* cupboard.

Schraube *f* screw.

schrauben *vt* to screw.

Schraubenzieher *m* screwdriver.

Schreck *m* terror; fright.

schrecken *vt* to frighten, scare.

schrecklich *adj* terrible, awful.

Schrei *m* shout; scream.

schreiben *vt vi* to write.

Schreibmaschine *f* typewriter.

Schreibtisch *m* desk.

schreien *vt vi* to scream, cry out.

Schrein *m* shrine.

schreiten *vi* to stride.

Schrift *f* (hand)writing; script; typeface.

schriftlich *adj* written:—*adv* in writing.

Schriftsteller(in) *m(f)* writer, author.

Schritt *m* step; walk; pace.

Schrittmacher *m* pacemaker.

schroff *adj* steep; brusque.

Schrott *m* scrap metal.

Schrotthaufen *m* scrap heap.

schrottreif *adj* ready for the scrap heap.

Schubkarren *m* wheelbarrow.

Schublade *f* drawer.

schüchtern *adj* shy, timid.

Schüchternheit *f* shyness, timidity.

Schuh *m* shoe.

Schuld *f* guilt, fault:—**~en** *pl* debts: — in ~**en geraten** to get into debt.

schuldig *adj* guilty.

Schuldner(in) *m(f)* debtor.

Schule *f* school.

schulen *vt* to train.

Schüler(in) *m(f)* pupil.

Schulter *f* shoulder.

schultern *vt* to shoulder.

Schulung *f* schooling, education.

Schuppe *f* (fish) scale:—**~n** *pl* dandruff.

Schürze *f* apron.

Schuß *m* shot.

Schüssel *f* dish.
schütteln *vt* to shake.
Schutz *m* shelter; protection.
Schütze *m* gunman; marksman; (*astrol*) Sagittarius.
schützen *vt* to protect.
Schutzmarke *f* trademark.
Schwaben *n* Swabia.
schwach *adj* weak, feeble.
Schwäche *f* weakness.
schwächen *vt* to weaken.
Schwachheit *f* weakness.
Schwager *m* brother-in-law.
Schwägerin *f* sister-in-law.
Schwalbe *f* swallow.
Schwamm *m* sponge.
Schwan *m* swan.
schwanger *adj* pregnant.
Schwangerschaft *f* pregnancy.
schwanken *vi* to sway; to fluctuate; to stagger.
Schwankung *f* fluctuation.
Schwanz *m* tail.
schwänzen *vt* to skip, cut:—*vi* to play truant.
Schwarm *m* swarm.
schwarz *adj* black.
schwärzen *vt* to blacken, slander.
Schwarzmarkt *m* black market.
Schwarzwald *m* (the) Black Forest.
Schwarzweißfilm *m* black and white film.
schweben *vi* to soar.
Schwede *m* Swede.
Schweden *n* Sweden.
Schwedin *f* Swede.
schwedisch *adj* Swedish.
Schwefel *m* sulphur.
Schwefelsäure *f* sulphuric acid.
Schweigen *n* silence.
schweigen *vi* to be silent.
schweigsam *adj* silent, taciturn.
Schweigsamkeit *f* quietness.

Schwein *n* pig.
Schweinefleisch *n* pork.
Schweinestall *m* pigsty.
Schweiß *m* sweat.
schweißen *vt vi* to weld.
Schweißer *m* welder.
Schweiz *f* Switzerland.
Schweizer(in) *m(f)* Swiss.
schweizerisch *adj* Swiss.
Schwelle *f* threshold.
schwellen *vi* to swell.
schwenken *vt* to swing; to wave:—*vi* to swivel.
schwer *adj* heavy; difficult, hard; serious.
Schwere *f* heaviness; gravity.
Schwergewicht *n* heavyweight; emphasis.
Schwerindustrie *f* heavy industry.
Schwerpunkt *m* centre of gravity; emphasis.
Schwert *n* sword.
Schwester *f* sister; nurse.
schwesterlich *adj* sisterly.
Schwiegereltern *pl* parents-in-law.
Schwiegermutter *f* mother-in-law.
Schwiegersohn *m* son-in-law.
Schwiegertochter *f* daughter-in-law.
Schwiegervater *m* father-in-law.
schwierig *adj* difficult.
Schwierigkeit *f* difficulty.
Schwimmbad *n* swimming baths.
schwimmen *vi* to swim.
Schwimmveste *f* life jacket.
schwinden *vi* to disappear; to decline.
schwingen *vi* to swing.
Schwingung *f* vibration; oscillation.
schwitzen *vi* to sweat.
schwören *vt vi* to swear.
schwül *adj* stuffy, close.
Schwung *m* swing; momentum.
Schwur *m* oath.
schwürzen *vi* to swear.

sechs *num* six.
sechste(r, s) *adj* sixth.
sechzehn *num* sixteen.
sechzig *num* sixty.
See *m* lake:—*f* sea.
Seehund *m* seal.
Seeigel *m* sea urchin.
seekrank *adj* seasick.
Seekrankheit *f* seasickness.
Seelachs *m* rock salmon.
Seele *f* soul.
seelisch *adj* mental.
Seelöwe *m* sea lion.
Seemann *m* sailor, seaman.
Seemöwe *f* seagull.
Seenot *f* distress.
Seepolyp *m* octopus.
Seeräuber *m* pirate.
Seerose *f* water lily.
Seestern *m* starfish.
Seetang *m* seaweed.
seetüchtig *adj* seaworthy.
Seeweg *m* sea route.
Seezunge *f* sole.
Segel *n* sail.
Segelboot *n* yacht.
segeln *vt vi* to sail.
Segelschiff *n* sailing vessel.
Segelsport *m* sailing.
Segen *m* blessing.
Segler *m* sailor, yachtsman.
segnen *vt* to bless.
sehen *vt vi* to see.
sehnen *vr*:—**sich ~ nach** to yearn for.
Sehnsucht *f* longing.
sehr *adv* very.
Seide *f* silk.
seiden *adj* silk.
Seidenraupe *f* silkworm.
Seife *f* soap.
Seil *n* rope, cable.
Seilbahn *f* cable railway.
Seiltänzer(in) *m(f)* tightrope walker.

sein *vi v aux* to be.
sein(e) *poss adj* his; its.
seine(r, s) *poss pn* his; its.
seit *prep conj* since.
seitdem *adv conj* since.
Seite *f* side; page.
seitens *prep* on the part of.
seither *adv conj* since (then).
seitwärts *adv* sidewards.
Sekretär(in) *m(f)* secretary.
Sekretariat *n* secretariat.
Sekt *m* champagne.
Sekunde *f* second.
selber = **selbst.**
Selbst *n* self.
selbst *pn*:—**ich ~** myself, **wir ~** ourselves, etc; alone, on one's own:—*adv* even.
selbständig *adj* independent; self-employed.
Selbständigkeit *f* independence; self-employment.
selbstbewußt *adj* self-confident.
selbstlos *adj* selfless, unselfish.
Selbstmord *m* suicide:—**~ begehen** to commit suicide.
Selbstmörder(in) *m(f)* suicide.
selbstmörderisch *adj* suicidal.
Selbstsucht *f* selfishness.
selbstsüchtig *adj* selfish.
selbstverständlich *adj* obvious:—*adv* naturally.
Selbstverteidigung *f* self-defence.
selig *adj* blessed; deceased, late.
Sellerie *m/f* celery.
selten *adj* rare, scarce:—*adv* seldom, rarely.
Seltenheit *f* rarity.
seltsam *adj* strange.
Seltsamkeit *f* strangeness.
Semikolon *n* semicolon.
senden *vt vi* to send; to transmit, broadcast.

Sender *m* station; transmitter.

Sendung *f* consignment; broadcast, transmission; programme.

Senf *m* mustard.

Senke *f* depression.

senken *vt* to lower:—*vr* to sink.

senkrecht *adj* vertical, perpendicular.

Sensation *f* sensation.

sensationell *adj* sensational.

Sense *f* scythe.

September *m* September.

Serie *f* series.

seriös *adj* serious.

Service *n* set, service:—*m* service.

servieren *vt vi* to serve.

Serviererin *f* waitress.

Serviette *f* serviette, napkin.

Sessel *m* armchair.

Sessellift *m* chairlift.

setzen *vt* to put, set; to plant:—*vr* to settle; to sit down:—*vi* to leap; to bet.

Seuche *f* epidemic.

seufzen *vi* to sigh.

Seufzer *m* sigh.

Sex *m* sex.

Sexualität *f* sexuality.

sexuell *adj* sexual.

Shampoo *n* shampoo.

Sibieren *n* Siberian.

sibirisch *adj* Siberian.

sich *pn* oneself, himself, herself, itself, themselves.

Sichel *f* sickle; crescent.

sicher *adj* safe; certain; secure.

Sicherheit *f* certainty; safety; security.

sicherlich *adv* surely, certainly.

sichern *vt* to protect; secure.

Sicherung *f* fuse; safety catch.

Sicht *f* sight.

sichtbar *adj* visible.

sichtlich *adj* obvious.

sie *pn nom* she, it, they; *acc* her, it, them.

Sie *pn nom acc* you.

Sieb *n* sieve; strainer.

sieben *num* seven:—*vt* to sift; to strain.

siebzehn *num* seventeen.

siebzig *num* seventy.

sieden *vt* to boil, simmer.

Siedler *m* settler.

Siedlung *f* settlement; housing estate.

Sieg *m* victory, triumph.

Siegel *m* seal.

siegen *vi* to win, be victorious.

Sieger *m* victor; winner.

siegreich *adj* victorious.

Signal *n* signal, call.

Silbe *f* syllable.

Silber *n* silver.

silbern *adj* silver.

Silhouette *f* silhouette.

Silvester(abend) *m* New Year's Eve.

Sims *n* mantelpiece; sill.

simulieren *vt* to simulate:—*vi* to feign illness.

simultan *adj* simultaneous.

Sinfonie *f* symphony.

singen *vt vi* to sing.

Singular *m* singular.

sinken *vi* to sink; to fall.

Sinn *m* sense; mind; meaning.

sinnen *vi* to ponder.

sinngemäß *adj* faithful.

sinnlich *adj* sensual; sensory.

Sinnlichkeit *f* sensuality.

sinnlos *adj* senseless; meaningless.

Sinnlosigkeit *f* senselessness; meaninglessness.

sinnvoll *adj* sensible.

Sirene *f* siren.

Sirup *m* syrup.

Sitte *f* custom:—**~n** *pl* morals.

sittlich *adj* moral.

Sittlichkeit *f* morality.

Situation *f* situation.

Sitz *m* seat.

sitzen *vi* to sit.

Sitzung f meeting.
Sizilien n Sicily.
Skandal m scandal.
skandalös adj scandalous.
Skandinavien n Scandinavia.
Skandinavier(in) m(f) Scandinavian.
skandinavisch adj Scandinavian.
Skelett n skeleton.
Skepsis f scepticism.
skeptisch adj sceptical.
Ski m ski:—~ **laufen** to ski.
Skiläufer m skier.
Skilehrer m ski instructor.
Skizze f sketch.
skizzieren vt vi to sketch.
Sklave m slave.
Sklaverei f slavery.
Sklavin f slave.
Skonto m discount.
Skorpion m scorpion; (astrol) Scorpio.
Skulptur f (piece of) sculpture.
Smaragd m emerald.
Smoking m dinner jacket.
so adv so; like this:—~ **daß** conj so that:—excl **so?** really?
Socke f sock.
soeben adv just (now).
sofern conj if, provided (that).
sofort adv immediately, at once.
Software f software.
sogar adv even.
sogenannt adj so-called.
sogleich adv straight away.
Sohle f sole.
Sohn m son.
solch pn such.
solche(r, s) adj:—ein ~ such a(n).
Soldat m soldier.
solidarisch adj in solidarity.
Solidarität f solidarity.
solid(e) adj solid; respectable.
Solist(in) m(f) soloist.
Soll n debit.

sollen v aux to be supposed to, should.
Solo n solo.
somit conj and so, therefore.
Sommer m summer.
Sonate f sonata.
Sonde f probe.
Sonderangebot m special offer.
sonderbar adj odd, strange.
Sonderfall m special case.
sonderlich adj particular; peculiar; remarkable.
sondern conj but:—vt to separate:—nicht nur... ~ auch not only... but also.
Sonnabend m Saturday.
Sonne f sun.
Sonnenaufgang m sunrise.
sonnenbaden vi to sunbathe.
Sonnenbrille f sunglasses.
Sonnenenergie f solar energy.
Sonnenfinsternis f solar eclipse.
Sonnenschein m sunshine.
Sonnenuntergang m sunset.
sonnig adj sunny.
Sonntag m Sunday.
sonst adv conj otherwise.
Sopran m soprano.
Sorge f care, worry.
sorgen vi:—für jdn ~ to look after somebody:—vr sich ~ (um) to worry (about).
sorgenfrei adj carefree.
sorgenvoll adj worried.
Sorgfalt f carefulness.
sorgfältig adj careful.
sorglos adj careless; carefree.
Sorte f sort; brand.
sortieren vt to sort (out).
Sortiment n assortment.
Soße f sauce; gravy.
soviel conj as far as (I know, etc).
soweit conj as far as.
sowenig conj as little as.
sowie conj as soon as; as well as.

sowohl *conj*:—~... **als auch** both... and.

sozial *adj* social.

Sozialismus *m* socialism.

Sozialist(in) *m(f)* socialist.

sozialistisch *adj* socialist.

sozialogisch *adj* sociological.

Spalte *f* column (in newspaper, etc).

Spanien *n* Spain.

Spanier(in) *m(f)* Spaniard.

spanisch *adj* Spanish.

spannen *vt* to tighten:—*vi* to be tight.

spannend *adj* exciting, gripping.

Spannung *f* tension; voltage; suspense.

sparen *vt vi* to save, economize.

Sparer *m* saver.

Spargel *m* asparagus.

Sparkasse *f* savings bank.

Sparkonto *n* savings account.

sparsam *adj* economical, thrifty.

Sparsamkeit *f* thrift.

Sparschwein *n* piggy bank.

Spaß *m* joke; fun:—**jdm ~ machen** to be fun (for somebody).

spaßen *vi* to joke.

spaßhaft *adj* jocular, funny.

spät *adj adv* late:—**wie ~ ist es?** what time is it?

Spaten *m* spade.

später *adj adv* later.

spätestens *adv* at the latest.

Spatz *m* sparrow.

spazieren *vi* to stroll, walk.

spazierenfahren *vi* to go for a drive.

spazierengehen *vi* to go for a walk.

Spaziergang *m* walk.

Spazierstock *m* walking stick.

Specht *m* woodpecker.

Speck *m* bacon.

Spediteur *m* carrier.

Spedition *f* carriage.

Speer *m* spear; javelin.

Speichel *m* saliva, spit.

Speicher *m* storehouse.

speichern *vt* to store.

speien *vt vi* to spit; to vomit.

Speise *f* food.

speisen *vt* to feed; to eat:—*vi* to dine.

Speisewagen *m* dining car.

Spekulant *m* speculator.

Spekulation *f* speculation.

spekulieren *vi* to speculate.

Spende *f* donation.

spenden *vt* to give, donate.

Spender *m* donor.

Sperling *m* sparrow.

Sperre *f* barrier; ban.

sperren *vt* to block; to bar:—*vr* to baulk.

Spiegel *m* mirror.

Spiegelei *n* fried egg.

Spiel *n* play, game, match.

spielen *vt vi* to play; to gamble.

Spieler(in) *m(f)* player; gambler.

Spielkarte *f* playing card.

Spielzeug *n* toy, plaything.

Spinat *m* spinach.

Spinn(en)gewebe *m* cobweb.

Spinne *f* spider.

spinnen *vt* to spin.

Spion *m* spy.

Spionage *f* espionage.

spitz *adj* acute, pointed.

Spitzen *pl* lace.

sponsern *vt* to sponsor.

Sport *m* sport.

Spott *m* mockery.

Sprache *f* language.

sprechen *vt vi* to speak.

sprengen *vt* to blow up; to sprinkle, water.

Sprengstoff *m* explosive.

Sprichwort *n* proverb, saying.

sprießen *vt* to sprout.

Springbrunnen *m* fountain.

springen *vi* to jump.

spritzen *vt* to squirt.

sprühen vi to sparkle.
spucken vi to spit.
spülen vt to wash up, rinse.
spüren vt to perceive.
Staat m state.
Staatsanwalt m public prosecutor.
Stachel m sting, prickle; thorn.
Stachelbeere f gooseberry.
Stadt f town.
Städter m citizen, townsman.
städtlich adj urban.
Stadtrat m town council(lor).
Stahl m steel.
Stamm m trunk, stem.
stampfen vt to mash, crush.
Stand m state, position, situation.
starr adj stiff; rigid; staring.
starren vi to stare.
Starrsinn m obstinacy.
Start m start; takeoff.
Startbahn f runway.
starten vt to start:—vi to take off.
Starter m starter.
statt conj prep instead of.
Stätte f place.
stattfinden vi to take place.
Statue f statue.
Status m status.
Staub m dust.
staubig adj dusty.
Staubsauger m vacuum cleaner.
Staubtuch n duster.
Staunen n astonishment, surprise.
staunen vi to be astonished, surprised (über at).
stechen vt to prick; to stab.
stecken vt to put, insert.
Steckrübe f turnip.
stehen vi to stand; to be.
stehenbleiben vi to stop.
stehlen vt to steal.
steif adj stiff.
Steifheit f stiffness.

Steigbügel m stirrup.
steigen vi to climb; to rise.
steigern vt to raise; to compare:—vi to bid:—vr to increase.
Steigung f incline, gradient, rise.
steil adj steep.
Stein m stone; jewel.
Steinbock m (astrol) Capricorn.
steinig adj stony.
Stelle f place; post, job; office.
stellen vt to put; to set.
Stellenangebot n job offer.
Stellung f position.
Stellungnahme f comment.
Stempel m stamp.
stempeln vt to stamp.
Stengel m stalk, stem.
Sterbefall m death.
Sterbehilfe f euthanasia.
sterben vi to die.
sterblich adj mortal.
Sterblichkeit f mortality.
steril adj sterile.
Stern m star.
Sternbild n constellation.
stet adj steady.
stetig adj constant, continual.
stets adv continually, always.
Steuer f tax:—n helm; rudder; steering wheel.
Steuerberater(in) m(f) tax consultant.
Steuerbord n (mar) starboard.
steuern vt to steer; to pilot.
Steuerrad n steering wheel.
Steuerzahler m taxpayer.
Steward(eß) m(f) steward(ess).
Stich m sting; stab; stitch; tinge.
Stichprobe f spot check.
Stichwort n cue; headword; note.
sticken vt vi to embroider.
Stickerei f embroidery.
stickig adj stuffy, close.
Stickstoff m nitrogen.

Stiefel m boot.
Stiefkind n stepchild.
Stiefmutter f stepmother.
Stiefmütterchen n pansy.
Stiefvater m stepfather.
Stier m bull; (astrol) Taurus.
Stierkampf m bullfight.
Stierkampfarena f bullring.
Stierkämpfer m bullfighter.
Stiftung f donation; foundation.
Stil m style.
still adj quiet; still; secret.
Stille f stillness, quietness.
stil(l)legen vt to close down.
stillschweigen vt to be silent.
Stillschweigen n silence.
stillschweigend adj (adv) silent(ly); tacit(ly).
Stimme f voice; vote.
stimmen vt to tune:—vi to be right.
Stimmung f mood.
stinken vi to stink.
Stirn f forehead; brow.
Stirnhöhle f sinus.
Stock m (walking) stick; storey, floor.
stocken vt to stop, pause.
Stockung f stoppage.
Stockwerk n storey, floor.
Stoff m material, cloth; matter; subject.
Stoffwechsel m metabolism.
stöhnen vi to groan.
stoisch adj stoical.
Stolz m pride, arrogance.
stolz adj proud.
stoppen vt vi to stop.
Stoppuhr f stopwatch.
Storch m stork.
stören vt to disturb; to interfere with.
störend adj disturbing, annoying.
Störung f disturbance; interference.
Stoß m push; blow; knock.
Stoßdämpfer m shock absorber.
stoßen vt to push, shove; to knock,

bump:—vr to get a knock:—vi ~ an/ auf +acc to bump into; to come across.
stottern vt vi to stutter.
strafbar adj punishable.
Strafe f punishment; penalty; sentence.
strafen vt to punish.
Strafgefangene(r) f(m) prisoner.
Strahl m ray, beam; jet.
strahlen vi to radiate.
Strahlung f radiation.
Strand m shore, strand; beach.
Strapaze f strain, exertion.
strapazieren vt to treat roughly; to wear out.
Straßburg n Strasbourg.
Straße f street, road.
Straßenbahn f tram(way).
Straßenbahnwagen m tram car.
Straßenbeleuchtung f street lighting.
Straßenkarte f street map.
Strategie f strategy.
strategisch adj strategic.
Strauch m shrub, bush.
Strauß m ostrich; bouquet, bunch.
streben vi to strive, endeavour.
Strecke f stretch; distance.
strecken vt to stretch.
Streich m trick, prank; blow.
streicheln vt to stroke.
streichen vt to stroke; to spread; to paint; to delete.
Streichholz n match.
Streife f patrol.
streifen vt to brush against; to touch on; to take off:—vi to roam.
Streifen m strip; stripe; film.
Streik m strike.
streiken vi to strike.
Streit m argument; dispute.
streiten vi to argue; to dispute.
streng adj strict; severe.
Strenge f strictness, severity.
Streß m stress.

stressen *vt* to put under stress.
streuen *vt* to strew, scatter.
Strich *m* line; stroke.
Strichkode *m* barcode.
Strichpunkt *m* semicolon.
Stroh *n* straw.
Strohhelm *m* (drinking) straw.
Strom *m* river; (electric) current; stream.
stromabwärts *adv* downstream.
stromaufwärts *adv* upstream.
strömen *vt* to stream, pour.
Stromkreis *m* circuit.
Strömung *f* current.
Strophe *f* verse, stanza.
Struktur *f* structure.
Strumpf *m* stocking.
Strumpfhose *f* (pair of) tights.
Stube *f* room.
Stück *n* play; piece, part.
Student(in) *m(f)* student.
Studie *f* study.
studieren *vt vi* to study.
Studio *n* studio.
Stufe *f* step; stage.
Stuhl *m* chair.
stumm *adj* silent; dumb.
stumpf *adj* blunt; dull; obtuse (of angle).
Stunde *f* hour; lesson.
stündlich *adj* hourly.
Sturm *m* storm, gale, tempest; attack, assault.
stürmen *vt vi* to storm.
stürmisch *adj* stormy.
Sturz *m* fall; overthrow.
stürzen *vt* to overthrow:—*vr* to rush: — *vi* to dash; to dive.
Stute *f* mare.
Stütze *f* support; help.
stützen *vt* to support.
Subjekt *n* subject.
subjektiv *adj* subjective.
Substantiv *n* noun, substantive.

Substanz *f* substance.
subtil *adj* subtle.
subtrahieren *vt* to subtract, deduct.
Subtraktion *f* subtraction.
Subvention *f* subsidy.
subventionieren *vt* to subsidize.
Suche *f* search.
suchen *vt vi* to seek.
Sucht *f* mania; addiction, craving.
süchtig *adj* addicted.
Süchtige(r) *f(m)* addict.
Südamerika *n* South America.
Südafrika *n* South Africa.
Süden *m* south.
südlich *adj* southern, southerly.
Südosten *m* southeast.
südöstlich *adj* southeastern.
Südpol *m* South Pole.
südwärts *adv* southwards.
Südwesten *m* southwest.
südwestlich *adj* southwestern.
Sultan(ine) *m(f)* sultan(a).
Summe *f* sum, total.
summen *vt vi* to buzz; to hum.
Sumpf *m* marsh, swamp.
sumpfig *adj* marshy.
Sünde *f* sin.
Sündenbock *m* scapegoat.
Sünder(in) *m(f)* sinner.
sündigen *vi* to sin.
Supermacht *f* superpower.
Supermarkt *m* supermarket.
Suppe *f* soup.
süß *adj* sweet.
Süße *f* sweetness.
süßen *vt* to sweeten.
Süßigkeit *f* sweetness, sweet.
Symbol *n* symbol.
symbolisch *adj* symbolic.
Symmetrie *f* symmetry.
symmetrisch *adj* symmetrical.
Sympathie *f* sympathy, liking.
sympathisch *adj* likeable.

sympathisieren *vi* to sympathize.
Symptom *n* symptom.
Synagoge *f* synagogue.
Synonym *n* synonym.
synonym *adj* synonymous.

synthetisch *adj* synthetic.
Syrien *n* Syria.
System *n* system.
systematisch systematic.
Szene *f* scene.

T

Tabak *m* tobacco.
Tabelle *f* table.
Tablett *n* tray.
Tablette *f* tablet, pill.
Tabu *n* taboo.
tabu *adj* taboo.
tadeln *vt* to scold.
Tafel *f* table; board; blackboard.
Tag *m* day, daylight:—**guten ~!** good
 morning/afternoon.
Tagebuch *n* diary, journal.
tagen *vi* to sit, meet.
Tagesanbruch *m* daybreak.
täglich *adj* daily.
tagsüber *adv* during the day.
Tagung *f* conference.
Taille *f* waist.
Takt *m* tact; (*mus*) time.
Taktik *f* tactics.
taktisch *adj* tactical.
taktlos *adj* tactless.
taktvoll *adj* tactful.
Tal *n* valley.
Talent *n* talent.
Talsperre *f* dam.
Tang *m* seaweed.
Tank *m* tank.
tanken *vi* to fill up with petrol; to refuel.
Tanker *m* tanker.
Tankstelle *f* service station.
Tanne *f* spruce, fir.
Tannenbaum *m* fir tree.

Tannenzapfen *m* fir cone.
Tante *f* aunt.
Tanz *m* dance.
tanzen *vt vi* to dance.
Tänzer(in) *m(f)* dancer.
Tanzsaal *m* dance hall, ballroom.
Tapete *f* wallpaper.
tapezieren *vt* to wallpaper.
Tapezierer *m* (interior) decorator.
tapfer *adj* gallant, brave.
Tapferkeit *f* courage, bravery.
Tarif *m* tariff, scale of charges.
tarnen *vt* to camouflage; to disguise.
Tasche *f* pocket; handbag.
Taschenbuch *n* paperback.
Taschendieb *m* pickpocket.
Taschengeld *n* pocket money.
Taschenlampe *f* torch.
Taschenmesser *m* penknife.
Taschentuch *n* handkerchief.
Tasse *f* cup.
Tastatur *f* keyboard.
Taste *f* key.
tasten *vt* to feel, touch:—*vi* to feel,
 grope:—*vr* to feel one's way.
Tat *f* deed, act, action:—**in der ~** as a
 matter of fact, indeed.
tatenlos *adj* inactive.
Täter(in) *m(f)* perpetrator, culprit.
tätig *adj* active, busy.
Tätigkeit *f* activity; occupation.
tätlich *adj* violent.

Tätlichkeit *f* violence.
tätowieren *vt* to tattoo.
Tatsache *f* fact.
tatsächlich *adj* actual:—*adv* really.
Tatze *f* paw.
Tau *n* rope:—*m* dew.
taub *adj* deaf.
Taube *f* pigeon; dove.
Taubheit *f* deafness.
taubstumm *adj* deaf-and-dumb.
tauchten *vt* to dip:—*vi* to dive; to submerge.
tauen *vt vi* to thaw.
Taufbecken *n* font.
Taufe *f* baptism, christening.
taufen *vt* to christen, baptize.
Taufschein *m* certificate of baptism.
taugen *vi* to be of use.
Taugenichts *m* good-for-nothing.
tauglich *adj* suitable; (*mil*) fit.
Taumel *m* dizziness; frenzy.
taumeln *vi* to reel, stagger.
Tausch *m* exchange.
tauschen *vt* to exchange, swap.
täuschen *vt* to deceive:—*vi* to be deceptive:—*vr* to be wrong.
täuschend *adj* deceptive.
Täuschung *f* deception.
tausend *num* thousand.
Tauwetter *n* thaw.
Taxi *n* taxi.
Taxifahrer(in) *m(f)* taxi driver.
Taxistand *m* taxi rank.
Technik *f* technology; technique.
Techniker *m* technician.
technisch *adj* technical.
Technologie *f* technology.
technologisch *adj* technological.
Tee *m* tea.
Teebeutel *m* tea bag.
Teekanne *f* teapot.
Teelöffel *m* teaspoon.
Teer *m* tar.

teeren *vt* to tar.
Teich *m* pond.
Teig *m* dough.
Teil *m/n* part; share; component:—**zum** ~ partly.
teilbar *adj* divisible.
Teilchen *n* (atomic) particle.
teilen *vt vr* to divide; to share.
teilhaben *vi*:—~ **an** +*dat* to share in.
Teilnahme *f* participation.
teilnehmen *vi*:—~ **an** +*dat* to take part in.
teilweise *adv* partially, in part.
Teint *m* complexion.
Telefax *n* fax.
Telefon *n* telephone.
Telefonbuch *n* telephone directory.
Telefonhörer *m* receiver.
telefonieren *vi* to telephone.
Telefonist(in) *m(f)* telephonist.
Telefonkarte *f* phonecard.
Telefonnummer *f* phone number.
Telefonzelle *f* telephone kiosk, callbox.
Telefonzentrale *f* telephone exchange.
Telegraf *m* telegraph.
telegrafieren *vt vi* to telegraph, wire.
Telegramm *n* telegram, cable.
Teleobjektiv *n* telephoto lens.
telepathisch *adj* telepathic.
Teleskop *n* telscope.
Telex *n* telex; telex machine.
Teller *m* plate.
Tempel *m* temple.
Temperament *n* temperament; liveliness.
temperamentvoll *adj* high-spirited, lively.
Temperatur *f* temperature.
Tempo *n* speed, pace; (*mus*) tempo.
Tendenz *f* tendency; intention.
tendieren *vi*:—~ **zu** to show a tendency to, incline towards.
Tennis *n* tennis.
Tennisball *m* tennis ball.

Tennisplatz *m* tennis court.
Tennisschläger *m* tennis racket.
Tennisspieler(in) *m(f)* tennis player.
Tenor *m* tenor.
Teppich *m* carpet.
Termin *m* date; time limit, deadline; appointment.
Termite *f* termite.
Terpentin *n* turpentine, turps.
Terrasse *f* terrace.
Terrine *f* tureen.
Territorium *m* territory.
Terror *m* terror.
terrorisieren *vt* to terrorize.
Terrorismus *m* terrorism.
Terrorist *m* terrorist.
Terz *f* (*mus*) third.
Terzett *n* trio.
Test *m* test.
Testament *n* will; (*rel*) Testament.
testen *vt* to test.
teuer *adj* expensive, dear.
Teufel *m* devil.
Text *m* text.
textil *adj* textile.
Textilien *pl* textiles.
Textverarbeitung *f* word processing.
Theater *n* theatre:—**ins ~ gehen** to go to the theatre.
Theaterbesucher *m* playgoer.
Theaterkasse *f* box office.
Theaterstück *n* (stage-)play.
Thema *n* theme, subject, topic.
Themse *f* Thames.
Theologe *m* theologian.
Theologie *f* theology.
theologisch *adj* theological.
theoretisch *adj* theoretical.
Theorie *f* theory.
Therapie *f* therapy.
Thermometer *m* thermometer.
Thermostat *m* thermostat.
These *f* thesis.

Thrombose *f* thrombosis.
Thron *m* throne.
Thunfisch *m* tuna.
Thymian *m* thyme.
Tick *m* tic; quirk.
ticken *vi* to tick.
tief *adj* deep; profound; low.
Tiefe *f* depth.
Tier *n* animal.
Tierarzt *n* vet, veterinary surgeon.
Tiergarten *m* zoo.
Tierkreis *m* zodiac.
Tierkunde *f* zoology.
Tiger(in) *m(f)* tiger (tigress).
Tinte *f* ink.
Tintenfisch *m* cuttlefish.
Tip *m* tip.
tippen *vi vt* to touch, tap; to type.
Tirol *n* the Tyrol.
Tiroler(in) *m(f)* Tyrolean.
tirolisch *adj* Tyrolean.
Tisch *m* table.
Tischdecke *f* tablecloth.
Tischler *m* joiner, carpenter.
tischlern *vi* to do carpentry.
Tischtennis *n* table tennis.
Tischtuch *n* tablecloth.
Titel *m* title.
Toast *m* toast.
Toaster *m* toaster.
toben *vi* to rage.
tobsüchtig *adj* maniacal.
Tochter *f* daughter.
Tod *m* death.
Todesanzeige *f* obituary.
Todesstrafe *f* death penalty.
tödlich *adj* fatal, deadly.
Toilette *f* toilet.
Toilettenpapier *n* toilet paper.
tolerant *adj* tolerant.
Toleranz *f* tolerance.
tolerieren *vt* to tolerate.
toll *adj* mad; wild.

tollen vi to romp.
Tollkirsche f deadly nightshade.
Tollwut f rabies.
Tomate f tomato.
Tombola f tombola.
Ton m clay; sound; note; tone; shade.
Tonart f (musical) key.
Tonband n sound-recording tape.
Tonbandgerät n tape recorder.
tönen vi to sound:—vt to shade; to tint.
tönern adj clay.
Tonleiter f (mus) scale.
Tonne f barrel; ton(ne).
Topas m topaz.
Topf m pot.
Topfblume f pot plant.
Töpfer m potter.
Tor m fool; gate; goal.
Torbogen m archway.
Torf m peat.
Torheit f foolishness.
töricht adj foolish.
torkeln vi to reel, stagger.
Torpedo m torpedo.
Torte f tart; cake.
Tortur f ordeal.
tosen vi to roar.
tot adj dead.
total adj total.
totalitär adj totalitarian.
Tote(r) f(m) dead (wo)man.
töten vt vi to kill.
Totenkopf m skull.
Totschlag m manslaughter.
Tötung f killing.
Toupet n toupee.
Tour f tour, excursion; revolution.
Tourist m tourist.
Trab m trot.
traben vi to trot.
Tracht f costume, dress.
trachten vi:—~ (nach) to strive (for).
trächtig adj pregnant.

Tradition f tradition.
traditionell adj traditional.
Tragbahre f stretcher.
tragbar adj portable; wearable; bearable.
träge adj sluggish; inert.
tragen vt to wear; to carry; to bear:—vi to be pregnant.
Träger m carrier; wearer; bearer.
Trägheit f laziness; inertia.
Tragik f tragedy.
tragisch adj tragic.
Tragödie f tragedy.
Tragweite f range; scope.
Trainer m trainer, coach; (football) manager.
trainieren vt to train, coach.
Training n training.
Traktor m tractor; tractor feed.
Tram f tram.
tranchieren vt to carve.
Träne f tear.
tränen vi to water.
Tränengas n teargas.
tränken vi to water.
transparent adj transparent.
Transparent n transparency.
Transplantation f transplantation; graft.
Transport m transport.
transportieren vt to transport.
Trapez n trapeze.
Traube f grape; bunch of grapes.
Traubenzucker m glucose.
trauen vi:—jdm/etw ~ to trust somebody/something:—vr to dare:—vt to marry.
Trauer f sorrow; mourning:—in ~ sein (um) be in mourning (for).
Trauerfall m death, bereavement.
Trauerfeier f funeral service.
Trauerkleidung f mourning.
trauern vi to mourn.
Trauerspiel n tragedy.
traulich adj cosy, intimate.
Traum m dream.

Trauma n trauma.
träumen vt vi to dream.
Träumer m dreamer.
Träumerei f dreaming.
träumerisch adj dreamy.
traumhaft adj dreamlike.
traurig adj sad.
Traurigkeit f sadness.
Trauring m wedding ring.
Trauschein m marriage certificate.
Trauung f wedding ceremony.
Trecker m tractor.
treffen vt to meet; to strike, hit:—vi to hit:—vr to meet.
Treffen n meeting.
treffend adj pertinent.
Treffpunkt m meeting place.
Treibeis n drift ice.
treiben vt to drive; to do, go in for; to pursue:—vi to drift; to sprout.
Treibhaus n greenhouse.
trennbar adj separable.
trennen vt to separate; to divide:—vr to separate.
Trennung f separation.
Trennungsstrich m hyphen.
Trennwand f partition wall.
treppab adv downstairs.
treppauf adv upstairs.
Treppe f stairs, staircase.
Treppenabsatz m landing.
Treppengeländer n banisters.
Tresor m safe; bank vault.
Tretboot n pedal boat.
treten vt to step; to appear:—vt to kick; to trample.
treu adj faithful, loyal.
Treubruch m breach of faith.
Treue f faithfulness, loyalty.
Treuhand f trust.
treulos adj unfaithful, disloyal.
Tribüne f grandstand; platform.
Trichter m funnel.

triefen vi to drip, be dripping.
triftig adj good, convincing.
trimmen vi to do keep fit exercises.
trinkbar adj drinkable.
trinken vt vi to drink.
Trinker m drinker.
Trinkgeld n tip, gratuity.
Trinkwasser n drinking water.
Tritt m step; kick.
Triumph m triumph.
triumphieren vi to triumph; to exult.
trocken adj dry.
trocknen vt vi to dry.
Trommel f drum.
Trommelfell n eardrum.
trommeln vt vi to drum.
Trompete f trumpet.
Trompeter m trumpeter.
tröpfeln vi to drop, trickle.
Tropfen m drop.
tropfen vt vi to drip.
tropisch adj tropical.
Trost m comfort, consolation.
trösten vt to comfort, console.
trostreich adj comforting.
Trott m trot; routine.
trotten vi to trot.
Trottoir n pavement.
trotz prep in spite of, despite.
trotzdem adv nevertheless, all the same:—conj although.
trüb adj dull; gloomy; cloudy.
trüben vt to cloud:—vr to become clouded.
Trübheit f dullness; cloudiness; gloom.
Trübsal f distress.
Trübsinn m depression.
trübsinnig adj gloomy, depressed.
trügen vt to deceive:—vi to be deceptive.
trügerisch adj deceptive.
Truhe f chest.
Trumpf m trump.
trumpfen vt vi to trump.

trunken *adj* intoxicated.
Trunkenheit *f* intoxication.
Truthahn *m* turkey.
Tscheche *m* Czech.
Tschechin *f* Czech.
tschechisch *adj* Czech.
tschüs *excl* cheerio.
T-Shirt *n* T-shirt.
Tube *f* tube.
Tuberkulose *f* tuberculosis.
Tuch *n* cloth; scarf; towel.
tüchtig *adj* efficient, able, capable.
Tüchtigkeit *f* efficiency, ability.
Tücke *f* malice; problem.
tückisch *adj* malicious.
Tugend *f* virtue.
tugendhaft *adj* virtuous.
Tüll *m* tulle.
Tüle *f* spout.
Tulpe *f* tulip.
Tumor *m* tumour.
Tümpel *m* pond, pool.
Tumult *m* tumult.
tun *vt* to do:—*vi* to act.
tunken *vt* to dunk.
Tunnel *m* tunnel.

Tupfen *m* dot, spot.
tupfen *vt vi* to dot.
Tür *f* door.
Turban *m* turban.
Turbine *f* turbine.
Türke *m* Turk.
Türkei *f* Turkey.
Türkin *f* Turk.
türkisch *adj* Turkish.
Turm *m* tower; steeple; rook, castle (in chess).
türmen *vr* to tower up:—*vi* to heap up.
Turnen *n* gymnastics; physical education.
Turner(in) *m(f)* gymnast.
Turnhalle *f* gym, gymnasium.
Turnier *n* tournament.
Tüte *f* bag.
tuten *vi* to hoot.
Typ *m* type.
Type *f* type.
typisch *adj* typical.
Tyrann *m* tyrant.
Tyrannei *f* tyranny.
tyrannisch *adj* tyrannical.
tyrannisieren *vt* to tyrannize.

U

U-Bahn *f* underground.
übel *adj* bad, wicked.
Übel *n* evil.
Übelkeit *f* nausea.
üben *vt vi* to exercise, practise.
über *prep* over, above; via; about.
überall *adv* everywhere.
Überblick *m* view; overview, survey.
überblicken *vt* to survey.
übereinkommen *vi* to agree.
Übereinkunft *f* agreement.

übereinstimmen *vi* to agree.
Übereinstimmung *f* agreement.
Überfall *m* assault.
überfallen *vt* to attack; to raid.
überfällig *adj* overdue.
Überfluß *m* excess.
überflüssig *adj* superfluous.
Übergewicht *n* excess weight.
überhaupt *adv* at all; in general; especially:—~ **nicht** not at all.
überholen *vt* to overtake; to overhaul.

überholt *adj* obsolete, out-of-date.
überhören *vt* not to hear; to ignore.
überleben *vi* to survive.
Überlebende(r) *f(m)* survivor.
überlegen *vt* to consider:—*adj* superior.
Überlegenheit *f* superiority.
Überlegung *f* consideration, deliberation.
überm = über dem.
Übermacht *f* superior force.
übermächtig *adj* superior; overpowering.
Übermaß *m* excess.
übermäßig *adj* excessive.
Übermensch *m* superman.
übermenschlich *adj* superhuman.
übermitteln *vt* to convey.
Übermittlung *f* transmission.
übermorgen *adv* the day after tomorrow.
übernachten *vi*:—(bei jdm) ~ to spend the night (at somebody's place).
übernatürlich *adj* supernatural.
überprüfen *vt* to check, examine.
überraschen *vt* to surprise.
Überraschung *f* surprise.
überreden *vt* to persuade.
Überredung *f* persuasion.
übers = über das.
Überschallgeschwindigkeit *f* supersonic speed.
Überschrift *f* heading, title.
Überschuß *m* surplus.
übersetzen *vt* to translate:—*vi* to cross.
Übersetzer(in) *m(f)* translator.
Übersetzung *f* translation.
Übersicht *f* overall view.
übersichtlich *adj* clear; open.
Übersichtlichkeit *f* clarity, lucidity.
übertragbar *adj* transferable; (*med*) infectious.
übertragen *vt* to transfer; to broadcast; to transmit (illness):—*vr* to spread.
Übertragung *f* broadcast; transmission.
übertreiben *vt* to exaggerate.

Übertreibung *f* exaggeration.
überwachen *vt* to supervise; to keep under surveillance.
Überwachung *f* supervision; surveillance.
überwältigen *vt* to overpower.
überwältigend *adj* overwhelming.
überweisen *vt* to transfer.
Überweisung *f* transfer.
überzeugen *vt* to convince, persuade.
überzeugend *adj* convincing.
Überzeugung *f* conviction, belief.
üblich *adj* usual.
U-Boot *n* submarine.
übrig *adj* remaining.
übrigbleiben *vi* to remain, be left (over).
übrigens *adv* besides; by the way.
übriglassen *vt* to leave (over).
Übung *f* practice; exercise:—~ **macht den Meister** practice makes perfect.
Ufer *n* bank; shore.
Uhr *f* watch; clock:—**20** ~ 8 o'clock: — **wieviel** ~ **ist es?** what time is it?
Uhrband *n* watch strap.
Uhrmacher *m* watchmaker.
Uhrwerk *n* clockwork.
Uhu *m* eagle owl.
ulkig *adj* funny.
Ulme *f* elm.
Ultimatum *n* ultimatum.
Ultraschall *m* ultrasound.
ultraviolett *adj* ultraviolet.
um *prep* (a)round; at (of time); by:— *adv* about:—~... **zu** in order to.
umarmen *vt* to embrace.
umbuchen *vi* to change one's flight/reservation.
umdrehen *vi vr* to turn (round).
Umdrehung *f* revolution; rotation.
Umfang *m* extent; range; area.
umfangreich *adj* extensive; voluminous.
umfassen *vt* to embrace; to surround; to include.

umfassend *adj* comprehensive, extensive.

Umfrage *f* poll.

Umgang *m* company; way of behaving; dealings.

Umgangssprache *f* colloquial language.

umgeben *vt* to surround.

Umgebung *f* surroundings; environment.

umgekehrt *adj* reverse(d); opposite:— *adv* vice versa, the other way round.

umher *adv* about, around.

umhergehen *vi* to walk about.

Umkreis *m* neighbourhood:—**im ~ von** within a radius of.

Umlauf *m* circulation.

Umlaufbahn *f* orbit.

Umlaut *m* umlaut.

umleiten *vt* to divert.

Umleitung *f* diversion.

umliegend *adj* surrounding.

umrechnen *vt* to convert.

Umrechnung *f* conversion.

Umrechnungskurs *m* rate of exchange.

Umriß *m* outline.

ums = **um das**.

Umsatz *m* turnover.

Umsatzsteuer *f* sales tax.

Umschlag *n* envelope.

umschulen *vt* to retrain.

umsehen *vr* to look around/about.

umseitig *adv* overleaf.

umsichtig *adj* cautious, prudent.

umsonst *adv* for nothing; in vain.

Umstand *m* circumstance.

umständlich *adj* cumbersome; longwinded.

Umstandskleid *n* maternity dress.

umsteigen *vi* to change (train, etc).

umstellen *vt* to rearrange; to convert: —*vr* to adapt (oneself).

Umstellung *f* change; conversion.

umstritten *adj* disputed.

Umsturz *m* overthrow.

Umtausch *m* exchange.

umtauschen *vt* to exchange.

Umweg *m* detour.

Umwelt *f* environment.

Umweltschützer *m* environmentalist.

Umweltverschmutzung *f* environmental pollution.

umziehen *vt vr* to change:—*vi* to move.

Umzug *m* procession; move, removal.

unabhängig *adj* independent.

Unabhängigkeit *f* independence.

Unart *f* bad manners; bad habit.

unartig *adj* badly behaved; naughty.

unbeabsichtigt *adj* unintentional.

unbegrenzt *adj* unlimited.

unbekannt *adj* unknown.

unbequem *adj* uncomfortable; inconvenient.

unbeweglich *adj* motionless.

unbewohnt *adj* unoccupied, vacant.

unbewußt *adj* unconscious.

und *conj* and:—**~ so weiter** and so on.

Undank *m* ingratitude.

undankbar *adj* ungrateful.

undeutich *adj* indistinct.

undicht *adj* leaky.

uneben *adj* uneven.

unendlich *adj* endless, infinite.

unfähig *adj* incapable, incompetent.

unfair *adj* unfair.

Unfall *m* accident.

unfreundlich *adj* unfriendly.

Unfreundlichkeit *f* unfriendliness.

Ungar(in) *m(f)* Hungarian.

ungarisch *adj* Hungarian.

Ungarn *n* Hungary.

Ungeduld *f* impatience.

ungeduldig *adj* impatient.

ungefähr *adj* approximate(ly).

ungeheuer *adj* huge:—*adv* enormously.

Ungeheuer *m* monster.

ungeheuerlich *adj* monstrous.

ungewöhnlich *adj* unusual.
ungläubig *adj* unbelievable.
unglaublich *adj* incredible.
Unglück *n* bad luck; misfortune; calamity; accident.
unglücklich *adj* unhappy; unlucky; unfortunate.
unglücklicherweise *adv* unfortunately.
Unglücksfall *m* accident, calamity.
ungültig *adj* invalid.
Ungültigkeit *f* invalidity.
Unheil *n* evil; misfortune.
unheilbar *adj* incurable.
Uniform *f* uniform.
Universität *f* university.
Universum *n* universe.
Unkraut *n* weed(s).
Unmensch *m* ogre, brute.
unmenschlich *adj* inhuman, brutal; awful.
unmittelbar *adj* immediate.
unmöglich *adj* impossible.
Unmöglichkeit *f* impossibility.
unmoralisch *adj* immoral.
unnötig *adj* unnecessary.
Unordnung *f* disorder.
unpersönlich *adj* impersonal.
unrecht *adj* wrong.
Unrecht *m* wrong.
unregelmäßig *adj* irregular.
Unregelmäßigkeit *f* irregularity.
Unruhe *f* unrest.
unruhig *adj* restless.
uns *pn acc dat* us; ourselves.
Unschuld *m* innocence.
unschuldig *adj* innocent.
unser(e) *poss adj* our.
unsere(r, s) *poss pn* ours.
unsichtbar *adj* invisible.
Unsinn *m* nonsense.
unsterblich *adj* immortal.
untätig *adj* idle.
unteilbar *adj* indivisible.

unten *adv* below; downstairs; at the bottom.
unter *prep* under; underneath, below; among(st).
Unterarm *m* forearm.
Unterbewußtsein *n* subconscious.
unterbrechen *vt* to interrupt.
Unterbrechung *f* interruption.
unterbringen *vt* to stow; to accommodate.
unterdessen *adv* meanwhile.
unterdrücken *vt* to suppress; to oppress.
untere(r, s) *adj* lower.
unterentwickelt *adj* underdeveloped.
unterernährt *adj* underfed, undernourished.
Unterernährung *f* malnutrition.
Untergang *m* downfall, decline; sinking.
untergeben *adj* subordinate.
untergehen *vi* to go down; to set (of the sun); to fall; to perish.
Untergeschoß *n* basement.
Untergewicht *n* underweight.
Untergrund *m* foundation; underground.
Untergrundbahn *f* underground, tube.
unterhalb *prep adv* below.
Unterhalt *m* maintenance.
unterhalten *vt* to maintain; to entertain:—*vt* to talk; to enjoy oneself.
unterhaltend *adj* entertaining, amusing.
Unterhaltung *f* maintenance; talk; amusement, entertainment.
Unterhemd *n* vest.
Unterhose *f* underpants.
Unterkunft *f* accommodation.
Unterlage *f* foundation; document.
unterlassen *vt* to refrain from; to fail to do.
Unterleib *m* abdomen.
unterliegen *vi* to be subject to.
unternehmen *vi* to undertake.
Unternehmen *n* undertaking, enterprise.

Unternehmer *m* businessman, entrepreneur.
Unterricht *m* instruction, lessons.
unterrichten *vt* to instruct; to teach.
untersagen *vt* to forbid.
unterschätzen *vt* to underestimate.
unterscheiden *vt* to distinguish:—*vr* to differ.
Unterscheidung *f* distinction; differentiation.
Unterschied *m* difference.
unterschreiben *vt* to sign.
Unterschrift *f* signature.
unterste(r, s) *adj* lowest, bottom.
unterstützen *vt* to support.
Unterstützung *f* support.
untersuchen *vt* to examine; to investigate.
Untersuchung *f* examination; investigation.
Untertan *m* subject (of a country).
Untertasse *f* saucer.
Untertitel *m* subtitle.
Unterwäsche *f* underwear.
unterwegs *adv* on the way.
unterzeichnen *vt* to sign.
untragbar *adj* intolerable.
untreu *adj* unfaithful.
Untreue *f* unfaithfulness.
unvollkommen *adj* imperfect.
unvollständig *adj* incomplete.
unwahr *adj* untrue.

unwahrscheinlich *adj* improbable, unlikely.
Unwetter *n* thunderstorm.
unwiderruflich *adj* irrevocable.
unwirklich *adj* unreal.
unwohl *adj* unwell, ill.
unwürdig *adj* unworthy.
Unze *f* ounce.
uralt *adj* very old, ancient.
Ural *m* (the) Urals.
Uran *n* uranium.
Urbild *n* original.
Urgroßmutter *f* great-grandmother.
Urgroßvater *m* great-grandfather.
Urin *m* urine.
Urkunde *f* deed, document.
Urlaub *m* holiday(s), leave.
Urlauber *m* holiday-maker.
Urlaubsort *m* holiday resort.
Urne *f* urn.
Ursache *f* cause.
Ursprung *m* origin, source.
ursprünglich *adj* original:—*adv* originally.
Urteil *m* judgment, sentence; opinion.
urteilen *vt* to judge.
Urwald *m* primeval forest; jungle.
Urzeit *f* prehistoric times.
usw (= **und so weiter**) etc.
Utopie *f* illusion, pipedream.
utopisch *adj* utopian.

V

vag(e) *adj* vague.
Vakuum *n* vacuum.
Vampir *m* vampire.
Vanille *f* vanilla.
Variation *f* variation.

variieren *vt vi* to vary.
Vase *f* vase.
Vater *m* father.
Vaterland *n* native country, fatherland.
väterlich *adj* fatherly.

Vaterschaft *f* paternity.
Vati *m* daddy.
Vatikan *m* (the) Vatican.
Vegetarier(in) *m(f)* vegetarian.
Veilchen *n* violet.
Vene *f* vein.
Venedig *n* Venice.
Ventil *n* valve.
verabscheuen *vt* to abhor, detest.
verabschieden *vt* to say goodbye to; to discharge:—*vr* to take one's leave.
Verabschiedung *f* leave-taking; discharge.
verachten *vt* to despise, scorn.
verächtlich *adj* contemptible, despicable.
Verachtung *f* contempt, scorn.
Veranda *f* veranda.
veränderlich *adj* changeable, unsettled.
verändern *vt vr* to change, alter.
Veränderung *f* change, alteration.
veranlassen *vt* to cause.
veranstalten *vt* to arrange, organize.
Veranstaltung *f* organising; function, event.
verantwortlich *adj* responsible.
Verantwortung *f* responsibility.
verarbeiten *vt* to process.
Verarbeitung *f* processing.
verärgern *vt* to annoy.
Verb *n* verb.
Verband *m* association, society; (*med*) bandage.
verbannen *vt* to banish.
Verbannung *f* exile.
verbergen *vt vr*:—(sich) ~ (vor +*dat*) to hide (from).
verbessern *vt vr* to improve.
Verbesserung *f* improvement.
verbeugen *vr* to bow.
Verbeugung *f* bow.
verbiegen *vi* to bend.
verbieten *vt* to forbid, prohibit.

verbinden *vt vr* to combine.
verbindlich *adj* binding.
Verbindung *f* combination; (*chem*) compound.
verblüffen *vt* to amaze.
Verblüffung *f* amazement.
Verbot *n* ban, prohibition.
verboten *adj* forbidden:—**Rauchen ~!** no smoking.
Verbrauch *m* consumption.
verbrauchen *vt* to use up.
Verbraucher *m* consumer.
verbraucht *adj* finished, used up; worn-out.
Verbrechen *n* crime, offence.
verbrechen *vi* to commit a crime.
Verbrecher *m* criminal.
verbrecherisch *adj* criminal.
verbreiten *vt vr* to spread.
verbreitern *vt* to broaden.
verbrennbar *adj* combustible.
verbrennen *vt* to burn; to cremate.
Verbrennung *f* burning; combustion; cremation.
verbringen *vt* to spend (of time).
verbunden *adj* connected.
Verdacht *f* suspicion.
verdächtig *adj* suspicious, suspect.
verdächtigen *vt* to suspect.
verdammen *vt* to damn, condemn.
verdammt *adj adv* damned.
verdampfen *vi* to evaporate, vaporize.
verdanken *vt*:—**jdm etw ~** to owe somebody something.
verdauen *vt* to digest.
verdaulich *adj* digestible.
Verdauung *f* digestion.
Verderben *n* ruin.
verderben *vt* to ruin; to spoil to corrupt:—*vi* to rot.
verderblich *adj* perishable; pernicious.
verdorben *adj* ruined; spoilt; corrupt.
verdrehen *vt* to twist; to roll (one's eyes).

verdrießen *vt* to annoy.
verdrießlich *adj* annoyed.
Verdruß *m* annoyance.
verehren *vt* to venerate, worship.
Verehrer(in) *m(f)* admirer, worshipper.
verehrt *adj* esteemed.
Verehrung *f* respect; worship.
Verein *m* association, club.
vereinbar *adj* compatible.
vereinbaren *vt* to agree upon.
Vereinbarung *f* agreement.
vereinen *vt* to unite; to reconcile.
vereinfachen *vt* to simplify.
vereinigen *vt vr* to unite.
Vereinigte Staaten *mpl* United States.
Vereinigung *f* union.
vereint *adj* united.
Vereinte Nationen *fpl* United Nations.
vererben *vt* to bequeath:—*vr* to be hereditary.
vererblich *adj* hereditary.
Vererbung *f* bequeathing; heredity.
Verfahren *n* procedure; process; (*jur*) proceedings.
Verfall *m* decline; dilapidation; expiry.
verfallen *vi* to decline; to lapse.
verfassen *vt* to prepare, work out.
Verfasser(in) *m(f)* writer, author.
Verfassung *f* constitution.
verfaulen *vi* to rot.
verfilmen *vt* to film.
verfluchen *vt* to curse.
verfolgen *vt* to pursue; to prosecute; to persecute.
Verfolger *m* pursuer.
Verfolgung *f* pursuit; prosecution; persecution.
verfügbar *adj* available.
verfügen *vt* to direct, order:—*vr* to proceed.
Verfügung *f* direction, order:—**zur ~ at** one's disposal.
verführen *vt* to tempt; to seduce.

Verführer *m* tempter; seducer.
verführerisch *adj* seductive.
Verführung *f* temptation; seduction.
vergangen *adj* past.
Vergangenheit *f* past.
vergeben *vt* to forgive.
vergebens *adv* in vain.
vergeblich *adv* in vain:—*adj* vain, futile.
Vergebung *f* forgiveness.
Vergehen *n* offence.
vergehen *vi* to pass away:—*vr* to commit an offence.
Vergeltung *f* retaliation, reprisal.
vergessen *vt* to forget.
Vergessenheit *f* oblivion.
vergeßlich *adj* forgetful.
Vergeßlichkeit *f* forgetfulness.
vergeuden *vt* to waste, squander.
vergewaltigen *vt* to rape; to violate.
Vergewaltigung *f* rape.
vergiften *vt* to poison.
Vergiftung *f* poisoning.
Vergißmeinnicht *n* forget-me-not.
Vergleich *m* comparison; (*jur*) settlement.
vergleichbar *adj* comparable.
vergleichen *vt* to compare:—*vr* to reach a settlement.
vergnügen *vt* to enjoy oneself.
Vergnügen *n* pleasure.
vergnügt *adj* cheerful.
Vergnügung *f* pleasure, amusement.
vergrößern *vt* to enlarge; to magnify.
Vergrößerung *f* enlargement; magnification.
Vergrößerungsglas *n* magnifying glass.
Vergütung *f* remuneration.
verhaften *vt* to arrest.
Verhaftung *f* arrest.
Verhalten *n* behaviour.
Verhältnis *n* relationship; proportion, ratio.

Verhandlung *f* negotiation; (*jur*) proceedings, trial.

verhaßt *adj* hateful, odious.

verheiraten *vr* to get married.

verheiratet *adj* married.

verhüten *vt* to prevent, avert.

Verhütung *f* prevention.

Verhütungsmittel *n* contraceptive.

verirren *vr* to go astray.

Verkauf *m* sale.

verkaufen *vt* to sell.

Verkäufer(in) *m(f)* seller; salesman (-woman); shop assistant.

Verkehr *m* traffic; circulation.

Verkehrsampel *pl* traffic lights.

Verkehrsamt *n* tourist office.

Verkehrsmittel *n* means of transport.

Verkehrszeichen *m* traffic sign.

verkehrt *adj* wrong; the wrong way round.

verkleinern *vt* to make smaller.

verkommen *vi* to decay, deteriorate; to come down in the world:—*adj* dissolute, depraved.

verkörpern *vt* to embody, personify.

Verlag *m* publishing house.

verlangen *vt* to demand; to desire.

Verlangen *n* desire.

verlängern *vt* to extend; to lengthen.

Verlängerung *f* extension.

verlangsamen *vi* to decelerate, slow down.

verlassen *vt* to leave:—*vr* sich ~ auf +*acc* to depend on:—*adj* desolate; abandoned.

verläßlich *adj* reliable.

verlegen *vt* to move; to mislay; to publish:—*adj* embarrassed.

Verleger *m* publisher.

verleihen *vt* to lend; to confer, bestow; to award.

Verleihung *f* lending; bestowal; award.

verletzen *vt* to injure; to violate (law, etc).

verletzend *adj* hurtful.

verletzlich *adj* vulnerable, sensitive.

Verletzte(r) *f(m)* injured person.

Verletzung *f* injury; infringement, violation.

verleumden *vt* to slander, defame.

Verleumdung *f* slander, libel.

verlieben *vr:*—**sich** ~ (**in** +*acc*) to fall in love (with).

verliebt *adj* in love.

verlieren *vt vi* to lose:—*vr* to get lost.

Verlierer *m* loser.

verloben *vr* to get engaged (to).

Verlobte(r) *f(m)* fiancé(e).

Verlobung *f* engagement.

verlocken *vt* to entice, lure.

Verlockung *f* attraction, enticement.

verloren *adj* lost; poached (of eggs).

Verlust *m* loss.

vermeiden *vt* to avoid.

vermeintlich *adj* supposed.

Vermerk *m* note; endorsement.

vermerken *vt* to note.

vermessen *vt* to survey:—*adj* presumptuous.

Vermessenheit *f* presumptuousness.

Vermessung *f* surveying.

vermieten *vt* to let, rent (out); to hire (out).

Vermieter(in) *m(f)* landlord(lady).

Vermietung *f* letting, renting (out); hiring (out).

vermindern *vt vr* to decrease, reduce; to diminish.

Verminderung *f* reduction.

vermissen *vt* to miss.

vermitteln *vi* to mediate:—*vt* to connect.

Vermittler *m* agent, mediator.

Vermittlung *f* procurement; agency; mediation.

vermögen *vi* to be capable of.

Vermögen *n* wealth; property; ability.

vermuten vt to suppose; to suspect.

vermutlich adj supposed, presumed: — adv probably.

Vermutung f supposition; suspicion.

vernachlässigen vt to neglect.

verneinen vi to deny; to answer in the negative.

verneinend adj negative.

Verneinung f negation.

vernichten vt to annihilate, destroy.

Vernunft f reason, judgement.

vernünftig adj reasonable, judicious.

veröffentlichen vt to publish.

Veröffentlichung f publication.

verordnen vt (med) to prescribe.

Verordnung f order, decree; (med) prescription.

verpassen vt to miss.

verpflichten vt to bind, oblige; to engage:—vr to undertake; (mil) to sign on:—vi to carry obligations.

Verpflichtung f duty, obligation.

Verrat m treason; treachery.

verraten vt to betray:—vr to give oneself away.

Verräter m traitor.

verringern vt to reduce:—vr to diminish.

Verringerung f reduction.

verrücken vt to shift, move.

verrückt adj mad, crazy.

Verrückte(r) f(m) lunatic.

Verrücktheit f madness, lunacy.

Vers m verse.

versagen vi to fail.

Versagen n failure.

Versager m failure.

versammeln vt vr to assemble, gather.

Versammlung f meeting, gathering.

Versand m dispatch, forwarding.

versäumen vt to miss; to neglect.

verschärfen vt vr to intensify.

verschieden adj different; various.

Verschleiß m wear and tear.

verschleißen vt to wear out.

verschleudern vt to squander.

verschlingen vt to devour, swallow up.

verschwenden vt to squander.

Verschwender m spendthrift.

verschwinden vi to disappear, vanish.

Verschwinden n disappearance.

versehen vt to supply, provide; to carry out (duty, etc):—vr to make a mistake.

Versehen n oversight:—aus ~ by mistake.

versichern vt to assure; to insure.

Versicherung f assurance; insurance.

versöhnen vt to reconcile:—vr to become reconciled.

versöhnlich adj forgiving, conciliatory.

Versöhnung f reconciliation.

versorgen vt to provide, supply; to look after.

Versorgung f provision; assistance, benefit.

verspäten vr to be late.

verspätet adj late; belated.

Verspätung f delay:—— haben to be late.

verspotten vt to mock.

versprechen vt to promise.

Versprechen n promise.

verstaatlichen vt to nationalize.

Verstand m intelligence; mind.

verständlich adj understandable.

Verständlichkeit f intelligibility.

Verständnis n understanding.

verstärken vt vr to intensify.

Verstärker m amplifier.

Verstärkung f strengthening; amplification.

verstecken vt vr to hide:—adj hidden.

verstehen vt to understand.

versteigern vt to auction.

Versteigerung f auction.

verstellbar adj adjustable, variable.

verstellen vt to shift, move; to adjust; to block; to disguise:—vr to pretend.

Verstellung f pretence.
Verstoß m infringement, violation.
verstoßen vt to disown, reject:—vi ~ **gegen** to offend against.
Versuch m attempt.
versuchen vi to try; to tempt.
Versuchung f temptation.
vertagen vt vi to adjourn.
verteidigen vt to defend.
Verteidiger m defender; (jur) defence counsel.
Verteidigung f defence.
verteilen vt to distribute; to assign.
Verteilung f distribution, allotment.
vertiefen vt to deepen.
Vertiefung f depression.
vertikal adj vertical.
Vertrag m contract, agreement; treaty.
vertragen vt to tolerate, stand:—vr to get along.
vertraglich adj contractual.
Vertrauen n trust, confidence.
vertrauen vi:—**jdm** ~ to trust somebody:—~ **auf** +acc to rely on.
vertraulich adj familiar; confidential.
vertraut adj familiar.
Vertrautheit f familiarity.
vertreiben vt to drive away; to expel; to sell.
vertreten vt to represent.
Vertreter m representative.
Vertretung f representation.
Vertrieb m marketing (department).
verursachen vt to cause.
verurteilen vt to sentence, condemn.
Verurteilung f sentence; condemnation.
vervielfachen vt to multiply.
vervielfältigen vt to copy, duplicate.
Vervielfältigung f copying, duplication.
vervollkommen vt to perfect.
vervollständigen vt to complete.
verwalten vt to administer; to manage.
Verwalter m manager; trustee.

Verwaltung f administration; management.
verwandeln vt to change, transform: — vr to change; to be transformed.
Verwandlung f change, transformation.
verwandt adj related.
Verwandte(r) f(m) relation.
Verwandtschaft f relationship; relations.
verwechseln vt to confuse.
Verwechslung f confusion.
Verweigerung f refusal.
Verweis m rebuke, reprimand; reference.
verweisen vt to refer.
verwendbar adj usable.
verwenden vt to use; to spend:—vr to intercede.
Verwendung f use.
verwirklichen vt to realize, put into effect.
Verwirklichung f realization.
verwirren vt to tangle; to confuse.
Verwirrung f confusion.
verwittern vt to weather.
verwitwet adj widowed.
verwöhnen vt to spoil, pamper.
verworfen adj depraved.
verwunden vt to wound.
Verwundete(r) f(m) wounded person, casualty.
Verwundung f wound.
verzagen vi to despair.
verzählen vr to miscount.
verzeichnen vt to list; to register.
Verzeichnis n list; index.
verzeihen vt vi to forgive.
verzeihlich adj pardonable.
Verzeihung f pardon, forgiveness:—~! excuse me!, sorry!
verzichten vi:—~ **auf** +acc to give up, forgo.
verzieren vi to decorate, ornament.
Verzierung f decoration.

verzögern *vt* to delay.
Verzögerung *f* delay.
verzollen *vt* to pay duty on:—**haben Sie etwas zu ~?** do you have anything to declare?
verzückt *adj* enraptured.
Verzug *m* delay.
verzweifeln *vi* to despair.
verzweifelt *adj* desperate.
Verzweiflung *f* despair, desperation.
Veto *n* veto.
Vetter *m* cousin.
vibrieren *vi* to vibrate.
Video *n* video.
Videorecorder *m* video recorder.
Vieh *n* cattle.
viel *adj adv* much, a lot (of).
vieles *pn* a lot.
vielleicht *adv* perhaps, maybe.
vielmal(s) *adv* many times:—**danke vielmals** many thanks.
vielmehr *adv* rather, on the contrary.
vier *num* four.
Viereck *n* quadrilateral; square.
viereckig *adj* four-sided; square.
vierte(r, s) *adj* fourth.
Viertel *n* quarter.
Vierteljahr *n* quarter.
vierteljährlich *adj* quarterly.
vierteln *vt* to divide into four/quarters.
Viertelnote *f* crotchet.
Viertelstunde *f* quarter of an hour.
Vierwaldstätter See *m* Lake Lucerne.
vierzehn *num* fourteen.
vierzehntägig *adj adv* fortnightly.
vierzig *num* forty.
Villa *f* villa.
Violine *f* violin.
Virus *m/n* virus.
Visite *f* (*med*) visit.
Visum *n* visa.
vital *adj* lively, vital.
Vitamin *n* vitamin.

Vogel *m* bird.
Vogelbauer *n* birdcage.
Vogelhäuschen *n* bird house.
Vogelperspektive *f* bird's-eye view.
Vogelscheuche *f* scarecrow.
Vokabel *f* word.
Vokabular *n* vocabulary.
Vokal *m* vowel.
Volk *n* people; nation.
Volksentscheid *m* referendum.
Volksfest *n* fair.
Volkslied *n* folksong.
Volkstanz *m* folk dance.
Volkswirtschaft *f* economics.
Volkszählung *f* census.
voll *adj* full:—*adv* fully.
vollauf *adv* amply.
Vollbart *m* full beard.
vollbringen *vt* to accomplish.
vollenden *vt* to finish, complete.
vollendet *adj* completed.
vollends *adv* completely.
Vollendung *f* completion.
voller *adj* fuller.
Volleyball *m* volleyball.
völlig *adj* complete:—*adv* completely.
volljährig *adj* of age.
vollkommen *adj* perfect.
Vollkommenheit *f* perfection.
Vollkornbrot *n* wholemeal bread.
Vollmacht *f* authority, full powers.
Vollmilch *f* full-cream milk.
Vollmond *m* full moon.
Vollpension *f* full board.
vollständig *adj* complete.
vollstrecken *vt* to execute.
vollziehen *vt* to carry out:—*vr* to happen.
Vollzug *m* execution.
Volt *n* volt.
Volumen *n* volume.
vom = **von dem**.
von *prep* of; from; by; about.

voneinander *adv* from each other.

vor *prep* in front of; before; with:—~ **allem** most of all:—~ **3 Tagen** 3 days ago.

Vorabend *m* eve, evening before.

voran *adv* before, ahead.

vorangehen *vi* to go ahead.

vorankommen *vi* to come along, make progress.

Voranschlag *m* estimate.

Vorarbeiter *m* foreman.

voraus *adv* ahead; in advance.

vorausgehen *vi* to go (on) ahead; to precede.

Voraussage *f* prediction.

voraussagen *vt* to predict.

voraussehen *vt* to foresee.

voraussetzen *vt* to assume:— **vorausgesetzt, daß...** provided that...

Voraussetzung *f* requirement.

Voraussicht *f* foresight.

voraussichtlich *adv* probably.

Vorbehalt *m* reservation, proviso.

vorbereiten *vt* to prepare.

Vorbereitung *f* preparation.

vordere(r, s) *adj* front.

Vordergrund *m* foreground.

voreingenommen *adj* biased.

Voreingenommenheit *f* bias.

Vorfahr *m* ancestor.

Vorfahrt *f* right of way.

Vorfall *m* incident.

vorfallen *vi* to occur.

vorfinden *vt* to find.

vorführen *vt* to show, display.

Vorgang *m* course of events; process.

Vorgänger(in) *m(f)* predecessor.

vorgefertigt *adj* prefabricated.

vorgehen *vi* to go (on) ahead; to proceed; to take precedence.

Vorgesetzte(r) *f(m)* superior.

vorgestern *adv* the day before yesterday.

vorhaben *vt* to intend.

Vorhaben *n* intention.

Vorhalle *f* entrance hall.

vorhalten *vt* to hold up:—*vi* to last.

vorhanden *adj* existing; available.

Vorhang *m* curtain.

Vorhängeschloß *m* padlock.

vorher *adv* before(hand).

vorherstimmen *vt* to preordain.

vorhergehen *vi* to precede.

vorherig *adj* previous.

Vorherrschaft *f* supremacy, predominance.

vorherrschen *vi* to predominate.

Vorhersage *f* forecast.

vorhersagen *vt* to forecast, predict.

vorhersehbar *adj* predictable.

vorhersehen *vt* to foresee.

vorhin *adv* just now, not long ago.

vorig *adv* last, previous.

Vorkämpfer(in) *m(f)* pioneer.

Vorkaufsrecht *n* purchase option.

Vorkehrung *f* precaution.

vorkommen *vi* to come forward; to happen, occur.

Vorkommen *n* occurrence.

Vorladung *f* summons.

Vorlage *f* pattern, model; bill (for a law).

vorlassen *vt* to admit.

vorläufig *adj* temporary, provisional.

vorlaut *adj* cheeky, impertinent.

vorlesen *vt* to read (out).

Vorleser(in) *m(f)* lecturer, reader.

Vorlesung *f* lecture:—**eine ~ halten** to give a lecture.

Vorliebe *f* preference, partiality.

vorliegen *vi* to be (here).

vorliegend *adj* present, at issue.

Vormachtstellung *f* supremacy.

Vormarsch *m* advance.

vormerken *vt* to book.

Vormittag *m* morning.

vormittags *adv* in the morning, before noon.

Vormund *m* guardian.

vorn *adv* in front.

Vorname *m* first/Christian name.

vornehm *adj* refined; distinguished; aristocratic.

vornehmen *vt* to carry out.

Vorort *m* suburb.

Vorrang *m* precedence, priority.

vorrangig *adj* of prime importance.

Vorrat *m* stock, supply.

vorrätig *adj* in stock.

Vorratskammer *f* pantry.

Vorrecht *n* privilege.

Vorrichtung *f* device, contrivance.

vorrücken *vi* to advance:—*vt* to move forward.

Vorsatz *m* intention; (*jur*) intent.

vorsätzlich *adj* intentional; (*jur*) premeditated:—*adv* intentionally.

Vorschau *f* (TV, etc) preview;(film) trailer.

Vorschlag *m* suggestion, proposal.

vorschlagen *vi* to suggest, propose.

vorschreiben *vt* to prescribe, specify.

Vorschrift *f* regulation(s); rule(s); instruction(s).

vorschriftsmäßig *adj* as per regulations/instructions.

Vorschuß *m* advance.

vorsehen *vt* to plan, provide for:—*vr* to be careful, take care:—*vi* to be visible.

Vorsehung *f* providence.

Vorsicht *f* caution, care.

vorsichtig *adj* cautious, careful.

vorsichtshalber *adv* just in case.

Vorsilbe *f* prefix.

vorsingen *vt* to sing (to); to audition (for):—*vi* to sing.

Vorsitz *m* chair(manship).

Vorsitzende(r) *f(m)* chairman (-woman).

Vorsorge *f* precaution(s), provision(s).

vorsorgen *vi*:—~ **für** to make provision(s) for.

Vorsorgeuntersuchung *f* check-up.

vorsorglich *adj* as a precaution.

Vorspeise *f* hors d'œuvre.

Vorspiel *n* prelude.

Vorsprung *m* projection; advantage, start.

Vorstadt *f* suburbs.

Vorstand *m* executive committee; board (of directors).

vorstehen *vi* to project.

vorstellbar *adj* conceivable.

vorstellen *vt* to introduce; to represent:—*vr* **sich** *dat* **etw** ~ to imagine something.

Vorstellung *f* introduction; performance; idea, thought.

Vorteil *m* advantage.

vorteilhaft *adj* advantageous.

Vortrag *m* lecture, talk.

vortragen *vt* to carry forward; to perform (song, etc).

vortreten *vi* to step forward; to protrude.

vorüber *adv* past, over.

Vorurteil *n* prejudice.

Vorwand *m* pretext.

vorwärts *adv* forward.

vorweg *adv* in advance.

vorweisen *vt* to show, produce.

vorwerfen *vi*:—**jdm etw** ~ to reproach somebody for something.

vorwiegend *adj* (*adv*) predominant(ly).

Vorwort *n* preface.

Vorwurf *m* reproach.

vorzeigen *vt* to show, produce.

vorzeitig *adj* premature.

vorziehen *vt* to pull forward; to prefer.

Vorzug *m* preference; advantage.

vorzüglich *adj* excellent.

vulgär *adj* vulgar.

Vulkan *m* volcano.

W

Waage *f* scale(s); balance; (*astrol*) Libra.

Wabe *f* honeycomb.

wach *adj* awake.

wachen *vi* to watch; to be awake.

wachhalten *vt* to keep awake.

wachhaltend *adj* on duty.

Wacholder *m* juniper.

Wachposten *m* guard, sentry.

wachrütteln *vt* to rouse; to shake up.

Wachs *n* wax.

wachsam *adj* watchful, on one's guard, vigilant.

wachsen *vi* to grow; to increase.

wachsen *vt* to wax.

wächsern *adj* waxy.

Wachstum *n* growth; increase.

Wachtel *f* quail.

Wächter *m* guard.

Wachtturm *m* watchtower.

wackelig *adj* shaky; loose.

wackeln *vi* to shake; to wobble, be loose.

Wade *f* calf.

Waffe *f* weapon.

Waffel *f* waffle; wafer.

Wagemut *m* daring.

wagen *vt* to dare; to risk.

Wagen *m* car; truck, lorry; cart, wag(g)on, carriage.

wägen *vt* to weigh (one's words, etc).

Waggon *m* wag(g)on.

waghalsig *adj* foolhardy.

Wagnis *n* risk.

Wahl *f* choice; option; selection; election; vote.

wählbar *adj* eligible.

wählen *vt vi* to choose, pick, select; to vote, elect.

Wähler(in) *m(f)* voter.

wählerisch *adj* fastidious, particular.

Wählerschaft *f* electorate.

Wahlgang *m* ballot.

Wahlkabine *f* polling booth.

Wahlkreis *m* constituency.

wahllos *adj* at random.

Wahlspruch *m* motto.

Wahlurne *f* ballot box.

Wahn *m* delusion; folly.

wähnen *vt* to believe (to be).

Wahnsinn *m* madness, insanity.

wahnsinnig *adj* mad, insane:—*adv* incredibly.

wahr *adj* true; real; genuine.

wahren *vt* to keep (secret, etc); to protect (interests, etc).

währen *vi* to last.

während *prep* during:—*conj* while; whereas.

wahrhaft *adv* truly.

wahrhaftig *adj* true, real:—*adv* really.

Wahrheit *f* truth.

wahrlich *adv* really, certainly.

wahrnehmen *vt* to perceive, notice.

Wahrnehmung *f* perception.

wahrsagen *vi* to tell fortunes, prophesy.

Wahrsager(in) *m(f)* fortune-teller.

wahrscheinlich *adj* probable:—*adv* probably.

Wahrscheinlichkeit *f* probability, likelihood.

Wahrung *f* protection; safeguarding.

Währung *f* currency.

Wahrzeichen *n* landmark.

Waise *f* orphan.

Waisenhaus *n* orphanage.

Wal *m* whale.

Wald *m* wood(s), forest.

Walfang *m* whaling.

Wall *m* dam, embankment; rampart.

Wallach *m* gelding.

wallen *vi* to flow.

Wallfahrer(in) *m(f)* pilgrim.

Wallfahrt *f* pilgrimage.

Walnuß *f* walnut.

Walroß *n* walrus.

walten *vi* to rule.

Walze *f* roller; cylinder.

walzen *vt* to roll.

wälzen *vt* to roll; to hunt through:—*vr* to wallow; to roll about.

Walzer *m* waltz.

Wand *f* wall; partition; precipice.

Wandalismus *m* vandalism.

Wandel *m* change.

wandelbar *adj* changeable, variable.

wandeln *vt vr* to change:—*vi* to walk.

Wanderer *m* hiker, rambler.

wandern *vi* to hike; to ramble, roam, wander.

Wandlung *f* change, transformation.

Wandtafel *f* blackboard.

Wandteppich *m* tapestry.

Wange *f* cheek.

wanken *vi* to stagger, reel; to rock; to waver.

wann *inter adv* when, at what time.

Wanne *f* tub; bathtub.

Wanze *f* bedbug.

Wappen *n* (coat of) arms, crest.

Ware *f* goods; article; product.

Warenhaus *n* department store.

Warenlager *n* stock, store.

Warenzeichen *n* trade mark.

warm *adj* warm; hot.

Wärme *f* warmth; heat.

wärmen *vt* to warm (up).

Warmwasserbereiter *m* water heater.

Warmwasserversorgung *f* hot-water supply.

warnen *vt* to warn, caution.

Warnung *f* warning, caution.

Warschau *n* Warsaw.

Warte *f* point of view; level.

warten *vi* to wait; to await:—*vt* to service, maintain.

Wärter *m* attendant; keeper.

Wartesaal *m* waiting room.

Wartung *f* maintenance.

warum *adv* why.

Warze *f* wart.

was *inter pn* what:—*rel pn* what.

waschbar *adj* washable.

Waschbecken *n* washbasin.

Wäsche *f* wash(ing), laundry; linen; underwear.

waschen *vt vr* to wash.

Wäscherei *f* laundry.

Waschmaschine *f* washing machine.

Wasser *n* water.

wasserdicht *adj* waterproof; watertight.

Wasserfall *m* waterfall; falls.

Wassermann *m* (*astrol*) Aquarius.

Wassermelone *f* watermelon.

wassern *vi* to land on water; to splash down.

wässern *vt* to soak; to water:—*vi* to water (of eyes, etc).

Wasserrohr *n* water pipe.

Wasserspiegel *m* water level.

Wasserstoff *m* hydrogen.

Wasserversorgung *f* water supply.

Wasserzeichen *n* watermark.

wäßrig *adj* watery.

waten *vi* to wade.

watscheln *vi* to waddle.

Watt *n* watt.

Watte *f* cotton wool.

wau *excl* woof.

weben *vt* to weave.

Weber *m* weaver.
Weberei *f* weaving mill.
Webstuhl *m* loom.
Wechsel *m* change; bill of exchange.
Wechselgeld *n* change.
wechselhaft *adj* variable.
Wechselkurs *m* rate of exchange.
wechseln *vt vi* to change.
Wechselstrom *m* alternating current.
Wechselwirkung *f* interaction.
wecken *vt* to wake (up).
Wecker *m* alarm clock.
weder *conj*:—~... **noch** neither... nor.
Weg *m* way; path; route.
weg *adv* away, off.
wegbleiben *vi* to stay away.
wegen *prep* because of.
weggehen *vi* to go away; to leave.
wegnehmen *vt* to take away.
wegwerfen *vt* to throw away.
wegwerfend *adj* disparaging.
weh *adj* sore:—~ **tun** to hurt.
wehen *vt vi* to blow.
wehmütig *adj* melancholy.
Wehrdienst *m* military service.
Weib *n* woman, female, wife.
weiblich *adj* female.
weich *adj* soft.
Weichheit *f* softness.
Weide *f* willow; pasture.
weiden *vi* to graze.
weigern *vt* to refuse.
Weigerung *f* refusal.
Weiher *m* pond.
Weihnachten *n* Christmas.
weihnachtlich *adj* Christmas.
Weihnachtsabend *m* Christmas Eve.
Weihnachtslied *n* Christmas carol.
Weinachtsmann *m* Father Christmas, Santa Claus.
Weihnachtstag *m* Christmas Day.
Weihrausch *m* incense.
Weihwasser *n* holy water.

weil *conj* because.
Weile *f* while, short time.
Wein *m* wine; vine.
Weinberg *m* vineyard.
Weinbrand *m* brandy.
weinen *vt vi* to cry.
Weinglas *n* wine glass.
Weinkarte *f* wine list.
Weinlese *f* vintage.
Weinprobe *f* wine-tasting.
Weinrebe *f* vine.
Weinstock *m* vine.
Weintraube *f* grape.
weise *adj* wise.
Weise *m* way, manner; tune:—**auf diese ~** in this way.
weisen *vt* to show.
Weisheit *f* wisdom.
Weisheitszahn *m* wisdom tooth.
weiß *adj* white.
Weißbrot *n* white bread.
weißen *vt* to whitewash.
Weißglut *f* incandescence.
Weißwein *m* white wine.
weit *adj* wide; broad; long.
weitaus *adv* by far.
weitblickend *adj* far-seeing.
Weite *f* width; space; distance.
weiten *vt vi* to widen.
weiter *adj* wider; broader; farther; further:—*adv* further:—**ohne ~es** without further ado.
weiterarbeiten *vi* to go on working.
weiterbilden *vr* to continue one's education.
Weiterfahrt *f* continuation of the journey.
weitergehen *vi* to go on.
weiterkommen *vi* to make progress.
weiterläufig *adj* spacious; lengthy; distant.
weiterleiten *vt* to pass on.
weitermachen *vt vi* to continue.

weitgehend *adj* considerable:—*adv* largely.

weitreichend *adj* long-range; far-reaching.

weitschweifig *adj* long-winded.

weitsichtig *adj* long-sighted; far-sighted.

Weitsprung *m* long jump.

weitverbreitet *adj* widespread.

Weizen *m* wheat.

welche(r, s) *inter pn* which:—*indef pn* some; any:—*rel pn* who; which, that.

Welle *f* wave; shaft.

Wellensittich *m* budgerigar.

Welt *f* world.

Weltall *n* universe,

Weltanschauung *f* philosophy of life.

weltberühmt *adj* world-famous.

Weltkrieg *m* world war.

weltlich *adj* worldly; secular.

Weltmacht *f* world power.

Weltmeister *m* world champion.

Weltraum *m* space.

weltweit *adj* worldwide.

wem *pn* (*dat of* **wer**) to whom.

wen *pn* (*acc of* **wer**) whom.

Wende *f* turn; change.

Wendekreis *m* tropic.

Wendeltreppe *f* spiral staircase.

wenden *vt vi vr* to turn.

Wendepunkt *m* turning point.

Wendung *f* turn; idiom.

wenig *adj* less; fewer:—*adv* less.

wenige *pn pl* few.

wenigste(r, s) *pn* least.

wenigstens *adv* at least.

wenn *conj* if; when.

wer *pn nom* who.

werben *vt* to recruit:—*vi* to advertise.

Werbung *f* advertisement; recruitment.

werden *vi v aux* to become.

werfen *vt* to throw.

Werft *f* shipyard.

Werk *n* work; job; works.

Werkstatt *f* workshop.

Werkzeug *n* tool.

Wert *m* worth; value.

wert *adj* worth; dear; worthy.

werten *vt* to rate.

wertlos *adj* worthless.

Wertpapier *n* security.

wertvoll *adj* valuable.

Wesen *n* being; nature.

wesentlich *adj* significant; considerable.

weshalb *adv* why.

Wespe *f* wasp.

wessen *pn* (*gen of* **wer**) whose.

Weste *f* waistcoat.

Westen *m* west.

Westeuropa *n* western Europe.

Westindien *n* (the) West Indies.

westlich *adj* western:—*adv* to the west.

wett *adj* even.

Wettbewerb *m* competition.

Wette *f* wager, bet.

wetten *vt vi* to bet.

Wetter *n* weather.

Wetterbericht *m* weather report.

Wettervorhersage *f* weather forecast.

Wettkampf *m* contest.

wettmachen *vt* to make good.

wichtig *adj* important.

Wichtigkeit *f* importance.

Widder *m* ram; (*astrol*) Aries.

wider *prep* against.

widerlegen *vt* to refute.

widerlich *adj* repulsive.

widerrechtlich *adj* unlawful.

Widerrede *f* contradiction.

Widerruf *m* retraction.

widerrufen *vt* to retract.

widerspiegeln *vt* to mirror, reflect:—*vr* to be reflected.

widersprechen *vt* to contradict.

Widerspruch *m* contraction.

Widerstand *m* resistance.

widerstandsfähig *adj* resistant.

widerstehen *vi:*—**jdm/etw ~** to withstand somebody/something.

widmen *vt* to dedicate; to devote:—*vr* to devote oneself.

widrig *adj* adverse.

wie *adv* how:—*conj:*—**so schön ~** as beautiful as.

wieder *adv* again.

Wiederaufbau *m* rebuilding.

wiederaufnehmen *vt* to resume.

wiederbekommen *vt* to get back.

wiederbringen *vt* to bring back.

wiedererkennen *vt* to recognize.

Wiedergabe *f* reproduction.

wiedergeben *vt* to return; to repeat.

wiedergutmachen *vt* to make up for.

Wiedergutmachung *f* reparation.

wiederherstellen *vt* to restore.

wiederholen *vt* to repeat.

Wiederholung *f* repeat.

Wiederkehr *f* return; recurrence.

wiedersehen *vt* to see again:—**auf Wiedersehen** goodbye.

wiederum *adv* again; on the other hand.

wiedervereinigen to reunite; to reunify.

Wiederwahl *f* re-election.

Wiege *f* cradle.

wlegen *vt* to rock; *vt vi* to weigh.

wiehern *vi* to neigh, whinny.

Wien *n* Vienna.

Wiese *f* meadow.

Wiesel *n* weasel.

wieso *adv* why.

wieviel *adj* how much.

wieweit *adv* to what extent.

wild *adj* wild.

Wild *n* game.

wildern *vi* to poach.

Wildheit *f* wildness.

Wildleder *n* suede.

Wildnis *f* wilderness.

Wildschwein *n* (wild) boar.

Wille *m* will.

willen *prep* +*gen* **um... ~** for the sake of…

willenstark *adj* strong-willed.

willig *adj* willing.

Willkommen *n* welcome.

willkommen *adj* welcome.

willkürlich *adj* arbitrary; voluntary.

wimmeln *vi:*—**~ (von)** to swarm (with).

wimmern *vi* to whimper.

Wind *m* wind.

Winde *f* winch, windlass; bindweed.

Windel *f* nappy.

winden *vi* to be windy:—*vt* to wind; to wave; to twist.

Windhund *m* greyhound.

windig *adj* windy; dubious.

Windmühle *f* windmill.

Windpocken *pl* chickenpox.

Windschutzscheibe *f* windscreen.

Windstärke *f* wind-force.

windstill *adj* still, windless.

Windstille *f* calm.

Windstoß *m* gust of wind.

Wink *m* wave; nod; hint.

Winkel *m* angle; set square; corner.

winkeln *vt vi* to wave.

winseln *vi* to whine.

Winter *m* winter.

winterfest *adj* (*bot*) hardy.

Wintergarten *m* conservatory.

winterlich *adj* wintry.

Winterreifen *m* winter tyre.

Wintersport *m* winter sports.

Winzer *m* vine grower.

winzig *adj* tiny.

Wipfel *m* treetop.

wir *pn nom* we.

Wirbel *m* whirl, swirl; fuss; vertebra.

wirbeln *vi* to whirl, swirl.

Wirbelsäule *f* spine.

wirken *vi* to have an effect; to work; to seem:—*vt* to work.

wirklich *adj* real:—*adv* really.
Wirklichkeit *f* reality.
wirksam *adj* effective.
Wirkung *f* effect.
wirr *adj* confused, wild.
Wirrwarr *m* chaos, disorder.
Wirt(in) *m(f)* landlord (landlady).
Wirtschaft *f* pub; economy.
wirtschaftlich *adj* economical; economic.
Wirtschaftskrise *f* economic crisis.
Wirtshaus *n* inn.
wischen *vt* to wipe.
Wischer *m* wiper.
wispern *vi* to whisper.
wissen *vt* to know.
Wissen *n* knowledge.
Wissenschaft *f* science.
Wissenschaftler(in) *m(f)* scientist.
wissenschaftlich *adj* scientific.
wissenswert *adj* worth knowing.
wissentlich *adj* knowing.
wittern *vt* to scent; to suspect.
Witterung *f* weather; scent.
Witwe *f* widow.
Witwer *m* widower.
Witz *m* joke.
witzig *adj* funny.
wo *adv* where; somewhere.
woanders *adv* elsewhere.
wobei *adv* by/with which.
Woche *f* week.
Wochenende *n* weekend.
wochenlang *adj adv* for weeks.
Wochenschau *f* newsreel.
wöchentlich *adj adv* weekly.
wodurch *adv* through which.
wofür *adv* for which.
wogegen *adv* against which.
woher *adv* where... from.
wohin *adv* where... to.
wohl *adv* well; probably; certainly; perhaps.

Wohl *n* welfare.
Wohlfahrt *f* welfare.
wohlhabend *adj* wealthy.
Wohlstand *m* prosperity.
Wohltat *f* relief; act of charity.
Wohltäter(in) *m(f)* benefactor.
wohltätig *adj* charitable.
Wohltun *vi* to do good.
Wohlwollen *n* goodwill.
wohnen *vi* to live, dwell, reside.
wohnhaft *adj* resident.
Wohnort *m* domicile.
Wohnsitz *m* place of residence.
Wohnung *f* house; flat, apartment.
Wohnzimmer *n* living room.
wölben *vt vr* to curve.
Wölbung *f* curve.
Wolf *m* wolf.
Wolke *f* cloud.
Wolkenkratzer *m* skyscraper.
wolkig *adj* cloudy.
Wolle *f* wool.
wollen *adj* woollen.
wollen *vt vi v aux* to want.
wollüstig *adj* lusty, sensual.
womit *adv* with which.
wonach *adv* after/for which.
woran *adv* on/at which.
worauf *adv* on which.
woraus *adv* from/out of which.
worin *adv* in which.
Wort *n* word.
Wörterbuch *n* dictionary.
Wortlaut *m* wording.
wortlos *adj* mute.
wortreich *adv* wordy, verbose.
Wortschatz *m* vocabulary.
Wortspiel *n* pun.
worüber *adv* over/about which.
worum *adv* about/round which.
worunter *adv* under which.
wovon *adv* from which.
wovor *adv* in front of/before which.

wozu *adv* to/for which.
Wrack *n* wreck.
wringen *vt* to wring.
Wucher *m* profiteering.
Wucherer *m* profiteer.
wuchern *vi* to grow wild.
Wucherung *f* growth, tumour.
Wuchs *m* growth; build.
Wucht *f* force.
wühlen *vi* to scrabble; to root; to burrow:—*vt* to dig.
Wulst *m* bulge; swelling.
wund *adj* sore, raw.
Wunde *f* wound.
Wunder *n* miracle.
wunderbar *adj* wonderful, marvellous.
Wunderkind *n* infant prodigy.
wunderlich *adj* odd, peculiar.
wundern *vr* to be surprised:—*vt* to surprise.
wunderschön *adj* beautiful.
wundervoll *adj* wonderful.

Wunsch *m* wish.
wünschen *vt* to wish, desire.
wünschenswert *adj* desirable.
Würde *f* dignity; honour.
würdevoll *adj* dignified.
würdig *adj* worthy.
würdigen *vt* to appreciate.
Wurf *m* throw; litter.
Würfel *m* dice; cube.
würfeln *vi* to play dice:—*vt* to dice.
würgen *vi* *vt* to choke.
Wurm *m* worm.
Wurst *f* sausage.
Würze *f* spice.
Würzel *f* root.
würzen *vt* to season, spice.
würzig *adj* spicy.
wüst *adj* untidy, messy; wild; waste.
Wüste *f* desert.
Wut *f* rage, fury.
wüten *vi* to rage.
wütend *adj* furious.

XY

xerokopieren *vt* to xerox, photocopy.
x-mal *adv* any number of times:—*n* times.

Xylophon *n* xylophone.
Yacht *f* yacht.
Ypsilon *n* the letter Y.

Z

zaghaft *adj* timid.
Zaghaftigkeit *f* timidity.
zäh *adj* tough; tenacious.
Zähigkeit *f* toughness; tenacity.
Zahl *f* number.
zahlbar *adj* payable.

zahlen *vt* *vi* to pay:—**zahlen bitte!** the bill please!
zählen *vt* *vi* to count.
Zähler *m* meter; numerator.
zahllos *adj* countless.
zahlreich *adj* numerous.

Zahlung f payment.
zahm adj tame.
zähmen vt to tame; to curb.
Zahn m tooth.
Zahnarzt m **Zahnärztin** f dentist.
Zahnbürste f toothbrush.
Zahnfleisch n gums.
Zahnpasta f toothpaste.
Zahnrad n cog.
Zahnschmerzen pl toothache.
Zange f pliers; tongs; pincers; forceps.
zanken vi vr to quarrel.
zänkisch adj quarrelsome.
zart adj soft; tender; delicate.
Zartheit f softness; tenderness.
zärtlich adj tender, affectionate.
Zauber m magic; spell.
Zauberei f magic.
zauberhaft adj magical, enchanting.
Zauberkünstler m conjuror.
zaubern vi to conjure, practise magic.
zaudern vi to hesitate.
Zaum m bridle.
Zaun m fence.
Zaunkönig m wren.
z.B. (= **zum Beispiel**) e.g.
Zebra n zebra.
Zebrastreifen m zebra crossing.
Zeche f bill; mine.
Zeh m toe.
Zehe f toe; clove.
zehn num ten.
zehnte(r, s) adj tenth.
Zeichen n sign.
zeichnen vt vi to draw; to sign.
Zeichnung f drawing.
zeigen vt to show:—vi to point:—vr to show oneself.
Zeiger m pointer; hand (of clock).
Zeile f line; row.
Zeit f time; (gr) tense:—**zur ~** at the moment.
Zeitalter n age.

Zeitgenosse m contemporary.
zeitig adj early.
zeitlich adj temporal.
Zeitlupe f slow motion.
Zeitraum m period.
Zeitrechnung f time, era:—**nach/vor unserer ~** AD/BC.
Zeitschrift f periodical.
Zeitung f newspaper.
Zeitvertreib m pastime, diversion.
zeitweilig adj temporary.
zeitweise adv for a time.
Zeitwort n verb.
Zeitzünder m time fuse.
Zelle f cell; callbox.
Zellstoff m cellulose.
Zelt n tent.
zelten vi to camp.
Zeltplatz m campsite.
Zement m cement.
zementieren vt to cement.
zensieren vt to censor.
Zentimeter m/n centimetre.
Zentner m hundredweight.
Zensur f censorship.
zentral adj central.
Zentrale f central office; (telephone) exchange.
Zentralheizung f central heating.
Zentrum n centre.
zerbrechen vt vi to break.
zerbrechlich adj fragile.
zerdrücken vt to smash, crush; to mash (of potatoes).
Zeremonie f ceremony.
Zerfall m decay.
zerfallen vi to disintegrate, decay.
zergehen vi to melt, dissolve.
zerkleinern vt to reduce to small pieces.
zerlegbar adj able to be dismantled.
zerlegen vi to take to pieces; to carve.
zermürben vt to wear down.
zerquetschen vt to squash.

Zerrbild *n* caricature.

zerreißen *vt* to tear to pieces:—*vi* to tear, rip.

zerren *vt* to drag:—*vi* ~ (**an** +*dat*) to tug (at).

zerrinnen *vi* to melt away.

zerrissen *adj* torn, tattered.

Zerrissenheit *f* tattered state.

Zerrung *f* (*med*) pulled muscle.

zerrütten *vt* to wreck, destroy.

zerrüttet *adj* wrecked, shattered.

zerschlagen *vt* to shatter, smash:—*vr* to fall through.

zerschneiden *vt* to cut up.

zersetzen *vt vr* to decompose.

zerspringen *vi* to shatter, burst.

Zerstäuber *m* atomiser.

zerstören *vt* to destroy.

Zerstörung *f* destruction.

zerstreuen *vt* to scatter, disperse; to dispel:—*vr* to scatter, disperse; to be dispelled.

zerstreut *adj* scattered; absent-minded.

Zerstreutheit *f* absent-mindedness.

Zerstreuung *f* dispersion.

zerteilen *vt* to divide into parts.

Zertifikat *n* certificate.

zertreten *vt* to crush underfoot.

zertrümmern *vt* to demolish, to shatter.

zetern *vi* to shout; to shriek.

Zettel *m* slip of paper; note; form.

Zeug *n* stuff; gear:—**das ~ haben zu** to have the makings of.

Zeuge *m* witness.

Zeugenaussage *f* evidence.

Zeugin *f* witness.

zeugen *vi* to testify, bear witness:—*vt* to father.

Zeugnis *n* certificate; report; evidence, testimony.

Zickzack *m* zigzag.

Ziege *f* goat.

Ziegel *m* brick; tile.

ziehen *vt* to draw; to pull; to move:—*vi* to draw; to move; to drift.

Ziehharmonika *f* concertina; accordion.

Ziehung *f* drawing.

Ziel *n* destination; finish; target; goal.

ziemlich *adj* quite a, fair:—*adv* rather; quite a bit.

zieren *vi* to act coy.

zierlich *adj* dainty.

Ziffer *f* figure, digit.

Zigarette *f* cigarette.

Zigarre *f* cigar.

Zigeuner(in) *m(f)* gypsy.

Zimmer *n* room.

Zimt *m* cinnamon.

Zink *n* zinc.

Zinn *n* tin; pewter.

Zins *m* interest.

zinslos *adj* interest-free.

Zinssatz *m* rate of interest.

zirka *adv* (round) about.

Zirkus *m* circus.

zischen *vi* to hiss.

Zitat *n* quotation, quote.

zitieren *vt* to quote.

Zitrone *f* lemon.

Zitronensaft *m* lemon juice.

zittern *vi* to tremble.

zivil *adj* civil; moderate.

Zivil *n* plain clothes.

Zivilbevölkerung *f* civil population.

Zivilisation *f* civilization.

zivilisieren *vt* to civilize.

Zivilist *m* civilian.

zögern *vi* to hesitate.

Zoll *m* customs; duty.

Zollamt *n* customs office.

Zollbeamte(r) *m* customs officer.

Zollerklärung *f* customs declaration.

zollfrei *adj* duty-free.

Zollkontrolle *f* customs check.

zollpflichtig *adj* liable to duty.

Zone *f* zone.

Zoo *m* zoo.

Zoologe *m* zoologist.

Zoologie *f* zoology.

zoologisch *adj* zoological.

Zorn *m* anger.

zornig *adj* angry.

zu *prep* to; at; with; for; into:—*conj* to:—*adv* too; towards; shut, closed.

zuallererst *adv* first of all.

zuallerletzt *adv* last of all.

Zubehör *n* accessories.

zubereiten *vt* to prepare.

zubilligen *vt* to grant.

zubinden *vt* to tie up.

zubringen *vt* to spend.

Zucchini *pl* courgette.

Zucht *f* breeding; cultivation; breed; discipline.

züchten *vt* to breed; to cultivate; to grow.

Züchter *m* breeder; grower.

Zuchthaus *n* prison.

züchtigen *vt* to chastise.

Züchtung *f* breed; variety.

zucken *vi* to jerk, twitch; to flicker:— *vi* to shrug.

Zucker *m* sugar; (*med*) diabetes.

Zuckerguß *m* icing.

zuckerkrank *adj* diabetic.

Zuckerkrankheit (*med*) diabetes.

zuckern *vt* to sugar.

Zuckerrohr *n* sugar cane.

Zuckerrübe *f* sugar beet.

Zuckung *f* convulsion, spasm; twitch.

zudecken *vt* to cover (up).

zudem *adv* in addition.

zudringlich *adj* forward, pushing, obtrusive.

zudrücken *vt* to close.

zueinander *adv* to one another; together.

zuerkennen *vt* to award.

zuerst *adv* first; at first.

Zufahrt *f* approach.

Zufahrtsstraße *f* approach road; slip road.

Zufall *m* chance; coincidence:—**durch** ~ by accident.

zufallen *vi* to close, shut; to fall.

zufällig *adj* chance:—*adv* by chance.

Zuflucht *f* recourse; refuge.

zufolge *prep* judging by; according to.

zufrieden *adj* content(ed), satisfied.

zufriedengeben *vr* to be content/satisfied (with).

zufriedenstellen *vt* to satisfy.

zufrieren *vi* to freeze up.

zufügen *vt* to add.

Zug *m* train; draught; pull; feature; move, stroke; breath; procession.

Zugabe *f* extra; encore.

Zugang *m* access, approach.

zugänglich *adj* accessible; approachable.

zugeben *vt* to add; to admit; to permit.

zugehen *vi* to shut.

Zugehörigkeit *f* membership; belonging (to).

Zügel *m* rein(s); curb.

Zugeständnis *n* concession.

zugestehen *vt* to admit; to concede.

Zugführer *m* guard.

zugig *adj* draughty.

zügig *adj* swift, speedy.

zugreifen *vi* to seize/grab at; to help.

zugrunde *adv*:—~ **gehen** to collapse: —**einer Sache dat etw** ~ **legen** to base something on something:—~ **richten** to destroy, ruin.

zugunsten *prep* in favour of.

Zugvogel *m* migratory bird.

zuhalten *vt* to keep closed:—*vi* **auf jdn/ etw** ~ to make a beeline for somebody/ something.

Zuhälter *m* pimp.

Zuhause *n* home.

zuhören *vi* to listen.

Zuhörer *m* listener.
zukleben *vi* to paste up.
zukommen *vi* to come up.
Zukunft *f* future.
zukünftig *adj* future:—*adv* in future.
Zulage *f* bonus.
zulassen *vt* to admit; to permit; to license.
zulässig *adj* permissible.
Zulassung *f* authorization; licensing.
zulaufen *vi*:—~ **auf jdn/etw** to run up to somebody or something:—~ **auf** to lead towards.
zuletzt *adv* finally, at last.
zum = **zu dem**.
zumachen *vt* to shut; to do up, fasten:— *vi* to shut; to hurry up.
zumal *conj* especially (as).
zumindest *adv* at least.
zumutbar *adj* reasonable.
zumuten *vt*:—**(jdm) etw** ~ to expect/ask something (of somebody).
Zumutung *f* unreasonable expectation, impertinence.
zunächst *adv* first of all.
Zunahme *f* increase.
Zuname *m* surname.
zünden *vi* to light, ignite; to fire.
zündend *adj* fiery.
Zünder *m* fuse; detonator.
Zündholz *n* match.
Zündkerze *f* spark plug.
Zündschlüssel *m* ignition key.
Zündung *f* ignition.
zunehmen *vi* to increase, grow; to put on weight.
Zuneigung *f* affection.
Zunft *f* guild.
zünftig *adj* proper; decent.
Zunge *f* tongue.
zuoberst *adv* at the top.
zupfen *vt* to pull, pick, pluck.
zur = **zu der**.
zurechtweisen *vt* to reprimand.

Zurechtweisung *f* reprimand, rebuff.
zureden *vi*:—**jdm** ~ to persuade/urge someone.
Zürich *n* Zurich.
zurück *adv* back.
zurückhaltend *adj* reserved.
Zurückhaltung *f* reserve.
zurückkehren *vi* to return.
Zuruf *f* cry, shout.
Zusage *f* promise; consent.
zusagen *vt* to promise:—*vi* to accept.
zusammen *adv* together.
Zusammenarbeit *f* cooperation.
zusammenarbeiten *vi* to cooperate.
zusammenbrechen *vt* to collapse; to break down.
Zusammenbruch *m* collapse.
zusammenfassen *vt* to summarize; to unite.
Zusammenfassung *f* summary.
Zusammenhang *m* connection.
zusammenkommen *vi* to assemble; to occur at once.
zusammenschließen *vt vi* to join (together).
Zusammenschluß *m* amalgamation.
zusammensetzen *vr* to be composed of; to get together.
Zusammensetzung *f* composition.
Zusammenstoß *m* collision.
zusätzlich *adj* additional:—*adv* in addition.
zuschauen *vt* to look on, watch.
Zuschauer(in) *m(f)* spectator.
Zuschlag *m* extra charge, surcharge.
zuschlagen *vt* to slam; to hit:—*vi* to shut; to hit, punch.
zuschreiben *vt* to ascribe, attribute.
Zuschrift *f* letter, reply.
Zuschuß *m* subsidy, allowance.
zusehen *vi* to watch; to take care.
zusehends *adv* visibly.
zusenden *vt* to forward, send on.

zuspielen *vt vi* to pass.

zuspitzen *vt* to sharpen:—*vr* to become critical.

zusprechen *vt* to award:—*vi* to speak.

Zustand *m* state, condition.

zustande *adv*:—~ **bringen** to bring about:—~ **kommen** to come about.

zuständig *adj* responsible.

Zuständigkeit *f* responsibility.

zustehen *vi*:—**jdm** ~ to be one's right.

zustellen *vt* to send; to block.

zustimmen *vi* to agree.

Zustimmung *f* agreement, consent.

zustoßen *vi* to happen.

zutage *adv*:—~ **bringen** to bring to light:—~ **treten** to come to light.

Zutaten *pl* ingredients.

zuteilen *vt* to designate, assign; to allocate.

zutiefst *adv* deeply.

zutragen *vt* to bring; to tell:—*vr* to happen.

Zutrauen *n* trust.

zutrauen *vt*:—**jdm etw** ~ to credit somebody with something.

zutraulich *adj* trusting, friendly.

zutreffen *vi* to be correct; to apply.

zutreffend *adj* accurate.

Zutritt *m* access, admittance.

Zutun *n* assistance.

zuverlässig *adj* reliable.

Zuverlässigkeit *f* reliability.

zuviel *adv* too much.

zuvor *adv* before, previously.

zuvorkommen *vt* +*dat* to anticipate.

zuvorkommend *adj* courteous, obliging.

Zuwachs *m* growth, increase.

zuwachsen *vi* to become overgrown; to heal (of wound).

zuwenig *adv* too little.

zuweilen *adv* at times, now and then.

zuwenden *vt* (+*dat*) to turn (towards).

zuziehen *vt* to draw, close; to call in (experts, etc):—*vi* to move in.

zuzüglich *prep* plus, with the addition of.

Zwang *m* compulsion, coercion.

zwängen *vt vr* to squeeze.

zwanglos *adj* informal.

zwanzig *num* twenty.

zwar *adv* indeed, to be sure.

Zweck *m* purpose, aim.

zwecklos *adj* pointless.

zwei *num* two.

zweideutig *adj* ambiguous.

zweifach *adj* double.

Zweifel *m* doubt.

zweifelhaft *adj* doubtful.

zweifellos *adj* doubtless.

zweifeln *vi*:—~ (**an etw** *dat*) to doubt (something).

Zweig *m* branch.

zweimal *adv* twice.

zweite(r, s) *adj* second.

Zwerg *m* dwarf.

Zwetsch(g)e *f* plum.

Zwieback *m* rusk.

Zwiebel *f* onion.

Zwilling *m* twin:—~**e** *pl* (*astrol*) Gemini.

zwingen *vt* to force, compel.

zwingend *adj* compulsive.

zwischen *prep* between.

Zwischenzeit *f* interval:—**in der** ~ meanwhile.

zwitschern *vt vi* to chirp, twitter.

zwo *num* two.

zwölf *num* twelve.

Zyklus *m* cycle.

Zylinder *m* cylinder; top hat.

Zyniker *m* cynic.

zynisch *adj* cynical.

Zypern *n* Cyprus.

Zyste *f* cyst.

English-German

A

a *art* ein, eine; per, pro, je.

abandon *vt* auf-, preisgeben; im Stich lassen.

abbey *n* Abtei *f*.

abbot *n* Abt *m*.

abbreviate *vt* (ab)kürzen.

abbreviation *n* Abkürzung *f*.

abdomen *n* Unterleib *m*, Bauch *m*.

ability *n* Fähigkeit *f*.

able *adj* fähig, tüchtig.

abnormal *adj* abnormal.

abnormality *n* Abnormalität *f*.

aboard *adv* an Bord.

abolish *vt* abschaffen, aufheben.

abolition *n* Abschaffung *f*, Aufhebung *f*.

abominable *adj* abscheulich.

about *prep* über; von; um... herum: — *adv* herum, umher; etwa, ungefähr.

above *prep* über, oberhalb:—*adv* oben, darüber:—~ **all** vor allem:—~ **mentioned** oben erwähnt.

abroad *adv* im Ausland, ~ ins Ausland.

absence *n* Abwesenheit *f*, Mangel *m*.

absent *adj* abwesend; fehlend.

absent-minded *adj* zerstreut.

absolute *adj* uneingeschränkt; vollkommen.

absorb *vt* aufsaugen; aufnehmen.

absorption *n* Aufnahme *f*; Vertieftsein *n*.

abstain *vi* sich enthalten.

abstract *adj* abstrakt:—*n* Auszug *m*; Übersicht *f*.

absurd *adj* absurd; lächerlich.

absurdity *n* Unsinn *m;* Lächerlichkeit *f*.

abundance *n* Überfluß *m*.

abundant *adj* reichlich.

abuse *vt* mißbrauchen; beleidigen:—*n* Mißbrauch *m*; Mißhandlung *f*.

abyss *n* Abgrund *m*.

academic *adj* akademisch; allgemeinbildend.

academy *n* Akademie *f*; Hochschule *f*.

accelerate *vt* beschleunigen.

acceleration *n* Beschleunigung *f*.

accent *n* Akzent *m*; Betonung *f*:—*vt* betonen.

accept *vt* annehmen.

acceptable *adj* annehmbar.

acceptance *n* Annahme *f*; Aufnahme *f*.

access *n* Zugang *m*; Zutritt *m*.

accident *n* Zufall *m*; Unfall *m*.

accidental *adj* zufällig; Unfalls-.

accommodate *vt* anpassen; unterbringen.

accommodation *n* Unterkunft *f*; Beilegung *f*.

accompany *vt* begleiten.

accord *n* Übereinstimmung *f*, Abkommen *n*.

accordance *n*:—**in ~ with** in Übereinstimmung mit, gemäß.

according *prep* gemäß, entsprechend:—~**ly** *adv* demnach, entsprechend.

account *n* Rechnung *f*; Konto *n*:—**on ~ of** wegen.

accountancy *n* Buchhaltung *f*.

accountant *n* Buchhalter(in) *m(f)*.

accuracy *n* Genauigkeit *f*.

accurate *adj* genau.

accuse *vt* anklagen; beschuldigen.

accustomed *adj* gewohnt, üblich; gewöhnt.

ace *n* As *n*.

ache n Schmerz m:—vi schmerzen, weh tun.

achieve vt erlangen; erreichen.

achievement n Leistung f; Ausführung f; Erreichung f.

acid adj sauer; scharf:—n Säure f.

acknowledge vt anerkennen; zugeben; bestätigen.

acknowledgment n Anerkennung f; Bestätigung f.

acorn n Eichel f.

acoustics n Akustik f.

acquaint vt bekannt machen, vertraut machen.

acquaintance n Bekanntschaft f; Bekannte(r) f(m); Kenntnis f.

acquire vt erwerben, erlangen.

acquisition n Erwerb m, Anschaffung f.

across adv hinüber; querdurch; drüben:—prep über; (mitten) durch.

act vi handeln; spielen:—n Tat f; Akt m.

action n Handlung f; (law) Klage f.

active adj aktiv; lebhaft.

activity n Aktivität f; Tätigkeit f.

actor n Schauspieler m.

actress n Schauspielerin f.

actual adj tatsächlich.

acute adj scharf; heftig; akut.

ad n Anzeige f.

adapt vt anpassen; umstellen.

add vt hinzufügen.

adder n Natter f.

addict n Süchtige(r) f(m).

addiction n Sucht f.

addition n Zusatz m.

additional adj zusätzlich.

address vt ansprechen; adressieren:—n Anschrift f; Rede f.

adequate adj angemessen; ausreichend.

adjective n Adjektiv n.

adjust vt anpassen; einstellen.

adjustment n Anpassung, Einstellung f.

administration n Verwaltung f.

administrator n Verwaltungsbeamte(r) f(m).

admiral n Admiral m.

admiration n Bewunderung f.

admire vt bewundern.

admission n Eintritt m; Einlaß m; Zulassung f.

admit vt einlassen; zulassen; zugeben.

adopt vt adoptieren; annehmen.

adoption n Adoption f; Annahme f.

adore vt anbeten; verehren.

adult adj erwachsen:—n Erwachsene(r) f(m).

adultery n Ehebruch m.

advance vt vi vorrücken:—n Vorrücken n; Fortschritt m.

advanced adj fortgeschritten.

advantage n Vorteil m.

adventure n Abenteuer n.

adventurous adj abenteuerlich.

adverb n Adverb n.

advertise vt ankündigen; werben für:—vi inserieren.

advertisement n Anzeige f.

advertising n Werbung f.

advice n Rat m; Nachricht f.

advise vt (be)raten; benachrichtigen.

aeroplane n Flugzeug n.

affair n Angelegenheit f; Sache f; Affäre f.

affection n Liebe f; Zuneigung f.

affectionate adj liebevoll, zärtlich.

affix vt befestigen; hinzufügen:—n (gr) Affix n; Anhang m.

affluence n Überfluß f; Wohlstand m.

afford vt sich leisten; aufbringen.

afraid adj:—be ~ Angst haben, sich fürchten.

after prep hinterher; nach:—adv nachher; darauf.

afternoon n Nachmittag m.

afterwards adv später, hinterher.

again adv wieder; außerdem:—~ **and** ~ immer wieder.

against prep gegen.

age n Alter n; Zeit f:—vi altern.

agency n Agentur f.

agent n Agent(in) m(f).

aggression n Agression f.

aggressive adj aggressiv.

agitate vt schütteln; aufregen; aufwiegeln.

ago adv vor.

agree vt vereinbaren:—vi zustimmen.

agreement n Vereinbarung f; Übereinstimmung f.

agricultural adj landwirtschaftlich, Agrar-.

agriculture n Landwirtschaft f.

ahead adv vorn; voraus.

aid vt helfen; fördern:—n Hilfe f; Beistand m; Helfer(in) m(f).

aim vt vi zielen:—n Ziel n; Absicht f.

air n Luft f.

air-conditioned adj klimatisiert.

air-conditioning n Klimaanlage f.

aircraft n Flugzeug n.

airline n Fluggesellschaft f.

airport n Flughafen m.

alarm n Alarm m; Wecker m; Alarmanlage f:—vt alarmieren.

alcohol n Alkohol m.

alcoholic adj alkoholisch; Alkohol-: —n Alkoholiker(in) m(f).

alert adj wachsam; munter.

alien adj fremd; ausländisch:—n Ausländer(in) m(f).

alike adj adv gleich; ähnlich.

alive adj lebendig; am Leben.

all adj all, ganz; jede(r, s); völlig:—adv ganz, völlig:—~ **at once** plötzlich:— ~ **the same** trotzdem:—**not at** ~ überhaupt nicht.

allergy n Allergie f.

alley n Gasse f.

alliance n Bund m, Bündnis n.

alligator n Alligator m.

allocate vt verteilen; zuweisen.

allocation n Verteilung f; Zuweisung f.

allow vt erlauben; bewilligen; zugeben.

allowance n Erlaubnis f; Zuschuß m.

ally n Verbündete(r) f(m):—vi sich verbünden.

almond n Mandel f.

almost adv fast, beinahe.

alone adj adv allein.

along prep entlang:—adv vorwärts, weiter.

aloud adv laut.

alphabet n Alphabet n.

already adv schon, bereits.

also adv auch, außerdem.

altar n Altar m.

alter vt (ver)ändern.

alteration n Änderung f; Umbau m.

alternative n Alternative f:—adj alternativ; andere(r, s):—~**ly** adv im anderen Falle, wahlweise.

although conj obwohl, wenn auch.

altogether adv insgesamt; ganz.

aluminium n Aluminium n.

always adv immer, jederzeit.

amateur n Amateur m; Liebhaber(in) m(f); Dilettant(in) m(f).

amaze vt überraschen, in Staunen versetzen.

amazement n (Er)staunen n; Überraschung f.

amazing adj erstaunlich; unglaublich.

ambassador n Botschafter m; Gesandte(r) f(m).

ambiguity n Zwei-, Vieldeutigkeit f.

ambiguous adj zwei-, vieldeutig.

ambition n Ehrgeiz m; Ziel n.

ambitious adj ehrgeizig.

ambulance n Krankenwagen m.

amend vt verbessern; abändern, ergänzen.

amendment n (Ver)Besserung f; Ergänzung f; Änderungsantrag m.

America n Amerika n.

American adj amerikanisch.

ammunition n Munition f.

among prep unter, inmitten.

amount n Betrag m; Menge f:—vi betragen.

ample adj weit, groß, geräumig; reichlich, genügend.

amplify vt erweitern, verstärken.

amuse vt amüsieren, unterhalten.

amusement n Unterhaltung f, Vergnügen n.

amusing adj amüsant.

anaesthetic n Betäubungsmittel n.

analogy n Entsprechung f.

analyse vt analysieren; untersuchen.

analysis n Analyse f; Untersuchung f.

analyst n (Psycho)Analytiker(in) m(f).

analytical adj analytisch.

anarchic adj anarchistisch.

anarchist n Anarchist(in) m(f).

anarchy n Anarchie f.

anatomy n Anatomie f.

ancestry n Abstammung f; Vorfahren mpl.

anchor n Anker m:—vi ankern.

anchovy n Sardelle f.

ancient adj (ur)alt.

and conj und.

anecdote n Anekdote f.

anew adv von neuem.

angel n Engel m.

anger n Ärger m; Wut f:—vt verärgern, erzürnen.

angle n Winkel m; Ecke f:—vt (ab)biegen; angeln.

angry adj verärgert; stürmisch.

anguish n Qual f; Schmerz m.

animal n Tier n.

animate vt beleben, aufmuntern:—adj lebendig, lebhaft.

ankle n (Fuß)Knöchel m; Fessel f.

annex vt beifügen, anhängen; annektieren:—n Anhang m; Anlage f.

annihilate vt vernichten.

annihilation n Vernichtung f.

anniversary n Jahrestag m; Jubiläum n.

announce vt ankündigen; bekanntgeben.

announcement n Ankündigung f; Ansage f.

annoy vt ärgern; belästigen.

annoyance n Ärgernis n; Belästigung f.

annoying adj ärgerlich; lästig.

annual adj jährlich, Jahres-.

anonymity n Anonymität f.

anonymous adj anonym.

another adj ein anderer; noch ein(er, e, es):—one ~ einander.

answer vt (be)antworten; verantworten:—n Antwort f.

ant n Ameise f.

Antarctic adj antarktisch.

antelope n Antilope f.

antenna n Antenne f; Fühler m.

anthology n Anthologie f.

anthropology n Anthropologie f

antibiotic n Antibiotikum n.

antibody n Antikörper m.

anticipate vt voraussehen; erwarten.

anticipation n (Vor)Ahnung f; Vorfreude f.

anticlockwise adv gegen den Uhrzeigersinn.

antidote n Gegengift, Gegenmittel n.

antifreeze n Frostschutzmittel n.

antipathy n Abneigung f.

antiquated adj veraltet.

antique n Antiquität f:—adj antik.

antisocial adj asozial; ungesellig.

antler n Geweih n.

anvil n Amboß m.

anxiety n Angst f; Beklemmung f.

anxious adj ängstlich, besorgt; gespannt.

any adj pn (irgend)eine(r); (irgend)welche; jede(r, s); ~**body** irgend jemand; jeder(mann):—~**how** irgendwie:—~**thing** etwas; alles.

apart adv für sich; getrennt.

apathetic adj teilnahmslos.

apathy n Teilnahmslosigkeit f.

ape n (Menschen)Affe m:—vt nachäffen.

apiary n Bienenhaus n.

apologetic adj entschuldigend; reumütig.

apologist n Verteidiger m.

apologize vu sich entschuldigen.

apology n Entschuldigung f.

apostrophe n Apostroph m.

appal vt erschrecken.

appalling adj entsetzlich.

apparatus n Apparat m.

apparent adj offensichtlich; scheinbar.

appeal vi Berufung einlegen; sich berufen; appellieren:—n (law) Berufung f; Appell m.

appear vi (er)scheinen.

appearance n Erscheinen n; Auftreten n; Erscheinung f.

appendix n Blinddarm m.

appetite n Appetit m.

applaud vt vi applaudieren.

applause n Beifall m.

apple n Apfel m.

apple tree n Apfelbaum m.

appliance n Gerät n.

applicable adj anwendbar.

application n Anwendung f; Antrag m.

apply vt anwenden; auftragen:—vi zutreffen; sich anwenden lassen.

appoint vt ernennen; bestimmen.

appointment n Ernennung f; Bestimmung f.

appreciate vt (ein)schätzen.

appreciation n (Ein)Schätzung f.

apprentice n Lehrling m.

approach vt vi sich nähern; nahekommen:—n Nahen n; Annäherung f.

appropriate adj passend, angemessen.

approval n Billigung f; Beifall m.

approve vt billigen; gutheißen.

approximate vi sich nähern:—adj annähernd.

approximation n Annäherung f.

apricot n Aprikose f.

April n April m.

apron n Schürze f; Schurz m.

apt adj passend; geneigt; geschickt.

aquarium n Aquarium n.

Aquarius n (astrol) Wassermann m.

aquatic adj Wasser-.

arch n Bogen m.

archaeological adj archäologisch.

archaeology n Archäologie f.

archaic adj archaisch.

archbishop n Erzbischof m.

archer n Bogenschütze m.

archery n Bogenschießen n.

architect n Architekt(in) m(f).

architectural adj architektonisch.

architecture n Architektur f.

Arctic adj arktisch.

area n Fläche f; Gebiet n.

arena n Arena f; Schauplatz m.

argue vi argumentieren; streiten.

argument n Auseinandersetzung f; Argument n.

aria n Arie f.

Aries n (astrol) Widder m.

arise vi entstehen; sich erheben.

aristocracy n Aristokratie f.

aristocrat n Aristokrat(in) m(f).

aristocratic adj aristokratisch, adlig.

arithmetic n Rechnen n.

arithmetical adj arithmetisch.

ark n Arche f.

arm n Arm m; Waffe f:—vt sich waffnen.

armchair n Sessel m.

armed adj bewaffnet.

armistice n Waffenstillstand m.

armour n Rüstung f; Panzer m.

armpit n Achselhöhle f.

army n Armee f; Heer n; Militär n.

aroma n Duft m.

aromatic adj aromatisch.

around prep um… herum; etwa:—adv (rund)herum.

arouse vt (auf)wecken; erregen.

arrange vt (ein)richten.

arrangement n (An)Ordnung f.

arrest n Festnahme f; Aufhalten n:—vt aufhalten; festnehmen.

arrival n Ankunft f.

arrive vi ankommen.

arrogance n Überheblichkeit f.

arrogant adj überheblich.

arrow n Pfeil m.

arsenic n Arsen n.

arson n Brandstiftung f.

art n Kunst f.

artery n Schlagader f.

arthritis n Arthritis f.

artichoke n Artischocke f.

article n Artikel m.

artificial adj künstlich, Kunst-.

artillery n Artillerie f.

artist n Künstler(in) m(f).

artistic adj künstlerisch.

as conj (so) wie; als; obwohl; weil.

asbestos n Asbest m.

ascend vi (auf)steigen.

ascent n Aufstieg m; Besteigung f.

ash n (bot) Esche f.

ashamed adj beschämt.

ashtray n Aschenbecher m.

ask vt fragen; bitten; verlangen:—~ for bitten um.

asleep adj schlafend:—**fall** ~ einschlafen.

asparagus n Spargel m.

aspect n Aspekt m; Aussehen n; Hinsicht f.

ass n Esel m:—**she** ~ Eselin f.

assassin n Attentäter(in) m(f).

assassinate vt ermorden.

assassination n Attentat.

assault n Angriff m:—vt angreifen.

assemble vt versammeln:—vi sich versammeln.

assembly n Versammlung f; Montage f.

assent n Zustimmung f:—vi zustimmen.

assert vt behaupten; durchsetzen.

assertion n Behauptung f.

assess vt festsetzen; (ab)schätzen; besteuern.

assessment n (Ab) Schätzung f; Beurteilung f.

asset n Vorzug m; Gewinn m; Vermögenswert m:—**s** pl Vermögen n.

assign vt zuweisen; bestimmen.

assignment n Zuweisung f; Bestimmung f; Aufgabe f.

assist vt helfen; unterstützen.

assistance n Hilfe f; Unterstützung f.

assistant n Assistent(in) m(f); Angestellte(r) f(m).

associate vt verbinden; anschließen: —n Partner m; Genosse m.

association n Vereinigung f; Verein m.

assume vt annehmen; voraussetzen; übernehmen; sich anmaßen.

assumption n Annahme f; Voraussetzung f; Anmaßung f.

assurance n Zusicherung f; Selbstsicherheit f.

assure vt (ver)sichern; zusichern; beruhigen.

asthma n Asthma n.

asthmatic adj asthmatisch.

astonish vt in Erstaunen setzen; verblüffen.

astonishing *adj* erstaunlich.
astonishment *n* (Er)Staunen *n*.
astound *vt* verblüffen; überraschen.
astrologer *n* Astrologe *m*.
astrological *adj* astrologisch.
astrology *n* Astrologie *f*.
astronaut *n* Astronaut *m*.
astronomer *n* Astronom *m*.
astronomical *adj* astronomisch.
astronomy *n* Astronomie *f*.
astute *adj* scharfsinnig; schlau.
at *prep* in; an; bei; zu; auf; nach; gegen; um; mit.
atheism *n* Atheismus *m*.
atheist *n* Atheist *m*.
athlete *n* (Leicht)Athlet(in) *m(f)*; Sportler(in) *m(f)*.
athletic *adj* Sport-; sportlich; muskulös.
atlas *n* Atlas *m*.
atmosphere *n* Atmosphäre *f*.
atmospheric *adj* Luft-; Wetter-; stimmungsvoll.
atom *n* Atom *n*.
atomic *adj* Atom-.
atrocious *adj* abscheulich; grauenhaft.
atrocity *n* Abscheulichkeit *f*; Greueltat *f*.
attach *vt* befestigen; beifügen; verbinden.
attaché *n* Attaché *m*.
attachment *n* Befestigung *f*; Anhängsel *n*; Zuneigung *f*; Zugehörigkeit *f*.
attack *vt* angreifen; in Angriff nehmen:—*n* Angriff *m*; Anfall *m*.
attacker *n* Angreifer(in) *m(f)*.
attain *vt* erreichen; erlangen.
attainable *adj* erreichbar.
attempt *vt* versuchen:—*n* Versuch *m*.
attend *vt vi* (be)achten; bedienen; teilnehmen an.
attendance *n* Dienst *m*; Bedienung *f*; Pflege *f*; Anwesenheit *f*.

attendant *n* Begleiter(in) *m(f)*; Diener(in) *m(f)*; Wart *m*.
attention *n* Aufmerksamkeit *f*; Beachtung *f*.
attentive *adj* aufmerksam.
attic *n* Dachgeschoß *n*; Mansarde *f*.
attitude *n* Haltung *f*; (Ein)Stellung *f*.
attract *vt* anziehen; gewinnen; erregen.
attraction *n* Anziehungskraft *f*; Attraktion *f*.
attractive *adj* anziehend; attraktiv.
auction *n* Versteigerung *f*.
audience *n* Publikum *n*; Audienz *f*; Gehör *n*.
augment *vt* vermehren; vergrößern: — *vi* zunehmen.
August *n* August *m*.
aunt *n* Tante *f*.
aura *n* Aura *f*.
auspicious *adj* günstig; glücklich.
austere *adj* streng; karg; hart.
austerity *n* Strenge *f*; Kargheit *f*.
authentic *adj* authentisch; echt.
authenticate *vt* beglaubigen; die Echtheit bescheinigen.
authenticity *n* Echtheit *f*; Glaubwürdigkeit *f*.
author(ess) *n* Urheber(in) *m(f)*; Verfasser(in) *m(f)*.
authoritarian *adj* autoritär.
authoritative *adj* herrisch; maßgebend.
authority *n* Autorität *f*; Vollmacht *f*.
authorize *vt* ermächtigen; genehmigen.
autograph *n* Autogramm *n*.
automated *adj* vollautomatisiert.
automatic *adj* automatisch.
automaton *n* Roboter *m*.
autonomy *n* Autonomie *f*; Selbständigkeit *f*.
autopsy *n* Autopsie *f*.
autumn *n* Herbst *m*.
auxiliary *adj* Hilfs-.
available *adj* verfügbar; vorhanden.

avalanche *n* Lawine *f.*
avarice *n* Geiz *m.*
avaricious *adj* geizig.
avenge *vt* rächen.
avenue *n* Weg *m*; Allee *f.*
average *vt* durchschnittlich betragen: —*n* Durchschnitt *m.*
aviary *n* Vogelhaus *n.*
avoid *vt* (ver)meiden.
avoidable *adj* vermeidbar.
await *vt* erwarten.
awake *vt* wecken:—*vi* aufwachen; erwachen:—*adj* wach; sich bewußt.
awakening *n* Erwachen *n*; Wecken *n.*

award *vt* zusprechen; verleihen:—*n* Urteil *n*; Zuerkennung *f.*
aware *adj* bewußt.
awareness *n* Bewußtsein *n.*
away *adv* weg; fort; entfernt.
awe *n* (Ehr)Furcht *f.*
awful *adj* furchtbar; schrecklich.
awkward *adj* ungeschickt; unangenehm; unhandlich.
axe *n* Axt *f.*
axiom *n* Axiom *n.*
axis *n* Achse *f.*
axle *n* Achse *f.*

B

baby *n* Baby *n.*
baboon *n* Pavian *m.*
bachelor *n* Bakkalaureus *m* Junggeselle *m.*
back *n* Rücken *m*; Rückseite *f:—adj* Hinter-; Rück-:—*adv* zurück:—*vt* unterstützen.
background *n* Hintergrund *m.*
backward *adj* Rück(wärts)-; rückständig:—~**s** *adv* rückwärts; zurück.
bacon *n* Speck *m.*
bad *adj* schlecht; böse; schlimm.
badge *n* Abzeichen *n.*
badger *n* Dachs *m.*
bag *n* Tasche *f*; Tüte *f.*
baggage *n* Gepäck *n.*
bagpipe *n* Dudelsack *m.*
bake *vt* backen; braten.
bakery *n* Bäckerei *f.*
baker *n* Bäcker *m.*
balance *n* Waage *f*; Gleichgewicht *n*; Kontostand *m:—vt* abwägen; balancieren; ausgleichen.

balance sheet *n* Bilanz *f.*
balcony *n* Balkon *m.*
bald *adj* kahl.
ball *n* Ball *m*; Kugel *f*; Ballen *m.*
ballet *n* Ballett *n.*
balloon *n* Ballon *m.*
ballroom *n* Ballsaal *m.*
bamboo *n* Bambus *m.*
ban *n* Verbot *n*; Sperre *f*; Ächtung *f*: — *vt* verbieten; sperren.
banana *n* Banane *f.*
band *n* Gruppe *f*; Bande *f.*
bandage *n* Bandage *f.*
bandit *n* Bandit *m*; Räuber *m.*
bang *n* Knall *m:—vt* dröhnend (zu) schlagen; knallen; (an)stoßen.
bank *n* Bank *f*; Ufer *n.*
banker *n* Bankier *m.*
banking *n* Bankwesen *n*; Bankgeschäft *n.*
bankrupt *adj* bankrott:—*n* Bankrotteur *m.*
bankruptcy *n* Bankrott *m*; Konkurs *m.*

banner n Banner n; Standarte f.
banquet n Bankett n; Festessen n.
baptise vt taufen.
baptism n Taufe f.
bar n Stange f; Riegel m:—vt verriegeln; versperren.
barbarian n Barbar(in) m(f):—adj barbarisch.
barbaric adj barbarisch; grausam.
barbecue n Grillfest n; Grill m.
barber n (Herren)Friseur m.
bar code n Strichcode m.
bard n Barde m.
bare adj bloß; nackt; kahl.
barefoot adj barfuß.
barely adv kaum; knapp.
bargain n Geschäft n; Sonderangebot n:—vi (ver)handeln.
baritone n Bariton m.
bark n Rinde f; Bellen n:—vi bellen.
barley n Gerste f.
barmaid n Bardame f.
barman n Barmann m.
barn n Scheune f; Stall m.
barometer n Barometer n.
baron(ess) n Baron(ess) m(f).
barrel n Faß m.
barren adj unfruchtbar; öde.
base n Basis f; Grundlage f:—vt stützen; gründen:—adj Grund-; gemein; niedrig; unecht.
basement n Keller(geschoß) m(n).
basic adj grundlegend; Grund-.
basin n Becken n; Schale f.
basis n Basis f; Grundlage f.
basket n Korb m.
basketball n Basketball m.
bass n (mus) Baß m.
bassoon n Fagott n.
bat n Fledermaus f; Schläger m.
bath n Bad n.
bathe vt vi baden.
bathroom n Badezimmer n.

bathtub n Badewanne f.
battalion n Bataillon n.
battery n Batterie f.
battle n Schlacht f; Kampf m:—vi kämpfen; streiten.
battlefield n Schlachtfeld n.
battleship n Schlachtschiff n.
bay n Bucht f.
bayonet n Bajonett n.
bazaar n Basar m.
be vi sein.
beach n Strand m.
beacon n Leuchtturm m; Leuchtfeuer n.
bead n Perle f; Tropfen m.
beak n Schnabel m.
beaker n Becher m.
beam n Strahl m; Balken m:—vi strahlen.
bean n Bohne f.
bear n Bär m:—**she ~** Bärin f:—vt vi tragen.
bearable adj erträglich.
beard n Bart m.
beast n Tier n; Bestie f; Vieh n.
beat vt vi schlagen:—n Schlag m.
beautiful adj schön; wunderbar.
beauty n Schönheit f.
beaver n Biber m.
because conj weil; da.
become vt (an)stehen; sich schicken für:—vi werden.
bed n Bett n; Lager n; Beet n.
bedroom n Schlafzimmer n.
bedtime n Schlafenszeit f.
bee n Biene f.
beech n Buche f.
beef n Rindfleisch n; Mastrind n.
beehive n Bienenstock m.
beer n Bier n.
beet n Bete f; Runkelrübe f.
beetle n Käfer m.
before adv vorn; vorher:—prep vor: — conj bevor; ehe.

beg vt erbetteln; (er)bitten:—vi betteln; bitten.

beggar n Bettler(in) m(f).

begin vt vi beginnen, anfangen.

beginner n Anfänger(in) m(f).

beginning n Anfang m; Beginn m.

behalf n:—**on ~ of** im Namen von; im Auftrag von.

behave vi sich benehmen; sich verhalten.

behaviour n Benehmen n; Verhalten n.

behind prep hinter:—adv (nach) hinten; hinterher.

being n (Da)Sein n; Existenz f; Wesen n.

belfry n Glockenturm m.

belief n Glaube m.

believable adj glaubhaft.

believe vt vi glauben.

bell n Glocke f; Klingel f; Läuten n.

belly n Bauch m; Magen m.

belong vi gehören.

beloved adj geliebt.

below adv unten; hinunter; (dar)unter: —prep unter; unterhalb.

belt n Gürtel m; Gurt m; Riemen m.

bench n Bank f; Sitz m; Gericht n.

bend vt biegen; krümmen; beugen:— vi sich krümmen; sich (ver)beugen: —n Kurve f; Krümmung f.

beneficial adj nützlich; wohltuend; nutznießend.

benefit n Vorteil m; Nutzen m; Unterstützung f:—vt nützen; zugute kommen:—vi Nutzen ziehen.

bent n Neigung f; Hang m; Veranlagung f.

berry n Beere f.

beside(s) prep neben; dicht bei; außer(halb):—adv außerdem; sonst.

best adj beste(r, s); größte(r, s):—adv am besten; am meisten:—n (der, die, das) Beste m/f/n.

bestial adj tierisch; bestialisch; gemein.

bestiality n Bestialität f; Greueltat f.

bestow vt schenken; verleihen.

bestseller n Bestseller m.

bet n Wette f:—vt wetten.

betray vt verraten; hintergehen.

betrayal n Verrat m.

better adj adv besser:—vt verbessern; übertreffen.

between prep zwischen.

beware vi sich hüten; sich in acht nehmen.

beyond prep jenseits; außer; über... hinaus.

Bible n Bibel f.

biblical adj biblisch.

bibliography n Bibliographie f.

bicycle n Fahrrad n.

bid vt bieten; gebieten:—n Gebot n.

big adj groß.

bilingual adj zweisprachig.

bill n Schnabel m; Rechnung f.

billion n Milliarde f.

bin n Kasten m; Behälter m.

bind vt (ver)binden.

biographer n Biograph m.

biographical adj biographisch.

biography n Biographie f.

biological adj biologisch.

biology n Biologie f.

birch n Birke f.

bird n Vogel m.

birth n Geburt f; Abstammung f; Entstehung f.

birthday n Geburtstag m.

biscuit n Keks m.

bishop n Bischof m.

bit n Gebiß n.

bitch n Hündin f.

bite vt beißen:—n Biß m; Bissen m; Schärfe f.

bitter adj bitter; erbittert; scharf.

bitterness n Bitterkeit f; Erbitterung f.
bitumen n Bitumen n; Asphalt m.
bizarre adj bizarr; absonderlich.
black adj schwarz; dunkel; düster:—n Schwarz n; Schwarze(r) f(m).
blackberry n Brombeere f.
blackbird n Amsel f.
blackboard n Tafel f.
blacken vt schwärzen.
blackmail n Erpressung f:—vt erpressen.
black market n Schwarzmarkt m.
black pudding n Blutwurst f.
blacksmith n Schmied m.
bladder n Blase f.
blade n Klinge f; Blatt n; Halm m.
blame vt tadeln; die Schuld geben:—n Tadel m; Schuld f.
bland adj mild; verbindlich; fad; langweilig.
blank adj blank; leer; Blanko-; verblüfft:—n Leere f; Lücke f.
blanket n Decke f.
blare vi schmettern; plärren; dröhnen; grell leuchten.
blaspheme vt lästern; schmähen.
blasphemous adj (gottes)lästerlich.
blasphemy n Blasphemie f; (Gottes)-Lästerung f.
blast n Windstoß m; Ton m; Explosion f; Sprengung f.
blatant adj lärmend; aufdringlich; eklatant.
blaze n loderndes Feuer n:—vi lodern.
bleach vt vi bleichen:—n Bleichmittel n.
bleak adj öde; rauh.
bleat n Blöken n:—vi blöken.
bleed vi bluten:—vt zur Ader lassen; abzapfen.
blend vt mischen.
bless vt segnen.
blessing n Segen m.

blind adj blind:—vt (ver)blenden:—n Rolladen m.
blindness n Blindheit f.
blink vi blinzeln; zwinkern.
bliss n (Glück)Seligkeit f.
blissful adj (glück)selig.
blister n Blase f; Bläschen n:—vi Blasen werfen.
blitz n heftiger (Luft)Angriff m; Blitzkrieg m.
blizzard n Schneesturm m.
block n Block m; Klotz m; Verstopfung f:—vt sperren; blockieren; verstopfen.
blond(e) adj blond; hell:—n Blondine f.
blood n Blut n.
bloody adj blutig.
bloom, blossom n Blüte f:—vi (er)-blühen.
blow vt vi blasen; wehen:—~ up sprengen:—n Blasen n; Schlag m.
blue adj blau.
bluebell n Glockenblume f; Sternhyazinthe f.
bluff n Bluff m:—vt bluffen.
blunt adj stumpf:—vt abstumpfen.
blur n Fleck m:—vt verwischen:—vi verschwimmen.
blush n Erröten n; Röte f:—vi erröten; rot werden.
boa n Boa f.
boar n Eber m:—**wild** ~ Keiler m.
board n Brett n; Tisch m; Tafel f; Bord m:—vt an Bord gehen.
boast vi prahlen; sich rühmen:—n Prahlerei f.
boat n Boot n; Schiff n.
body n Körper m; Leiche f; Masse f.
bodyguard n Leibwächter m.
bog n Sumpf m.
boil vt vi kochen.
bold adj kühn; mutig.

bolt n Bolzen m; Riegel m.
bomb n Bombe f.
bond n Bund m; (Ver)Bindung f; Anleihe f.
bone n Knochen m.
book n Buch n.
bookkeeper n Buchhalter(in) m(f).
bookkeeping n Buchhaltung f; Buchführung f.
bookshop n Buchhandlung f.
boost n Förderung f; Auftrieb m:—vt nachhelfen; steigern.
boot n Stiefel m; Kofferraum m.
booth n Bude f; Zelle f; Kabine f.
border n Rand m; Grenze f:—vt säumen; grenzen an.
bore vt langweilen; bohren:—n Langweiler m; Bohrung f.
boredom n Langeweile f.
boring adj langweilig.
born adj geboren; angeboren.
borrow vt borgen; leihen.
boss n Boß m; Chef m; Vorgesetzer m.
botanical adj botanisch.
botany n Botanik f.
both adj beide(r, s):—conj sowohl... als.
bottle n Flasche f.
bottom n Boden m; Unterseite f; Hintern m:—adj unterste(r, s); Grund-.
bounce vi aufprallen; springen:—n Aufprall m; Sprung m.
bound n Grenze f; Sprung m:—adj gebunden; verpflichtet.
boundary n Grenze f.
bouquet n Blumenstrauß m.
bovine adj Rinder-.
bow vt biegen; beugen:—vi sich (ver)beugen:—n Verbeugung f; n Bogen m.
bowl n Schüssel f; Schale f; Napf m, Becken n.
bowling n Bowling n; Kegeln n.

box n Kiste f; Kasten m; Dose f:—vi boxen.
boxer n Boxer m.
boxing n Boxen n.
box office n Kasse f.
boy n Junge m.
boyfriend n Freund m.
bra n BH m.
bracket n Klammer f.
brain n Gehirn n; Verstand m.
brake n Bremse f:—vt vi bremsen.
branch n Zweig m; Zweigstelle f.
brand n Marke f; Art f; Brand m.
brandy n Weinbrand m.
brass n Messing n.
brave adj mutig; tapfer.
bravery n Mut m; Tapferkeit f.
bread n Brot n.
breadcrumbs npl Paniermehl n.
breadth n Breite f.
break vt vi brechen.
breakdown n Panne f; Zusammenbruch m.
breakfast n Frühstück n.
breast n Brust f.
breath n Atem(zug) m.
breathe vt vi atmen.
breeze n Brise f.
brew vt brauen:—n Gebräu n.
brewer n Brauer m.
brewery n Brauerei f.
bribe n Bestechung f:—vt bestechen.
bribery n Bestechung f.
brick n Ziegelstein m.
bride n Braut f.
bridegroom n Bräutigam m.
bridesmaid n Brautjungfer f.
bridge n Brücke f.
bridle n Zaum m:—vt zäumen; zügeln.
brief adj kurz; knapp.
bright adj hell; leuchtend.
brighten vi sich aufhellen; aufleuchten.

brightness *n* Helligkeit *f*; Glanz *m*.
brilliant *adj* leuchtend; glänzend.
bring *vt* (mit)bringen.
brink *n* Rand *m*; Ufer *n*.
broad *adj* breit; weit.
broadbean *n* Saubohne *f*.
broadcast *n* Übertragung *f*; Sendung *f*:—*vt vi* senden; übertragen.
broaden *vt vi* verbreitern; erweitern.
broccoli *n* Brokkoli *m*.
brochure *n* Broschüre *f*; Prospekt *m*.
broken *adj* gebrochen; kaputt.
broker *n* Makler *m*; Vermittler *m*.
bronze *n* Bronze *f*:—*vt* bronzieren.
brook *n* Bach *m*.
broom *n* Besen *m*; (Besen)Ginster *m*.
broth *n* Suppe *f*; Brühe *f*.
brothel *n* Bordell *n*.
brother *n* Bruder *m*.
brother-in-law *n* Schwager *m*.
brotherly *adj* brüderlich.
brow *n* Braue *f*; Stirn *f*.
brown *adj* braun.
brush *n* Bürste *f*; Pinsel *m*:—*vt* bürsten.
Brussels sprouts *npl* Rosenkohl *m*.
brutal *adj* brutal; roh.
bubble *n* (Seifen)Blase *f*; Schwindel *m*:—*vi* sprudeln; brodeln.
bucket *n* Eimer *m*; Kübel *m*; Schaufel *f*.
bud *n* Knospe *f*; Auge *n*; Keim *m*:—*vi* knospen; keimen; heranreifen.
Buddhism *n* Buddhismus *m*.
buddy *n* Kumpel *m*; Kamerad *m*.
budge *vi* sich rühren; sich bewegen.
budgerigar *n* Wellensittich *m*.
budget *n* Budget *n*; Etat *m*; Haushaltsplan *m*; Finanzen *pl*.
buffalo *n* Büffel *m*; Bison *m*.
buffer *n* Puffer *m*; Prellbock *m*.
buffoon *n* Possenreißer *m*; Hanswurst *m*.
bug *n* Wanze *f*; Insekt *n*; Bazillus *m*; Fanatiker(in) *m(f)*; Defekt *m*.

build *vt* (er)bauen; errichten; aufbauen.
builder *n* Erbauer *m*; Bauunternehmer *m*; Bauhandwerker *m*.
building *n* Gebäude *n*; (Er)Bauen *n*; Bau *m*.
bulb *n* Knolle *f*; Zwiebel *f*; Kugel *f*; (Glüh)Birne *f*.
bulk *n* Masse *f*; Umfang *m*; Volumen *n*:—**in ~** lose; in großen Mengen.
bull *n* Bulle *m*; Stier *m*.
bulldog *n* Bulldogge *f*.
bulldozer *n* Planierraupe *f*.
bullet *n* Kugel *f*.
bullfight *n* Stierkampf *m*.
bullfighter *n* Stierkämpfer *m*.
bullring *n* Stierkampfarena *f*.
bully *n* Schläger *m*; brutaler Kerl *m*: —*vt* tyrannisieren.
bum *n* Hintern *m*; Herumtreiber *m*; Tippelbruder *m*.
bump *n* heftiger Stoß *m*; Beule *f*.
bun *n* süßes Brötchen; (Haar)Knoten *m*.
bundle *n* Bündel *n*:—*vt* bündeln.
bungalow *n* Bungalow *m*.
bunk *n* Koje *f*.
bunker *n* Bunker *m*.
buoy *n* Boje *f*; Bake *f*.
buoyant *adj* schwimmend; lebhaft.
burden *n* Last *f*; Ladung *f*; Bürde *f*:—*vt* belasten.
bureau *n* Schreibpult *n*; Büro *n*; Amt *n*.
bureaucracy *n* Bürokratie *f*.
bureaucrat *n* Bürokrat *m*.
burglar *n* Einbrecher *m*.
burglary *n* Einbruch *m*.
burial *n* Begräbnis *n*; Beerdigung *f*.
burn *vt vi* (ver)brennen:—*n* Verbrennung *f*; verbrannte Stelle *f*.
burner *n* Brenner *m*.
burning *adj* brennend; glühend.
burrow *n* Bau *m*; Höhle *f*:—*vi* graben; sich vergraben.

bursar n Quästor m; Finanzverwalter m.

burst vi bersten; platzen:—n Platzen n; (Aus)Bruch m; Stoß m.

bury vt vergraben; begraben; beerdigen.

bus n Bus m; Omnibus m.

bush n Busch m, Strauch m; Gebüsch n; Schopf m.

business n Geschäft n; Arbeit f; Unternehmen n; Sache f; Angelegenheit f.

businessman n Geschäftsmann m.

businesswoman n Geschäftsfrau f.

bus-stop n Bushaltestelle f.

bust n Büste f; Busen m.

busy adj beschäftigt; belebt; arbeitsreich.

but conj aber, jedoch; sondern.

butcher n Metzger m, Fleischer m, Schlachter m:—vt (ab)schlachten.

butcher's n Metzgerei f.

butler n Butler m.

butter n Butter f:—vt buttern.

buttercup n Butterblume f.

butterfly n Schmetterling m.

button n Knopf m; Taste f:—vt (zu)knöpfen.

buy vt (ein)kaufen.

buyer n (Ein)Käufer(in) m(f).

buzz n Summen n; Schwirren n:—vi summen; schwirren.

by prep bei; an; neben; durch; nach; von; mit; um.

by-law n Satzung f; Ortsstatut.

bypass n Umgehungsstraße f.

by-product n Nebenprodukt n.

byte n Byte n.

C

cab n Taxi n; Führerhaus n.

cabbage n Kohl m.

cabin n Hütte f; Kabine f.

cabinet n Kabinett n; Schrank m.

cable n Kabel n; Tau n.

cable car n Seilbahn f.

cactus n Kaktus m.

café n Café n.

cafeteria n Cafeteria f; Kantine f.

cage n Käfig m; Förderkorb m.

cake n Kuchen m, Torte f.

calculate vt berechnen; kalkulieren.

calculation n Berechnung f; Kalkulation f.

calculator n Rechner m.

calendar n Kalender m.

calf n Kalb n; Wade f.

call vt (an)rufen; (ein)berufen:—n Ruf m; Anruf m; Berufung f.

calm n Ruhe f; Stille f:—adj ruhig; still:—vt beruhigen; besänftigen.

calorie n Kalorie f.

camel n Kamel n.

camera n Kamera f.

camouflage n Tarnung f; Verschleierung f.

camp n Lager n:—vi kampieren; lagern; zelten.

campaign n Kampagne f; Wahlkampf m.

camping n Zelten n; Camping n.

campsite n Lagerplatz m; Zeltplatz m.

can v aux können:—vt eindosen:—n Kanne f; Dose f.

canal n Kanal m.

cancel vt kündigen.

cancellation n Kündigung f.

cancer, Cancer (astrol) n Krebs m.

candidate n Kandidat(in) m(f); Bewerber(in) m(f).

candle *n* Kerze *f.*

cane *n* Rohr *n*; (Spazier)Stock *m.*

canine *adj* Hunde-; hündisch.

cannabis *n* Cannabis *m*; Haschisch *n.*

cannibal *n* Kannibale *m.*

cannibalism *n* Kannibalismus *m.*

cannon *n* Kanone *f*; Geschütz *n.*

canoe *n* Kanu *n.*

canon *n* Kanon *m.*

canopy *n* Baldachin *m.*

canteen *n* Kantine *f*; Feldflasche *f.*

canter *n* Arbeitsgalopp *m.*

canvas *n* Segeltuch *n*; (Zelt)Leinwand *f.*

canyon *n* Felsschlucht *f.*

cap *n* Mütze *f.*

capable *adj* fähig; tüchtig; imstande.

capacity *n* Kapazität *f*; Fähigkeit *f*; Leistung *f.*

cape *n* Umhang *m*; Cape *n*; Kap *n.*

capital *adj* kapital; Haupt-; groß(artig): —*n* Hauptstadt *f*; Großbuchstabe *m*; Kapital *n.*

capitalism *n* Kapitalismus *m.*

capitalist *n* Kapitalist *m.*

Capricorn *n* (*astrol*) Steinbock *m.*

captain *n* Kapitän *m*; Hauptmann *m.*

capture *n* Gefangennahme *f*:—*vt* gefangennehmen.

car *n* Auto *n*; Wagen *m.*

caravan *n* Karawane *f*; Wohnwagen *m.*

carbon *n* Kohlenstoff *m*; Kohle *f*; Kohlepapier *n.*

card *n* Karte *f.*

care *n* Sorge *f*; Sorgfalt *f*; Pflege *f*:—*vi* sich sorgen.

career *n* Karriere *f*; Beruf *m*:—*vi* rasen, rennen.

careful *adj* vorsichtig; sorgfältig.

careless *adj* unvorsichtig; sorglos.

caress *n* Liebkosung *f*:—*vt* liebkosen; streicheln.

caretaker *n* Hausmeister(in) *m(f).*

car-ferry *n* Autofähre *f.*

cargo *n* Fracht *f*; Ladung *f.*

carnation *n* Nelke *f*; Blaßrot *n.*

carnival *n* Karneval *m*; Fasching *m*; Volksfest *n.*

carol *n* Weihnachtslied *n.*

carpenter *n* Zimmermann *m*; Tischler *m.*

carpentry *n* Zimmerei *f*; Zimmerhandwerk *n.*

carpet *n* Teppich *m.*

carriage *n* Wagen *m*; Kutsche *f*; Transport *m*; Fracht *f.*

carrot *n* Karotte *f*; Möhre *f.*

carry *vi vt* tragen:—~ **on** weitermachen; fortsetzen.

cart *n* Karre *f*; Karren *m*; Wagen *m*:— *vt* karren.

carton *n* Karton *m*; Schachtel *f.*

cartoon *n* Cartoon *m*; Zeichentrickfilm *m.*

carve *vt* schnitzen; tranchieren.

case *n* Kiste *f*; Koffer *m*; Behälter *m*; Gehäuse *n*; Fall *m*; Sache *f*, **in** ~ im Falle.

cash *n* Bargeld *n*:—*vt* einlösen; zu Geld machen.

casino *n* Kasino *n.*

cassette *n* Kassette *f.*

cast *vt* werfen; gießen:—*n* Wurf *m*; Besetzung *f*; Guß *m.*

castle *n* Schloß *n*; Burg *f*; Turm *m.*

casual *adj* zufällig; gelegentlich.

casualty *n* Unfall *m*; Opfer *n.*

cat *n* Katze *f.*

catalogue *n* Katalog *m.*

catastrophe *n* Katastrophe *f.*

catch *vt* (ein)fangen:—*n* Fang *m*; Fangen *n.*

category *n* Kategorie *f.*

caterpillar *n* Raupe *f.*

cathedral *n* Kathedrale *f*; Dom *m.*

catholic *adj* katholisch:—*n* Katholik(in) *m(f).*

Catholicism n Katholizismus m.

cattle n Vieh n.

cauliflower n Blumenkohl m.

cause n Ursache f; Grund m:—vt verursachen.

caution n Vorsicht f; Verwarnung f.

cautious adj vorsichtig; achtsam.

cave n Höhle f.

cavern n Höhle f.

cease vt vi aufhören.

ceasefire n Waffenruhe f.

cedar n Zeder f.

cede vt abtreten; überlassen.

ceiling n Decke f.

celebrate vt feiern.

celebration n Feier f; Verherrlichung f.

celebrity n Berühmtheit f; Ruhm m.

celery n Sellerie m.

cell n Zelle f.

cellar n (Wein)Keller m.

cello n Cello n.

cement n Zement m; Mörtel m; Kitt m.

cemetery n Friedhof m.

censor n Zensor m.

censorship n Zensur f.

centenary n Jahrhundert n; hundertjähriges Jubiläum n.

centre n Zentrum n; Mitte f; Mittelpunkt m; Zentrale f.

centigrade adj Celsius.

centilitre n Zentiliter m.

centimetre n Zentimeter m.

centipede n Hundertfüßer m.

central adj zentral; Haupt-.

century n Jahrhundert n.

ceramic adj keramisch.

ceremony n Zeremonie f.

certain adj sicher; bestimmt; gewiß.

certainty n Sicherheit f; Bestimmtheit f.

certificate n Bescheinigung f; Urkunde f.

certify vt bescheinigen; beglaubigen.

chain n Kette f:—vt (an)ketten.

chair n Stuhl m; Sessel m; Vorsitz m.

chairman n Vorsitzender m.

chalk n Kreide f; Kalk m.

challenge n Herausforderung f:—vt herausfordern.

chamber n Kammer f; Zimmer n.

champagne n Sekt m.

champion n Sieger m; Meister m.

championship n Meisterschaft f.

chance n Chance f; Zufall m:—by ~ zufällig.

chancellor n Kanzler m.

change vt (ver)ändern; wechseln:—vi sich (ver)ändern; wechseln; sich umziehen:—n (Ver)Änderung f; Wechsel m; Wechselgeld n.

channel n Kanal m; Rinne f.

chaos n Chaos n; Durcheinander n.

chaotic adj chaotisch.

chapel n Kapelle f; Gottesdienst m.

chapter n Kapitel n.

character n Charakter m; Figur f; Rolle f; Buchstabe m.

charge vt (be)laden; beauftragen; anklagen; belasten:—n Ladung f; Belastung f; Angriff m; Anklage f.

charity n Nächstenliebe f; Wohltätigkeit f.

charm n Charme m; Zauber m; Talismann m:—vt bezaubern; verzaubern.

charming adj bezaubernd; charmant.

chart n Tabelle f; Karte f; Schaubild n.

charter n Urkunde f; Freibrief m; Charta f; Chartern n:—vt chartern.

chase vt jagen; verfolgen:—n Jagd f; Verfolgung f.

chat vi plaudern:—n Plauderei f; Schwätzchen n.

chatter vi schnattern; klappern:—n Geschnatter n; Klappern n.

cheap adj billig; preiswert; schäbig; ordinär.

cheapen vt verbilligen; herabsetzen.

cheat *vt vi* betrügen:—*n* Betrüger(in) *m*(*f*).

check *vt* überprüfen; kontrollieren; Schach bieten:—*n* Schach *n*; Hindernis *n*; Kontrolle *f*; Karo(muster) *n*.

checkmate *n* Matt *n*.

cheek *n* Wange *f*.

cheekbone *n* Wangenknochen *m*.

cheer *n* Beifall *m*; Aufmunterung *f*:—*vt* Beifall spenden; aufmuntern.

cheerful *adj* fröhlich; freundlich.

cheese *n* Käse *m*.

chef *n* Küchenchef *m*.

chemical *adj* chemisch.

chemist *n* Chemiker(in) *m*(*f*); Apotheker(in) *m*(*f*); Drogist(in) *m*(*f*).

chemistry *n* Chemie *f*.

cheque *n* Scheck *m*.

cherish *vt* (wert)schätzen; in Ehren halten; hegen; zugetan sein.

cherry *n* Kirsche *f*; Kirschrot *n*:—*adj* kirschrot:—~ **tree** *n* Kirschbaum *m*.

chess *n* Schach *n*.

chessboard *n* Schachbrett *n*.

chessman *n* Schachfigur *f*.

chest *n* Truhe *f*; Kiste *f*; Kasten *m*; Brust *f*.

chestnut *n* Kastanie *f*; Kastanienbraun *n*.

chestnut tree *n* Kastanienbaum *m*.

chew *vt* kauen; sinnen.

chewing gum *n* Kaugummi *m*.

chicken *n* Huhn *n*; Hähnchen *n*.

chief *adj* wichtigste(r, s); hauptsächlich; Haupt-; oberste(r, s):—~**ly** *adv* hauptsächlich; vor allem:—*n* Chef *m*; (Ober)Haupt *n*; Häuptling *m*.

child *n* Kind *n*.

childhood *n* Kindheit *f*.

childish *adj* kindisch.

childless *adj* kinderlos.

childlike *adj* kindlich.

chimney *n* Schornstein *m*; Kamin *m*.

chimpanzee *n* Schimpanse *m*.

chin *n* Kinn *n*.

china(ware) *n* Porzellan *n*.

chip *n* Splitter *m*; Schnitzel *n*:—~**s** *npl* Pommes frites *pl*.

chocolate *n* Schokolade *f*; Praline *f*; Schokoladenbraun *n*.

choice *n* (Aus)Wahl *f*; Auslese *f*:—*adj* ausgesucht; wählerisch.

choir *n* Chor *m*.

choke *vt* (er)würgen; ersticken.

choose *vt* (aus)wählen; aussuchen; vorziehen.

chop *vt* (zer)hacken:—*n* Hieb *m*; Schlag *m*; Kotelett *n*.

choral *adj* Chor-.

chord *n* Saite *f*; Akkord *m*.

Christ *n* Christus *m*.

christen *vt* taufen.

christening *n* Taufe *f*.

Christian *adj* christlich:—*n* Christ(in) *m*(*f*):—~ **name** Vorname *m*.

Christianity *n* Christentum *n*; Christenheit *f*.

Christmas *n* Weihnachten *n*.

Christmas Eve *n* Heiligabend *m*.

chronic *adj* chronisch.

chronicle *n* Chronik *f*.

chronology *n* Chronologie *f*.

church *n* Kirche *f*.

cider *n* Apfelwein *m*; Apfelmost *m*.

cigar *n* Zigarre *f*.

cigarette *n* Zigarette *f*.

cinema *n* Kino *n*.

cinnamon *n* Zimt *m*.

circle *n* Kreis *m*.

circuit *n* Kreislauf *m*; Stromkreis *m*.

circular *adj* kreisförmig; rund:—*n* Rundschreiben *n*.

circulate *vi* im Umlauf sein; kursieren; kreisen.

circulation *n* Zirkulation *f*; Kreislauf *m*; Umlauf *m*.

circumstance n Umstand m; Sachverhalt m:—~s pl Verhältnisse npl.

circus n Zirkus m.

citizen n Bürger(in) m(f).

city n (Groß)Stadt f.

civil adj staatlich; Bürger-; bürgerlich; zivil(rechtlich).

civilian n Zivilist m.

civilization n Zivilisation f.

civilize vt zivilisieren.

claim vt fordern; beanspruchen; in Anspruch nehmen; behaupten:—n Forderung f; Anspruch m; Behauptung f.

clam n Muschel f.

clamber vi klettern.

clap vt klatschen; schlagen; klopfen.

clarification n Klärung f.

clarify vt (er)klären; klarstellen.

clarinet n Klarinette f.

clarity n Klarheit f.

clash vi klirren; zusammenstoßen:—n Geklirr n; Zusammenstoß m.

class n Klasse f; Kurs m:—vt klassifizieren.

classic(al) adj klassisch; erstklassig:—n Klassiker m.

classification n Klassifikation f.

classify vt klassifizieren.

classroom n Klassenzimmer n.

clause n Klausel f; Abschnitt m; Satz m.

claw n Klaue f; Kralle f:—vt (zer)-kratzen; krallen; packen.

clay n Lehm m; Ton m.

clean adj sauber; rein:—vt reinigen; säubern.

cleaner n Reinigung f; Reinigungsmittel n; Raumpfleger(in) m(f).

clear adj klar; hell:—vt (auf)klären; (weg)räumen:—vi sich klären; sich aufhellen.

clef n (Noten)Schlüssel m.

clever adj klug.

click vt klicken; schnalzen:—vi klikken; schnalzen; zuschnappen.

client n Kunde m, Kundin f; Klient(in) m(f).

cliff n Klippe f; Felswand f.

climate n Klima n.

climax n Höhepunkt m.

climb vt erklettern; besteigen:—vi klettern; steigen.

clinic n Klinik f.

clip vt (be)schneiden:—n Klammer f; Schur f.

cloak n Umhang m; (Deck)Mantel m.

cloakroom n Garderobe f.

clock n Uhr f.

close vt vi schließen:—adj dicht; eng:—adv nahe.

closed adj geschlossen.

cloth n Tuch n.

clothe vt kleiden; einhüllen.

clothing n Kleidung f.

cloud n Wolke f.

cloudy adj bewölkt; Wolken-.

clover n Klee m.

clown n Clown m.

club n Keule f; Knüppel m; Schläger m; Klub m.

clue n Hinweis m; Anhaltspunkt m.

clumsy adj ungeschickt; unbeholfen.

coach n Reisebus m; Kutsche f; Trainer m; Nachhilfelehrer m:—vt trainieren.

coal n Kohle f.

coalmine n Kohlenbergwerk n.

coarse adj grob.

coast n Küste f.

coastal adj Küsten-.

coat n Mantel m; Schicht f:—vt beschichten.

coax vt überreden.

cobweb n Spinnwebe f.

cock n Hahn m.

cocktail n Cocktail m.

cocoa n Kakao m.
coconut n Kokosnuß f.
cocoon n Kokon m.
cod n Kabeljau m.
coffee n Kaffee m.
coffeepot n Kaffeekanne f.
coffin n Sarg m.
cog n Zahnrad n.
coil n Rolle f; Spirale f.
coin n Münze f:—vt münzen; prägen.
coincide vi zusammentreffen.
cold adj kalt; kühl:—n Kälte f; Erkältung f.
collaborate vt zusammenarbeiten; kollaborieren.
collaboration n Zusammenarbeit f; Kollaboration f.
collapse vi zusammenbrechen:—n Zusammenbruch m.
collar n Kragen m.
colleague n Kollege m, Kollegin f; Mitarbeiter(in) m(f).
collect vt (ein)sammeln; abholen; versammeln.
collection n (An)Sammlung f; Kollektion f.
collide vi kollidieren; zusammenstoßen.
collision n Zusammenstoß m; Kollision f.
colloquial adj umgangssprachlich.
colon n Doppelpunkt m.
colonel n Oberst m.
colony n Kolonie f; Siedlung f.
colossal adj kolossal; riesig.
colour n Farbe f.
colourful adj farbenprächtig; bunt.
colt n Fohlen n.
column n Spalte f; Kolonne f.
comb n Kamm m; Wabe f; Striegel m: —vt (durch)kämmen; striegeln.
combat n Kampf m; Gefecht n:—vt (be)kämpfen.

combination n Kombination f; Verbindung f; Vereinigung f.
combine vt verbinden; kombinieren: —vi sich vereinigen; sich verbünden.
come vi kommen.
comedy n Komödie f.
comet n Komet m.
comfortable adj bequem.
comic(al) adj komisch.
comma n (gr) Komma n.
command vt befehlen beherrschen:— n Befehl m; Beherrschung f.
commander n Befehlshaber m; Kommandant m.
commemorate vt gedenken; feiern; erinnern an.
commemoration n Gedenkfeier f; Gedenken n.
commence vt vi beginnen; anfangen.
comment n Kommentar m; Bemerkung f:—vt bemerken:—vi kommentieren.
commentary n Kommentar m.
commerce n Handel m; Verkehr m.
commercial adj Handels-; kommerziell.
commission n Auftrag m; Provision f: —vt beauftragen.
commit vt anvertrauen; verpflichten.
commitment n Verpflichtung f; Überantwortung f.
committee n Komitee n; Ausschuß m.
common adj gemeinsam; all(gemein): —n Gemeinsamkeit f; Gemeindeland n.
communicate vt mitteilen; übertragen:—vi kommunizieren.
communication n Kommunikation f; Mitteilung f.
communism n Kommunismus m.
communist n Kommunist(in) m(f).
community n Gemeinschaft f.
compact adj kompakt.
compact disc n Compact Disc f.

companion n Begleiter(in) m(f).
company n Gesellschaft f; Firma f.
comparable adj vergleichbar.
compare vt vergleichen.
comparison n Vergleich m.
compartment n Abteil n; Abteilung f.
compassion n Mitleid n; Mitgefühl n.
compassionate adj mitfühlend; mitleidig.
compel vt (er)zwingen; (ab)nötigen.
compensate vt entschädigen.
compensation n Entschädigung f.
compete vi in Wettbewerb treten; konkurrieren.
competence n Kompetenz f; Fähigkeit f.
competent adj fähig; fachkundig; gekonnt.
competition n Wettbewerb m; Konkurrenz f.
competitive adj konkurrierend; Wettbewerbs-.
competitor n Mitbewerber(in) m(f); Konkurrent(in) m(f).
compile vt zusammenstellen; kompilieren.
complain vi sich beschweren; klagen; beanstanden.
complaint n Beschwerde(n) f(pl); Klage f; Reklamation f.
complete adj vollständig; völlig:—vt vollenden.
completion n Beendigung f; Vervollständigung f.
complex adj komplex; vielschichtig.
complicate vt komplizieren.
complicated adj kompliziert.
compliment n Kompliment n; Lob n:
—vt ein Kompliment machen.
complimentary adj Höflichkeits-; Frei-; Gratis-.
compose vt zusammensetzen; verfassen.
composer n Komponist(in) m(f).

composition n Komposition f; Zusammensetzung f.
comprehensive adj umfassend.
compress vt zusammenpressen.
compulsion n Zwang m.
compulsory adj Zwangs-; obligatorisch.
computer n Computer m.
conceal vt verbergen.
conceit n Einbildung f; Selbstgefälligkeit f.
conceited adj eingebildet; selbstgefällig.
conceive vt sich vorstellen; ausdenken:—vi schwanger werden; trächtig werden.
concentrate vt konzentrieren.
concentration n Konzentration f.
concept n Vorstellung f; Begriff m.
concern vt betreffen; beunruhigen; beschäftigen:—n Angelegenheit f.
concerning prep betreffend; hinsichtlich.
concert n Konzert n.
concerto n Konzert n.
concise adj kurz; bündig; knapp.
conclude vt beenden; (ab)schließen; entscheiden.
conclusion n (Ab)Schluß m; Ende n; Entscheidung f.
concrete n Beton m.
condemn vt verurteilen; verdammen; verwerfen.
condense vt kondensieren; kürzen; zusammenfassen.
condition n Bedingung f; Abmachung f; Zustand m; Lage f.
conditional adj bedingt; abhängig; konditional.
condom n Kondom n.
conduct n (Durch)Führung f:—vt (durch)führen.
conductor n Schaffner m; Dirigent m.

cone *n* Kegel *m*; Zapfen *m*.

confer *vi* sich beraten:—*vt* verleihen; erteilen.

conference *n* Konferenz *f*; Besprechung *f*.

confess *vt vi* gestehen; zugeben.

confession *n* Geständnis *n*.

confidence *n* Vertrauen *n*; Selbstbewußtsein *n*.

confident *adj* gewiß; (selbst)sicher; zuversichtlich.

confidential *adj* vertraulich; Vertrauens-.

confine *vt* begrenzen; beschränken; einsperren.

confirm *vt* bestätigen; festigen.

confirmation *n* Bestätigung *f*; Festigung *f*.

conflict *n* Konflikt *m*; Kampf *m*.

conform *vt vi* (sich) anpassen; übereinstimmen.

confuse *vt* verwechseln; verwirren.

confusing *adj* verwirrend.

confusion *n* Verwirrung *f*; Verwechslung *f*.

congested *adj* überfüllt; verstopft.

congestion *n* Stauung *f*; Stockung *f*; Andrang *m*.

congratulate *vt* gratulieren; beglückwünschen.

congratulation *n* Glückwunsch *m*.

congregate *vt* (sich) (ver)sammeln.

congregation *n* Versammlung *f*.

congress *n* Kongreß *m*.

conjugate *vt* (*gr*) konjugieren.

conjugation *n* Konjugation *f*.

conjunction *n* Verbindung *f*; Konjunktion *f*.

connect *vt* verbinden; verknüpfen.

connection *n* Verbindung *f*; Zusammenhang *m*.

connoisseur *n* Kenner *m*.

conquer *vt* erobern; besiegen; unterwerfen; überwinden.

conqueror *n* Eroberer *m*; Sieger *m*.

conquest *n* Eroberung *f*; Überwindung *f*; Bezwingung *f*.

conscience *n* Gewissen *n*.

conscientious *adj* gewissenhaft; Gewissens-.

conscious *adj* bewußt; bei Bewußtsein.

consciousness *n* Bewußtsein *n*.

consent *n* Zustimmung *f*; Einwilligung *f*:—*vi* zustimmen; einwilligen.

consequence *n* Folge *f*; Konsequenz *f*; Bedeutung *f*; Einfluß *m*.

consequent *adj* (nach)folgend; konsequent:—**~ly** *adv* in der Folge; folglich.

conservation *n* Naturschutz *m*; Umweltschutz *m*; Konservieren *n*.

conserve *vt* erhalten; bewahren; einmachen:—*n* Eingemachtes *n*.

consider *vt vi* nachdenken.

considerable *adj* beachtlich; beträchtlich; ansehnlich; erheblich.

considerate *adj* rücksichtsvoll; aufmerksam; taktvoll; besonnen.

consideration *n* Erwägung *f*; Überlegung *f*; Berücksichtigung *f*.

consist *vi* bestehen; vereinbar sein.

consistent *adj* konsequent; übereinstimmend; konsistent.

consolation *n* Trost *m*.

console *vt* trösten.

consolidate *vt vi* (ver)stärken; konsolidieren.

consolidation *n* (Ver)Stärkung *f*; Konsolidierung *f*.

consonant *n* (*gr*) Konsonant *m*.

conspicuous *adj* deutlich sichtbar; auffällig; bemerkenswert.

conspiracy *n* Verschwörung *f*.

conspirator *n* Verschwörer *m*.

conspire *vi* sich verschwören; ein Komplott schmieden.

constant *adj* (be)ständig; standhaft; konstant.

constituency n Wählerschaft f; Wahlkreis m.

constituent n Bestandteil m; Wähler(in) m(f).

constitute vt ernennen; erlassen; gründen; darstellen.

construct vt errichten; bauen; konstruieren.

construction n Konstruktion f; Bau m; Bauwerk n; Auslegung f.

consul n Konsul m.

consult vt um Rat fragen; konsultieren.

consume vt zerstören; verzehren:—vi (dahin)schwinden.

consumer n Verbraucher(in) m(f).

contact n Kontakt m; Kontaktperson f; Berührung f; Verbindung f.

contain vt enthalten; umfassen; zügeln; in Schach halten; eindämmen.

container n Behälter m; Container m.

contaminate vt verunreinigen; infizieren; vergiften; verseuchen.

contemplate vt betrachten.

contemplation n Betrachtung f.

contemporary adj zeitgenössisch; gleichzeitig; gleichaltrig.

contempt n Verachtung f; Mißachtung f; Schande f.

contemptible adj verächtlich; verachtenswert; gemein.

content adj zufrieden; bereit:—n Zufriedenheit f; Inhalt m.

contest vt kämpfen um; bestreiten:—n (Wett)Kampf m; (Wett)Streit m.

contestant n Wettkämpfer(in) m(f).

context n Zusammenhang m; Umgebung f.

continent n Kontinent m.

continental adj kontinental.

continual adj fortwährend.

continuation n Fortsetzung f.

continue vt fortsetzen:—vi fortfahren.

continuity n Kontinuität f.

continuous adj ununterbrochen; (an)dauernd; kontinuierlich.

contour n Kontur f; Umriß m.

contraception n Empfängnisverhütung f.

contraceptive n empfängnisverhütendes Mittel n:—adj empfängnisverhütend.

contract vt zusammenziehen:—vi sich zusammenziehen; (ein)schrumpfen; einen Vertrag schließen:—n Vertrag m.

contractor n Unternehmer m; Lieferant m.

contradict vt widersprechen.

contradiction n Widerspruch m.

contradictory adj widersprechend.

contrary adj widersprechend; gegensätzlich; widrig:—n Gegenteil n; on the ~ im Gegenteil.

contrast n Kontrast m:—vt kontrastieren.

contrasting adj kontrastierend.

contribute vt beitragen.

contribution n Beitrag m.

control n Beherrschung f; Kontrolle f:—vt beherrschen; kontrollieren.

controversial adj umstritten; kontrovers.

controversy n Kontroverse f; Streit m.

convenience n Bequemlichkeit f.

convenient adj bequem; praktisch; günstig.

conventional adj konventionell.

conversation n Unterhaltung f; Gespräch n.

converse vi sich unterhalten; srechen.

conversion n Umwandlung f; Umbau m; Umstellung f.

convert vt umwandeln:—n Bekehrte(r) f(m); Konvertit(in) m(f).

convertible adj umwandelbar.

convict vt für schuldig erklären; verurteilen:—*n* Strafgefangene(r) *f(m)*; Verurteilte(r) *f(m)*.

conviction *n* Schuldspruch *m*; Verurteilung *f*; Überzeugung *f*.

convince *vt* überzeugen.

convincing *adj* überzeugend.

cook *n* Koch *m*, Köchin *f*:—*vt vi* kochen.

cooker *n* Herd *m*; Kocher *m*; Kochfrucht *f*.

cookery *n* Kochen *n*; Kochkunst *f*.

cool *adj* kühl; frisch.

cooperate *vi* zusammenarbeiten; mitwirken.

cooperation *n* Zusammenarbeit *f*; Mitarbeit *f*.

coordinate *vt* koordinieren.

coordination *n* Koordination *f*.

cope *vi* fertig werden; gewachsen sein; bewältigen.

copier *n* Kopierer *m*.

copper *n* Kupfer(rot) *n*.

copy *n* Kopie *f*; Abschrift *f*; Exemplar *n*:—*vt* kopieren; abschreiben; nachahmen.

copyright *n* Urheberrecht *n*.

core *n* Kern *m*; Kerngehäuse *n*; Innerste *n*; Herz *n*.

cork *n* Kork(en) *m*.

corkscrew *n* Korkenzieher *m*.

corn *n* Korn *n*.

corner *n* Ecke *f*.

coronation *n* Krönung *f*.

corporation *n* Körperschaft *f*; (Aktien)Gesellschaft *f*.

corpse *n* Leiche *f*.

correct *vt* korrigieren:—*adj* korrekt; richtig; genau.

correction *n* Korrektur *f*.

correspond *vi* korrespondieren; entsprechen.

correspondence *n* Korrespondenz *f*; Entsprechung *f*.

correspondent *n* Korrespondent(in) *m(f)*.

corridor *n* Flur *m*; Korridor *m*; Gang *m*.

corrupt *vt vi* verderben:—*adj* korrupt; bestechlich; verderbt.

corruption *n* Korruption *f*; Bestechlichkeit *f*; Verderbtheit *f*.

cosmetic *adj* kosmetisch; Schönheits-: —*n* Kosmetik *f*; Schönheitsmittel *n*.

cosmic *adj* kosmisch.

cost *n* Kosten *pl*; Preis *m*:—*vi* kosten.

costly *adj* kostspielig; teuer.

costume *n* Kostüm *n*; Kleidung *f*.

cosy *adj* gemütlich.

cottage *n* kleines Landhaus *n*; Hütte *f*.

cotton *n* Baumwolle *f*.

couch *n* Sofa *n*; Liege *f*.

cough *n* Husten *m*:—*vi* husten.

count *vt* zählen; (be)rechnen:—*n* Graf *m*; Zählung *f*; (Be)Rechnung *f*.

counter *n* Ladentisch *m*; Schalter *m*; Zähler *m*.

countess *n* Gräfin *f*; Komteß *f*.

country *n* Land *n*.

couple *n* Paar *n*; Koppel *f*; Verbindungsglied *n*.

courage *n* Mut *m*; Tapferkeit *f*.

courageous *adj* mutig; beherzt; tapfer.

course *n* Kurs *m*; Lauf *m*; Weg *m*; Richtung *f*:—**of** ~ selbstverständlich; natürlich.

court *n* Hof *m*; Gericht *n*.

courteous *adj* höflich.

courtesy *n* Höflichkeit *f*.

courtroom *n* Gerichtssaal *m*.

cóusin *n* Cousin(e) *m(f)*, Vetter *m*, Base *f*.

cover *n* Decke *f*:—*vt* bedecken.

cow *n* Kuh *f*.

coward *n* Feigling *m*.

cowardice *n* Feigheit *f*.

cowardly *adj* feig(e).

cowboy *n* Cowboy *m*.

coy *adj* schüchtern; scheu; spröde.
crab *n* Krabbe *f*; Krebs *m*.
crack *n* Knall *m*; Schlag *m*:—*vt vi* knallen; knacken.
cradle *n* Wiege *f*.
craft *n* Gewerbe *n*; Handwerk *n*; Kunst (fertigkeit) *f*; Schiff *n*; Flugzeug *n*.
crafty *adj* schlau; verschlagen.
crane *n* Kran *m*; (*zool*) Kranich *m*.
crash *n* Krach *m*; *vi* (zusammen) krachen .
crass *adj* grob; krass; derb.
crate *n* Kiste *f*; Kasten *m*.
crater *n* Krater *m*.
crawl *vi* kriechen; krabbeln.
crazy *adj* verrückt; wahnsinnig.
creak *vi* knarren; quietschen.
cream *n* Sahne *f*; Creme *f*.
crease *n* Falte *f*; Kniff *m*:—*vt* falten; kniffen.
create *vt* (er)schaffen.
creation *n* Schöpfung *f*; (Er)Schaffung *f*.
creative *adj* schöpferisch; kreativ.
creator *n* Schöpfer *m*.
creature *n* Kreatur *f*; Geschöpf *n*.
credibility *n* Glaubwürdigkeit *f*.
credible *adj* glaubwürdig.
credit *n* Kredit *m*; (Gut)Haben *n*.
creditor *n* Gläubiger *m*.
creep *vi* kriechen; schleichen; kribbeln.
cremate *vt* (Leichen) verbrennen; einäschern.
cremation *n* (Leichen)Verbrennung *f*; Einäscherung *f*.
crematorium *n* Krematorium *n*.
crescent *n* Halbmond *m*; Mondsichel *f*.
cress *n* Kresse *f*.
crest *n* Kamm *m*; Mähne *f*.
crew *n* Mannschaft *f*.
cricket *n* Grille *f*; Kricket *n*.
crime *n* Verbrechen *n*; Straftat *f*; Frevel *m*.

criminal *adj* kriminell; verbrecherisch; strafrechtlich; Straf-:—*n* Kriminelle (r) *f(m)*; Verbrecher(in) *m(f)*.
cripple *n* Krüppel *m*:—*vt* lähmen.
crippled *adj* verkrüppelt; gelähmt.
crisis *n* Krise *f*.
crisp *adj* knusprig; kraus.
criterion *n* Kriterium *n*; Maßstab *m*.
critic *n* Kritiker(in) *m(f)*; Rezensent(in) *m(f)*.
critical *adj* kritisch.
criticism *n* Kritik *f*.
criticize *vt* kritisieren; rezensieren.
croak *vi* quaken; krächzen.
crockery *n* Geschirr *n*; Töpferware *f*.
crocodile *n* Krokodil *m*.
crooked *adj* krumm; gewunden; unehrlich.
crop *n* (Feld)Frucht *f*; Ernte *f*.
cross *n* Kreuz(zeichen) *n*:—*adj* ärgerlich; entgegengesetzt; quer:—*vt* kreuzen; überqueren.
crossing *n* Kreuzung *f*.
crow *n* Krähe *f*; Krähen *n*.
crowd *n* Menge *f*; Masse *f*; Haufen *m*: —*vt* zusammendrängen; hineinstopfen; bevölkern:—*vi* sich drängen.
crown *n* Krone *f*; Kranz *m*; Scheitel(punkt) *m*; Kopf *m*; Gipfel *m*:—*vt* krönen; überkronen.
crucial *adj* kritisch; entscheidend.
crude *adj* roh; grob.
cruel *adj* grausam.
cruelty *n* Grausamkeit *f*.
cruise *n* Kreuzfahrt *f*.
crumb *n* Krümel *m*; Brösel *m*.
crumble *vt* zerkrümeln; zerbröckeln: —*vi* zerbröckeln; zerfallen.
crusade *n* Kreuzzug *m*.
crush *vt* (zer)quetschen; (zer)drücken: —*n* (zermalmender) Druck *m*; Gedränge *n*; Schwärmerei *f*.
crust *n* Kruste *f*; Rinde *f*.

cry *vt vi* schreien; rufen; weinen:—*n* Schrei *m*; Ruf *m*; Geschrei *n*.
crypt *n* Krypta *f*.
crystal *n* Kristall *m/n*.
cub *n* Junge *n*; Bengel *m*; Anfänger *m*.
cube *n* Würfel *m*.
cubic *adj* Kubik-; kubisch.
cuckoo *n* Kuckuck *m*.
cucumber *n* Gurke *f*.
cuddle *vt vi* schmusen:—*n* enge Umarmung *f*.
cult *n* Kult *m*; Sekte *f*.
cultivate *vi* kultivieren.
cultivation *n* Kultivierung *f*.
cultural *adj* kulturell; Kultur-.
culture *n* Kultur *f*.
cunning *adj* geschickt; schlau.
cup *n* Tasse *f*.
cupboard *n* Schrank *m*.
cure *n* Kur *f*; Heilung *f*:—*vt* heilen; kurieren.
curiosity *n* Neugier *f*.
curious *adj* neugierig.
curl *n* Locke *f*:—*vi* sich locken.
currant *n* Korinthe *f*; Johannisbeere *f*.
currency *n* Währung *f*; Umlauf *m*.
current *adj* (um)laufend; gegenwärtig; aktuell:—*n* Strom *m*; Strömung *f*.
currently *adv* gegenwärtig; flüssig.
curry *n* Curry *m, n*.

curse *vt* verfluchen:—*vi* fluchen:—*n* Fluch *m*.
curt *adj* kurz (angebunden); knapp; barsch.
curtail *vt* beschneiden; (ab)kürzen; einschränken.
curtain *n* Gardine *f*; Vorhang *m*.
curve *vt* biegen; krümmen:—*n* Kurve *f*; Krümmung *f*; Biegung *f*.
cushion *n* Kissen *n*; Polster *n*; Bande *f*.
custom *n* Brauch *m*; Sitte *f*; Kundschaft *f*.
customary *adj* üblich; gebräuchlich; gewohnt.
customer *n* Kunde *m*; Kundin *f*.
customs *npl* Zoll *m*.
customs officer *n* Zollbeamter *m*.
cut *vt vi* schneiden:—*n* Schnitt *m*.
cutlery *n* Besteck *n*.
cyanide *n* Zyanid *n*.
cycle *n* Zyklus *m*; Kreis(lauf) *m*; Periode *f*; Fahrrad *n*:—*vi* radfahren.
cyclist *n* Radfahrer(in) *m(f)*.
cyclone *n* Zyklon *m*.
cygnet *n* junger Schwan *m*.
cylinder *n* Zylinder *m*; Walze *f*; Trommel *f*.
cylindrical *adj* zylindrisch.
cynical *adj* zynisch.
cynicism *n* Zynismus *m*.
cypress *n* Zypresse *f*.

D

daffodil *n* Narzisse *f*; Osterglocke *f*.
dagger *n* Dolch *m*.
daily *adj adv* (all)täglich.
dairy *n* Molkerei *f*.
daisy *n* Gänseblümchen *n*; Margerite *f*.
damage *n* Schaden(ersatz) *m*; Verlust *m*:—*vt* (be)schädigen.

dame *n* Freifrau *f*.
damn *vt* verdammen.
damp *adj* feucht; klamm.
dampen *vt* befeuchten.
dance *n* Tanz *m*:—*vi* tanzen.
dancer *n* Tänzer(in) *m(f)*.
dandelion *n* Löwenzahn *m*.

danger n Gefahr f.
dangerous adj gefährlich.
dare vt vi wagen.
dark adj dunkel; finster.
darken vt verdunkeln:—vi sich ver-dunkeln.
darkness n Dunkelheit f; Finsternis f.
darling n Liebling m.
dash vi stürmen; stürzen:—n Schlag m; Schuß m.
data n Daten pl.
database n Datenbank f.
date n Datum n; Dattel f.
daughter n Tochter f.
daughter-in-law Schwiegertochter f.
dawn n (Morgen)Dämmerung f; (Ta-ges)Anbruch m.
day n Tag m.
daze vt betäuben; verwirren.
dazzle vt blenden.
dazzling adj blendend.
dead adj tot.
deadly adj tödlich; Todes-.
deaf adj taub.
deal n Geschäft n; vi handeln.
dealer n Händler(in) m(f).
dear adj lieb; teuer.
death n Tod m.
debate n Debatte f:—vt debattieren.
debit n Soll n; (Konto)Belastung f:—vt belasten.
debt n Schuld f; Forderung f.
debtor n Schuldner(in) m(f).
decade n Jahrzehnt n.
decadence n Dekadenz f; Verfall m.
decanter n Karaffe f.
decay vi verfallen:—n Verfall m.
deceit n Betrug m.
deceitful adj betrügerisch.
deceive vt (be)trügen.
December n Dezember m.
decency n Anstand m; Anständigkeit f.
decent adj anständig.

deceptive adj (be)trügerisch.
decide vt vi (sich) entscheiden.
decision n Entscheidung f.
deck n Deck n; (Karten)Spiel n.
declaration n (Zoll)Erklärung f
declare vt erklären; verkünden.
decline vt neigen:—vi sich neigen:—n Abhang m.
decor n Dekor n.
decorate vt schmücken.
decoration n Verzierung f; Schmuck m.
decrease vt vermindern:—n Vermin-derung f.
dedicate vt widmen.
dedication n Widmung f.
deduce vt folgern; schließen.
deduct vt abziehen; absetzen.
deduction n Abzug m; Subtraktion f.
deed n Tat f; Handlung f; Urkunde f.
deep adj tief.
deepen vt vertiefen.
deer n Hirsch m; Rotwild n; Reh n.
defeat n Niederlage f:—vt besiegen; (nieder)schlagen.
defect n Defekt m; Fehler m; Mangel m.
defection n Abfall m; Überlaufen n.
defence n Verteidigung f; Schutz m.
defend vt verteidigen; schützen.
defer vt verschieben; (ver)zögern.
defiance n Trotz m; Herausforderung f.
defiant adj trotzig; herausfordernd.
deficiency n Mangel m; Unzulän-glichkeit f.
deficient adj unzulänglich; mangel-haft; fehlend.
deficit n Defizit n; Mangel m; Verlust m.
define vt definieren; bestimmen.
definite adj bestimmt; festgelegt.
definition n Definition f.
definitive adj definitiv; endgültig.

defuse *vt* entschärfen.

defy *n* trotzen; herausfordern.

degree *n* Grad *m*; Rang *m*; Stufe *f*; (Aus)Maß *n*.

deity *n* Gottheit *f*.

delay *vt* verzögern:—*n* Verzögerung *f*.

delegate *vt* delegieren:—*n* Delegierte(r) *f(m)*.

delegation *n* Delegation *f*.

deliberate *adj* absichtlich.

delicate *adj* zart; fein(fühlig).

delicious *adj* köstlich.

delight *n* Entzücken *n*:—*vt* entzücken.

delighted *adj* entzückt.

delightful *adj* entzückend; köstlich.

deliver *vt* (aus)liefern.

delivery *n* (Aus)Lieferung *f*.

demand *n* (An)Forderung *f*; Verlangen *n*; Nachfrage *f*:—*vt* (er)fordern; verlangen.

democracy *n* Demokratie *f*.

democrat *n* Demokrat(in) *m(f)*.

democratic *adj* demokratisch.

demolish *vt* demolieren.

demolition *n* Demolierung *f*.

demonstrate *vt* beweisen:—*vi* demonstrieren.

demonstration *n* Demonstration *f*.

dense *adj* dicht.

density *n* Dichte *f*.

dental *adj* Zahn-; zahnärztlich.

dentist *n* Zahnarzt *m*, Zahnärztin *f*.

dentistry *n* Zahnmedizin *f*.

deny *vt* (ver)leugnen.

depart *vi* fortgehen; abreisen; abfahren.

department *n* Abteilung *f*.

department store *n* Kaufhaus *n*.

departure *n* Abreise *f*; Abfahrt *f*; Abflug *m*.

depend *vi*:—~ **on** sich verlassen auf.

dependent *adj* abhängig; angewiesen; bedingt; vertrauend.

depict *vt* darstellen.

deposit *vt* (hinter)legen; deponieren:—*n* Anzahlung *f*; Pfand *n*.

depot *n* Depot *n*; Lagerhaus *n*.

depress *vt* deprimieren; (be)drücken.

depressed *adj* deprimiert; nieder-geschlagen.

depression *n* Depression *f*; Niedergeschlagenheit *f*.

depth *n* Tiefe *f*.

derive *vt* herleiten.

descend *vi* herabsteigen; hinuntergehen; niedergehen.

descendant *n* Nachkomme *m*; Deszendent *m*.

descent *n* Abstieg *m*; Niedergang *m*.

describe *vt* beschreiben.

description *n* Beschreibung *f*.

descriptive *adj* beschreibend.

desert *n* Wüste *f*; Ödland *n*.

deserve *vt* verdienen.

design *vt* gestalten:—*n* Design *n*; Gestaltung *f*; Konstruktion *f*.

designer *n* Designer(in) *m(f)*; Konstrukteur *m*.

desire *n* Wunsch *m*:—*vt* wünschen.

desk *n* Schreibtisch *m*; Pult *n*.

despair *n* Verzweiflung *f*:—*vi* verzweifeln.

desperate *adj* verzweifelt; hoffnungslos.

despise *vt* verachten.

despite *prep* trotz.

dessert *n* Nachtisch *m*; Dessert *n*.

destination *n* Bestimmungsort *m*; Ziel *n*.

destiny *n* Schicksal *n*.

destroy *vt* zerstören; vernichten.

destruction *n* Zerstörung *f*; Vernichtung *f*.

destructive *adj* zerstörend; vernichtend.

detail *n* Detail *n*; Einzelheit *f*:—**in** ~ detailliert.

detective n Detektiv(in) m(f).
deter vt abschrecken; abhalten.
deteriorate vt verschlechtern; (ver)mindern.
deterioration n Verschlechterung f; Wertminderung f.
determination n Feststellung f.
determine vt feststellen.
determined adj entschlossen.
detest vt verabscheuen; hassen.
detonate vi detonieren.
detonation n Detonation f.
detour n Umweg m.
develop vt entwickeln.
development n Entwicklung f.
deviate vi abweichen.
deviation n Abweichung f.
devil n Teufel m.
devote vt weihen.
devoted adj ergeben.
devotion n Ergebenheit f.
devour vt verschlingen; vernichten.
devout adj fromm; andächtig; innig.
dew n Tau m.
diabetic n Diabetiker(in) m(f).
diagnosis n Diagnose f.
diagonal adj diagonal:—n Diagonale f.
diagram n Diagramm n.
dial n Zifferblatt n; Wählscheibe f.
dialect n Dialekt m; Mundart f.
diameter n Durchmesser m.
diamond n Diamant m; Karo n.
diarrhoea n Durchfall m.
diary n Tagebuch n.
dictate vt diktieren:—n Diktat n.
dictation n Diktat n.
dictatorship n Diktatur f.
dictionary n Wörterbuch n.
die vi sterben:—n Würfel m.
diesel n Diesel m.
diet n Diät f; Ernährung f; Kost f:—vi Diät halten.
differ vi sich unterscheiden.

difference n Unterschied m.
different adj verschieden; anders:—
~ly adv verschieden; unterschiedlich.
differentiate vt differenzieren.
difficult adj schwierig; schwer.
difficulty n Schwierigkeit f.
diffidence n Schüchternheit f.
diffident adj schüchtern.
dig vt (ein)graben:—n (Aus)Grabung f.
digest vt verdauen.
digestion n Verdauung f.
digit n Finger m; Zehe f; Ziffer f.
digital adj digital; Finger-.
dignity n Würde f.
diligent adj fleißig.
dim adj (halb)dunkel; trüb:—vt verdunkeln; trüben.
diminish vt vermindern:—vi sich vermindern.
diminution n (Ver)Minderung f.
din n Lärm m; Getöse n.
dine vi speisen.
dinner n Abendessen n.
dinosaur n Dinosaurier m.
dip vt (ein)tauchen; (ein)tunken.
diploma n Diplom n; Urkunde f.
diplomacy n Diplomatie f.
diplomat n Diplomat m.
diplomatic adj diplomatisch.
direct adj direkt; gerade; unmittelbar.
direction n Richtung f.
director n Direktor m; Regisseur m.
dirt n Schmutz m.
dirty adj schmutzig.
disadvantage n Nachteil m.
disadvantageous adj nachteilig.
disagreement n Unstimmigkeit f.
disappear vi verschwinden.
disappearance n Verschwinden n.
disappoint vt enttäuschen.
disappointed adj enttäuscht.
disappointing adj enttäuschend.
disappointment n Enttäuschung f.

disaster *n* Katastrophe *f*.
disastrous *adj* katastrophal.
discern *vt* erkennen;n.
discipline *n* Disziplin *f*:—*vt* disziplinieren.
disco *n* Disko *f*.
discount *n* Preisnachlaß *m*; Skonto *n*; Abzug *m*.
discover *vt* entdecken.
discovery *n* Entdeckung *f*.
discreet *adj* diskret.
discriminate *vt* diskriminieren.
discrimination *n* Diskriminierung *f*.
discuss *vt* diskutieren.
discussion *n* Diskussion *f*.
disease *n* Krankheit *f*.
disgrace *n* Schande *f*.
disgraceful *adj* schändlich.
disguise *vt* verkleiden:—*n* Verkleidung *f*.
disgust *n* Ekel *m*:—*vt* (an)ekeln.
disgusting *adj* ekelhaft.
dish *n* (Servier)Platte *f*; Gericht *n*.
dishonest *adj* unehrlich.
dishonesty *n* Unehrlichkeit *f*.
dishonour *n* Unehre *f*.
disillusion *vt* Ernüchterung *f*.
disillusioned *adj* ernüchtert.
disk *n* Scheibe *f*; (Schall)Platte *f*.
diskette *n* Diskette *f*.
dismantle *vt* demontieren; abbauen.
dismay *n* Entsetzen *f*; Bestürzung *f*.
dismiss *vt* entlassen; fortschicken.
disorder *n* Unordnung *f*; Durcheinander *n*.
dispatch *vt* (ab)senden:—*n* (Ab)Sendung *f*.
dispel *vt* zerstreuen.
display *vt* ausbreiten; (her)zeigen:—*n* (Her)Zeigen *n*; Ausstellung *f*.
dispute *n* Streit *m*:—*vt* streiten über.
disrupt *vt* unterbrechen.
disruption *n* Unterbrechung *f*.

dissolve *vt* (auf)lösen; schmelzen:—*vi* sich auflösen.
distance *n* Entfernung *f*.
distant *adj* entfernt.
distinct *adj* deutlich.
distinction *n* Unterschied *m*; Unterscheidung *f*; Auszeichnung *f*.
distinctive *adj* Unterscheidungs-.
distinguish *vt* unterscheiden; ausmachen; auszeichnen.
distract *vt* ablenken.
distraction *n* Ablenkung *f*.
distress *n* Qual *f*; Elend *n*:—*vt* quälen; bedrücken.
distressing *adj* quälend; bedrückend.
distribute *vt* verteilen; verbreiten.
distribution *n* Verteilung *f*; Verbreitung *f*.
district *n* Gegend *f*.
disturb *vt* stören; beunruhigen.
disturbance *n* Störung *f*; Beunruhigung *f*.
disturbed *adj* gestört; beunruhigt.
disturbing *adj* störend; beunruhigend.
ditch *n* Graben *m*.
dive *vi* tauchen.
diversion *n* Umleitung *f*.
divert *vt* umleiten.
divide *vt* (ver)teilen.
dividend *n* Dividende *f*; Gewinnanteil *m*.
divine *adj* göttlich.
diving *n* Tauchen *n*.
division *n* (Ver)Teilung *f*.
divorce *n* (Ehe)Scheidung *f*:—*vi* sich scheiden lassen.
divorced *adj* geschieden.
dizzy *adj* schwindlig.
do *vt* tun; machen.
dock *n* Dock *n*:—*vi* (an)docken.
docker *n* Hafenarbeiter *m*.
dockyard *n* Werft *f*.
doctor *n* Doktor *m*; Arzt *m*, Ärztin *f*.
document *n* Dokument *n*; Urkunde *f*.

dog n Hund m.
dogmatic adj dogmatisch.
doll n Puppe f.
dollar n Dollar m.
dolphin n Delphin m.
domain n Domäne f; Gebiet n.
dome n Kuppel f; Dom m.
domestic adj häuslich.
dominant adj dominant; (vor)herrschend.
dominate vi dominieren; (vor)herrschen.
domination n (Vor)Herrschaft f.
donate vt schenken.
donation n Schenkung f.
donkey n Esel m.
donor n Schenker(in) m(f).
door n Tür f.
dormouse n Schlafmaus f; Haselmaus f.
dosage n Dosierung f.
dose n Dosis f:—vt dosieren.
dot n Punkt m; Tupfen m.
double adj (ver)doppelt:—vt verdoppeln.
doubt n Zweifel m:—vt bezweifeln.
doubtful adj zweifelhaft.
doubtless adv zweifellos.
dough n Teig m.
dove n Taube f.
down prep hinunter.
downstairs adv (nach) unten.
downward(s) adv abwärts; hinunter.
dozen n Dutzend n.
draft n Entwurf m.
drag vt schleppen.
dragon n Drache(n) m.
dragonfly n Libelle f.
drain n Entwässerungsgraben m; (Straßen)Rinne f.
drake n Enterich m.
drama n Drama n; Schauspielkunst f.
dramatic adj dramatisch; Theater-.
dramatist n Dramatiker(in) m(f).

drastic adj drastisch.
draught n Zug m; Tiefgang m.
draughts npl Damespiel n.
draughty adj zugig.
draw vt (an)ziehen; zeichnen.
drawer n Schublade f; Zeichner m.
drawing n Zeichnung f.
dread n Furcht f:—vt fürchten.
dreadful adj furchtbar; schrecklich.
dream n Traum m:—vi träumen.
dress vt bekleiden; anziehen:—vi sich anziehen:—n Kleid n; Kleidung f.
dried adj getrocknet; Dörr-.
drill n Bohrer m; Bohrmaschine f; Drill m:—vt bohren; drillen.
drink vt vi trinken; saufen:—n Getränk m.
drinking water n Trinkwasser n.
drip vi tropfen:—n Tropfen n; Tropf m.
drive vt vi fahren; treiben:—n Fahrt f; Treiben n.
driver n Fahrer(in) m(f).
drop n Tropfen m:—vt (herab)tropfen; fallen lassen.
drought n Dürre f.
drown vt ertränken; überschwemmen:—vi ertrinken.
drug n Droge f; Medikament n.
drum n Trommel f:—vi trommeln.
drunk adj betrunken.
drunkard n Trinker(in) m(f); Säufer(in) m(f).
drunken adj betrunken.
dry adj trocken:—vt vi trocknen.
duck n Ente f.
due adj fällig.
duel n Duell n.
duet n Duett n.
dull adj stumpf.
dumb adj stumm.
dump n Schutthaufen m.
dumpling n Knödel m.
durable adj dauerhaft.

duration *n* Dauer *f.*
during *prep* während.
dust *n* Staub *m.*
duster *n* Staubtuch *n.*
dusty *adj* staubig.
duty *n* Pflicht *f.*
dwarf *n* Zwerg *m.*

dye *vt* färben:—*n* Farbstoff *m*; Färbung *f.*
dynamic *adj* dynamisch.
dynamics *n* Dynamik *f.*
dynamite *n* Dynamit *n.*
dynamo *n* Dynamo *m.*
dynasty *n* Dynastie *f.*

E

each *pn* jede(r, s):—~ **other** einander.
eager *adj* eifrig; begierig.
eagle *n* Adler *m.*
ear *n* Ohr *n.*
earache *n* Ohrenschmerzen *mpl.*
eardrum *n* Trommelfell *n.*
early *adj adv* früh.
earn *vt* verdienen.
earnest *adj* ernst; ernsthaft.
earring *n* Ohrring *m.*
earth *n* Erde *f*; Boden *m.*
earthquake *n* Erdbeben *n.*
ease *n* Bequemlichkeit *f*; Ruhe *f.*
east *n* Osten *m.*
Easter *n* Ostern *n.*
Easter egg *n* Osterei *n.*
eastern *adj* östlich; Ost-.
easy *adj* leicht; mühelos; einfach.
eat *vt vi* essen; fressen; nagen.
ebb *n* Ebbe *f*:—*vi* zurückgehen; abebben.
ebony *n* Ebenholz *n.*
eccentric *adj* exzentrisch.
echo *n* Echo *n*:—*vi* (wider)hallen.
ecology *n* Ökologie *f.*
economic(al) *adj* wirtschaftlich; sparsam.
economics *npl* Volkswirtschaft(slehre) *f.*
economist *n* Volkswirt *m.*
economy *n* Sparsamkeit *f*; Wirtschaftlichkeit *f.*

edge *n* Rand *m.*
edible *adv* eßbar.
edition *n* Ausgabe *f*; Auflage *f.*
editor *n* Redakteur(in) *m(f).*
educate *vt* erziehen; unterrichten; (aus)bilden.
education *n* Erziehung *f*; (Aus)Bildung *f.*
eel *n* Aal *m.*
effect *n* Effekt *m*; Wirkung *f.*
effective *adj* effektiv; (rechts)wirksam.
efficiency *n* Effizienz *f*; (Leistungs)-Fähigkeit *f.*
efficient *adj* effizient; (leistungs)fähig.
effort *n* Anstrengung *f*; Mühe *f.*
effortless *adj* mühelos.
effrontery *n* Unverschämtheit *f.*
egg *n* Ei *n.*
eggcup *n* Eierbecher *m.*
ego(t)ism *n* Egoismus *m*; Selbstsucht *f.*
ego(t)ist *n* Egoist(in) *m(f)*; selbstgefälliger Mensch *m.*
eight *num* acht.
eighteen *num* achtzehn.
eighth *adj* achte(r, s).
eighty *num* achtzig.
either *conj* entweder.
elastic *adj* elastisch; dehnbar; Gummiband.
elbow *n* Ell(en)bogen *m.*

elder *adj* ältere(r, s).
eldest *adj* älteste(r, s).
elect *vt* wählen.
election *n* Wahl *f*.
elector *n* Wähler(in) *m(f)*.
electric(al) *adj* elektrisch; Elektro-.
electrician *n* Elektriker *m*.
electricity *n* Elektrizität *f*.
electron *n* Elektron *n*.
electronic *adj* elektronisch:—**s** *npl* Elektronik *f*.
elegance *n* Eleganz *f*.
elegant *adj* elegant.
element *n* Element *n*.
elephant *n* Elefant *m*.
eleven *num* elf.
elk *n* Elch *m*; Wapiti *n*.
elm *n* Ulme *f*.
eloquence *n* Beredsamkeit *f*.
eloquent *adj* beredt.
else *adv* sonst; weiter; andere(r, s).
elsewhere *adv* anderswo; woanders hin.
embarrass *vt* verlegen machen; in Verlegenheit bringen.
embarrassed *adj* verlegen.
embarrassing *adj* unangenehm; peinlich.
embarrassment *n* Verlegenheit *f*.
embassy *n* Botschaft *f*.
embitter *vt* bitter(er) machen.
embrace *vt* umarmen; umfassen:—*n* Umarmung *f*.
embroider *vt* (be)sticken.
embroidery *n* Stickerei *f*.
emerald *n* Smaragd *m*.
emerge *vi* auftauchen; sich herausstellen.
emergency *n* Not(lage) *f*; Notfall *m*.
emigrant *n* Emigrant(in) *m(f)*; Auswanderer *m*.
emigrate *vi* auswandern; emigrieren.
emigration *n* Auswanderung *f*; Emigration *f*.

eminence *n* Anhöhe *f*; Eminenz *f*.
eminent *adj* eminent; hervorragend.
emit *vt* ausstoßen; ausstrahlen.
emotion *n* Gefühl *n*; Erregung *f*; Rührung *f*.
emotional *adj* emotionell; gefühlsmäßig.
emperor *n* Kaiser *m*.
emphasis *n* Betonung *f*; Schwerpunkt *m*.
emphasize *vt* betonen; hervorheben.
empire *n* Reich *n*; Imperium *n*.
employ *vt* beschäftigen; einstellen.
employee *n* Arbeitnehmer(in) *m(f)*; Angestellte(r) *f(m)*.
employer *n* Arbeitgeber(in) *m(f)*; Unternehmer(in) *m(f)*.
employment *n* Beschäftigung *f*; Arbeit *f*.
empress *n* Kaiserin *f*.
empty *adj* leer.
enable *vt* ermächtigen; befähigen; ermöglichen.
enact *vt* erlassen; verfügen; aufführen; darstellen.
enclose *vt* einschließen.
enclosure *n* Einfriedung *f*.
encounter *n* Begegnung *f*:—*vt* begegnen.
encourage *vt* ermutigen.
encouragement *n* Ermutigung *f*.
encyclopedia *n* Enzyklopädie *f*.
end *n* Ende *n*; Folge *f*; Zweck *n*; Ziel *n*:—*vt* beenden:—*vi* enden.
endless *adj* endlos; unendlich.
enemy *n* Feind(in) *m(f)*.
energetic *adj* energisch.
energy *n* Energie *f*.
engage *vt* verpflichten; anstellen.
engaged *adj* verlobt; verpflichtet; besetzt.
engagement *n* Verpflichtung *f*; Verlobung *f*.
engine *n* Motor *m*.

engineer *n* Ingenieur *m*.
engineering *n* Ingenieurwesen *n*.
enigma *n* Rätsel *n*.
enjoy *vt* genießen.
enjoyable *adj* genießbar.
enjoyment *n* Genuß *m*.
enlarge *vt* vergrößern.
enlargement *n* Vergrößerung *f*.
enormous *adj* ungeheuer(lich); enorm; riesig.
enough *adv* genug; ausreichend.
enrage *vt* wütend machen.
enrich *vt* bereichern; anreichern.
ensure *vt* sichern; sicherstellen; sorgen für.
enter *vt* eintreten (in).
enterprise *n* Unternehmen *n*; Unternehmung *f*.
entertain *vt* unterhalten.
entertainer *n* Unterhaltungskünstler(in) *m(f)*.
entertainment *n* Unterhaltung *f*.
enthusiasm *n* Begeisterung *f*.
enthusiastic *adj* begeistert.
entice *vt* (ver)locken.
entire *adj* ganz; vollständig:—**~ly** *adv* völlig; durchaus.
entrance *n* Eintritt *m*; Eingang *m*.
entrant *n* Teilnehmer(in) *m(f)*; Eintretende(r) *f(m)*.
entrepreneur *n* Unternehmer *m*.
entrust *vt* anvertrauen; betrauen.
entry *n* Eintritt *m*; Einreise *f*; Auftritt *m*.
envelope *vt* (Brief)Umschlag *m*.
enviable *adj* beneidenswert.
envious *adj* neidisch.
environment *n* Umgebung *f*; Umwelt *f*.
environmental *adj* Umwelt-.
envy *n* Neid *m*:—*vt* beneiden.
epidemic *n* Epidemie *f*; Seuche *f*.
epilogue *n* Epilog *m*; Nachwort *n*.
Epiphany *n* Dreikönigstag *m*.
episode *n* Episode *f*; Ereignis *n*.

epoch *n* Epoche *f*; Zeitalter *n*.
equal *adj* gleich(förmig); gleichberechtigt:—*n* Gleichgestellte(r) *f(m)*: —*vt* gleichen; entsprechen.
equality *n* Gleichheit *f*; Gleichberechtigung *f*.
equate *vt* gleichmachen; ausgleichen.
equation *n* Gleichung *f*.
equator *n* Äquator *m*.
equip *vt* ausrüsten; ausstatten.
equipment *n* Ausrüstung *f*; Ausstattung *f*; Einrichtung *f*.
equivalent *adj* äquivalent:—*n* Äquivalent *n*.
era *n* Ära *f*; Zeitalter *n*.
eradicate *vt* ausreißen; ausrotten.
eradication *n* Ausrottung *f*; Entwurzelung *f*.
erase *vt* ausradieren; (aus)löschen; tilgen.
erect *vt* aufrichten; errichten:—*adj* aufgerichtet; aufrecht.
erection *n* Errichtung *f*; Montage *f*; Erektion *f*.
erode *vt* zerfressen; erodieren.
erotic *adj* erotisch.
err *vi* irren; falsch sein.
errand *n* Auftrag *m*; (Boten)Gang *m*; Besorgung *f*.
erratic *adj* (umher)wandernd; regellos.
error *n* Irrtum *m*; Fehler *m*; Versehen *n*.
erupt *vi* ausbrechen; durchbrechen.
eruption *n* Ausbruch *m*.
escalator *n* Rolltreppe *f*.
escape *vt vi* entkommen:—*n* Flucht *f*; Rettung *f*.
escort *n* Eskorte *f*; Begleitung *f*:—*vt* eskortieren; begleiten.
especially *adv* besonders.
essay *n* Essay *n*; Aufsatz *m*.
essence *n* Essenz *f*; Wesen *n*.
essential *adj* wesentlich:—**~ly** *adv* im wesentlichen.

establish vt festsetzen; einrichten; (be)gründen.

establishment n Festsetzung f; Gründung f; Einrichtung f.

estate n Vermögen n; Nachlaß m.

estimate vt (ein)schätzen.

eternal adj ewig; unveränderlich.

eternity n Ewigkeit f.

ethical adj ethisch; moralisch.

ethics npl Ethik f; Moral f; Ethos m.

ethnic adj ethnisch.

ethos n Ethos m.

etiquette n Etikette f.

evacuate vt evakuieren; entleeren; räumen.

evacuation n Evakuierung f; Entleerung f; Räumung f.

evaporate vi verdampfen.

evaporation n Verdampfung f.

eve n Vorabend m; Vortag m.

even adj eben; gerade; glatt:—adv sogar; gerade; eben; ganz.

evening n Abend m.

event n Ereignis n; (Vor)Fall m.

eventual adj schließlich.

ever adv immer (wieder); je(mals); irgend:—~ **since** seitdem.

every adj jede(r, s):—~**where** überall(hin):—~**thing** alles:—~**one,** ~**body** jeder (einzelne).

evidence n Beweis m.

evident adj offensichtlich; augenscheinlich.

evil adj böse; übel:—n Böse n; Übel n.

evolution n Evolution f.

ewe n Mutterschaf n.

exact adj exakt.

exaggerate vt übertreiben.

exaggeration n Übertreibung f.

examination n Untersuchung f; Prüfung f.

examine vt untersuchen; prüfen.

examiner n Prüfer(in) m(f).

example n Beispiel n.

exceed vt überschreiten; übersteigen.

excellent adj ausgezeichnet.

except prep ausgenommen.

exception n Ausnahme f.

excerpt n Auszug m.

excess n Übermaß n; Exzeß m.

exchange vt (aus)tauschen; (um)wechseln:—n (Aus)Tausch m; (Um)Wechseln n; Börse f.

excite vt erregen; aufregen; reizen.

excited adj aufgeregt; erregt.

excitement n Erregung f; Aufregung f; Reizung f.

exciting adj aufregend; erregend; spannend.

exclaim vt ausrufen; hervorstoßen.

exclamation n Ausruf m; (Auf)Schrei m.

exclude vt ausschließen.

exclusion n Ausschluß m; Ausschließung f.

exclusive adj exklusiv; ausschließlich.

excursion n Exkursion f; Ausflug m.

excuse vt entschuldigen; verzeihen: — n Entschuldigung f; Vorwand m.

execute vt ausführen; hinrichten.

execution n Ausführung f; Hinrichtung f.

executioner n Henker m; Scharfrichter m.

exempt adj befreit.

exemption n Befreiung f.

exercise n (Aus)Übung f.

exhaust n Abgas n; Auspuff m:—vt erschöpfen.

exhausted adj erschöpft.

exhaustion n Erschöpfung f.

exhibit vt ausstellen.

exhibition n Ausstellung f.

exile n Exil n; Verbannung f:—vt verbannen.

exist vi existieren; bestehen.

existence n Existenz f; Bestand m.

existent *adj* existierend; bestehend.

exit *n* Ausgang *m*; Ausfahrt *f*; Abgang *m*:—*vi* abgehen; abtreten.

exotic *adj* exotisch.

expand *vt* erweitern; ausbreiten.

expansion *n* Ausbreitung *f*; Erweiterung *f*.

expect *vt* erwarten; annehmen.

expectation *n* Erwartung *f*.

expel *vt* vertreiben; hinauswerfen.

expenditure *n* Ausgabe *f*; Aufwand *m*.

expensive *adj* teuer; kostspielig.

experience *n* Erfahrung *f*, Erlebnis *n*:—*vt* erfahren; erleben.

experienced *adj* erfahren; erprobt.

experiment *n* Experiment *n*:—*vi* experimentieren.

expert *adj* Experte *m*, Expertin *f*; Sachverständige(r) *f(m)*.

expertise *n* Expertise *f*; Sachkenntnis *f*.

explain *vt* erklären.

explanation *n* Erklärung *f*.

explode *vi* explodieren; platzen.

exploit *vt* verwerten; ausnutzen.

exploitation *n* Ausnutzung *f*; Verwertung *f*.

exploration *n* Erforschung *f*.

explore *vt* (er)forschen.

explorer *n* Forscher(in) *m(f)*.

explosion *n* Explosion *f*; Ausbruch *m*.

explosive *adj* explosiv; Explosions-:—*n* Sprengstoff *m*.

export *vt* exportieren; ausführen:—*n* Export *m*; Ausfuhr *f*.

exporter *n* Exporteur *m*.

expose *vt* aussetzen; bloßstellen.

exposed *adj* ausgesetzt; ungeschützt.

exposure *n* Aussetzung *f*; Bloßstellung *f*.

express *vt* ausdrücken; äußern:—*adj* ausdrücklich; Expreß-; Eil-:—*n* Schnellzug *m*.

expression *n* Ausdruck *m*.

expressive *adj* ausdrucksvoll; Ausdrucks-.

extend *vt* (aus)dehnen:—*vi* sich ausdehnen.

extension *n* Ausdehnung *f*.

extensive *adj* ausgedehnt; weitläufig.

extent *n* Ausdehnung *f*; Umfang *m*.

exterior *adj* äußerlich.

external *adj* äußere(r, s).

extinct *adj* ausgestorben; erloschen.

extinction *n* Aussterben *n*; (Aus)Löschen *n*; Vernichtung *f*.

extinguish *vt* (aus)löschen; vernichten.

extinguisher *n* Feuerlöscher *m*.

extra *adv* extra.

extract *vt* usziehen:—*n* Auszug *m*.

extraordinary *adj* außerordentlich.

extreme *adj* extrem; äußerste(r, s):— ~ly *adv* äußerst; höchst.

eye *n* Auge *n*.

eyeball *n* Augapfel *m*.

eyebrow *n* Augenbraue *f*.

eyelash *n* Wimper *f*.

eyelid *n* Augenlid *n*.

eyesight *n* Sehkraft *f*.

eyrie *n* Horst *m*.

F

fable *n* Fabel *f*; Sage *f*.

fabric *n* Stoff *m*; Gewebe *n*.

fabulous *adj* sagenhaft; fabelhaft.

facade *n* Fassade *f*.

face *n* Gesicht *n*; Miene *f*.

facial *adj* Gesichts-.

facility n Leichtigkeit f; Gelassenheit f.

fact n Tatsache f:—**in** ~ in der Tat.

factor n Faktor m; Umstand m.

factory n Fabrik f.

fade vi (ver)welken; verblassen; sich auflösen.

fail vt vi versagen; durchfallen.

faint vi ohnmächtig werden:—n Ohnmacht f.

fair adj schön; hell; blond; fair:—n Ausstellung f; Messe f.

fairly adv ziemlich; leidlich.

fairy n Fee f.

fairy tale n Märchen n.

faith n Treue f.

faithful adj treu.

fake n Fälschung f:—vt fälschen.

fall vi fallen:—n Fall m.

false adj falsch.

falsehood n Unwahrheit f; Lüge f; Falschheit f.

fame n Ruhm m, Berühmtheit f.

familiar adj vertraut.

family n Familie f.

famous adj berühmt.

fan n Fächer m; Fan m.

fanatic adj fanatisch:—n Fanatiker(in) m(f).

fancy n Laune f; Phantasie f; Vorliebe f.

fantastic adj phantastisch.

fantasy n Phantasie f.

far adv weit (entfernt); fern.

fare n Fahrpreis m; Fahrgast m.

farm n Bauernhof m.

farmer n Landwirt(in) m(f); Bauer m, Bäuerin f.

farmhouse n Bauernhaus n.

farmyard n Hof m.

farther adv weiter; mehr:—adj weiter (weg); entfernter.

fascinate vt faszinieren.

fascination n Faszination f.

fascism n Faschismus m.

fashion n Mode f.

fashionable adj modisch.

fast n Fasten n:—adj schnell; fest(gemacht):—adv (zu) schnell; rasch; fest.

fasten vt befestigen; festbinden.

fat adj dick; fett; beleibt:—n Fett n.

fatal adj tödlich; fatal.

fate n Schicksal n.

father n Vater m; Pater m.

fatherhood n Vaterschaft f.

father-in-law n Schwiegervater m.

fatherland n Vaterland n.

fatherly adj väterlich; Vater-.

fatigue n Ermüdung f.

fault n Fehler m; Mangel m; Irrtum m.

fauna n Fauna f.

favour n Gunst f; Begünstigung f:—vt begünstigen.

favourable adj wohlgesinnt; günstig.

favourite adj Lieblings-.

fax n Fax n:—vt faxen.

fear vi (sich) fürchten:—n Furcht f.

fearful adj furchtbar.

feast n Fest(mahl) n; Feiertag m.

feather n Feder f.

feature n (Gesichts)Zug m.

February n Februar m.

federal adj Bundes-.

federation n Föderation f; Staatenbund m.

fee n Gebühr f; Honorar n.

feed vt (ver)füttern; ernähren.

feel vt vi fühlen.

feeling n Gefühl n.

fellow n Kerl m.

felt n Filz m.

female, feminine adj weiblich.

feminist n Feminist(in) m(f).

fence n Zaun m:—vt einzäunen:—vi fechten.

ferry n Fähre f:—vt übersetzen.

fertile adj fruchtbar; reich.

fertilizer n Dünger m; Befruchter m.

festival n Fest n.

fetch vt (ab)holen.

fever n Fieber n.

few adj wenige:—**a ~** einige; ein paar.

fiancé(e) n Verlobte(r) f(m).

field n Feld n.

fieldmouse n Feldmaus f.

fierce adj wild; grimmig.

fifteen num fünfzehn.

fifth adj fünfte(r, s).

fifty num fünfzig.

fig n Feige f.

fight vt vi kämpfen:—n Kampf m.

fighter n Kämpfer(in) m(f).

figure n Zahl f; Ziffer f; Figur f; Gestalt f.

file n Ordner m; Akte f:—vt ablegen; (ein)ordnen; zu den Akten nehmen.

fill vt (ab)füllen; erfüllen; ausfüllen; besetzen.

film n Film m; dünne Schicht f:—vt (ver)filmen:—vi einen Film drehen.

filter n Filter m:—vt filtern; filtrieren; (durch)seihen.

filth n Schmutz m; Dreck m; Schweinerei f.

filthy adj schmutzig; dreckig; schweinisch; scheußlich.

fin n Finne f; Flosse f; Kühlrippe f.

final adj letzte(r, s); endgültig; End-; Schluß-:—**~ly** adv endlich; schließlich; zum Schluß; endgültig.

finale n Finale n.

finalist n Endkampfteilnehmer(in) m(f).

finalize vt beenden; abschließen.

finance n Finanzwesen n; pl Finanzen pl; Einkünfte pl.

financial adj finanziell; Finanz-.

financier n Finanzier m.

find vt (heraus)finden; feststellen:—**~ out** entdecken:—n Fund m; Entdeckung f.

fine adj fein; schön:—n Geldstrafe f; Bußgeld n:—vt zu einer Geldstrafe verurteilen.

finger n Finger m.

fingernail n Fingernagel m.

fingerprint n Fingerabdruck m.

finish vt (be)enden.

fir (tree) n Tanne f.

fire n Feuer n; Brand m:—vt (ab)feuern; abschießen:—vi feuern.

firearm n Schußwaffe f.

fireman n Feuerwehrmann m.

fireplace n (offener) Kamin m.

fireproof adj feuerfest.

fireworks npl Feuerwerk n.

firm adj fest:—n Firma f; Betrieb m.

first adj erste(r, s); erstklassig:—adv zuerst.

fish n Fisch m:—vi fischen; angeln.

fisherman n Fischer m; Angler m.

fishmonger n Fischhändler m.

fist n Faust f.

fit n Paßform f; Zusammenpassen n; Anfall m:—adj passend; geeignet; tauglich; fähig; gesund:—vt (an)passen; ausrüsten.

five num fünf.

fix vt befestigen; festsetzen; reparieren.

fixture n festes Inventar n; Installationsteil n; Spannvorrichtung f.

fizzy adj zischend; sprudelnd.

flag n Flagge f; Fahne f.

flake n Flocke f:—vi flocken.

flaky adj flockig; blätterig.

flamboyant adj extravagant; auffallend.

flame n Flamme f.

flamingo n Flamingo m.

flank n Flanke f; Seite f:—vt flankieren.

flannel n Flanell m; Waschlappen m.

flap n Flattern n; Schlag m; Klappe f.

flash n Aufleuchten n:—vt aufleuchten lassen.

flat *adj* flach; platt; glatt; (*mus*) erniedrigt:—*n* Fläche *f*; Ebene *f*; (*mus*) B *n*.

flatten *vt* (ein)ebnen; flach machen.

flatter *vt* schmeicheln.

flattering *adj* schmeichelhaft.

flattery *n* Schmeichelei *f*.

flavour *n* Geschmack *m*; Aroma *n*; Würze *f*:—*vt* würzen.

flaw *n* Fehler *m*; Mangel *m*; Makel *m*; Defekt *m*.

flax *n* Flachs *m*; Lein *m*.

flea *n* Floh *m*.

flee *vt* fliehen vor; fliehen aus; meiden:—*vi* fliehen; flüchten.

fleet *n* Flotte *f*.

fleeting *adj* flüchtig.

flesh *n* Fleisch *f*.

flesh wound *n* Fleischwunde *f*.

fleshy *adj* fleischig.

flex *n* Kabel *n*; Schnur *f*; Beugen *n*:—*vt* biegen; beugen; anspannen.

flexibility *n* Flexibilität *f*; Biegsamkeit *f*.

flexible *adj* flexibel; biegsam.

flick *n* Klaps *m*; schnelle Bewegung *f*; Knall *m*:—*vt* leicht schlagen; knallen mit.

flicker *vi* flackern; zucken; flimmern.

flier *n* Flieger *m*; Schwungrad *n*; Flugblatt *n*.

flight *n* Flug *m*; Fliegen *n*; Schwarm *m*; Treppe *f*; Flucht *f*.

flimsy *adj* dünn; leichtzerbrechlich.

flinch *vi* zurückschrecken; (zurück)zucken.

fling *vt* werfen; schleudern.

flint *n* Flint *m*; Feuerstein *m*.

flip *vt* schnippen; schnellen.

flippant *adj* respektlos; schnippisch.

flipper *n* Flosse *f*.

flirt *vi* herumsausen; flirten; liebäugeln:—*n* Schäker(in) *m(f)*.

flirtation *n* Flirten *n*; Flirt *m*; Liebäugeln *n*.

flit *vi* flitzen; huschen; flattern.

float *vt* treiben lassen; flößen:—*vi* schwimmen; treiben:—*n* Floß *n*; Prahm *m*.

flock *n* Herde *f*; Schwarm *m*; Flocke *f*.

flog *vt* prügeln; auspeitschen; antreiben.

flogging *n* Prügel(strafe) *f*; Auspeitschen *n*.

flood *n* Flut *f*; Überschwemmung *f*; Schwall *m*:—*vt* (über)fluten; überschwemmen.

flooding *n* Überschwemmung *f*; Überflutung *f*.

floodlight *n* Flutlicht *n*.

floor *n* (Fuß)Boden *m*.

florist *n* Blumenhändler(in) *m(f)*.

flour *n* Mehl *n*; Pulver *n*.

flourishing *adj* blühend; gedeihend.

flout *vt* verspotten; mißachten.

flow *vi* fließen; strömen; rinnen; wallen; entspringen:—*n* Fließen *n*; Fluß *m*; Schwall *m*; Flut *f*.

flower *n* Blume *f*; Blüte *f*:—*vi* blühen.

flowerpot *n* Blumentopf *m*.

flowery *adj* geblümt.

fluctuate *vi* schwanken; fluktuieren.

fluency *n* Flüssigkeit *f*; (Rede)Gewandtheit *f*.

fluent *adj* flüssig; fließend; gewandt.

fluff *n* Staubflocke *f*; Fussel *f*; Flaum *m*.

fluffy *adj* flaumig; flockig; locker.

fluid *adj* flüssig:—*n* Flüssigkeit *f*.

flute *n* Flöte *f*; Riefe *f*.

flutter *vi* flattern; zittern:—*n* Flattern *n*; Verwirrung *f*.

fly *vt* vi fliegen:—*n* Fliege *f*; Flug *m*; Hosenschlitz *m*.

foal *n* Fohlen *n*.

foam *n* Schaum *m*:—*vi* schäumen.

foamy *adj* schaumig.

focus *n* Brennpunkt *m*; Scharfeinstellung *f*; Herd *m*.

fodder n Futter n.

foe n Feind(in) m(f); Widersacher(in) m(f).

fog n Nebel m; Schleier m.

foggy adj neblig; nebelhaft.

foil n Folie f.

fold n Falte f:—vt falten.

folder n Mappe f; Schnellhefter m; Faltprospekt m.

folio n Blatt n; Foliant m.

folk n Leute pl; Volk n; Folk m.

folklore n Folklore f; Volkskunde f; Volkstum n.

follow vt vi (nach)folgen.

folly n Torheit f; Verrücktheit f.

fond adj zärtlich; liebevoll.

fondle vt streicheln; spielen mit.

food n Essen n; Nahrung f; Verpflegung f; Lebensmittel pl; Futter n.

fool n Narr m; Närrin f; Dummkopf m:—vt zum Narren halten; reinlegen; betrügen.

foolish adj dumm; töricht; albern; unklug; lächerlich.

foot n Fuß m:—**on/by ~** zu Fuß.

football n Fußball m.

footpath n Pfad m; Fußweg m.

footprint n Fußabdruck m.

for prep für:—conj denn.

forbid vt verbieten.

force n Kraft f; Stärke f:—vt (er)zwingen.

forearm n Unterarm m.

foreboding n (böse) Vorahnung f; (böses) Vorzeichen.

forecast vt vorhersagen; voraussagen:—n Vorhersage f; Prognose f.

forecourt n Vorhof m; Vorplatz m.

forefather n Ahn m; Vorfahr m.

forefinger n Zeigefinger m.

forefront n:—**in the ~ of** in vorderster Linie.

forego vt vorangehen; vorhergehen.

foregone adj vorhergehend; früher; von vornherein feststehend.

foreground n Vordergrund m.

forehead n Stirn f.

foreign adj fremd; ausländisch; Auslands-; Außen-.

foreigner n Ausländer(in) m.

foresee vt vorhersehen; voraussehen.

foresight n Weitblick m; Voraussicht f.

forest n Wald m; Forst m.

foretell vt vorhersagen; voraussagen.

forewarn vt vorher warnen.

foreword n Vorwort n.

forfeit n (Ein)Buße f; Strafe f; Verlust m; Pfand n:—vt verwirken; verlieren; einbüßen.

forge n Schmiede f; Esse f; Hammerwerk n:—vt schmieden; formen; erfinden; fälchen.

forger n Fälscher m; Schmied m.

forgery n Fälschung f; Fälchen n.

forget vt vergessen:—vi vergessen.

forgetful adj vergeßlich; nachlässig.

forget-me-not n (bot) Vergißmeinnicht n.

forgive vt vergeben; verzeihen.

fork n Gabel f.

forlorn adj verlassen; einsam; verzweifelt; verloren.

form n Form f; Gestalt f:—vt formen; bilden.

formal adj förmlich; formell; feierlich.

formality n Förmlichkeit f; Formalität f.

format n Format n; Gestaltung f:—vt formatieren.

formation n Formation f; Bildung f; Entstehung f; Gründung f.

former adj früher; ehemalig:—**~ly** adv früher; ehemals.

formula n Formel f; Rezept n.

fort n Fort n; Festung f.

forthwith adj sofort; umgehend; unverzüglich.

fortification n Befestigung f; Festung f; (Ver)Stärkung f; Untermauerung f.

fortify vt befestigen; (ver)stärken; untermauern.

fortnight n vierzehn Tage mpl:—~**ly** adj adv vierzehntägig; alle 14 Tage.

fortress n (mil) Festung f.

fortunate adj glücklich; glückverheißend:—~**ly** adv glücklicherweise; zum Glück.

fortune n Vermögen n; Reichtum m; (glücklicher) Zufall; Glück n; Schicksal n.

forty num vierzig.

forum n Forum n; Gericht n.

forward adj vorwärts; vordere(r, s); frühreif; fortschrittlich; vorlaut; vorschnell; bereitwillig:—~**s** adv vor; nach vorn; vorwärts; voraus; voran:—vt beschleunigen; fördern; schicken; (nach)senden.

fossil n Fossil n; Versteinerung f.

foster vt aufziehen; in Pflege nehmen/ geben; hegen; fördern.

foul adj stinkend; widerlich; schlecht; faul; schmutzig:—vt beschmutzen; verunreinigen; foulen; kollidieren mit.

found vt gründen.

foundation n Fundament n; Gründung f; Stiftung f.

fountain n Quelle f; Fontäne f; Springbrunnen m.

four num vier.

fourteen num vierzehn.

fourth adj vierte(r, s).

fowl n Geflügel n; Federvieh n.

fox n Fuchs m.

fraction n Fraktion f; Bruch(teil) m.

fracture n Bruch m; Fraktur f.

fragile adj gebrechlich.

fragment n Fragment n.

fragrance n Duft m.

fragrant adj duftend.

frame n Rahmen m.

France n Frankreich n.

frank adj offen; aufrichtig; freimütig.

fraud n Betrug m.

free adj frei:—vt befreien.

freedom n Freiheit f.

freeze vi frieren.

freezing adj eiskalt; Gefrier-.

freight n Fracht f; Ladung f.

freighter n Frachter m; Transportflugzeug n.

French adj französisch.

frequency n Frequenz f; Häufigkeit f.

frequent adj häufig.

fresh adj frisch.

friction n Reibung f.

Friday n Freitag m:—**Good ~** Karfreitag m.

friend n Freund(in) m(f); Bekannte(r) f(m).

friendly adj freundlich.

friendship n Freundschaft f.

fright n Schreck(en) m; Entsetzen n.

frighten vt erschrecken; Angst einjagen.

frightened adj erschrocken; verängstigt.

frightful adj schrecklich; furchtbar.

frigid adj kalt; frostig; frigid.

fringe n Franse f; Rand m; Ponyfrisur f.

frisk vt wedeln mit; durchsuchen.

frog n Frosch m.

from prep von; aus; seit; von... aus.

front n Vorderseite f; Fassade f; Vorderteil n; Front f:—vt Front-; Vorder-.

frontier n Grenze f; Grenzbereich m.

frost n Frost m; Reif m.

frown vi die Stirn runzeln:—n Stirnrunzeln n.

frozen adj (ein)gefroren.

fruit n Obst n; Frucht f.

frustrate vt vereiteln; frustrieren.

frustrated adj frustriert; vereitelt.

frustration n Frustration f; Vereitelung f.

fry *vt* braten.
fuchsia *n* Fuchsie *f*.
fuel *n* Brennstoff *m*.
fulfil *vt* erfüllen.
fulfilment *n* Erfüllung *f*.
full *adj* voll; weit; rund.
fully *adv* voll; völlig; ganz.
fun *n* Spaß *m*.
function *n* Funktion *f*; Feier *f*; Veranstaltung *f*.
functional *adj* funktionell; funktionsfähig.
fund *n* Kapital *n*; Fonds *m*:—*vt* fundieren; finanzieren.
fundamental *adj* fundamental; grundlegend; grundsätzlich; Grund-:—**ly** *adv* im Grunde; im wesentlichen.
funeral *n* Beerdigung *f*; Bestattung *f*; Begräbnis *n*.
fungus *n* Pilz *m*; Schwamm *m*; Fungus *m*.
funnel *n* Trichter *m*; Schornstein *m*.
funny *adj* komisch.

fur *n* Fell *n*; Pelz *m*.
furious *adj* wütend; wild; heftig.
furnace *n* Ofen *m*; Kessel *m*; Feuerung *f*.
furnish *vt* versorgen; ausstatten; möblieren; liefern.
furniture *n* Möbel *pl*; Einrichtung *f*.
further *adj adv* weiter:—*vt* fördern; unterstützen.
furthermore *adv* ferner; überdies; außerdem.
fury *n* Wut *f*; Wildheit *f*; Heftigkeit *f*; Furie *f*.
fuse *vt* einen Zünder anbringen:—*vi* durchbrennen:—*n* Zünder *m*; Sicherung *f*.
fusion *n* Fusion *f*; Schmelzen *n*; Verschmelzung *f*; Vereinigung *f*.
fuss *n* Aufregung *f*; Ärger *m*; Wirbel *m*; Theater *n*.
fussy *adj* aufgeregt; pedantisch.
futile *adj* zwecklos.
future *adj* (zu)künftig; Zukunfts-:—*n* Zukunft *f*; Futur *n*.

G

gain *n* Gewinn *m*:—*vt* verdienen; gewinnen.
galaxy *n* Galaxie *f*.
gale *n* Sturm *m*.
gallery *n* Gallerie *f*.
gallop *n* Galopp *m*:—*vi* galoppieren.
gamble *vi* spielen; spekulieren:—*n* Glücksspiel *n*.
gambler *n* Spieler(in) *m(f)*.
gambling *n* Spielen *n*.
game *n* Spiel *n*.
gander *n* Gänserich *m*.
gap *n* Lücke *f*.
garage *n* Garage *f*; Reparaturwerkstatt *f*.

garden *n* Garten *m*.
gardener *n* Gärtner(in) *m(f)*.
gardening *n* Gärtnerei *f*.
garlic *n* Knoblauch *m*.
garment *n* Kleidungsstück *n*; Gewand *n*.
gas *n* Gas *n*.
gasp *vi* keuchen:—*n* Keuchen *n*.
gate *n* Tor *n*; Pforte *f*.
gather *vt* versammeln:—*vi* sich versammeln.
gay *adj* fröhlich; bunt; schwul.
gaze *vi* starren:—*n* (starrer) Blick *m*.
gear *n* Getriebe *n*; Gang *m*; Gerät *n*; Ausrüstung *f*.

gem *n* Edelstein *m*; Juwel *n*.

Gemini *n* (*astrol*) Zwillinge *pl*.

gene *n* Gen *n*.

general *adj* allgemein:—**in** ~ im allgemeinen:—*n* General *m*.

generate *vt* erzeugen.

generation *n* Generation *f*, (Er)Zeugung *f*.

generator *n* Generator *m*; Erzeuger *m*.

generic *adj* Gattungs-; allgemein.

generosity *n* Großzügigkeit *f*.

generous *adj* großzügig.

genetics *npl* Genetik *f*.

genius *n* Genie *n*; Genialität *f*; Geist *m*.

gentle *adj* sanft.

gentleman *n* Ehrenmann *m*; Herr *m*.

gentleness *n* Sanftheit *f*.

genuine *adj* echt; aufrichtig; natürlich; ernsthaft.

geographer *n* Geograph(in) *m(f)*.

geographical *adj* geographisch.

geography *n* Geographie *f*; Erdkunde *f*.

geological *adj* geologisch.

geologist *n* Geologe *m*; Geologin *f*.

geology *n* Geologie *f*.

geometric(al) *adj* geometrisch.

geometry *n* Geometrie *f*.

geranium *n* (*bot*) Geranie *f*; Storchschnabel *m*.

germ *n* Keim *m*; Mikrobe *f*; Krankheitserreger *m*.

gesture *n* Geste *f*; Gebärde *f*.

get *vt* bekommen; erhalten; kriegen; holen; beschaffen; erreichen.

ghost *n* Gespenst *n*; Geist *m*.

ghostly *adj* geisterhaft; gespenstisch.

giant *n* Riese *m*.

giddy *adj* schwindlig; schwindelerregend.

gift *n* Geschenk *n*; Spende *f*; Schenkung *f*; Gabe *f*; Talent *n*.

gifted *adj* begabt; talentiert.

gigantic *adj* gigantisch; riesig.

giggle *vi* kichern.

gild *vt* vergolden.

gill *n* Kieme *f*; Lamelle *f*.

gimmick *n* Trick *m*; Masche *f*.

gin *n* Gin *m*; Wacholderschnaps *m*.

ginger *n* Ingwer *m*.

gingerbread *n* Lebkuchen *m*.

gipsy *n* Zigeuner(in) *m(f)*.

giraffe *n* Giraffe *f*.

girl *n* Mädchen *n*.

girlfriend *n* Freundin *f*.

give *vt vi* geben:—~ **up** *vi* aufgeben.

glacier *n* Gletscher *m*.

glad *adj* froh; erfreut:—~**ly** *adv* gern; mit Freuden.

glamorous *adj* bezaubernd.

glamour *n* Zauber *m*; Glanz *m*.

glance *n* (flüchtiger) Blick:—*vi* (flüchtig) blicken.

gland *n* Drüse *f*.

glare *n* greller Schein *m*; wütender Blick *m*:—*vi* grell leuchten; wütend starren.

glass *n* Glas *n*; Spiegel *m*:—~**es** *pl* Brille *f*:—*adj* Glas-.

glassware *n* Glaswaren *fpl*.

glaze *vt* verglasen; glasieren; glasig machen.

glide *vi* gleiten; schweben; segelfliegen.

glimmer *n* Schimmer *m*; Glimmer *m*:—*vi* glimmen; schimmern.

glimpse *n* flüchtiger Blick *m*; flüchtiger Eindruck *m*:—*vt* einen flüchtigen Blick erhaschen von.

glint *vi* glitzern; glänzen.

global *adj* global; Welt-; umfassend.

globe *n* (Erd)Kugel *f*; Erde *f*; Globus *m*.

gloomy *adj* düster; schwermütig; trübsinnig; hoffnungslos.

glorious *adj* ruhmreich; glorreich; herrlich; prächtig.

glory *n* Ruhm *m*; Ehre *f*; Stolz *m*; Herrlichkeit *f*; Pracht *f*.

gloss *n* Glanz *m*; Glosse *f*.

glossary *n* Glossar *n*.

glove *n* Handschuh *m*.

glow *vi* glühen:—*n* Glühen *n*.

glue *n* Leim *m*; Klebstoff *m*:—*vt* leimen, kleben.

glut *n* Übersättigung *f*; Überangebot *n*; Schwemme *f*.

gnome *n* (Garten)Zwerg *m*; Gnom *m*.

go *vi* (fort)gehen; (ab)fahren.

goal *n* Ziel *n*; Tor *n*.

goalkeeper *n* Torhüter(in) *m(f)*.

god *n* Gott *m*.

godchild *n* Patenkind *n*.

goddaughter *n* Patentochter *f*.

goddess *n* Göttin *f*.

godfather *n* Pate *m*, Patenonkel *m*.

godmother *n* Patin *f*, Patentante *f*.

godson *n* Patensohn *m*.

gold *n* Gold *n*; Goldgelb *n*.

golden *adj* golden; Gold-.

goldfish *n* Goldfisch *m*.

goldsmith *n* Goldschmied(in) *m(f)*.

golf *n* Golf *m*.

golf ball *n* Golfball *m*.

golf club *n* club de golf *m*.

golf course *n* Golfplatz *m*.

golfer *n* Golfspieler(in) *m(f)*.

gondolier *n* Gondoliere *m*.

gong *n* Gong *m*.

good *adj* gut.

goodbye! *excl* auf Wiedersehen! auf Wiederhören!

Good Friday *n* Karfreitag *m*.

goodness *n* Güte *f*.

goose *n* Gans *f*.

gooseberry *n* Stachelbeere *f*.

gorilla *n* Gorilla *m*.

gorse *n* Stechginster *m*.

gospel *n* Evangelium *n*.

gossip *n* Klatsch *m*; Schwatz *m*:—*vi* klatschen; schwatzen.

govern *vt* regieren.

government *n* Regierung *f*.

grab *vt* ergreifen; packen; schnappen.

grace *n* Anmut *f*; Gnade *f*.

graceful *adj* anmutig; graziös.

gracious *adj* gnädig.

grade *n* Grad *m*; Klasse *f*; Stufe *f*.

gradient *n* Steigung *f*; Gefälle *n*; Gradient *m*.

gradual *adj* allmählich:——**ly** *adv* nach und nach.

grain *n* Korn *n*; Getreide *n*.

gram *n* Gramm *n*.

grammar *n* Grammatik *f*.

grammatical *adj* grammatisch.

granary *n* Kornkammer *f*; Getreidespeicher *m*.

grand *adj* groß(artig).

grandchild *n* Enkelkind *n*.

granddaughter *n* Enkeltochter *f*, Enkelin *f*:—**great-~** Urenkelin *f*.

grandfather *n* Großvater *m*:—**great-~** Urgroßvater *m*.

grandmother *n* Großmutter *f*:—**great-~** Urgroßmutter *f*.

grandparents *npl* Großeltern *pl*.

grandson *n* Enkelsohn *m*, Enkel *m*:—**great-~** Urenkel *m*.

granite *n* Granit *m*.

granny *n* Oma *f*.

grant *vt* gewähren, bewilligen:—*n* Bewilligung *f*.

grape *n* Weintraube *f*.

grapefruit *n* Grapefruit *f*; Pampelmuse *f*.

graph *n* graphische Darstellung *f*; Diagramm *n*; Kurve *f*.

graphic(al) *adj* anschaulich; plastisch; graphisch; Schrift-.

graphics *n* Graphik *f*; graphische Darstellung *f*.

grasp *vt* packen; (er)greifen; an sich reißen:—*n* Griff *m*; Gewalt *f*; Auffassungsgabe *f*; Verständnis *n*.

grass *n* Gras *n*; Rasen *m*.

grasshopper n Grashüpfer m; Heuschrecke f.

grate n Gitter n; Rost m:—vt vergittern; reiben.

grateful adj dankbar.

gratitude n Dankbarkeit f.

grave n Grab n:—adj ernst; gewichtig.

gravedigger n Totengräber m.

gravel n Kies m; Schotter m; Geröll n.

gravestone n Grabstein m.

graveyard n Friedhof m.

gravity n Schwere f; Gravitation f.

graze vt vi weiden.

grease n Fett n; Schmalz n:—vt (ein)fetten.

greasy adj fettig; schmierig; ölig.

great adj groß; großartig.

greed n (Hab)Gier f; Gierigkeit f.

greedy adj (hab)gierig; gefräßig.

Greek n Griechisch n; Grieche m, Griechin f.

green adj grün; unreif.

greengrocer n Obst- und Gemüsehändler m.

greenhouse n Gewächshaus n; Treibhaus n.

greet vt (be)grüßen; empfangen.

greeting n Gruß m; Begrüßung f.

grenade n (mil) Granate f; Tränengaspatrone f.

grey adj grau.

greyhound n Windhund m.

grid n Gitter n; Rost m; Netz n.

grief n Gram m; Kummer m.

grill n Grill m; Gegrilltes n:—vt grillen.

grim adj grimmig; erbittert.

grime n Schmutz m; Ruß m.

grimy adj schmutzig; rußig.

grin n Grinsen n:—vi grinsen; feixen.

grind vt schleifen; wetzen.

grip n Griff m; Halt m:—vt ergreifen; packen.

grit n (Streu)Sand m; Kies m.

groan vi (auf)stöhnen; ächzen:—n Stöhnen n; Ächzen n.

grocer n Lebensmittelhändler m.

groom n Pferdepfleger(in) m(f); Bräutigam m:—vt pflegen.

gross adj brutto; Gesamt-; schwer; grob; anstößig; unfein.

grotesque adj grotesk.

ground n Grund m; (Erd)Boden m:—vt niederlegen; auf Grund setzen.

group n Gruppe f; Konzern m:—vt gruppieren.

grow vi wachsen.

growl vi knurren; grollen:—n Knurren n; Grollen n.

growth n Wachstum n.

grumble vi murren; knurren; grollen.

grumpy adj mürrisch; mißmutig; verdrießlich.

grunt vi grunzen; murren; ächzen:—n Grunzen n; Ächzen n.

guarantee n Garantie f; Bürgschaft f; Sicherheit f:—vt garantieren; (ver)bürgen für; sichern.

guard n Wache f; Wächter m:—vt bewachen.

guerrilla n Guerilla f.

guess vi raten.

guest n Gast m.

guide vt (an)leiten; führen:—n Führer(in) m(f); Leitfaden m.

guilt n Schuld f.

guilty adj schuldig.

guitar n Gitarre f.

gulf n Golf m; Bucht f; Abgrund m.

gull n Möwe f.

gullible adj leichtgläubig.

gum n Zahnfleisch n; Gummi m.

gun n Geschütz n; Feuerwaffe f.

gunfire n Geschützfeuer n.

gunman n Revolverheld m; Bewaffnete(r) f(m).

gunpowder n Schießpulver n.

gush *vi* strömen; sich ergießen.
gust *n* Bö *f*; Windstoß *m*; Ausbruch *m*; Sturm *m*.
gutter *n* Rinnstein *m*; Gosse *f*, (Dach) Rinne *f*.

guy *n* Kerl *m*; Typ *m*.
guzzle *vt* saufen; fressen.
gym(nasium) *n* Turnhalle *f*.
gymnast *n* Turner(in) *m(f)*.
gymnastics *npl* Turnen *n*; Gymnastik *f*.

H

habit *n* (An)Gewohnheit *f*; Sucht *f*.
habitat *n* Habitat *n*.
habitual *adj* gewohnheitsmäßig.
haddock *n* Schellfisch *m*.
hail *n* Hagel *m*:—*vi* hageln.
hair *n* Haar *n*; Haare *pl*.
hairbrush *n* Haarbürste *f*; Haarpinsel *m*.
haircut *n* Haarschnitt *m*; Frisur *f*.
hairdresser *n* Friseur *m*, Friseuse *f*.
hairy *adj* haarig.
half *n* Hälfte *f*:—*adj* halb.
hall *n* Halle *f*; Saal *m*.
halt *vi* anhalten:—*n* Halt *m*.
halve *vt* halbieren.
ham *n* Schinken *m*.
hamburger *n* Hamburger *m*.
hammer *n* Hammer *m*:—*vt* hämmern.
hand *n* Hand *f*.
handbag *n* Handtasche *f*.
handbrake *n* Handbremse *f*.
handcuff *n* Handschelle *f*.
handicap *n* Handikap *n*; Behinderung *f*.
handicapped *adj* behindert.
handkerchief *n* Taschentuch *n*.
handle *n* (Hand)Griff *m*:—*vt* anfassen.
handsome *adj* hübsch; stattlich.
hang *vt vi* hängen.
hangman *n* Henker *m*.
hangover *n* Kater *m*.
happen *vi* geschehen; passieren.
happiness *n* Glück *n*; Glückseligkeit *f*.
happy *adj* glücklich; froh.

harass *vt* belästigen; schikanieren.
harbour *n* Hafen *m*.
hard *adj* hart; schwierig.
hardly *adv* kaum; hart; streng.
hardware *n* Hardware *f*.
hare *n* Hase *m*.
harm *n* Schaden *m*; Unrecht *m*; Übel *n*:—*vt* schaden; verletzen.
harmful *adj* nachteilig; schädlich.
harmless *adj* harmlos.
harmonious *adj* harmonisch.
harmony *n* Harmonie *f*.
harness *n* Geschirr *n*:—*vt* anschirren.
harp *n* Harfe *f*.
harpist *n* Harfenist(in) *m(f)*.
harsh *adj* rauh; grell.
harvest *n* Ernte *f*.
haste *n* Eile *f*.
hasten *vt vi* (sich be)eilen.
hasty *adj* hastig; (vor)eilig; übereilt.
hat *n* Hut *m*.
hatch *vt* ausbrüten:—*n* Brut *f*; Luke *f*; Durchreiche *f*.
hate *n* Haß *m*; Abscheu *f*:—*vt* hassen, verabscheuen.
hateful *adj* hassenswert; abscheulich.
hatred *n* Haß *m*; Abscheu *f*.
have *vt v aux* haben.
hawk *n* Falke *m*; Habicht *m*; Mörtelbrett *n*.
hawthorn *n* Weißdorn *m*.
hay *n* Heu *n*.

hazard n Gefahr f; Risiko m:—vt riskieren; wagen.

hazardous adj gewagt; gefährlich.

haze n Dunst(schleier) m, Schleier m.

hazel n Haselnuß f; Nußbraun n:—adj nußbraun.

hazelnut n Haselnuß f.

hazy adj dunstig.

he pn er.

head n Kopf m; Haupt n.

headache n Kopfschmerzen mpl.

headlight n Scheinwerfer m.

headline n Schlagzeile f; Überschrift f.

headmaster n Direktor m; Rektor m.

headquarters npl Hauptquartier n.

heal vt vi heilen.

health n Gesundheit f.

healthy adj gesund.

heap n Haufen m:—vt (über)häufen.

hear vt vi hören.

hearse n Leichenwagen m.

heart n Herz n:—by ~ auswendig.

heat n Hitze f.

heater n Heizgerät n.

heating n Heizung f.

heatwave n Hitzewelle f.

heaven n Himmel m.

heavenly adj himmlisch.

heavy adj schwer; heftig.

hectic adj hektisch.

hedge n Hecke f.

hedgehog n Igel m.

heel n Ferse f.

heifer n Färse f.

height n Höhe f; Größe f.

heighten vt erhöhen; hervorheben.

heir n Erbe m:—~ apparent rechtmäßiger Erbe m.

heiress n Erbin f.

heirloom n Erbstück n.

helicopter n Hubschrauber m.

hell n Hölle f.

helm n (mar) Helm m; Ruder n.

helmet n Helm m.

help vt vi helfen:—n Hilfe f.

helper n Helfer(in) m(f).

helpful adj hilfsbereit; hilfreich.

helpless adj hilflos; unbeholfen.

hem n Saum m; Rand m:—vt säumen.

hemisphere n Hemisphäre f; Halbkugel f.

hen n Henne f; Huhn f; Weibchen n.

her poss adj ihr, ihre.

herb n Kraut n:—~s pl Kräuter pl.

herd n Herde f; Rudel n; Hirt(in) m(f).

here adv hier; hierher.

heritage n Erbe n.

hermit n Einsiedler m; Eremit m.

hero n Held m; Heros m; Halbgott m.

heroic adj heroisch; heldenhaft; Helden-; grandios.

heroine n Heldin f; Halbgöttin f.

heron n Reiher m.

herring n Hering m.

hers poss pn (der, die, das) ihrige.

herself pn sie selbst; ihr selbst; sich (selbst).

hesitant adj zögernd.

hesitate vi zögern.

hesitation n Zögern n.

heterosexual adj heterosexuell:—n Heterosexuelle(r) f(m).

hibernate vi überwintern; Winterschlaf halten.

hiccup n Schluckauf m:—vi den Schluckauf haben.

hide vt verbergen; verstecken.

hideous adj scheußlich; gräßlich.

hierarchy n Hierarchie f.

high adj hoch.

hijack vt entführen; überfallen.

hijacker n (Flugzeug)Entführer m; Räuber m.

hike vi wandern; marschieren.

hilarious adj lustig; vergnügt.

hill n Hügel m; Anhöhe f; Haufen m.

hilt n Heft n; Griff m.

him pn ihn; ihm.

himself pn sich (selbst); selbst.

hinder vt aufhalten; (be)hindern.

hindrance n Behinderung f; Hindernis n.

hinge n Scharnier n; Angel f.

hint n Wink m; Andeutung f:—vt andeuten.

hip n Hüfte f; Hagebutte f.

hippopotamus n Flußpferd n.

hire vt (ver)mieten; engagieren:—n Miete f; Lohn m.

his poss adj sein, seine:—poss pn (der, die, das) seine.

hiss vt vi zischen.

historian n Historiker(in) m(f).

historic(al) adj historisch; geschichtlich.

history n Geschichte f.

hit vt schlagen:—n Schlag m.

hitch vt ankoppeln; per Anhalter fahren:—n Knoten m; Problem n.

hive n Bienenstock m; Bienenschwarm n.

hoard n Hort m:—vt horten.

hoarse adj heiser.

hobby n Steckenpferd n; Hobby n; Liebhaberei f.

hockey n Hockey n.

hoe n Hacke f:—vt hacken.

hog n (Haus)Schwein n.

hold vt (fest)halten:—n Halt m; Griff m.

hole n Loch n.

holiday n Feiertag m; freier Tag m:—~s pl Ferien pl.

hollow adj hohl:—n Höhle f.

holly n Stechpalme f.

hollyhock n Stockrose f.

holocaust n Holocaust m; Katastrophe f.

holster n Halfter n.

holy adj heilig; geweiht.

him pn ihn; ihm.

homage n Huldigung f; Homage f.

home n Heim n; Zuhause n; Heimat f.

homeless adj obdachlos.

home-made adj hausgemacht.

homesick adj heimwehkrank.

homeward adj Heim-; Rück-:—adv heimwärts; nach Hause.

homosexual adj homosexuell:—n Homosexuelle(r) f(m).

honest adj ehrlich.

honesty n Ehrlichkeit f.

honey n Honig m.

honeycomb n Honigwabe f.

honeymoon n Flitterwochen fpl.

honeysuckle n Geißblatt n.

honour n Ehre f:—vt ehren.

honourable adj ehrenwert.

hood n Kapuze f; Kappe f.

hoof n Huf m.

hook n (Angel)Haken m:—vt (zu)haken.

hooligan n Rowdy m.

hoop n Reif(en) m; Ring m; Bügel m.

hop n (bot) Hopfen m; Sprung m:—vi hüpfen; springen.

hope n Hoffnung f; Aussicht f:—vi (er)hoffen.

hopeful adj hoffnungsvoll:—~ly adv hoffentlich.

hopeless adj hoffnungslos.

horizon n Horizont m.

horizontal adj horizontal.

horn n Horn n; Hupe f; Schalltrichter m; Sattelknopf m.

hornet n Hornisse f.

horoscope n Horoskop n.

horrible adj schrecklich; furchtbar.

horrific adj schrecklich; entsetzlich.

horrify vt entsetzen; mit Schrecken erfüllen.

horror n Entsetzen n; Schrecken m.

horse n Pferd n; Bock m.

horse chesnut n Roßkastanie f.

horsefly n (Pferde)Bremse f.
horsepower n Pferdestärke f.
horseradish n Meerrettich m.
horseshoe n Hufeisen n.
hospitable adj gastfreundlich; gastlich.
hospital n Krankenhaus n.
hospitality n Gastfreundschaft f; Gastlichkeit f.
host n Gastgeber(in) m(f); (Gast)Wirt m; Moderator(in) m(f).
hostage n Geisel f.
hostess n Gastgeberin f; (Gast)Wirtin f; Hostess f.
hostile adj feindlich; feindselig.
hostility n Feindschaft f; Feindseligkeit f.
hot adj heiß; warm.
hotel n Hotel n.
hound n Jagdhund m.
hour n Stunde f.
hourly adv stündlich.
house n Haus n:—vt unterbringen.
household n Haushalt m.
housekeeper n Haushälter(in) m(f).
houskeeping n Haushaltsführung f.
housewife n Hausfrau f.
housework n Hausarbeit f.
housing n Unterbringung f.
hover vi schweben; sich herumtreiben; schwanken.
how adv wie.
however adv wie auch (immer):—conj dennoch; (je)doch; aber.
howl vi heulen; brüllen:—n Heulen n; Schrei m; Brüllen n.
hub n (Rad)Nabe f.
hubcap n Radkappe f.
hug vt umarmen:—n Umarmung f.
huge adj riesig; gewaltig; mächtig.
hull n Rumpf m.
hum vi summen; brummen.
human adj menschlich; Menschen-.

humanity n Menschheit f; Humanität f; Menschlichkeit f.
humble adj bescheiden; demütig:—vt demütigen; erniedrigen.
humid adj feucht; humid.
humidity n Feuchtigkeit f.
humiliate vt demütigen.
humiliation n Demütigung f.
humility n Demut f; Bescheidenheit f.
humour n Humor m.
humorous adj humorvoll.
hump n Buckel m; Höcker m; (kleiner) Hügel m.
hundred num hundert.
hundredth adj hundertste(r, s).
hunger n Hunger m:—vi Hunger haben; hungern.
hungry adj hungrig.
hunt vt vi jagen:—n Jagd f.
hunter n Jäger m.
hurdle n Hürde f; Hindernis n; Geflecht n.
hurricane n Hurrikan m; Wirbelsturm m; Orkan m.
hurry vi eilen; hasten; sich beeilen:—n Hast f; Eile f.
hurt vt verletzen; verwunden:—n Schmerz m; Verletzung f; Wunde f.
hurtful adj verletzend; schmerzlich; schädlich.
husband n Ehemann m; Gatte m.
hut n Hütte f; Baracke f.
hyacinth n Hyazinthe f.
hydraulic adj hydraulisch.
hydrogen n Wasserstoff m.
hydrophobia n Tollwut f; Hydrophobie f.
hyena n Hyäne f.
hygiene n Hygiene f; Gesundheitspflege f.
hygienic adj hygienisch.
hyphen n (gr) Bindestrich m; Trennungszeichen n.

hypocrisy *n* Heuchelei *f*; Scheinheilig-keit *f*.
hypocrite *n* Heuchler(in) *m(f)*.
hypocritical *adj* heuchlerisch; schein-heilig.

hypothesis *n* Hypothese *f*.
hypothetical *adj* hypothetisch.
hysteria *n* Hysterie *f*.
hysterical *adj* hysterisch.

I

I *pn* ich.
ice *n* Eis *n*.
iceberg *n* Eisberg *m*.
ice cream *n* Eis *n*; Eiscreme *f*.
ice rink *n* Eisbahn *f*.
ice skating *n* Eislauf *m*; Eislaufen *n*.
icicle *n* Eiszapfen *m*.
icy *adj* eisig; vereist; eiskalt.
idea *n* Idee *f*.
ideal *adj* ideal.
identical *adj* identisch.
identification *n* Identifizierung *f*.
identify *vt* identifizieren.
identity *n* Identität *f*.
idiom *n* Idiom *n*; Redewendung *f*.
idiomatic *adj* idiomatisch.
idiot *n* Idiot *m*; Trottel *m*.
idiotic *adj* idiotisch; blöd.
Idle *adj* untätig; müßig; faul.
idleness *n* Untätigkeit *f*; Faulheit *f*.
idol *n* Idol *n*; Götze *m*.
if *conj* wenn (auch); falls; ob:—~ **not** wenn nicht.
igloo *n* Iglu *n*.
ignite *vt* (ent)zünden.
ignition *n* (*chem*) Erhitzung *f*; Entzün-den *n*; Zündung *f*.
ignorance *n* Unwissenheit *f*; Unkennt-nis *f*; Ignoranz *f*.
ignorant *adj* unwissentlich.
ignore *vt* ignorieren; nicht beachten.
ill *adj* schlimm; schlecht; übel; widrig; unheilvoll; krank:—*n* Übel *n*.

illegal *adj* illegal; verboten; gesetzwid-rig; regelwidrig.
illegality *n* Ungesetzlichkeit *f*; Gesetz-widrigkeit *f*; Illegalität *f*.
illegible *adj* unleserlich.
illegitimate *adj* unehelich; inkorrekt; illegal; gesetzwidrig.
illicit *adj* unzulässig; gesetzwidrig.
illiterate *adj* analphabetisch; ungebildet.
illness *n* Krankheit *f*.
illogical *adj* unlogisch.
illusion *n* Illusion *f*; Sinnestäuschung *f*, Einbildung *f*; Wahn *m*.
illustrate *vt* erläutern; veranschauli-chen; illustrieren.
illustration *n* Illustration *f*; Erläute-rung *f*; Veranschaulichung *f*.
illustrative *adj* erläuternd; veran-schaulichend; illustrativ.
illustrious *adj* glanzvoll; erlaucht; be-rühmt.
ill-will *n* Übelwollen *n*; böse Absicht *f*.
image *n* Bild(nis) *n*; Ebenbild *n*; Bild-säule *f*; Symbol *n*; Metapher *f*.
imaginable *adj* vorstellbar; denkbar.
imaginary *adj* imaginär; eingebildet; Phantasie-.
imagination *n* Einbildung(skraft) *f*; Vorstellung *f*.
imaginative *adj* einfallsreich; phanta-sievoll; phantastisch.
imagine *vt* sich vorstellen; sich (aus) denken; sich einbilden.

imbalance n Unausgewogenheit f; Ungleichgewicht n.

imbue vt durchtränken; tief färben.

imitate vt nachahmen; nachbilden.

imitation n Nachahmung f; Nachbildung f.

immature adj unreif; unausgereift.

immediate adj unmittelbar; unverzüglich; sofortig:—~ly adv unmittelbar; sofort; unverzüglich.

immense adj riesig; enorm; immens.

immigrant n Einwanderer m, Einwanderin f; Immigrant(in) m(f).

immigration n Einwanderung f; Immigration f.

imminent adj drohend.

immoral adj unmoralisch; unsittlich.

immortal adj unsterblich.

immortality n Unsterblichkeit f; Unvergänglichkeit f.

immune adj immun; unempfänglich.

impact n Aufprall m; Einschlag m; Impakt m.

impatience n Ungeduld f.

impatient adj ungeduldig; unduldsam; intolerant.

impersonal adj unpersönlich.

impetus n Antrieb m; Anstoß m.

implicit adj impliziert; vorbehaltlos.

imply vt implizieren.

impolite adj unhöflich.

import vt importieren; einführen:—n Import m; Einfuhr f.

importance n Wichtigkeit f.

important adj wichtig.

importer n Importeur m.

impose vt auferlegen; aufdrängen.

impossibility n Unmöglichkeit f.

impossible adj unmöglich.

impractical adj unpraktisch; unklug; undurchführbar.

imprecise adj ungenau.

impress vt beeindrucken; imponieren;

durchdringen; tief einprägen; (auf) drücken; einprägen.

impression n Eindruck m; Nachahmung f; (Ab)Druck m; Aufdruck m; Vertiefung f; Abzug m; Auflage f.

impressive adj eindrucksvoll; imposant; wirkungsvoll.

imprison vt inhaftieren; einsperren; einschließen.

imprisonment n Freiheitsstrafe f; Haft f; Inhaftierung f.

improbable adj unwahrscheinlich.

improve vt verbessern:—vi sich (ver) bessern.

improvement n (Ver)Besserung f; Veredelung f; Steigerung f.

impulse n Impuls m; Antrieb m; (An) Stoß m.

impulsive adj impulsiv; spontan; Trieb-.

impure adj unrein; verunreinigt; verfälscht.

in prep in; innerhalb; an; auf; bei; mit.

inability n Unfähigkeit f; Unvermögen n.

inaccuracy n Ungenauigkeit f.

inaccurate adj ungenau; unrichtig.

inactive adj untätig; träge; lustlos; inaktiv.

inactivity n Untätigkeit f; Inaktivität f.

inadequate adj unzulänglich; unangemessen.

inadmissible adj unzulässig; unstatthaft.

inane adj leer; albern.

inaudible adj unhörbar.

inauspicious adj ungünstig; unheilvoll.

incapable adj unfähig; hilflos; ungeeignet; untauglich.

incapacity n (Erwerbs)Unfähigkeit f; Untauglichkeit f.

inch n Zoll m:—~ by ~ Zentimeter um Zentimeter.

incidence n Vorkommen n; Häufigkeit f.

incident n Vorfall m; Zwischenfall.

incinerator n Verbrennungsanlage f.

incite vt anregen; anspornen.

inclination n Neigung f; (Ab)Hang m.

incline vt vi neigen.

include vt einschließen; umfassen.

including prep einschließlich.

inclusion n Einschluß m; Einbeziehung f.

inclusive adj einschließlich; inklusive.

income n Einkommen n.

incomparable adj unvergleichbar.

incompatibility n Unvereinbarkeit f; Unverträglichkeit f.

incompatible adj unvereinbar; unverträglich.

incompetence n Unfähigkeit f; Inkompetenz f.

incompetent adj unfähig; unqualifiziert.

incomplete adj unvollständig; unvollendet.

incomprehensible adj unbegreiflich; unverständlich.

inconclusive adj nicht überzeugend; ergebnislos.

inconsistent adj inkonsequent; unbeständig; unvereinbar; widersprüchlich.

inconvenience n Unbequemlichkeit f; Ungelegenheit f; Unannehmlichkeit f:—vt stören; zur Last fallen; Unannehmlichkeiten bereiten.

inconvenient adj unbequem; ungelegen; lästig.

incorporate vt vereinigen; einverleiben; aufnehmen; enthalten; einbauen; verkörpern; vi sich vereinigen; (law) eine Gesellschaft gründen.

incorporation n Vereinigung f; Einverleibung f; Eintragung f.

incorrect adj unrichtig; fehlerhaft; inkorrekt.

increase vt vergrößern; vermehren; steigern; erhöhen:—vi zunehmen; sich vermehren:—n Vergrößerung f; Zunahme f; Steigerung f; Erhöhung f; Vermehrung f.

incredible adj unglaublich; unglaubwürdig.

incur vt sich zuziehen; sich aussetzen; geraten in.

incurable adj unheilbar.

indeed adv in der Tat; tatsächlich; wirklich; freilich.

indefinite adj unbestimmt; unbegrenzt.

independence n Unabhängigkeit f; Selbständigkeit f.

independent adj unabhängig; selbständig.

indescribable adj unbeschreiblich.

indeterminate adj unbestimmt; ungewiß; unentschieden.

index n Index m; (Inhalts)Verzeichnis n; Register n.

indicate vt zeigen auf; hinweisen auf; andeuten; anzeigen.

indication n Zeigen n; (An)Zeichen n; Hinweis m; Andeutung f; Indikation f.

indifferent adj gleichgültig; mittelmäßig; indifferent.

indigenous adj einheimisch.

indigent adj arm; bedürftig; mittellos.

indigestible adj unverdaulich.

indigestion n Verdauungsstörung f; Magenverstimmung f.

indignant adj entrüstet; empört.

indignation n Entrüstung f; Empörung f.

indigo n Indigo m.

indirect adj indirekt; mittelbar.

indiscreet adj unbesonnen; indiskret.

indiscretion n Unbedachtheit f; Indiskretion f.

indiscriminate *adj* nicht wählerisch; wahllos.

indistinct *adj* undeutlich.

individual *adj* einzeln; Einzel-; individuell.

indoors *adv* im Haus; drinnen; ins Haus.

industrial *adj* industriell; Industrie-.

industrialist *n* Industrielle(r) *f(m)*.

industrious *adj* fleißig.

industry *n* Industrie *f*; Gewerbe *n*; Arbeit *f*; Fleiß *m*.

inefficient *adj* ineffizient; (leistungs)unfähig.

inequality *n* Ungleichheit *f*; Verschiedenheit *f*.

inert *adj* träge; inert.

inertia *n* Trägheit *f*.

inevitable *adj* unvermeidlich.

inexcusable *adj* unentschuldbar; unverzeihlich.

inexpensive *adj* billig; nicht teuer.

inexperience *n* Unerfahrenheit *f*.

inexperienced *adj* unerfahren.

inexplicable *adj* unerklärlich.

infant *n* Säugling *m*; Kleinkind *n*.

infantry *n* Infanterie *f*.

infatuated *adj* betört; vernarrt.

infatuation *n* Vernarrtheit *f*; Schwarm *m*.

infect *vt* infizieren; anstecken; befallen.

infection *n* Infektion(skrankheit) *f*; Ansteckung *f*; Befall *m*.

infectious *adj* ansteckend; infektiös.

infer *vt* schließen; folgern; andeuten.

inference *n* (Schluß)Folgerung *f*; (Rück)Schluß *m*.

inferior *adj* untergeordnet; niedriger; minderwertig; Unter-:—*n* Untergebene(r) *f(m)*; Unterlegene(r) *f(m)*.

inferiority *n* Unterlegenheit *f*; Minderwertigkeit *f*.

infiltrate *vt* einsickern in; infiltrieren.

infinite *adj* unendlich; grenzenlos; endlos.

infinity *n* Unendlichkeit *f*; Grenzenlosigkeit *f*.

infirm *adj* schwach; gebrechlich; fragwürdig.

inflate *vt* aufblasen; aufpumpen; aufblähen.

inflation *n* Inflation *f*; Aufgeblasenheit *f*; Aufpumpen *n*.

influence *n* Einfluß *m*:—*vt* beeinflussen; bewegen.

influential *adj* einflußreich; maßgeblich.

influenza *n* Grippe *f*.

inform *vt* informieren; mitteilen.

informal *adj* zwanglos; inoffiziell.

informality *n* Zwanglosigkeit *f*.

information *n* Information *f*; Auskunft *f*.

infrastructure *n* Infrastruktur *f*.

infuriate *vt* wütend machen.

ingot *n* Barren *m*.

ingratitude *n* Undankbarkeit *f*.

ingredient *n* Bestandteil *m*; Zutat *f*.

inhabit *vt* bewohnen; leben in.

inhabitant *n* Bewohner(in) *m(f)*; Einwohner(in) *m(f)*.

inhale *vt* einatmen; inhalieren.

inherit *vt* (er)erben; beerben.

inheritance *n* Erbschaft *f*; Erbgut *n*.

initial *adj* anfänglich; Ausgangs-; erste(r, s):—*n* Initiale *f*.

initiate *vt* initiieren.

initiation *n* Initiation *f*.

initiative *n* Initiative *f*.

inject *vt* injizieren; einspritzen.

injection *n* Injektion *f*; Spritze *f*; Einspritzung *f*.

injure *vt* verletzen.

injury *n* Verletzung *f*.

injustice *n* Ungerechtigkeit *f*; Unrecht *n*.

ink *n* Tinte *f*; Tusche *f*; Druckfarbe *f*.

inland *adj* inländisch; Binnen-; einheimisch:—*adv* landeinwärts.

inn *n* Gasthaus *n*; Wirtshaus *n*.

innate *adj* angeboren; innewohnen.

inner *adj* Innen-; innere(r, s).
innkeeper *n* (Gast)Wirt(in) *m(f)*.
innocence *n* Unschuld *f*; Unwissenheit *f*.
innocent *adj* unschuldig.
inoculate *vt* (ein)impfen.
inoculation *n* (Ein)Impfung *f*.
inoffensive *adj* harmlos; friedfertig.
inorganic *adj* unorganisch.
inquire *vi* (nach)fragen; sich erkundigen; nachforschen.
inquiry *n* Erkundigung *f*; (An)Frage *f*.
inquisitive *adj* wißbegierig; neugierig.
insane *adj* wahnsinnig.
insanity *n* Wahnsinn *m*.
insect *n* Insekt *n*.
insecure *adj* unsicher; ungesichert.
insecurity *n* Unsicherheit *f*.
insert *vt* einführen; einwerfen.
insertion *n* Einführung *f*; Einwurf *m*.
inside *adv* (dr)innen; innerhalb; hinein; herein.
insight *n* Einblick *m*; Einsicht *f*.
insignificant *adj* bedeutungslos; unwichtig.
insincere *adj* unaufrichtig; falsch.
insinuate *vt* andeuten; anspielen auf.
insinuation *n* Andeutung *f*; Anspielung *f*.
insist *vi* bestehen.
insistence *n* Bestehen *n*.
insistent *adj* beharrlich.
insomnia *n* Schlaflosigkeit *f*.
inspect *vt* untersuchen; prüfen.
inspection *n* Untersuchung *f*; Prüfung *f*.
inspector *n* Inspektor *m*; Aufsichtsbeamte(r) *f(m)*; Prüfer(in) *m(f)*.
inspiration *n* Inspiration *f*.
inspire *vt* inspirieren.
install *vt* installieren; einbauen; einsetzen.
installation *n* Installation *f*; Einbau *m*; Einrichtung *f*; Einsetzung *f*.
instalment *n* Rate *f*.

instance *n* Beispiel *n*; Fall *m*; Instanz *f*:—**for ~** zum Beispiel.
instant *n* Moment *m*; Augenblick *m*.
instead (of) *prep* (an)statt.
instinct *n* Instinkt *m*.
instinctive *adj* instinktiv.
institute *n* Institut *n*; Anstalt *f*.
institution *n* Institution *f*.
instruct *vt* unterrichten.
instruction *n* Unterricht *m*.
instrument *n* Instrument *n*.
insulate *vt* isolieren.
insulation *n* Isolierung *f*.
insult *vt* beleidigen:—*n* Beleidigung *f*.
insulting *adj* beleidigend; unverschämt.
insurance *n* Versicherung *f*; (Ab)Sicherung *f*.
insure *vt* versichern.
intact *adj* intakt.
integrate *vt* integrieren.
integration *n* Integration *f*.
integrity *n* Integrität *f*.
intellect *n* Intellekt *m*; Verstand *m*.
intellectual *adj* intellektuell; geistig.
intelligence *n* Intelligenz *f*.
intelligent *adj* intelligent.
intend *vi* beabsichtigen; vorhaben.
intense *adj* intensiv.
intensity *n* Intensität *f*; Stärke *f*.
intensive *adj* intensiv; stark; heftig; gründlich.
intent *n* Absicht *f*; Vorsatz *m*; Ziel *n*; Zweck *m*.
intention *n* Absicht *f*; Vorhaben *n*; Vorsatz *m*; Zweck *m*; Ziel *n*.
interest *vt* interessieren:—*n* Interesse *n*; Zinsen *pl*.
interesting *adj* interessant.
interfere *vi* stören; eingreifen; sich einmischen.
interference *n* Störung *f*; Einmischung *f*.
interior *adj* innere(r, s); Innen-; inländisch; intern.

internal *adj* innere(r, s); innerlich.
international *adj* international.
interpret *vt* auslegen; interpretieren; dolmetschen.
interpreter *n* Dometscher(in) *m(f)*.
interrogate *vt* verhören.
interrogation *n* Verhör *n*.
interrupt *vt* unterbrechen; aufhalten.
interruption *n* Unterbrechung *f*; Störung *f*.
interval *n* Abstand *m*; Intervall *n*; Pause *f*.
interview *n* Interview *n*.
interviewer *n* Interviewer(in) *m(f)*.
intimate *n* Vertraute(r) *f(m)*:—*adj* vertraut.
intimidate *vt* einschüchtern.
into *prep* in.
intoxicate *vt* berauschen.
intoxication *n* Rausch *m*.
intricate *adj* verschlungen.
introduce *vt* einführen; vorstellen; einleiten.
introduction *n* Einführung *f*; Vorstellung *f*; Einleitung *f*.
introvert *n* introvertierter Mensch *m*.
intrude *vi* sich eindrängen; sich aufdrängen; stören.
intruder *n* Eindringling *m*; Störenfried *m*.
intuition *n* Intuition *f*.
intuitive *adj* intuitiv.
invade *vt* einfallen in.
invalid *adj* ungültig:—*n* Invalide *m*; Kranke(r) *f(m)*.
invalidate *vt* entkräften.
invaluable *adj* unschätzbar.
invariable *adj* unveränderlich.
invasion *n* Einfall *m*.
invent *vt* erfinden.
invention *n* Erfindung *f*.
inventive *adj* erfinderisch.
inventor *n* Erfinder(in) *m(f)*.

inverse *adj* umgekehrt.
inversion *n* Umkehrung *f*.
invert *vt* umkehren.
invest *vt* investieren; anlegen.
investigate *vt* untersuchen.
investigation *n* Untersuchung *f*.
investment *n* Investition *f*; Anlage *f*.
invisible *adj* unsichtbar.
invitation *n* Einladung *f*.
invite *vt* einladen.
invoice *n* Rechnung *f*.
involve *vt* verwickeln.
involved *adj* verwickelt.
involvement *n* Verwicklung *f*.
iris *n* Iris *f*.
iron *n* Eisen *n*; Bügeleisen *n*:—*adj* eisern; Eisen-:—*vt* bügeln.
ironic *adj* ironisch.
irony *n* Ironie *f*.
irrational *adj* irrational.
irrelevant *adj* irrelevant.
irritate *vt* reizen; (ver)ärgern; irritieren.
irritating *adj* ärgerlich; irritierend; Reiz-.
irritation *n* Ärger *m*; Verärgerung *f*; Reizung *f*; Irritation *f*.
Islam *n* Islam *m*.
island *n* Insel *f*.
isolate *vt* isolieren.
isolation *n* Isolation *f*.
issue *n* Ausgabe *f*; Erteilung *f*:—*vt* (her)ausgeben; erteilen.
it *pn* es; er; ihn; sie.
italic *n* Kursivschrift *f*.
itch *n* Jucken *n*; Juckreiz *m*:—*vi* jukken; kratzen.
item *n* Gegenstand *m*; Posten *m*.
itinerary *n* Reiseweg *m*; Reisebericht *m*; Reiseführer *m*.
its *poss adj* sein, seine; ihr, ihre.
itself *pn* sich; sich selbst; selbst.
ivory *n* Elfenbein *n*.
ivy *n* Efeu *m*.

J

jack *n* Wagenheber *m*; Bube *m*.
jackal *n* Schakal *m*.
jacket *n* Jacke *f*; Jackett *n*.
jade *n* Jade *f*.
jaguar *n* Jaguar *m*.
jail *n* Gefängnis *n*.
jailer *n* Gefängniswärter *m*.
jam *n* Gedränge *n*; Verstopfung *f*; Marmelade *f*.
January *n* Januar *m*, Jänner *m*.
jar *n* Krug *m*.
javelin *n* Wurfspieß *m*; Speer *m*.
jaw *n* Kiefer *m*.
jay *n* Eichelhäher *m*.
jazz *n* Jazz *m*.
jealous *adj* eifersüchtig.
jealousy *n* Eifersucht *f*.
jeer *vi* höhnisch lachen:—*n* Hohngelächter *n*.
jelly *n* Gallerte *f*; Gelee *n*; Aspik *m*; Götterspeise *f*.
jellyfish *n* Qualle *f*.
jeopardize *vt* gefährden.
jet *n* Düsenflugzeug *n*; Strahl *m*; Düse *f*; Jett *m*.
jettison *vt* über Bord werfen; abwerfen.
jetty *n* Mole *f*; Pier *m*.
Jew *n* Jude *m*.
jewel *n* Juwel *n*; Edelstein *m*.
jeweller *n* Juwelier *m*.
jewellery *n* Juwelen *pl*; Schmuck *m*.
Jewish *adj* jüdisch.
jig *n* Gigue *f*; Einspannvorrichtung *f*.
jigsaw *n* Puzzle *n*; Dekupiersäge *f*.
job *n* Arbeit *f*; Beschäftigung *f*; Stelle *f*; Arbeitsplatz *m*.

jockey *n* Jockey *m*.
jog *vi* trottenn; joggen.
join *vt* verbinden; vereinigen.
joint *n* Verbindung(sstelle) *f*; Gelenk *n*:—*adj* gemeinsam; gemeinschaftlich; vereint.
joke *n* Witz *m*; Scherz *m*; Spaß *m*:—*vi* scherzen; Witze machen.
joker *n* Spaßvogel *m*; Joker *m*.
jolly *adj* lustig; fröhlich; vergnügt.
journal *n* Tagebuch *n*; Journal *n*.
journalism *n* Journalismus *m*.
journalist *n* Journalist(in) *m(f)*.
journey *n* Reise *f*:—*vt* reisen.
joy *n* Freude *f*.
jubilation *n* Jubel *m*.
jubilee *n* Jubiläum *n*.
judge *n* Richter(in) *m(f)*:—*vt* richten; beurteilen.
judgment *n* Urteil *n*; Beurteilung *f*.
jug *n* Krug *m*.
juggle *vi* jonglieren.
juggler *n* Jongleur *m*; Schwindler *m*.
juice *n* Saft *m*.
juicy *adj* saftig.
July *n* Juli *m*.
jumble *vt* durcheinanderwerfen:—*n* Durcheinander *n*; Ramsch *m*.
jump *vi* (über)springen:—*n* (Ab)-Sprung *m*.
jumper *n* Pullover *m*.
June *n* Juni *m*.
jungle *n* Dschungel *m*.
junior *adj* junior; jünger; Unter-.
juniper *n* Wacholder *m*.
junk *n* Plunder *m*; Schrott *m*.
junta *n* Junta *f*.

jurisdiction n Rechtssprechung f; Gerichtsbarkeit f.

jury n Jury f; Preisgericht n.

just adj gerecht; rechtmäßig; bere

tigt; richtig:—adv gerade; (so)eben.

justice n Gerechtigkeit f; Rechtmäßigkeit f.

~tify vt rechtfertigen.

K

kangaroo n Känguruh n.

karate n Karate n.

keen adj scharf; fein; heftig; begeistert.

keep vt (be)halten; erhalten.

keeper n Wächter m; Verwalter m; Inhaber m; Halter m.

kennel n Hundehütte f.

kerb n Bordstein m.

kernel n Kern m; Korn n.

kettle n Kessel m.

key n Schlüssel m; (mus) Tonart f; Taste f.

keyboard n Tastatur f; Klaviatur f.

kick vt treten; (mit dem Fuß) stoßen:—n (Fuß)Tritt m; (Rück)Stoß m.

kid n Zicklein n; Kitz n.

kidnap vt kidnappen; entführen.

kidney n Niere f.

kill vt (ab)töten; umbringen; ermorden; totschlagen.

killer n Mörder m; Schlächter m.

kilo n Kilo n.

kilobyte n Kilobyte n.

kilogram n Kilogramm n.

kilometre n Kilometer m.

kilt n Kilt m; Schottenrock m.

kind adj freundlich; liebenswürdig: —n Art f, Sorte f.

kindergarten n Kindergarten m.

king n König m.

kingdom n Königreich n; Reich n.

kingfisher n Eisvogel m.

kiosk n Kiosk m; Telefonzelle f.

kipper n Räucherhering m.

kiss n Kuß m:—vt küssen.

kissing n Küssen n.

kit n Ausrüstung f; Montur f; Arbeitsgerät n.

kitchen n Küche f.

kite n Drachen m; Gabelweihe f.

kitten n Kätzchen n.

knack n Trick m; Kniff m; Geschick n; Talent n.

knave n Bube m; Schurke m.

knead vt kneten.

knee n Knie(stück) n.

kneel vi (sich hin)knien.

knell n Totengeläut n.

knife n Messer n.

knight n Ritter m; (Schach) Springer m; Pferd n.

knit vt vi tejer, stricken.

knob n Knauf m; Griff m; Höcker m; Stück(chen) n; Knorren m.

knock vt vi schlagen; klopfen:—n Schlag m; Klopfen n.

knot n Knoten m; Schleife f:—vt (ver)knoten; verheddern.

know vt wissen; können; (er)kennen: —vi wissen.

know-how n Know-how n.

knowledge n Wissen n; Kenntnis f.

knuckle n Knöchel m.

L

label n Etikett n.
laboratory n Labor(atorium) n.
labour n Arbeit f; Mühe f.
labyrinth n Labyrinth n.
lace n Spitze f.
lack vi fehlen:—n Mangel m.
lad n junger Kerl m; Junge m.
ladder n Leiter f; Laufmasche f.
ladle n (Schöpf)Kelle f.
lady n Dame f; Herrin f.
ladybird n Marienkäfer m.
lager n Lagerbier n.
lagoon n Lagune f.
lake n See m.
lamb n Lamm n:—vi lammen.
lame adj lahm.
lamp n Lampe f; Laterne f; Leuchte f.
lampshade n Lampenschirm m.
land n Land n; Boden m:—vt vi landen.
landlady n Vermieterin f; Wirtin f.
landlord n Vermieter m; Wirt m.
landmark n Grenzstein m; Landmarke f.
landowner n Grundbesitzer(in) m(f).
landscape n Landschaft f.
landslide n Erdrutsch m.
lane n Weg m; Gasse f.
language n Sprache f.
lantern n Laterne f.
larch n Lärche f.
larder n Speisekammer f.
large adj groß.
lark n Lerche f.
last adj letzte(r, s):—at ~ adv zuletzt:
—vi (an)dauern.
late adj spät; verspätet.
laugh vi lachen:—n Lachen n.
laughter n Gelächter n.

launder vt waschen.
laundry n Wäsche f; Wäscherei f.
lava n Lava f.
lavatory n Toilette f.
lavender n Lavendel m.
law n Gesetz n; Recht n; Rechtswissen-
schaft f.
lawn n Rasen m.
lawyer n Rechtsanwalt m, Rechtsanwältin f.
lay vt vi legen.
layer n Schicht f; Lage f.
layman n Laie m.
lazy adj faul.
lead n Blei n; Führung f:—vt vi führen.
leader n Führer(in) m(f).
leaf n Blatt n; Flügel m.
leaflet n Flugblatt n; Prospekt m.
leak n Leck n:—vi lecken.
lean vt neigen; lehnen:—vi sich neigen; sich lehnen:—adj mager.
leap vi springen:—n Sprung m.
learn vt vi lernen.
least adj wenigste(r, s):—at ~ wenigstens.
leather n Leder n.
leave vt verlassen; weggehen; abreisen.
lecture n Vortrag m; Vorlesung f.
lecturer n Vortragende(r) f(m).
leek n Porree m.
left adj linke(r, s); Links-:—on the ~
links.
left-handed adj linkshändig.
leg n Bein n.
legal adj gesetzlich.
legality n Gesetzlichkeit f.
legend n Legende f.

legendary *adj* legendär.
legible *adj* leserlich.
legion *n* Legion *f*.
legislation *n* Gesetzgebung *f*.
legitimate *adj* legitim.
leisure *n* Freizeit *f*.
lemon *n* Zitrone *f*.
lemon tree *n* Zitronenbaum *m*.
lend *vt* (ver)leihen.
length *n* Länge *f*.
lengthen *vt* verlängern:—*vi* sich verlängern.
lens *n* Linse *f*; Objektiv *n*.
Lent *n* Fastenzeit *f*.
lentil *n* Linse *f*.
leopard *n* Leopard *m*.
lesbian *n* Lesbierin *f*.
less *adj adv* weniger.
lessen *vt* vermindern:—*vi* sich vermindern.
lesson *n* (Unterrichts)Stunde *f*.
let *vt* lassen; erlauben; vermieten, verpachten.
letter *n* Brief *m*; Buchstabe *m*.
lettuce *n* Salat *m*.
level *adj* eben; waagerecht:—*n* Wasserwaage *f*; Ebene *f*.
lever *n* Hebel *m*.
liability *n* Verantwortlichkeit *f*; Haftung *f*.
liable *adj* verantwortlich; haftpflichtig.
liar *n* Lügner(in) *m(f)*.
liberal *adj* liberal.
liberate *vt* befreien.
liberation *n* Befreiung *f*.
liberty *n* Freiheit *f*.
Libra *n* (*astrol*) Waage *f*.
library *n* Bibliothek *f*.
licence *n* Erlaubnis *f*; Lizenz *f*.
lick *vt* (ab)lecken.
lid *n* Deckel *n*.
lie *n* Lüge *f*:—*vi* lügen; liegen.
lieutenant *n* Leutnant *m*.

life *n* Leben *n*.
lifeboat *n* Rettungsboot *n*.
lift *vt* (hoch)heben; erheben.
light *n* Licht *n*; Helligkeit *f*; Beleuchtung *f*:—*adj* hell; leicht:—*vt* anzünden; (er)leuchten.
lighthouse *n* Leuchtturm *m*.
lighting *n* Beleuchtung *f*.
lightning *n* Blitz *m*.
like *adj* gleich; wie; ähnlich:—*adv* (so) wie:—*vt* gern haben; mögen.
likely *adj* wahrscheinlich; voraussichtlich.
lily *n* Lilie *f*.
lime *n* Kalk *m*; Linde *f*; Limone *f*.
limit *n* Grenze *f*; Beschränkung *f*:—*vt* beschränken; begrenzen.
limp *vi* hinken; humpeln.
line *n* Linie *f*:—*vt* linieren.
linen *n* Leinen *n*; Wäsche *f*.
link *n* Verbindung *f*:—*vt* verbinden.
lion *n* Löwe *m*.
lioness *n* Löwin *f*.
lip *n* Lippe *f*.
lipstick *n* Lippenstift *m*.
liqueur *n* Likör *m*.
liquid *adj* flüssig:—*n* Flüssigkeit *f*.
lisp *vi* lispeln.
list *n* Liste *f*; Verzeichnis *n*:—*vt* verzeichnen.
listen *vi* (zu)hören.
litre *n* Liter *n*.
literature *n* Literatur *f*.
little *adj* klein; wenig.
live *vi* leben; wohnen.
lively *adj* lebendig.
liver *n* Leber *f*.
lizard *n* Eidechse *f*.
load *vt* (be)laden:—*n* Ladung *f*; Last *f*.
loaf *n* Laib *m*; Brot *n*.
loan *n* (Ver)Leihen *n*.
lobe *n* Lappen *m*.
lobster *n* Hummer *m*.

local *adj* lokal; örtlich.
location *n* Stelle *f*; Lage *f*.
lock *n* Schloß *n*:—*vt* verschließen.
loft *n* Dachboden *m*.
logic *n* Logik *f*.
logical *adj* logisch.
loneliness *n* Einsamkeit *f*.
lonely *adj* einsam.
long *adj* lang.
longing *n* Sehnsucht *f*.
long-term *adj* langfristig.
long wave *n* Langwelle *f*.
look *vi* (aus)schauen; aussehen:—*n* Blick *m*; Miene *f*.
loose *adj* lose; locker.
loosen *vt* lösen; lockern.
lose *vt vi* verlieren.
loss *n* Verlust *m*.
lot *n* Los *n*; Anteil *m*; Menge *f*; **a ~** viel.
lottery *n* Lotterie *f*.
loud *adj* laut.
lounge *n* Wohnzimmer *n*; Salon *m*.
louse *n* (*pl* **lice**) Laus *f*.
love *n* Liebe *f*:—**fall in ~** sich verlieben:—*vt* lieben.

lovely *adj* (wunder)schön; reizend.
lover *n* Liebhaber(in) *m(f)*; Geliebte(r) *f(m)*.
low *adj* niedrig.
loyal *adj* loyal; treu.
loyalty *n* Loyalität *f*; Treue *f*.
luck *n* Glück *n*.
lucky *adj* glücklich.
luggage *n* Gepäck *n*.
lullaby *n* Wiegenlied *n*.
lump *n* Klumpen *m*; Brocken *m*.
lunar *adj* lunar; Mond-.
lunch *n* Mittagessen *n*.
lungs *npl* Lunge *f*.
lure *vt* (ver)locken; verführen; ködern.
lust *n* Lust *f*; Wollust *f*.
lute *n* Laute *f*; Kitt *m*.
luxurious *adj* luxuriös.
luxury *n* Luxus *m*.
lymph *n* Lymphe *f*.
lynch *vt* lynchen.
lynx *n* Luchs *m*.
lyrical *adj* lyrisch.
lyrics *npl* (Lied)Text *m*.

M

machine *n* Maschine *f*.
mackerel *n* Makrele *f*.
mad *adj* verrückt.
magazine *n* Zeitschrift *f*, Illustrierte *f*.
magic *n* Zauber *m*:—*adj* zauberhaft, magisch.
magician *n* Zauberkünstler *m*.
magnet *n* Magnet *n*.
magnetic *adj* magnetisch.
magnetism *n* Magnetismus *m*.
magnificent *adj* herrlich.
magnify *vt* vergrößern.

magpie *n* Elster *f*.
mahogany *n* Mahagoni *n*.
maid *n* Dienstmädchen *n*.
maiden *n* Maid *f*.
mail *n* Post *f*.
main *adj* Haupt-.
mainly *adv* hauptsächlich, größtenteils.
maintain *vt* aufrechterhalten; instand halten; warten.
maintenance *n* Instandhaltung *f*; Wartung *f*.
maize *n* Mais *m*.

majestic *adj* majestätisch.
majesty *n* Majestät *f*.
majority *n* Mehrheit *f*.
make *vt* machen:—*n* Marke *f*.
make-up *n* Make-up *n*.
malaria *n* Malaria *f*.
male *adj* männlich.
malfunction *n* Funktionsstörung *f*.
malice *n* Bosheit *f*.
malicious *adj* böswillig, boshaft.
malt *n* Malz *n*.
mammal *n* Säugetier *n*.
man *n* Mann *m*.
manage *vt vi* führen, leiten; schaffen.
manageable *adj* handlich, fügsam.
management *n* Leitung *f*, Geschäftsführung *f*.
manager *n* Leiter(in) *m(f)*, Manager *m*.
mania *n* Manie *f*.
maniac *n* Verrückte(r) *f(m*).
manic *adj* hektisch.
manner *n* Weise *f*; Art *f*.
manslaughter *n* Totschlag *m*.
mantelpiece *n* Kaminsims *m*.
manual *adj* manuell; Hand-:—*n* Handbuch *n*.
manufacture *n* Herstellung *f*:—*vt* herstellen.
manufacturer *n* Hersteller *m*.
manure *n* Dünger *m*, Mist *m*.
manuscript *n* Manuskript *n*.
many *adj* viel(e):—~ **a** manche(r, s):— **how ~?** wie viele?
map *n* Landkarte *f*; Stadtplan *m*.
maple *n* Ahorn *m*.
mar *vt* verderben.
marathon *n* Marathonlauf *m*.
marble *n* Marmor *m*, Murmel *f*.
March *n* März *m*.
march *n* Marsch *m*:—*vi* marschieren.
mare *n* Stute *f*.
margin *n* Rand *m*.
marigold *n* Ringelblume *f*.

mark *n* Sput *f*; Zeichen *n*; Note *f*:—*vt* markieren; benoten.
market *n* Markt *m*.
marketing *n* Marketing *n*.
marmalade *n* Orangenmarmelade *f*.
marriage *n* Ehe *f*; Trauung *f*; Heirat *f*.
married *adj* verheiratet.
marrow *n* Knochenmark *m*; Speisekürbis *m*.
marry *vt vi* heiraten.
marsh *n* Sumpf *m*.
marshal *n* Marschall *m*.
martial *adj* Kriegs-.
martyr *n* Martyrer(in) *m(f)*.
marvel *n* Wunder *n*:—*vi* sich wundern.
marvellous *adj* wunderbar, fabelhaft.
masculine *adj* männlich.
mash *vt* zu Brei zerdrücken.
mask *n* Maske *f*:—*vt* maskieren.
mass *n* Messe *f*; Masse *f*.
massacre *n* Massaker *n*:—*vt* massakrieren.
massage *n* Massage *f*; *vt* massieren.
massive *adj* massiv.
mast *n* Mast *m*.
master *n* Meister *m*:—*vt* meistern; beherrschen.
masterpiece *n* Meisterwerk *n*.
mat *n* Matte *f*; Abtreter *m*.
match *n* Streichholz *n*, Spiel *n*:—*vt* passen zu.
matchbox *n* Streichholzschachtel *f*.
mate *n* Gehilfe *m*; Kumpel *m*:—*vt* sich paaren.
material *adj* materiell:—*n* Stoff *m*, Material *n*.
maternal *adj* mütterlich.
maternity *n* Mutterschaft *f*.
mathematical *adj* mathematisch.
mathematician *n* Mathematiker *m*.
mathematics *npl* Mathematik *f*.
matrimonial *adj* ehelich, Ehe-.
matt *adj* matt.

matter *n* Materie *f*; Sache *f*; Angelegenheit *f*:—**what's the ~?** was ist los?:—*vi* von Bedeutung sein.

mattress *n* Matratze *f*.

mature *adj* reif:—*vt vi* reifen.

maturity *n* Reife *f*.

mauve *adj* lila.

maxim *n* Maxime *f*.

maximum *n* Maxmium *n*:—*adj* maximal.

may *v aux* können:—**~be** vielleicht.

May *n* Mai *m*.

mayor *n* Bürgermeister(in) *m(f)*.

maze *n* Irrgarten *m*; Labyrinth *n*.

me *pn* mich; mir.

meadow *n* Wiese *f*.

meal *n* Mahlzeit *f*.

mean *adj* gemein; geizig:—*vt vi* meinen.

meaning *n* Bedeutung *f*.

meantime, meanwhile *adv* inzwischen.

measure *n* Maß *n*; Maßnahme *f*:—*vt* messen.

measurement *n* Messung *f*.

meat *n* Fleisch *n*.

mechanic *n* Mechaniker *m*.

mechanical *adj* mechanisch.

mechanics *npl* Mechanik *f*.

mechanism *n* Mechanismus *m*.

medal *n* Medaille *f*.

media *npl* die Medien *pl*.

medical *adj* medizinisch; ärztlich.

medicine *n* Medizin *f*.

medieval *adj* mittelalterlich.

mediocre *adj* mittelmäßig.

Mediterranean *adj*:—**the ~ (Sea)** das Mittelmeer.

medium *n* Mittel *n*:—*adj* Mittel-.

meet *vt* treffen; begegnen:—*vi* sich treffen.

meeting *n* Begegnung *f*.

melody *n* Melodie *f*.

melon *n* Melone *f*.

melt *vi* schmelzen.

member *n* Mitglied *n*.

membership *n* Mitgliedschaft *f*.

memorable *adj* denkwürdig.

memorandum *n* Mitteilung *f*.

memorial *n* Denkmal *n*.

memory *n* Gedächtnis *n*; Erinnerung *f*.

menace *n* Drohung *f*:—*vt* drohen.

mend *vt* reparieren.

mental *adj* geistig.

mentality *n* Mentalität *f*.

mention *n* Erwähnung *f*:—*vt* erwähnen.

menu *n* Speisekarte *f*.

merchant *n* Kaufmann *m*.

merciful *adj* barmherzig.

merciless *adj* erbarmungslos.

mercury *n* Quecksilber *n*.

mercy *n* Barmherzigkeit *f*.

mere(ly) *adj (adv)* bloß.

merge *vt* verbinden; fusionieren.

merger *n* Fusion *f*.

merit *n* Verdienst *m*; Wert *m*:—*vt* verdienen.

mermaid *n* Meerjungfrau *f*.

merry *adj* fröhlich.

mesh *n* Masche *f*.

mess *n* Unordnung *f*.

message *n* Botschaft *f*.

messenger *n* Bote *m*.

metal *n* Metall *n*.

metallic *adj* metallisch.

metaphor *n* Metapher *f*.

metaphorical *adj* metaphorisch.

meteor *n* Meteor *m*.

meter *n* Meßgerät *n*.

method *n* Methode *f*.

methodical *adj* systematisch.

Methodist *n* Methodist(in) *m(f)*.

metre *n* Meter *m/n*.

metric *adj* metrisch.

mew *vi* miauen.
microbe *n* Mikrobe *f.*
microphone *n* Mikrofon *n.*
microscope *n* Mikroskop *n.*
microscopic *adj* mikroskopisch.
midday *n* Mittag *m.*
middle *adj* Mittel-:—*n* Mitte *f.*
midnight *n* Mitternacht *f.*
midsummer *n* Hochsommer *m.*
might *n* Kraft *f*, Macht *f.*
mighty *adj* mächtig, gewaltig.
migrate *vi* abwandern.
migration *n* Abwanderung *f.*
Milan *n* Mailand.
mild *adj* mild, leicht.
mile *n* Meile *f.*
mileage *n* Meilenzahl *f.*
militant *adj* militant.
military *adj* militärisch, Militär-.
milk *n* Milch *f*:—*vt* melken.
milky *adj* milchig.
Milky Way *n* Milchstraße *f.*
mill *n* Mühle *f*:—*vt* mahlen.
millennium *n* Jahrtausend *n.*
miller *n* Müller *m.*
millet *n* Hirse *f.*
milligram *n* Milligramm *n.*
millilitre *n* Milliliter *m.*
millimetre *n* Millimeter *m/n.*
million *n* Million *f.*
millionaire *n* Millionär(in) *m(f).*
mimic *vt* nachäffen.
mince *vt* durchdrehen.
mind *n* Sinn *m*; Geist *m*:—*vi* sich kümmern.
mine *poss pn* meiner, meine, mein(e)s:
—*n* Bergwerk *n*; Mine *f.*
miner *n* Bergarbeiter *m.*
mineral *n* Mineral *n.*
mineral water *n* Mineralwasser *n.*
minimal *adj* minimal.
minimize *vt* auf ein Minimum beschränken.

minimum *n* Minimum *n.*
mining *n* Bergbau *m.*
minister *n* Minister *m*; Pastor *m.*
ministry *n* Ministerium *n.*
minor *adj* klein:—*n* Minderjährige(r)
(f)m.
minority *n* Minderheit *f.*
mint *n* (*bot*) Minze *f*; Münzanstalt *f*: —
vt prägen.
minus *adv* minus.
minute *adj* winzig:—*n* Minute *f.*
miracle *n* Wunder *n.*
mirror *n* Spiegel *m.*
miscellaneous *adj* verschieden.
mischief *n* Unfug *m.*
mischievous *adj* durchtrieben.
miser *n* Geizhals *m.*
miserable *adj* elend, trübsinnig.
misery *n* Elend *n.*
misfortune *n* Unglück *n.*
mishap *n* Mißgeschick *n.*
mislead *vt* irreführen.
Miss *n* Fräulein *n.*
miss *vt* verfehlen; verpassen.
missile *n* Geschoß *n.*
missing *adj* fehlend; vermißt.
mission *n* Aufgabe *f*; Mission *f.*
mist *n* Dunst *m*, Nebel *m.*
mistake *vt* verwechseln:—*n* Fehler *m.*
Mister *n* Herr *m.*
mistress *n* Herrin *f*; Geliebte *f.*
mistrust *vt* mißtrauen:—*n* Mißtrauen *n.*
misty *adj* neblig, dunstig.
misunderstand *vt* mißverstehen.
misuse *n* Mißbrauch *m*:—*vt* mißbrauchen.
mix *vt* mischen.
mixture *n* Mischung *f*, Gemisch *n.*
moan *vi* ächzen, stöhnen.
mobile *adj* beweglich, fahrbar.
mock *vt vi* verspotten.
mockery *n* Spott *m.*
mode *n* Weise *f.*

model n Modell n:—vt modellieren.

moderate adj mäßig, gemäßigt:—vt mäßigen.

moderation n Mäßigung f.

modern adj modern.

modernize vt modernisieren.

modest adj bescheiden.

modesty n Bescheidenheit f.

modification n Änderung f.

modify vt ändern.

moist adj feucht.

moisten vt befeuchten.

moisture n Feuchtigkeit f.

mole n Leberfleck m; Maulwurf m.

molecule n Molekul n.

moment n Moment m, Augenblick m.

monarch n Monarch m.

monarchy n Monarchie f.

monastery n Kloster n.

monastic adj mönchisch.

Monday n Montag m.

money n Geld n.

monk n Monch m.

monkey n Affe m.

monopoly n Monopol n.

monotony n Monotonie f; Eintönigkeit f.

monster n Ungeheuer n.

monstrous adj unerhört.

month n Monat m.

monthly adj monatlich.

monument n Denkmal n.

moo vi muhen.

mood n Stimmung f; Laune f.

moon n Mond m.

moonlight n Mondlicht n.

moor n Heide f:—vt festmachen.

moose n Elch m.

moral adj moralisch.

morale n Moral f.

morality n Sittlichkeit f.

morbid adj krankhaft.

more adj adv mehr:—~ and ~ immer mehr.

moreover adv außerdem.

morning n Morgen m:—**good ~** guten Morgen.

mortal adj sterblich.

mortality n Sterblichkeit f.

mortar n Mörser m.

mortgage n Hypothek f:—vt mit einer Hypothek belasten.

mosaic n Mosaik n.

Moscow n Moskau n.

mosque n Moschee f.

mosquito n Moskito m.

moss n Moos n.

most adj meist:—adv am meisten:— **for the ~ part** zum größten Teil.

mostly adv meistens.

moth n Nachtfalter m.

mother n Mutter f.

motherhood n Mutterschaft f.

mother-in-law n Schwiegermutter f.

motherly adj mütterlich.

mother tongue n Muttersprache f.

motion n Bewegung f.

motivated adj motiviert.

motive n Motiv n.

motor n Motor m.

motto n Motto n.

mould n Form f:—vt formen.

mouldy adj schimm(e)lig.

mound n Erdhügel m.

mount vt besteigen.

mountain n Berg m.

mountaineer n Bergsteiger m.

mountaineering n Bergsteigen n.

mountainous adj gebirgig.

mourn vt betrauern.

mourner n Trauernde(r) (f)m.

mournful adj trauervoll.

mourning n Trauer f.

mouse n (pl **mice**) Maus f.

mousse n Creme f.

moustache n Schnurrbart m.

mouth n Mund m; Maul n.

movable *adj* beweglich.
move *vt* bewegen:—*vi* sich bewegen:
—*n* Bewegung *f*; Zug *m*.
movement *n* Bewegung *f*.
mow *vt* mähen.
mower *n* Rasenmäher *m*.
Mrs *n* Frau *f*.
much *adj adv* viel.
muck *n* Mist *m*; Dreck *m*.
mud *n* Schlamm *m*.
muddy *adj* schlammig.
muffle *vt* dämpfen.
mug *n* Becher *m*.
mule *n* Maultier *n*.
multiple *adj* vielfach.
multiplication *n* Multiplikation *f*.
multiply *vt* multiplizieren.
mumble *vt vi* undeutlich sprechen.
mummy *n* Mumie *f*; Mutti *f*.
munch *vt vi* mampfen.
Munich *n* München.
murder *n* Mord *m*:—*vt* ermorden.

murderer *n* Mörder *m*.
murderess *n* Mörderin *f*.
murmur *n* Gemurmel *n*:—*vi* murmeln.
muscle *n* Muskel *m*.
museum *n* Museum *n*.
mushroom *n* Pilz *m*.
music *n* Musik *f*.
musical *adj* musikalisch.
musician *n* Musiker(in) *m(f)*.
mussel *n* Muschel *f*.
must *v aux* müssen.
mustard *n* Senf *m*.
mutter *vt vi* murmeln.
mutton *n* Hammelfleisch *n*.
mutual *adj* gegenseitig.
my *poss adj* meine(r, s).
myself *pn* selbst; mich (selbst).
mysterious *adj* geheimnisvoll, rätselhaft.
mystery *n* Geheimnis *n*, Rätsel *n*.
myth *n* Mythos *m*.
mythology *n* Mythologie *f*.

N

nail *n* Nagel *m*.
naive *adj* naiv.
naked *adj* nackt.
name *n* Name *m*:—*vt* nennen.
namely *adv* nämlich.
nap *n* Nickerchen *n*.
napkin *n* Serviette *f*.
nappy *n* Windel *f*.
narcissus *n* Narzisse *f*.
narcotic *n* Betäubungsmittel *n*.
narrate *vt* erzählen.
narrative *n* Erzählung *f*.
narrow *adj* eng.
nasal *adj* nasal.
nasty *adj* ekelhaft, fies.

nation *n* Nation *f*.
national *adj* National-.
nationalism *n* Nationalismus *m*.
nationalist *n* Nationalist *m*.
nationality *n* Staatsangehörigkeit *f*.
nationalize *vt* verstaatlichen.
native *adj* einheimisch:—*n* Einhei-
mische(r) *f(m)*.
natural *adj* natürlich.
nature *n* Natur *f*.
naughty *adj* unartig.
nausea *n* Ekel *m*.
nauseate *vt* anekeln.
nautical, naval *adj* nautisch, See-.
navigate *vi* navigieren.

navigation n Navigation f.
navy n Marine f.
Nazi n Nazi m.
near prep nahe, in der Nähe:—adv nah(e):—vt sich nähern.
nearby adj nahegelegen.
nearly adv fast, beinahe.
neat adj pur; ordentlich; gepflegt.
necessary adj notwendig.
necessitate vt benötigen.
necessity n Notwendigkeit f.
neck n Hals m.
necklace n Halskette f.
need n Notwendigkeit f, Bedarf m:—vt brauchen.
needle n Nadel f.
negative adj negativ.
neglect vt vernachlässigen:—n Vernachlässigung f.
negligence n Nachlässigkeit f, Fahrlässigkeit m.
negligent adj nachlässig, fahrlässig.
negotiate vi verhandeln.
negotiation n Verhandlung f.
neigh vi wiehern.
neighbour n Nachbar(in) m(f).
neighbouring adj benachbart, Nachbar-.
neither conj:—~... nor weder... noch.
nephew n Neffe m.
nerve n Nerv m.
nervous adj nervös.
nest n Nest n.
net n Netz n.
Netherlands npl:—the ~ die Niederlande pl.
nettle n Nessel f.
network n Netz n.
neuter adj sächlich:—n Neutrum n.
neutral adj neutral.
neutrality n Neutralität f.
never adv nie, niemals, nimmer.
nevertheless adv trotzdem.
new adj neu.

news npl Nachrichten pl.
newspaper n Zeitung f.
New Year n das Neue Jahr n.
New Year's Eve n Silvester n.
New Zealand n Neuseeland n.
next adj nächste(r, s).
nibble vt knabbern.
nice adj nett; sympathisch.
nickel n Nickel n.
nickname n Spitzname m.
niece n Nichte f.
night n Nacht f:—**good** ~ gute Nacht.
nightclub n Nachtklub m.
nightingale n Nachtigall f.
nightly adj nächtlich:—adv jede Nacht.
nightmare n Alptraum m.
nimble adj beweglich.
nine num neun.
nineteen num neunzehn.
ninety num neunzig.
ninth adj neunte(r, s).
nitrogen n Stickstoff m.
no adv nein:—adj kein(er, e, es).
noble adj adlig, edel.
nobody pn niemand.
nod n Nicken n:—vi nicken.
noise n Lärm m, Geräusch m.
noisy adj laut.
nominal adj nominell.
nominate vt ernennen, aufstellen.
none pn keiner, keine, kein(e)s.
nonetheless adv nichtsdestoweniger.
nonexistent adj nicht vorhanden.
non-fiction n Sachliteratur f.
nonsense n Unsinn m, Quatsch m.
non-smoker n Nichtraucher m.
nonstop adv ununterbrochen.
noon n Mittag m.
noose n Schlinge m.
nor conj:—**neither**... ~ weder... noch.
norm n Norm m.
normal adj normal.
normally adv normalerweise.

north *n* Norden *m*.
North Africa *n* Nordafrika *n*.
North America *n* Nordamerika *n*.
northeast *n* Nordosten *m*.
northern *adj* nördlich, Nord-.
Northern Ireland *n* Nordirland *n*.
North Pole *n* Nordpol *m*.
North Sea *n* Nordsee *f*.
northwards *adv* nach Norden.
northwest *n* Nordwesten *m*.
Norway *n* Norvegen *n*.
Norwegian *adj* norwegisch:—*n* Norweger(in) *m(f)*; Norwegisch *n*.
nose *n* Nase *f*.
nostalgia *n* Nostalgie *f*, Sehnsucht *f*.
nostril *n* Nasenloch *f*.
not *adv* nicht.
notable *adj* bemerkenswert, bedeutend.
notary *n* Notar *m*.
notch *n* Kerbe *f*.
note *n* Note *f*; Ton *m*; Anmerkung *f*:—*vt* zur Kenntnis nehmen; aufschreiben.
noted *adj* bekannt.
nothing *n* nichts.
notice *n* Anzeige *f*, Anschlag *m*:—*vt* bemerken.
noticeable *adj* bemerkbar.
notify *vt* benachrichtigen.
notion *n* Idee *f*.
notorious *adj* berüchtigt.
notwithstanding *adv* troztdem.
nought *n* Null *f*.
noun *n* (*gr*) Substantiv *m*.
nourish *vt* ernähren, nähren.
nourishing *adj* nahrhaft.

nourishment *n* Nahrung *m*.
novel *n* Roman *m*.
novelist *n* Romanschriftsteller *m*.
novelty *n* Neuheit *f*.
November *n* November *m*.
novice *n* Neuling *m*.
now *adv* jetzt, nun:—~ **and then** hin und wieder.
nowadays *adv* heutzutage.
nowhere *adv* nirgends.
nuclear *adj* nuklear, Kern-.
nucleus *n* Kern *m*.
nude *adj* nackt.
nudist *n* Nudist(in) *m(f)*.
nudity *n* Nacktheit *f*.
nuisance *n* lästiger Mensch *m*, Quälgeist *m*.
null *adj* nichtig.
nullify *vt* für nichtig erklären.
numb *adj* gefühllos:—*vt* betäuben.
number *n* Zahl *f*, Anzahl *f*:—*vt* numerieren.
numeral *n* Ziffer *f*.
numerical *adj* numerisch.
numerous *adj* zahlreich.
nun *n* Nonne *f*.
nurse *n* Krankenschwester *f*:—*vt* pflegen.
nursery *n* Kinderzimmer *n*; Gärtnerei *f*.
nursery school *n* Vorschule *f*.
nurture *vt* nähren.
nut *n* Nuß *f*.
nutritious *adj* nahrhaft.
nylon *n* Nylon *n*.
nymph *n* Nymphe *f*.

O

oak *n* Eiche *f*:—*adj* Eichen(holz)-.
oar *n* Ruder *n*.

oasis *n* Oase *f*.
oath *n* Eid *m*, Schwur *m*; Fluch *m*.

oatmeal *n* Haferschrot *m*.

oats *npl* Hafer *m*.

obedience *n* Gehorsam *m*.

obedient *adj* gehorsam.

obey *vt vi* gehorchen.

obituary *n* Nachruf *m*.

object *n* Gegenstand *m*; Object *n*; Ziel *n*:—*vi* dagegen sein.

objection *n* Einwand *m*, Einspruch *m*.

objective *n* Ziel *n*:—*adj* objektiv.

obligation *n* Verpflichtung *f*.

obligatory *adj* verpflichtend, verbindlich.

oblige *vt* zwingen; einen Gefallen tun.

oblique *adj* schräg, schief:—*n* Schrägstrich *m*.

oblivion *n* Vergessenheit *f*.

oblivious *adj* nichr bewußt.

oboe *n* Oboe *f*.

obscene *adj* obszön.

obscenity *n* Obszönität *f*.

obscure *adj* unklar; undeutlich; unbekannt, obskur; düster.

obscurity *n* Unklarheit *f*; Dunkelheit *f*.

observant *adj* aufmerksam.

observation *n* Bemerkung *f*; Beobachtung *f*.

observatory *n* Sternwarte *f*, Observatorium *n*.

observe *vt* beobachen; bemerken.

observer *n* Beobachter(in) *m(f)*.

obsess *vt* verfolgen, quälen.

obsession *n* Besessenheit *f*, Wahn *m*.

obsessive *adj* krankhaft.

obsolete *adj* überholt, verlaltet.

obstacle *n* Hindernis *n*.

obstinate *adj* hartnäckig, stur.

obstruct *vt* versperren; verstopfen; hemmen.

obstruction *n* Versperrung *f*; Verstopfung *f*; Hindernis *n*.

obtain *vt* erhalten, bekommen; erzielen.

obtainable *adj* erhältlich.

obvious *adj* offenbar, offensichtlich.

occasion *n* Gelegenheit *f*; Ereignis *n*; Anlaß *m*.

occasional *adj* gelegentlich.

occupant *n* Inhaber(in) *m(f)*; Bewohner(in) *m(f)*.

occupation *n* Tâtigkeit *f*; Beruf *m*; Beschäftigung *f*.

occupier *n* Bewohner(in) *m(f)*.

occupy *vt* besetzen; belegen; bewohnen.

occur *vi* vorkommen.

occurrence *n* Ereignis *n*.

ocean *n* Ozean *m*; Meer *n*.

octagonal *adj* achteckig.

octane *n* Oktan *n*.

octave *n* Oktave *f*.

October *n* Oktober *m*.

octopus *n* Krake *f*.

odd *adj* sonderbar; ungerade; einzeln.

odious *adj* verhaßt; abscheulich.

odour *n* Geruch *m*.

of *prep* von; aus.

off *adv* weg, fort; aus, ab:—*prep* von.

offence *n* Vorgehen *n*, Straftat *f*; Beleidigung *f*.

offend *vt* beleidigen.

offer * *n* Angebot *f*:—*vt* anbieten.

office *n* Büro *n*; Amt *n*.

officer *n* Offizier *m*; Beamte(r) *m*.

official *adj* offiziell, amtlich:—*n* Beamte(r) *m*.

offshore *adj* küstennah, Küsten-.

oil *n* Öl *n*:—*vt* ölen.

oilfield *n* Ölfeld *n*.

oil painting *n* Ölgemälde *n*.

oil tanker *n* Öltanker *m*.

ointment *n* Salbe *f*.

old *adj* alt.

olive *n* Olive *f*.

omelette *n* Omelett *n*.

omen *n* Omen *n*.

ominous *adj* bedrohlich.

omission *n* Auslassung *f*; Versäumnis *n*.

omit vt auslassen; versäumen.

on prep auf; an; über:—adv an; weiters:—adj an; aufgedreht.

once adv einmal:—**at ~ sofort:—~ more** noch einmal:—**~ upon a time** es war einmal.

one num eins; ein/eine; adj einzige(r, s); pn eine(r, s):—**~ by ~** einzeln:—**~ another** einander.

oneself pn sich; sich selbst/selber; selbst.

onion n Zwiebel f.

only adv nur, bloß.

open adj offen; aufgeschlossen:—vt öffnen, aufmachen; eröffnen.

opera n Oper f.

operate vt bedienen; betätigen:—vi laufen, in Betrieb sein.

operation n Betrieb m; Operation f.

opinion n Meinung f; Ansicht f.

opponent n Gegner m.

opportunity n Gelegenheit f.

oppose vt entgegentreten; ablehnen.

opposite prep gegenüber:—n Gegenteil n.

opposition n Widerstand m; Opposition f; Gegensatz m.

oppress vt unterdrücken.

optical adj optisch.

optician n Optiker m.

optimist n Optimist m.

optimistic adj optimistisch.

option n Wahl f; Option f.

optional adj freiwillig; wahlfrei.

or conj oder.

oracle n Orakel n.

oral adj mündlich.

orange n Apfelsine f, Orange f:—adj orange.

orator n Redner(in) m(f).

orbit n Umlaufbahn f.

orchard n Obstgarten m.

orchestra n Orchester n.

orchid n Orchidee f.

order n Ordnung f; Befehl m; Auftrag m; Bestellung f:—vt befehlen; bestellen.

ordinary adj normal, gewöhnlich.

ordnance n Artillerie f.

ore n Erz n.

organ n Orgel f; Organ n.

organic adj organisch.

organism n Organismus m.

organist n Organist m.

organization n Organisation f.

organize vt organisieren.

orgasm n Orgasmus m.

orgy n Orgie f.

origin n Ursprung m, Quelle f; Herkunft f.

original adj ursprünglich, original; originell.

originality n Originalität f.

originate vi entstehen; stammen.

ornament n Schmuck m.

ornamental adj Zier-.

orphan n Waise f.

orthodox adj orthodox.

oscillate vi schwingen; schwanken.

osprey n Fischadler m.

ostrich n Strauß m.

other adj pn andere(r, s):—**~ than** anders als.

otherwise adv anders; sonst.

otter n Otter m.

ought v aux sollen.

ounce n Unze f.

our poss adj unser(er, e, es)

ourselves pn uns (selbst).

out adv hinaus/heraus; draußen:—**~ of** prep aus; außerhalb.

outbreak n Ausbruch m.

outcast n Ausgestoßene(r) f(m).

outcome n Ergebnis n.

outcry n Protest m.

outdo vt übertrumpfen.

outdoors adv im Freien.

outer *adj* äußere(r, s).
outfit *n* Kleidung *f*.
outlay *n* Auslage *f*.
outline *n* Umriß *m*.
outlook *n* Aussicht *f*; Einstellung *f*.
outmoded *adj* veraltet.
output *n* Leistung *f*, Produktion *f*.
outrage *n* Ausschreitung *f*; Skandal *m*:—*vt* verstoßen gegen; empören.
outrageous *adj* unerhöht.
outshine *vt* überstrahlen.
outside *n* Außenseite *f*:—*adj* äußere(r, s), Außen-:—*adv* außen: —*prep* außerhalb.
outstanding *adj* hervorragend; ausstehend.
outstretched *adj* ausgestreckt.
outward *adj* äußere(r, s); Hin-; ausgehend:—*adv* nach außen.
outweigh *vt* überwiegen.
oval *n* Oval *n*:—*adj* oval.
ovary *n* Eierstock *m*.
oven *n* Backofen *m*.
over *adv* hinüber/herüber; vorbei; *prep* über.
overall *adj* allgemein; Gesamt-:—*adv* insgesamt.
overawe *vt* einschüchtern; überwältigen.
overcast *adj* bedeckt.
overcoat *n* Mantel *m*.
overcome *vt* überwinden.
overcrowded *adj* überfüllt.
overdose *n* Überdosis *f*.
overdraft *n* Überziehung *f*.

overdrawn *adj* überzogen.
overdue *adj* überfällig.
overestimate *vt* überschätzen.
overgrown *adj* verwildert.
overhaul *vt* überholen; überprüfen:—*n* Überholung *f*.
overhead *adv* oben:—*adj* Hoch-; überirdisch, Decken-.
overjoyed *adj* überglücklich.
overleaf *adv* umseitig.
overload *vt* überladen.
overlook *vt* überblicken; übersehen.
overriding *adj* vorherrschend.
overseas *adv* nach/in Übersee:—*adj* Übersee-, überseeisch.
oversee *vt* beaufsichtigen.
overshadow *vt* überschatten.
oversight *n* Versehen *n*.
oversleep *vi* verschlafen.
overt *adj* offen(kundig).
overtake *vt vi* überholen.
overtime *n* Überstunden *fpl*.
overture *n* Ouvertüre *f*.
overwhelm *vt* überwaltigen.
overwhelming *adj* überwaltigend.
owe *vt* schulden.
owing to *prep* wegen.
owl *n* Eule *f*.
own *vt* besitzen:—*adj* eigen.
owner *n* Besitzer(in) *m(f)*.
ownership *n* Besitz *m*.
ox *n* Ochse *f*.
oxygen *n* Sauerstoff *m*.
oyster *n* Auster *f*.

P

pace *n* Schritt *m*; Gang *m*; Tempo *n*.
pack *n* Packung *f*; Meute *f*:—*vt* pakken.

package *n* Paket *n*.
packet *n* Päckchen *n*.
pad *n* Block *m*; Polster *n*:—*vt* polstern.

padding n Polsterung f.
paddock n Koppel f.
page n Seite f.
pail n Eimer m.
pain n Schmerz m.
painful adj schmerzhaft; peinlich.
painstaking adj gewissenhaft.
paint n Farbe f:—vt anstreichen; malen.
paintbrush n Pinsel m.
painter n Maler m.
painting n Malerei f; Gemälde n.
pair n Paar n.
pal n Kumpel m.
palace n Schloß n.
palate n Gaumen m.
pale adj blaß, bleich.
palm n Handfläche f; Palme f.
pamphlet n Broschüre f.
pan n Pfanne f:—vi schwenken.
pancake n Pfannkuchen m.
pane n Fensterscheibe f.
panel n Tafel f.
panic n Panik f:—vi in Panik geraten.
pansy n Stiefmütterchen n.
pant vi keuchen; hecheln.
panther n Panther m.
pantry n Vorratskammer f.
pants npl Schlüpfer m; Unterhose f.
paper n Papier n:—adj Papier-, aus Papier.
paperback n Taschenbuch n.
parachute n Fallschirm m:—vi (mit dem Fallschirm) abspringen.
parade n Parade f:—vt aufmaschieren lassen; zur Schau stellen:—vi paradieren, vorbeimarschieren.
paradise n Paradies n.
paradox n Paradox n.
paragraph n Absatz m.
parallel adj parallel:—n Parallele f.
paralyse vt lähmen, paralysieren; lahmlagen.

paralysis n Lähmung f.
paranoid adj paranoid.
parasite n Schmarotzer m, Parasit m.
parasol n Sonnenschirm m.
parcel n Paket n.
pardon n Verzeihung f:—vt begnadigen.
parent n Elternteil m:—~s pl Eltern pl.
parental adj elterlich, Eltern-.
parish n Gemeinde f.
park n Park m:—vt vi parken.
parking n Parken n.
parliament n Parlament n.
parliamentary adj parlamentarisch, Parlaments-.
parody n Parodie f:—vt parodieren.
parrot n Papagei m.
parsley n Petersilie m.
parsnip nPastinake f.
part n Teil m; Rolle f; Teil n:—vt trennen; scheiteln:—vi sich trennen.
participant n Teilnehmer(in) m(f).
participate vi teilnehmen (in an).
participation n Teilname f; Beteiligung f.
particle n Teilchen n; (gr) Partikel m.
particular adj bestimmt; genau; eigen:—in ~ besonders.
partition n Trennwand f; Teilung f:—vt aufteilen.
partly adv zum Teil, teilweise.
partner n Partner m.
partnership n Partnerschaft f.
partridge n Rebhuhn n.
party n Partei f; Party f.
pass vt vorbeigehen an +dat; vorbeifahren an +dat; weitergeben; verbringen:—vi vorbeigehen; vorbeifahren; vergehen:—n Paß m; Passierschein m.
passage n Gang m; Textstelle f; Überfahrt f.
passenger n Passagier m.
passion n Leidenschaft f.
passionate adj leidenschaftlich.

passive *adj* passiv; passivisch.
passport *n* Reisepaß *m*.
password *n* Parole *f*, Kennwort *n*.
past *adj* vergangen; ehemalig:—*n* Vergangenheit *f*:—*prep* an +*dat* vorbei; hinter +*dat*.
pasta *n* Teigwaren *pl*.
paste *n* Paste *f*:—*vt* kleben.
pastor *n* Pfarrer *m*.
pastry *n* Blätterteig *m*.
pasture *n* Weide *f*.
pat *vt* tätscheln.
patch *n* Fleck *m*:—*vt* flicken.
patent *adj* offenkundig:—*n* Patent *n*: —*vt* patentieren.
paternal *adj* väterlich.
paternity *n* Vaterschaft *f*.
path *n* Pfad *m*; Weg *m*.
pathetic *adj* kläglich.
pathological *adj* pathologisch.
pathology *n* Pathologie *f*.
pathos *n* Rührseligkeit *f*.
patience *n* Geduld *f*.
patient *adj* geduldig:—*n* Patient(in) *m(f)*.
patriotic *adj* patriotisch.
patrol *n* Patrouille *f*; Streife *f*:—*vi* patrouillieren.
patron *n* Kunde *m*; Gast *m*; Förderer *m*.
patronage *n* Schirmherrschaft *f*.
patronize *vt* unterstützen; besuchen; von oben herab behandeln.
patter *n* Trappeln *n*; Prasseln *n*:—*vi* trappeln; prasseln.
pattern *n* Muster *n*.
pause *n* Pause *f*:—*vi* innehalten.
pavement *n* Bürgersteig *m*.
paw *n* Tatze *f*.
pawn *n* Pfand *n*; Bauer *m*:—*vt* verpfänden.
pay *n* Bezahlung *f*, Lohn *m*:—*vt* zahlen.
payment *n* paga *f*; Bezahlung *f*.
pea *n* Erbse *f*.

peace *n* Friede(n) *m*.
peaceful *adj* friedlich, ruhig.
peach *n* Pfirsich *m*.
peacock *n* Pfau *m*.
peak *n* Spitze *f*; Gipfel *m*.
peanut *n* Erdnuß *f*.
pear *n* Birne *f*.
pearl *n* Perle *f*.
peasant *n* Bauer *m*.
peat *n* Torf *m*.
pebble *n* Kiesel *m*.
peck *n* Schnabelhieb *m*:—*vt vi* picken.
peculiar *adj* seltsam.
peculiarity *n* Besonderheit *f*; Eigenartigkeit *f*.
pedal *n* Pedal *n*.
pedestrian *n* Fußgänger *m*.
peek *vi* gucken.
peel *vt* schälen:—*vi* abblättern:—*n* Schale *f*.
peer *n* Peer *m*; Ebenbürtige(r) *f(m)*:— *vi* gucken; starren.
peg *n* Pflock *m*; Wäschenklammer *f*.
pelican *n* Pelikan *m*.
pellet *n* Kügelchen *n*.
pelt *n* Pelz *m*, Fell *n*:—*vt* bewerfen:— *vi* schüttern.
pen *n* Fedelhalter *m*; Kuli *m*; Pferch *m*.
penalty *n* Strafe *f*; Elfmeter *m*.
pencil *n* Bleistift *m*.
pendant *n* Anhänger *m*.
pending *adj* noch offen.
pendulum *n* Pendel *n*.
penetrate *vt* durchdringen.
penguin *n* Pinguin *m*.
penicillin *n* Penizillin *n*.
peninsula *n* Halbinsel *f*.
penis *n* Penis *m*.
penitence *n* Reue *f*.
penitent *adj* reuig.
penknife *n* Federmesser *n*.
penniless *adj* mittellos.
penny *n* Penny *m*.

pension n Rente f.
pensioner n Rentner(in) m(f).
pension fund n Rentenfonds m.
people n Volk n:—npl Leute pl; Bevölkerung f:—vt besiedeln.
pepper n Pfeffer m; Paprika m.
peppermint n Pfefferminz n.
per prep pro.
perceive vt wahrnehmen; verstehen.
per cent n Prozent n.
perception n Wahrnehmung f; Einsicht f.
perfect adj vollkommen; perfekt:—n (gr) Perfekt n:—vt vervollkommen.
perfection n Vollkommenheit f.
perforate vt durchlöchern.
perforation n Perforation f.
perform vt durchführen; verrichten; spielen:—vi auftreten.
performance n Durchführung f; Leistung f; Vorstellung f.
performer n Künstler(in) m(f).
perfume n Duft m; Parfüm n.
perhaps adv vielleicht.
peril n Gefahr f.
period n Periode f; Punkt m.
periodic adj periodisch.
periodical n Zeitschrift f.
peripheral adj Rand-:—n Peripheriegerät n.
perish vi umkommen; verderben.
perm n Dauerwelle f.
permanent adj dauernd, ständig.
permeate vt vi durchdringen.
permissible adj zulässig.
permission n Erlaubnis f.
permissive adj nachgiebig.
permit vt erlauben, zulassen:—n Zulassung f.
perpendicular adj senkrecht.
perpetrate vt begehen.
perpetual adj dauernd, ständig.
perpetuate vt verewigen.

perplex vt verblüffen.
persecute vt verfolgen.
persecution n Verfolgung f.
perseverance n Ausdauer f.
persevere vi durchhalten.
Persian adj persisch:—n Perser(in) m(f).
persist vi bleiben; andauern.
persistence adj Beharrlichkeit f.
persistent adj beharrlich; ständig.
person n Person f.
personal adj persönlich; privat.
personality n Persönlichkeit f.
personify vt verkörpern.
personnel n Personal n.
perspective n Perspektive f.
perspiration n Transpiration f.
perspire vi transpirieren.
persuade vt überreden; überzeugen.
persuasion n Überredung f; Überzeugung f.
persuasive adj überzeugend.
pertinent adj relevant.
perturb vt beunruhigen.
pervade vt erfüllen.
perverse adj pervers; eigensinnig.
pervert n perverser Mensch m:—vt verdrehen; verderben.
pessimist n Pessimist m.
pessimistic adj pessimistisch.
pet n Haustier n.
petal n Blütenblatt n.
petition n Bittschrift f.
petroleum n Petroleum n.
petticoat n Unterrock m.
petty adj unbedeutend; kleinlich.
pew n Kirchenbank f.
pewter n Zinn n.
phantom n Phantom n.
pharmacist n Pharmazeut m; Apotheker m.
pharmacy n Pharmazie f; Apotheke f.
phase n Phase f.
pheasant n Fasan m.

phenomenon *n* Phänomen *n*.
philanthropist *n* Philanthrop *m*.
philosopher *n* Philosopher *m*.
philosophical *adj* philosophisch.
philosophy *n* Philosophie *f*.
phlegm *n* Schleim *m*.
phlegmatic *adj* gelassen.
phobia *n* Phobie *f*.
phone *n* Telefon *n*:—*vt vi* telefonieren, anrufen.
phone call *n* Telefonanruf *m*.
phosphorus *n* Phosphor *m*.
photocopier *n* Kopiergerät *n*.
photocopy *n* Fotokopie *f*:—*vt* fotokopieren.
photograph *n* Fotografie *f*, Aufnahme *f*:—*vt* fotografieren.
photographer *n* Fotograf *m*.
photographic *adj* fotografisch.
photography *n* Fotografie *f*.
phrase *n* Satz *m*; Ausdruck *m*:—*vt* ausdrücken, formulieren.
physical *adj* physikalisch; körperlich, physisch.
physician *n* Arzt *m*.
physicist *n* Physiker(in) *m(f)*.
physiotherapy *n* Heilgymnastik *f*, Physiotherapie *f*.
physique *n* Körperbau *m*.
pianist *n* Pianist(in) *m(f)*.
piano *n* Klavier *n*.
pick *n* Pickel *m*; Auswahl *f*:—*vt* pflücken; aussuchen.
picnic *n* Picknick *n*.
picture *n* Bild *n*:—*vt* sich *dat* vorstellen.
picturesque *adj* malerisch.
pie *n* Pastete *f*; Torte *f*.
piece *n* Stück *n*.
pier *n* Pier *m*, Mole *f*.
pierce *vt* durchstechen.
piety *n* Frömmigkeit *f*.
pig *n* Schwein *n*.
pigeon *n* Taube *f*.

pigsty *n* Schweinestall *m*.
pike *n* Hecht *m*.
pile *n* Pfahl *m*, Haufen *m*, Stapel *m*:— *vt* aufschichten, stapeln.
pilgrim *n* Pilger *m*.
pilgrimage *n* Pilgerfahrt *f*.
pill *n* Pille *f*:—**be on the ~** die Pille nehmen.
pillar *n* Pfeiler *m*, Säule *f*.
pillow *n* Kopfkissen *n*.
pilot *n* Pilot *m*, Pilotin *f*; (*mar*) Lotse:—*vt* führen; (*mar*) lotsen.
pimple *n* Pickel *m*.
pin *n* Nadel *f*.
pinch *vt* zwicken:—*n* Zwicken *n*.
pine *n* Kiefer *f*:—*vi*:—**~ for** sich sehnen nach.
pineapple *n* Ananas *f*.
pink *n* Rosa *n*:—*adj* rosa *inv*.
pinnacle *n* Spitze *f*.
pint *n* Pint *n*.
pioneer *n* Pionier *m*.
pious *adj* fromm.
pip *n* Kern *m*.
pipe *n* Pfeife *f*; Rohr *n*; Rohrleitung *f*; **~s** Dudelsack *m*.
piper *n* Pfeifer *m*; Dudelsackbläser *m*.
piracy *n* Piraterie *f*; Seeräuberei *f*.
pirate *n* Pirat *m*; Seeräuber *m*.
Pisces *n* (*astrol*) Fische *pl*.
piss *vi* pissen.
pistol *n* Pistole *f*.
piston *n* Kolben *m*.
pit *n* Grube *f*; Miete *f*.
pitch *n* Pech *n*; Tonhöhe *f*.
pitiful *adj* bedauenswert; jämmerlich.
pity *n* Mitleid *n*:—*vt* Mitleid haben mit.
pizza *n* Pizza *f*.
place *n* Platz *m*; Stelle *f*; Ort *m*:—*vt* setzen, stellen, legen.
plague *n* Pest *f*; Plage *f*:—*vt* plagen.
plaice *n* Scholle *f*.
plain *adj* klar, deutlich:—*n* Ebene *f*.

plan *n* Plan *m:—vt vi* planen.

plane *n* Ebene *f;* Flugzeug *n;* Hobel *m;* Platane *f.*

planet *n* Planet *m.*

plank *n* Brett *n.*

plant *n* Pflanze *f;* Anlage *f:—vt* pflanzen.

plaster *n* Gips *m;* Verputz *m;* Pflaster *n.*

plastic *n* Plastik *n/f:—adj* Plastik-.

plate *n* Teller *m.*

platform *n* Plattform *f;* Bahnsteig *m.*

platinum *n* Platin *n.*

plausible *adj* plausibel.

play *n* Spiel *n;* Theaterstück *n:—vt vi* spielen.

player *n* Spieler(in) *m(f).*

plea *n* Bitte *f;* Plädoyer *n.*

pleasant *adj* angenehm.

please *vt* gefallen +*dat;* ~! bitte!

pleased *adj* zufrieden.

pleasure *n* Freude *f.*

pledge *n* Pfand *f;* Versprechen *n:—vt* verpfänden; versprechen.

plenty *n* Fülle *f.*

plight *n* Notlage *f.*

plot *n* Komplott *n;* Handlung *f;* Grundstück *n:—vi* sich verschwören.

plough *n* Pflug *m:—vt* pflügen.

pluck *vt* pflücken:—*n* Mut *m.*

plug *n* Stöpsel *m;* Stecker *m;* Zündkerze *f:—vt* stopfen.

plum *n* Pflaume *f,* Zwetsch(g)e *f.*

plumber *n* Klempner *m,* Installateur *m.*

plume *n* Feder *f,* Fahne *f.*

plump *adj* ründlich, füllig.

plunder *n* Plünderung *f,* Beute *f:—vt* plündern.

plunge *vt* stoßen:—*vi* (sich) stürzen.

plural *n* Plural *m,* Mehrzahl *f.*

plus *n* Plus(zeichen) *n:—prep* plus, und.

ply *vt* betreiben:—*vi* verkehren.

pneumatic *adj* pneumatisch; Luft-.

pneumonia *n* Lüngenentzündung *f.*

poach *vt* pochieren; stehlen:—*vi* wildern.

poached *adj* (egg) verloren.

poacher *n* Wilddieb *m.*

pocket *n* Tasche *f.*

pocket money *n* Taschengeld *n.*

pod *n* Hülse *f.*

poem *n* Gedicht *n.*

poet *n* Dichter *m,* Poet *m.*

poetic *adj* poetisch.

poetry *n* Poesie *f.*

point *n* Punkt *m;* Spitze *f,* Zweck *m:—vt* zeigen mit; richten:—*vi* zeigen.

pointed *adj* spitz, scharf.

poison *n* Gift *n:—vt* vergiften.

poisoning *n* Vergiftung *f.*

poisonous *adj* Gift-, giftig.

poke *vt* stecken; schüren.

poker *n* Schürhaken *m;* Poker *n.*

Poland *n* Polen *n.*

polar *adj* Polar-, polar.

Pole *n* Pole *n,* Polin *f.*

pole *n* Stange *f,* Pfosten *m;* Mast *m;* Pol *m.*

police *n* Polizei *f.*

policeman *n* Polizist *m.*

police station *n* Polizeirevier *n,* Wache *f.*

policewoman *n* Polizistin *f.*

policy *n* Politik *f,* Versicherungspolice *f.*

polio *n* Polio *f.*

Polish *adj* polnisch:—*n* Polnisch *n.*

polish *n* Politur *f;* Wachs *n;* Creme *f:—vt* polieren; putzen.

polite *adj* höflich.

politeness *n* Höflichkeit *f.*

political *adj* politisch.

politician *n* Politiker *m.*

politics *npl* Politik *f.*

poll *n* Abstimmung *f;* Wahl *f;* Umfrage *f.*

pollen *n* (bot) Blütenstaub *m,* Pollen *m.*

pollute *vt* verschmutzen, verunreinigen.

pollution n Verschmutzung f.
polo n Polo n.
polytechnic n technische Hochschule f.
pomegranate n Granatapfel m.
pompous adj aufgeblasen.
pond n Teich m.
ponder vt nachdenken über +acc.
pony n Pony n.
ponytail n Pferdeschwanz m.
pool n Schwimmbad n; Lache f:—vt zusammenlegen.
poor adj arm; schlecht.
pop n Knall m; Popmusik f; Limo f.
pope n Papst m.
poplar n Pappel f.
poppy n Mohn m.
popular adj beliebt, populär; volkstümlich.
popularity n Beliebtheit f, Popularität f.
populate vt bevölkern.
population n Bevölkcrung f.
populous adj dicht besiedelt.
porcelain n Porzellan n.
porch n Vorbau m, Veranda f.
porcupine n Stachelschwein n.
pore n Pore f:—vi ~ over vt brüten über.
pork n Schweinefleisch n.
pornography n Pornographie f.
porpoise n Tümmler m.
porridge n Haferbrei m.
port n Hafen m; (mar) Backbord n; Portwein m.
porter n Pförtner(in) m(f); Gepäckträger m.
portion n Teil m, Stück n.
portrait n Porträt n.
portray vt darstellen.
Portugal n Portugal n.
Portuguese adj portugiesisch:—n Portugiese m Portugiesin f; Portugiesisch n.
pose n Stellung f, Pose f:—vi posieren:—vt stellen.

position n Stellung f; Lage f; Stelle f:—vt aufstellen.
positive adj positiv.
possess vt besitzen.
possession n Besitz m.
possessive adj besitzergreifend.
possibility n Möglichkeit f.
possible adj möglich.
post n Post f; Pfosten m; Stelle f:—vt anschlagen; aufgeben; aufstellen.
postage n Porto n.
postcard n Postkarte f.
poster n Plakat n.
postman n Briefträger m.
post office n Postamt n; Post f.
postpone vt verschieben.
postwar adj Nachkriegs-.
pot n Topf m; Kanne f.
potato n Kartoffel f.
potent adj stark; zwingend.
potential adj potentiell:—n Potential n.
pottery n Töpferei f.
pouch n Beutel m.
poultry n Geflügel n.
pound n Pfund n.
pour vt gießen.
poverty n Armut f.
powder n Pulver n, Puder m:—vt sich pudern.
power n Macht f; Fähigkeit f; Stärke f:—vt antreiben.
powerful adj mächtig.
powerless adj machtlos.
power station n Kraftwerk n.
practical adj praktisch.
practice n Übung f; Praxis f.
practise vt vi üben.
pragmatic adj pragmatisch.
praise n Lob n:—vt loben.
praiseworthy adj lobenswert.
prawn n Garnele f.
pray vi beten.
prayer n Gebet n.

preach *vi* predigen.
precede *vt vi* vorausgehen.
precious *adj* wertvoll; preziös.
precise *adj* genau, präzis.
precision *n* Präzision *f*.
predict *vt* voraussagen.
predictable *adj* vorhersagbar.
prediction *n* Voraussage *f*.
preface *n* Vorwort *n*.
prefer *vt* vorziehen, lieber mögen.
preferable *adj* vorzugsweise, am liebsten.
preference *n* Vorzug *m*.
preferential *adj* Vorzugs-.
prefix *n* Präfix *n*.
pregnancy *n* Schwangerschaft *f*.
pregnant *adj* schwanger.
prejudice *n* Vorurteil *n*; Voreingenommenheit *f*:—*vt* beeinträchtigen.
prejudiced *adj* voreingenommen.
prelude *n* Vorspiel *n*.
premature *adj* vorzeitig; Früh-.
premier *n* Premier *m*.
premiere *n* Premiere *f*.
premium *n* Prämie *f*.
preparation *n* Vorbereitung *f*.
prepare *vt* vorbereiten:—*vi* sich vorbereiten.
preposition *n* Präposition *f*, Verhältniswort *n*.
prescribe *vi* vorschreiben; (*med*) verschreiben.
prescription *n* (*med*) Rezept *n*.
presence *n* Gegenwart *f*.
present *adj* anwesend; gegenwärtig:—*n* Gegenwart *f*; Geschenk *n*:—*vt* vorlegen; vorstellen; zeigen.
preservation *n* Erhaltung *f*.
preservative *n* Konservierungsmittel *n*.
preserve *vt* erhalten; einmachen.
president *n* Präsident *m*.
press *n* Presse *f*; Druckerei *f*:—*vt* drücken; drängen:—*vi* drücken.

press conference *n* Pressekonferenz *f*.
pressing *adj* dringend.
pressure *n* Druck *m*.
prestige *n* Prestige *n*.
presume *vt* annehmen.
presumption *n* Annahme *f*.
pretend *vi* so tun.
pretentious *adj* angeberisch.
pretty *adj* hübsch:—*adv* ganz schön.
prevent *vt* verhindern, verhüten.
prevention *n* Verhütung *f*.
preview *n* Vorschau *f*.
previous *adj* früher, vorherig.
prewar *adj* Vorkriegs-.
prey *n* Beute *f*.
price *n* Preis *m*.
priceless *adj* unbezahlbar.
prick *n* Stich *m*:—*vt vi* stechen.
prickle *n* Stachel *m*, Dorn *m*.
pride *n* Stolz *m*.
priest(ess) *n* Priester(in) *m(f)*.
priesthood *n* Priesteramt *n*.
primary *adj* Haupt-.
prime minister *n* Premierminister *m*.
primitive *adj* primitiv.
primrose *n* (*bot*) Primel *f*.
prince *n* Prinz *m*; Fürst *m*.
princess *n* Prinzessin *f*; Fürstin *f*.
principal *adj* Haupt-:—*n* Direktor *m*.
principle *n* Grundsatz *m*; Prinzip *n*.
print *n* Druck *m*; Abdruck *m*; Abzug *m*:—*vt* drucken.
printer *n* Drucker *m*.
priority *n* Priorität *f*.
prison *n* Gefängnis *n*.
prisoner *n* Gefangene(r) *(f)m*.
privacy *n* Ungestörtheit *f*; Privatleben *n*.
private *adj* privat, Privat-.
privilege *n* Privileg *n*.
prize *n* Preis *m*:—*vt* (hoch)schätzen.
prizewinner *n* Preisträger(in) *m(f)*.
probability *n* Wahrscheinlichkeit *f*.
probable *adj* wahrscheinlich.

probation *n* Probe *f*.
probe *n* Sonde *f*; Untersuchung *f*:—*vt vi* erforschen.
problem *n* Problem *n*.
problematic *adj* problematisch.
procedure *n* Verfahren *n*.
proceed *vi* vorrücken; fortfahren:—~**s** *npl* Erlös *m*.
proceedings *n* Verfahren *n*.
process *n* Prozeß *m*; Verfahren *n*.
procession *n* Prozession *f*.
proclaim *vt* verkünden.
proclamation *n* Verkündung *f*.
procure *vt* beschaffen.
prodigy *n* Wunder *n*.
produce *n* Produkte *pl*; Erzeugnis *n*:—*vt* herstellen, produzieren; erzeugen.
producer *n* Hersteller *m*, Produzent *m*; Erzeuger *m*.
product *n* Produkt *n*; Erzeugnis *n*.
production *n* Produktion *f*, Herstellung *f*.
productive *adj* produktiv.
productivity *n* Produktivität *f*.
profess *vt* zeigen; vorgeben.
profession *n* Beruf *m*.
professional *adj* Berufs-.
professor *n* Professor *m*.
profile *n* Profil *n*.
profit *n* Gewinn *m*.
profitability *n* Rentabilität *f*.
profitable *adj* rentabel.
profound *adj* tief.
program(me) *n* Program *n*:—*vt* planen; programmieren.
programmer *n* Programmierer(in) *m(f)*.
programming *n* Programmieren *n*.
progress *n* Fortschritt *m*:—*vi* fortschreiten, weitergehen.
progression *n* Folge *f*.
progressive *adj* fortschrittlich, progressiv.

prohibit *vt* verbieten.
prohibition *n* Verbot *n*.
project *n* Projekt *n*:—*vt* vorausplanen; projizieren.
projection *n* Projektion *f*.
projector *n* Projektor *m*.
prolific *adj* produktiv.
prologue *n* Prolog *m*; Vorspiel *n*.
prolong *vt* verlängern.
promenade *n* Promenade *f*.
prominence *n* (große) Bedeutung *f*.
prominent *adj* prominent; bedeutend; auffallend.
promiscuous *adj* lose.
promise *n* Versprechen *n*:—*vt vi* versprechen.
promising *adj* vielversprechend.
promote *vt* befördern; fördern, unterstützen.
promotion *n* Beförderung *f*; Förderung *f*; Werbung *f*.
prompt *adj* prompt, schnell.
pronoun *n* Fürwort *n*.
pronounce *vt* aussprechen.
pronounced *adj* ausgesprochen.
pronouncement *n* Erklärung *f*.
pronunciation *n* Aussprache *f*.
proof *n* Beweis *f*; Korrekturfahne *f*; Alkoholgehalt *m*:— *adj* sicher.
prop *n* Stütze *f*; Requisit *n*:—*vt* (ab)stützen.
propaganda *n* Propaganda *f*.
propel *vt* (an)treiben.
propeller *n* Propeller *m*.
proper *adj* richtig; schicklich.
property *n* Eigentum *n*.
prophet *n* Prophet *m*.
proportion *n* Verhältnis *n*; Teil *m*.
proportional *adj* proportional.
proportionate *adj* verhältnismäßig.
proposal *n* Vorschlag *m*.
propose *vt* vorschlagen.
proposition *n* Angebot *n*.

proprietor *n* Besitzer *m*, Eigentümer *m*.

prose *n* Prosa *f*.

prosecute *vt* (strafrechtlich) verfolgen.

prosecution *n* strafrechtliche Verfolgung *f*; Anklage *f*.

prosecutor *n* Vertreter *m* der Anklage.

prospect *n* Aussicht *f*.

prospectus *n* Prospekt *m*.

prosper *vi* blühen, gedeihen; erfolgreich sein.

prosperity *n* Wohlstand *m*.

prosperous *adj* reich, wohlhabend.

prostitute *n* Prostituierte *f*, Dirne *f*.

protect *vt* (be)schützen.

protection *n* Schutz *m*.

protective *adj* Schutz-, (be)schützend.

protector *n* Schützer *m*.

protégé *n* Schützling *m*.

protein *n* Protein *n*.

protest *n* Protest *m*:—*vi* protestieren.

Protestant *adj* protestantisch:—*n* Protestant(in) *m(f)*.

protester *n* Demonstrant(in) *m(f)*.

protrude *vi* (her)vorstehen.

proud *adj* stolz.

prove *vt* beweisen.

proverb *n* Sprichwort *n*.

provide *vt* versehen:—— **for** *vt* sorgen für.

provided *conj*:—— **that** vorausgesetzt, daß.

province *n* Provinz *f*.

provincial *adj* provinziell.

provision *n* Vorkehrung *f*; Bestimmung *f*.

provisional *adj* provisorisch.

proviso *n* Bedingung *f*.

provocation *n* Herausforderung *f*.

provocative *adj* herausfordernd.

provoke *vt* provozieren; hervorrufen.

proximity *n* Nähe *f*.

prudence *n* Umsicht *f*.

prudent *adj* klug, umsichtig.

prudish *adj* prüde.

prune *n* Backpflaume *f*:—*vt* ausputzen.

pry *vi*:—— **into** seine Nase stecken (in +*acc*)

pseudonym *n* Pseudonym *n*, Deckname *m*.

psychiatric *adj* psychiatrisch.

psychiatrist *n* Psychiater *m*.

psychiatry *n* Psychiatrie *f*.

psychological *adj* psychologisch.

psychologist *n* Psychologe *m*, Psychologin *f*.

psychology *n* Psychologie *f*.

pub *n* Kneipe *f*.

puberty *n* Pubertät *f*.

public *adj* öffentlich:—*n* Öffentlichkeit *f*.

publican *n* Wirt *m*.

publication *n* Veröffentlichung *f*.

publicity *n* Publicity *f*, Werbung *f*.

publicize *vt* bekannt machen; Publicity machen für.

public opinion *n* öffentliche Meinung *f*.

publish *vt* veröffentlichen.

publisher *n* Verleger *m*.

publishing *n* Verlagswesen *n*.

pudding *n* Nachtisch *m*; Pudding *m*.

puddle *n* Pfütze *f*.

puff *n* Stoß *m*; Puderquaste *f*:—*vt vi* paffen.

pull *n* Ruck *m*; Beziehung *f*:—*vt vi* ziehen.

pulley *n* Rolle *f*, Flaschenzug *m*.

pullover *n* Pullover *m*.

pulp *n* Brei *m*; Fruchtfleisch *n*.

pulse *n* Puls *m*.

pump *n* Pumpe *f*:—*vt* pumpen.

pumpkin *n* Kürbis *m*.

pun *n* Wortspiel *n*.

punch *n* Locher *m*; Faustschlag *m*; Punsche *n*, Bowle *f*:—*vt* lochen; schlagen, boxen.

punctual *adj* pünktlich.

punctuate *vt* mit Satzzeichen versehen; unterbrechen.
punctuation *n* Zeichensetzung *f.*
punish *vt* bestrafen.
punishment *n* Strafe *f;* Bestrafung *f.*
pupil *n* Schüler(in) *m(f);* Pupille *f.*
puppet *n* Puppe *f;* Marionette *f.*
puppy *n* junger Hund *m.*
purchase *n* Kauf *m:—vt* kaufen.
purchaser *n* Käufer(in) *m(f).*
pure *adj* rein.
purify *vt* reinigen.
purity *n* Reinheit *f.*
purple *adj* violett; dunkelrot.

purpose *n* Zweck *m,* Ziel *n:—on ~* absichtlich.
purr *vi* schnurren.
purse *n* Portemonnaie *n,* Geldbeutel *m.*
pursue *vi* verfolgen.
pursuit *n* Verfolgung *f;* Beschäftigung *f.*
push *n* Stoß *m,* Schub *m;* Vorstoß *m:—vt* stoßen, schieben.
put *vt* setzen, stellen, legen.
puzzle *n* Rätsel *m;* Verwirrung *f.*
pyjamas *npl* Schlafanzug *m,* Pyjama *m.*
pylon *n* Mast *m.*
pyramid *n* Pyramide *f.*
python *n* Pythonschlange *m.*

Q

quack *vi* quaken:—*n* Quaken *n.*
quadrangle *n* Hof *m;* Viereck *n.*
quadruple *adj* vierfach.
quadruplet *n* Vierling *m.*
quagmire *n* Morass *m.*
quail *n* Wachtel *f.*
quaint *adj* malerisch, kuriös.
quake *vi* beben; zittern.
qualification *n* Qualifikation *f.*
qualified *adj* qualifiziert.
qualify *vt* befähigen:—*vi* qualifizieren.
quality *n* Qualität *f.*
qualm *n* Bedenken *n.*
quandary *n* Verlegenheit *f.*
quantity *n* Quantität *f,* Menge *f,* Anzahl *f.*
quarantine *n* Quarantän *f.*
quarrel *n* Streit *m:—vi* sich streiten.
quarrelsome *adj* streitsüchtig.
quarry *n* Steinbruch *m;* Wild *n.*
quarter *n* Viertel *n;* Quartal *n.*
quartet *n* Quartett *n.*
quartz *n* Quarz *m.*
quay *n* Kai *m.*

queen *n* Königin *f;* Dame *f.*
queer *adj* seltsam.
quell *vt* unterdrucken.
quench *vt* löschen.
quest *n* Suche *f.*
question *n* Frage *f:—vt* befragen.
questionable *adj* fragwürdig, zweifelhaft.
question mark *n* Fragezeichen *n.*
questionnaire *n* Fragebogen *m.*
quick *adj* schnell.
quicken *vt* beschleunigen:—*vi* sich beschleunigen.
quiet *adj* leise:—*n* Ruhe *f.*
quintet *n* Quintett *n.*
quit *vt* verlassen:—*vi* aufhören.
quite *adv* ganz, ziemlich; völlig.
quits *adj* quitt.
quiver *vi* zittern:—*n* Köcher *m.*
quiz *n* Quiz *n:—vt* prüfen, ausfragen.
quota *n* Quote *f.*
quotation *n* Zitat *n.*
quote *vt* zitieren.

R

rabbit n Kaninchen n.
rabies n Tollwut f.
race n Rasse f; Rennen n:—vi rennen.
radiant adj strahlend.
radiate vt vi ausstrahlen.
radiation n Strahlung f.
radiator n Heizkörper m.
radical adj radikal.
radio n Radio n.
radioactive adj radioactiv.
radish n Rettich m.
raft n Floß n.
rag n Fetzen m.
rage n Wut f:—vi toben.
raid n Razzia f.
rail n Schiene f; Gelände n; Reling f.
railway n Eisenbahn f.
rain n Regen m:—vt vi regnen.
rainbow n Regebogen m.
rainy adj regnerisch.
raise vt heben; erhohen.
raisin n Rasine f.
rake n Harke f:—vt harken.
ram n Widder m; Ramme f:—vt rammen.
ramp n Rampe f.
random adj ziellos, wahllos.
range n Reihe f; Sortiment n:—vt anordnen, aufstellen,
rank n Reihe f; Rang m; Stand m.
ransom n Lösegeld n.
rape n Vergewaltigung f:—vt vergewaltigen.
rapid adj schnell, rasch.
rapist n Vergewaltiger m.
rare adj selten, rar.
rarity n Seltenheit f.
raspberry n Himbeere f.

rat n Ratte f.
rate n Rate f, Tarif m; Tempo n:—vt (ein)schätzen.
rather adv lieber, eher; ziemlich.
ratio n Verhältnis n.
ration n Ration f.
rational adj rational.
rattle n Rasseln n; Rassel f:—vt vi ratteln.
rattlesnake n Klapperschlange f.
rave vi toben.
raven n Rabe m.
raw adj roh.
ray n Strahl m.
razor n Rasierapparat m.
reach vt (er)reichen.
react vi reagieren.
reaction n Reaktion f.
read vt vi lesen.
ready adj bereit.
real adj wirklich; eigentlich; echt.
reality n Wirklichkeit f.
realize vt begreifen; verwirklichen.
realm n Reich n.
reap vt ernten.
rear n Rückseite f; Schluß m:—vt aufziehen.
reason n Grund m; Verstand m.
reasonable adj vernünftig.
reassure vt beruhigen.
rebel n Rebell m:—vi rebellieren.
rebellion n Rebellion f, Aufstand m.
rebellious adj rebellisch.
receipt n Quittung f; Empfang m.
receive vt erhalten; empfangen.
recently adv neulich.
reception n Empfang m.

recession n Rezession f.
recipe n Rezept n.
recital n Vortrag m.
recite vt vortragen.
reckon vt rechnen, berechnen.
reclaim vt zurückverlangen.
recline vi sich zurücklehnen.
recognition n Erkennen n; Anerkennung f.
recognize vt erkennen; anerkennen.
recommend vt empfehlen.
recommendation n Empfehlung f.
record n Aufzeichnung f; Schallplatte f;
Rekord m:—vt aufzeichnen; aufnehmen.
recount vt berichten.
recover vi erholen.
recovery n Erholung f.
recruit vt Rekrut m:—vt rekrutieren.
recruitment n Rekrutierung f.
rectangle n Rechteck n.
red adj rot.
reduce vt vermindern.
reduction n Verminderung f.
redundancy n Entlassung f.
redundant adj überflüssig.
reed n Schilf n.
reel n Spule f, Rolle f:—vi taumeln.
refer vi:—~ to nachschlagen in +dat.
referee n Schiedsrichter m.
reference n Referenz f; Verweis m.
reflect vt reflektieren; spiegeln:—vi
nachdenken.
reflection n Reflexion f; Spiegelbild n.
reform n Reform f:—vt bessern.
refresh vt erfrischen.
refrigerator n Kühlschrank m.
refuge n Zuflucht f.
refugee n Flüchtling m.
refund n Rückvergütung f:—vt zurück-
erstatten.
refuse vt abschlagen:—vi sich weigern:—n Abfall n.
regain vt wiedergewinnen.

regard n Achtung f:—vt ansehen.
region n Region f.
register n Register n:—vt registrieren;
eintragen.
registration n Registrierung f.
regret n Bedauern n:—vt bedauern.
regular adj regelmäßig.
regulate vt regeln, regulieren.
regulation n Vorschrift f; Regulierung f.
rehearsal n Probe f.
rehearse vt proben.
reign n Herrschaft f:—vi herrschen.
rein n Zügel m.
reindeer n Ren n.
reinforce vt verstärken.
reject vt ablehnen.
rejection n Zurückweisung f.
relate vt erzählen; verbinden.
related adj verwandt.
relationship n Verhältnis n.
relative n Verwandte(r) f(m):—adj relativ.
relax vi sich entspannen.
relaxation n Entspannung f.
relay n Staffel f:—vt weiterleiten.
release n Entlassung f:—vt befreien;
entlassen.
relevant adj relevant.
reliable adj zuverlässig.
relief n Erleichterung f; Hilfe f.
religion n Religion f.
religious adj religiös.
reluctance n Widerstreben n.
reluctant adj widerwillig.
remain vi bleiben; übrigbleiben.
remainder n Rest m.
remark n Bemerkung f:—vt bemerken.
remarkable adj bemerkenswert.
remedy n Mittel n:—vt abhelfen +dat.
remember vt sich erinnern an +acc.
remembrance n Erinnerung f; Gedenken n.
reminder n Mahnung f.

remote *adj* abgelegen.
removable *adj* entfernbar.
removal *n* Beseitigung *f*; Umzug *m*.
remove *vt* beseitigen, entfernen.
remuneration *n* Vergütung *f*.
render *vt* machen; übersetzen.
renew *vt* erneuern.
renewal *n* Erneuerung *f*.
renounce *vt* verzichten auf +*acc*.
renovate *vt* renovieren.
renown *n* Ruf *m*.
rent *n* Miete *f*:—*vt* mieten.
rental *n* Miete *f*.
reorganize *vt* reorganisieren.
repair *n* Reparatur *f*:—*vt* reparieren; wiedergutmachen.
repay *vt* zurückzahlen.
repayment *n* Rückzahlung *f*.
repeat *vt* wiederholen.
repetition *n* Wiederholung *f*.
replace *vt* ersetzen; zurückstellen.
reply *n* Antwort *f*:—*vi* antworten.
report *n* Bericht *m*:—*vt* berichten; melden; anzeigen:—*vi* Bericht erstatten.
reporter *n* Reporter *m*.
represent *vt* darstellen; vertreten.
representation *n* Darstellung *f*; Vertretung *f*.
representative *n* Vertreter *m*.
repress *vt* unterdrücken.
repression *n* Unterdrückung *f*.
reproach *n* Vorwurf *m*:—*vt* Vorwürfe machen +*dat*.
reproduce *vt* reproduzieren.
reproduction *n* Reproduktion *f*.
reptile *n* Reptil *n*.
republic *n* Republik *f*.
repudiate *vt* zurückweisen.
repugnant *adj* widerlich.
repulse *vt* zurückschlagen.
repulsive *adj* abstoßend.
reputation *n* Ruf *m*.

repute *n* hohes Ansehen *n*.
request *n* Bitte *f*:—*vt* erbitten.
require *vt* brauchen; erfordern.
requirement *n* Bedarf *m*; Anforderung *f*.
rescue *n* Rettung *f*:—*vi* retten.
research *n* Forschung *f*:—*vi* forschen:—*vt* erforschen.
resemblance *n* Ähnlichkeit *f*.
resemble *vt* ähneln +*dat*.
reservation *n* Reservierung *f*; Vorbestellung *f*; Vorbehalt *m*.
reserve *n* Vorrat *m*; Reserve *f*:—*vt* reservieren.
reside *vi* wohnen.
residence *n* Wohnsitz *m*.
resident *n* Bewohner *m*; Einwohner *m*.
resign *vt vi* zurücktreten.
resignation *n* Kündigung *f*; Rucktritt *m*.
resist *vt* widerstehen +*dat*.
resistance *n* Widerstand *m*.
resolute *adj* resolut, entschlossen.
resolution *n* Entschlossenheit *f*.
resolve *vt* beschliessen:—*vi* sich lösen.
resort *n* Erholungsort *m*; Zuflucht *f*.
respect *n* Hinsicht *f*; Achtung *f*:—**with ~ to** hinsichtlich:—*vt* respektieren.
respectable *adj* solide.
respectful *adj* ehrerbietig, respektvoll.
respective *adj* jeweilig.
respiration *n* Atmung *f*.
respite *n* Atempause *f*, Ruhepause *f*.
respond *vi* antworten; reagieren.
response *n* Antwort *f*; Reaktion *f*.
responsibility *n* Verantwortung *f*.
responsible *adj* verantwortlich.
rest *n* Ruhe *f*, Ruhepause *f*; Pause *f*; Stütze *f*:—*vi* ruhen, sich ausruhen.
restful *adj* erholsam, ruhig, friedlich.
restive *adj* unruhig, nervös.
restless *adj* ruhelos, unruhig.

restoration n Rückerstattung f; Restaurierung f.

restore vt wiedergeben; restaurieren.

restrain vt zurückhalten, unterdrükken.

restraint n Zurückhaltung f.

restrict vt einschränken.

restriction n Einschränkung f.

restrictive adj einschränkend.

result n Ergebnis n.

resume vt fortsetzen; wieder einnehmen.

resurrection n Auferstehung f.

retail n Einzelhandel m.

retain vt behalten.

retire vi in den Ruhestand treten; sich zurückziehen.

retired adj im Ruhestand, pensioniert.

retirement n Ruhestand m.

retrace vt zurückverfolgen.

retract vt zurücknehmen.

retrain vt umschulen.

retreat n Rückzug m:—vi sich zurückziehen.

retrieve vt wiederbekommen.

return n Rückkehr f; Ertrag m:—adj Rück-:—vi zurückkommen, zurückkehren:—vt zurückgeben, zurücksenden.

reunion n Wiedervereinigung f.

reunite vt wiedervereinigen.

reveal vt enthülen.

revelation n Offenbarung f.

revelry n Rummel m.

revenge n Rache f.

revenue n Einnahmen pl.

reverse n Rückseite f; Rückwärtsgang m:—adj entgegengesetzt:—vt umkehren:—vi rückwärts fahren.

review n Rezension f; Zeitschrift f:—vt rezensieren.

revise vt revidieren; überarbeiten.

revision n Wiederholung f; Prüfung f.

revival n Wiederbelebung f; Wiederaufnahme f.

revive vt wiederbeleben:—vi wiedererwachen.

revolt n Aufstand m:—vi sich auflehnen.

revolting adj widerlich.

revolution n Umdrehung f; Revolution f.

revolutionary adj revolutionär.

revolve vi kreisen; sich drehen.

revolver n Revolver m.

revolving door n Drehtür f.

revulsion n Ekel m.

reward n Belohnung f:—vt belohnen.

rheumatism n Rheumatismus m.

rhinoceros n Nashorn n.

rhubarb n Rhabarber m.

rhyme n Reim m.

rhythm n Rhythmus m.

rib n Rippe f.

ribbon n Band n.

rice n Reis m.

rich adj reich.

rid vt befreien.

riddle n Rätsel n.

ride n Fahrt f; Ritt m:—vt vi reiten, fahren.

ridge n Kamm m; Spott m.

ridicule n Spott m:—vt lächerlich machen.

ridiculous adj lächerlich.

rifle n Gewehr n:—vt berauben.

right adj richtig, recht; rechte(r, s):—n Recht n; Rechte f:—adj rechts; nach rechts; richtig, recht.

rigid adj starr, steif.

rigidity n Starrheit f.

rigorous adj streng.

rigour n Strenge f.

rim n Rand m.

ring n Ring m; Kreis m; Klingeln n:—vt vi läufen; anrufen.

rinse n Spülen n:—vt spülen.
riot n Aufruhr m:—vi randalieren.
rip n Riß m:—vt vi rreißen.
ripe adj reif.
rise n Steigung f; Erhöhung f:—vi auf-
  gehen; aufsteigen; steigen.
risk n Risiko n:—vt riskieren.
risky adj riskant.
rival n Rivale m:—vt rivalisieren mit.
rivalry n Rivalität f.
river n Fluß m; Strom m.
road n Straße f.
roam vi umherstreifen.
roar n Brüllen n:—vi brüllen.
roast vt braten.
rob vt bestehlen, berauben.
robber n Räuber m.
robbery n Raub m.
robe n Gewand n; Robe f.
robin n Rotkehlchen m.
rock n Felsen m:—vt vi wiegen, schaukeln.
rocket n Rakete f.
rod n Stange f; Rute f.
rodent n Nagtier n.
roe n Reh n; Rogen m.
roll n Rolle f; Brötchen n; Liste f:—vt
  rollen, wälzen:—vi schlingern.
roller n Rolle f, Walze f.
Roman adj römisch:—n Römer(in) m(f).
Roman Catholic adj römisch-katholisch:—n Katholik(in) m(f).
romance n Romanze f; Liebesroman m.
romantic adj romantisch.
roof n Dach n.
rook n Saatkräke f; Turm m.
room n Zummer n, Raum m; Platz m;
  Spielraum m.
rooster n Hahn m.
root n Wurzel f.
rope n Seil n.
rose n Rose f.
rosebud n Rosenknospe m.

rosemary n Rosmarin m.
rot n Fäulnis n; Quatsch m:—vi verfaulen.
rotate vi rotieren.
rotation n Umdrehung f.
rotten adj faul; schlecht, gemein.
rough adj rauh; uneben; grob.
roughen vt aufrauhen.
round adj rund; aufgerundet:—adv
  um... herum.
rouse vt wecken; aufrütteln; erregen.
route n Route f, Weg m; Strecke f.
row n Lärm f; Streit f; n Reihe f:—vi
  sich streiten:—vt vi rudern.
royal adj königlich, Königs-.
rub vt reiben.
rubber n Gummi m; Radiergummi m.
rubbish n Abfall m; Quatsch m.
rubbish bin n Mülleimer m.
ruby n Rubin m:—adj rubinrot.
rude adj unverschämt; hart; unsanft;
  grob.
rudiment n Grundlage f.
rug n Brücke f; Bettvorleger m.
ruin n Ruine f; Ruin m:—vt ruinieren.
rule n Regel f; Regierung f:—vt regieren; linieren:—vi herrschen.
ruler n Lineal n; Herrscher m.
rum n Rum m.
rumour n Gerücht n.
run vi laufen, rennen.
runaway adj flüchtig; ausgebrochen.
rung n Sprosse f.
runner n Läufer(in) m(f); Kufe f.
runner-bean n Stangenbohne f.
runway n Startbahn f.
rupture n Bruch f.
rush n Eile f, Hetze f:—vi eilen.
Russia n Rußland n.
Russian adj russisch:—n Russe m,
  Russin f; Russisch f.
rust n Rost m:—vi rosten.
rusty adj rostig.
rye n Roggen m.

S

sack n Sack m:—vt hinauswerfen; plündern.
sacrifice n Opfer n:—vt opfern.
sad adj traurig.
saddle n Sattel m.
sadness n Traurigkeit f.
safe adj sicher; vorsichtig:—n Safe m.
safety n Sicherheit f.
sage n (bot) Salbei f; Weise(r) f(m).
Sagittarius n (astrol) Schütze m.
sail n Segel n:—vt segeln:—vi segeln; auslaufen.
sailing n Segeln n.
sailor n Matrose m, Seemann m.
saint n Heilige(r) f(m).
sake n:—for the ~ of um... willen.
salad n Salat m.
salami n Salami f.
salary n Gehalt n.
sale n Verkauf m.
saliva n Speichel m.
salmon n Lachs m.
saloon n Salon m.
salt n Salz n.
salty adj salzig.
salute n Gruß m:—vt salutieren.
same adj pn gleiche(r, s); derselbe/dieselbe/dasselbe.
sample n Probe f:—vt probieren.
sanction n Sanktion f.
sand n Sand m.
sandal n Sandale f.
sandwich n Sandwich m/n.
sane adj geistig gesund.
sanity n geistige Gesundheit f.
sapphire n Saphir m.
sarcasm n Sarkasmus m.

sarcastic adj sarkastisch.
sardine n Sardine f.
satisfaction n Befriedigung f.
satisfactory adj zufriedenstellend.
satisfy vt befriedigen, zufriedenstellen.
Saturday n Samstag m, Sonnabend m.
sauce n Soße f, Sauce f.
saucepan n Kassrolle f.
saucer n Untertasse f.
saucy adj frech, keck.
saunter vi schlendern.
sausage n Wurst f.
savage adj wild:—n Wilde(r) f(m).
save vt retten; sparen:—prep conj außer, ausgenommen.
saving n Sparen n, Ersparnis f.
savings account n Sparkonto n.
savings bank n Sparkasse f.
saviour n Erlöser m.
savour vt schmecken.
savoury adj würzig, pikant.
saw n Sage f:—vt vi sägen.
sawdust n Sägemehl n.
say vt vi sagen.
scab n Schorf m.
scaffold n Schafott n.
scaffolding n Baugerüst n.
scald vt verbrühen.
scale n Schuppe f; Tonleiter f; Maßstab m:—vt erklimmen.
scan vt genau prüfen; absuchen; skandieren.
scandal n Skandal m.
Scandinavia n Skandinavien n.
Scandinavian adj skandinavisch:—n Skandinavier(in) m(f).
scapegoat n Sündenbock m.

scar n Narbe f.

scarce adj selten, rar.

scarcely adv kaum.

scarcity n Mangel m.

scare n Schrecken m:—vt erschrecken.

scarecrow n Vogelscheuche f.

scarf n Schal m.

scatter vt streuen; zerstreuen:—vi sich zerstreuen.

scenario n Szenario n.

scene n Ort m; Szene f.

scenery n Bühnenbild n; Landschaft f.

scent n Parfüm n; Duft m:—vt parfümieren.

sceptical adj skeptisch.

schedule n Liste f; Programm n; Zeitplan m.

scheme n Schema n; Intrige f; Plan m:—vt planen:—vi intrigieren.

school n Schule f.

science n Wissenschaft f.

scientific adj wissenschaftlich.

scientist n Wissenschaftler(in) m(f).

scissors npl Schere f.

scope n Ausmaß n; Spielraum m.

scorch n Brandstelle f:—vt versengen.

score n Punktzahl f; Spielergebnis n; Partitur f:—vi Punkte zählen.

scorn n Verachtung f:—vt verhöhnen.

Scorpio n (astrol) Skorpion m.

Scot n Schotte m, Schottin f.

Scotch n Scotch m.

Scotland n Schottland n.

Scotsman n Schotte m.

Scotswoman n Schottin f.

Scottish adj schottisch.

scour vt absuchen; schrubben.

scourge n Geißel f; Qual f.

scout n Pfadfinder m.

scrap n Stückchen n; Kellerei f; Schrott m:—vt verwerfen.

scrape n Kratzen n; Klemme f:—vt vi kratzen.

scratch n Kratzer m, Schramme f:—vt kratzen.

scream n Schrei m:—vi schreien.

screen n Schutzschirm m; Leinwand f; Bildschirm m.

screw n Schraube f.

screwdriver n Schraubenzieher m.

script n Handschrift f; Manuskript n.

scrub n Schrubben n; Gestrüpp n:—vt schrubben.

sculptor n Bildhauer(in) m(f).

sculpture n Bildhauerei f.

sea n Meer n, See f.

seagull n Möwe f.

seal n Seehund m; Siegel n:—vt versiegeln.

seam n Saum m.

search n Suche f; Durchsuchung f:—vi suchen:—vt durchsuchen.

seashore n Meeresküste f.

seasick adj seekrank.

season n Jahreszeit f; Saison f:—vt würzen.

seasonal adj Saison-.

seat n Sitz m, Platz m; Gesäß n:—vt setzen.

seaweed n Seetang m.

seaworthy adj seetüchtig.

second adj zweite(r, s); adv an zweiter Stelle:—n Sekunde f.

secondhand adj gebraucht.

secrecy n Geheimhaltung f.

secret adj geheim:—n Geheimnis n.

secretary n Sekretär(in) m(f).

section n Teil m; Abschnitt m.

sector n Sektor m.

secular adj weltlich, profan.

secure adj sicher; fest:—vt sichern.

security n Sicherheit f; Pfand n; Wertpapier n.

seduce vt verführen.

seduction n Verführung f.

seductive adj verführerisch.

see *vt vi* sehen.
seed *n* Samen *m*:—*vt* plazieren.
seek *vt* suchen.
seem *vi* scheinen.
seesaw *n* Wippe *f*.
seize *vt* greifen, ergreifen, packen.
seizure *n* Anfall *m*.
seldom *adv* selten.
select *adj* ausgewählt:—*vt* auswählen.
selection *n* Auswahl *f*.
selfish *adj* selbstsüchtig.
selfishness *n* Selbstsucht *f*.
sell *vt vi* verkaufen.
seller *n* Verkäufer *m*.
semicolon *n* Semikolon *n*.
send *vt* senden, schicken.
senior *adj* älter; Ober-.
sensation *n* Gefühl *n*; Sensation *f*.
sense *n* Sinn *m*; Verstand *m*; Gefühl *n*.
senseless *adj* sinnlos.
sensible *adj* vernünftig.
sensitive *adj* empfindlich.
sensual *adj* sinnlich.
sentence *n* Satz *m*; Strafe *f*; Urteil *n*.
sentiment *n* Gefühl *n*; Gedenke *m*.
sentimental *adj* sentimental.
separate *adj* getrennt, separat:—*vt* trennen:—*vi* sich trennen.
separation *n* Trennung *f*.
September *n* September *m*.
sequel *n* Folge *f*.
sequence *n* Reihenfolge *f*.
Serbia *n* Serbien *n*.
serene *adj* heiter.
sew
series *n* Serie *f*.
serious *adj* ernst; schwer.
sermon *n* Predigt *f*.
servant *n* Diener(in) *m(f)*.
serve *vt vi* dienen.
service *n* Dienst *m*; Service *m*, Bedienung *f*:—*vt* warten, überholen.
session *n* Sitzung *f*.

set *n* Satz *m*; Apparat *m*:—*adj* festgelegt; bereit:—*vt* setzen, stellen, legen:—*vi* untergehen; fest werden.
settle *vt* beruhigen; bezahlen; regeln: —*vi* sich einleben; sich setzen.
settlement *n* Regelung *f*; Begleichung *f*; Siedlung *f*.
seven *num* sieben.
seventeen *num* siebzehn.
seventh *adj* siebte(r, s).
seventy *num* siebzig.
several *adj* mehrere(r, s).
severe *adj* streng; schwer.
sew *vt vi* nähen.
sex *n* Sex *m*; Geschlecht *n*.
sexual *adj* sexuell.
sexy *adj* sexy.
shade *n* Schatten *m*; Schirm *m*:—*vt* beschatten; abschirmen.
shadow *n* Schatten *m*.
shake *vt* schütteln:—*vi* schwanken; zittern.
shallow *adj* seicht.
shame *n* Scham *m*; Schande *f*:—*vt* beschämen.
shameful *adj* schändlich.
shameless *adj* schamlos.
shampoo *n* Shampoo *n*.
shamrock *n* Kleeblatt *n*.
shape *n* Form *f*:—*vt* formen, gestalten.
share *n* Anteil *m*; (*fin*) Aktie *f*:—*vt* teilen.
shareholder *n* Aktionär(in) *m(f)*.
shark *n* Hai *m*.
sharp *adj* scharf; spitz; (*mus*) erhöht: —*n* Kreuz *n*.
sharpen *vt* schärfen.
shatter *vt* zerschmettern:—*vi* zerspringen.
shave *n* Rasur *f*:—*vt* rasieren:—*vi* sich rasieren.
shaver *n* Rasierapparat *m*.
she *pn* sie.

shed n Schuppen m; Stall m.

sheep n Schaf n.

sheer adj bloß, rein; steil.

sheet n Bettuch n; Blatt n.

shelf n Regal n.

shell n Schale f; Muschel f; Granate f.

shellfish n Schalentier n.

shelter n Schutz m; Bunker m:—vt schützen:—vi sich unterstellen.

shepherd n Schäfer m.

shield n Schild m; Schirm m:—vt schirmen.

shift n Verschiebung f; Schicht f:—vt rücken, verschieben.

shine n Glanz m, Schein m:—vi scheinen.

shiny adj glänzend.

ship n Schiff n.

shirt n Hemd n.

shiver vi zittern.

shock n Erschütterung f; Schock m; Schlag m:—vt erschüttern; schockieren.

shoe n Schuh m; Hufeisen n:—vt beschlagen.

shoot vt schießen.

shop n Laden m, Geschäft n.

shopping n Einkaufen n.

shopping centre n Einkaufszentrum n.

shore n Strand m.

short adj kurz.

shorten vt abkürzen.

short-sighted adj kurzsichtig.

shot n Schuß m.

shoulder n Schulter f.

shout n Schrei m:—vi schreien.

shove n Stoß m:—vt schieben, stoßen.

show n Schau f; Ausstellung f; Vorstellung f:—vt zeigen.

shower n Schauer m; Dusche f.

shred n Fetzen m:—vt zerfetzen.

shrewd adj clever.

shriek n Schrei m:—vi schreien.

shrimp n Garnele f.

shrink vi schrumpfen.

shroud n Leichentuch n.

Shrove Tuesday n Fastnachtsdienstag m.

shrub n Strauch m.

shun vt scheuen.

shut vt schließen, zumachen:—vi sich schließen.

shutter n Fensterladen m.

shy adj schüchtern.

sick adj krank; makaber.

sicken vt krankmachen:—vi krank werden.

sickle n Sichel f.

sickness n Krankheit f.

side n Seite m.

siege n Belagerung f.

sieve n Sieb n:—vt sieben.

sift vt sieben.

sigh n Seufzer m:—vi seufzen.

sight n Sehvermögen n; Blick m; Anblick m.

sign n Zeichen n; Schild n:—vt unterschreiben.

signal n Signal n.

signature n Unterschrift f.

significance n Bedeutung f.

significant adj bedeutend.

signify vt bedeuten.

signpost n Wegweiser m.

silence n Stille f; Schweigen n.

silent adj still; schweigsam.

silk n Seide f.

silky adj seidig.

silly adj dumm, albern.

silver n Silber n:—adj Silber-.

similar adj ähnlich.

similarity n Ähnlichkeit f.

simmer vi sieden.

simple adj einfach.

simplicity n Einfachheit f; Einfältigkeit f.

simplify vt vereinfachen.

simultaneous adj gleichzeitig.

sin n Sünde f:—vi sündigen.
since adv seither:—prep conj seit.
sincere adj aufrichtig.
sincerity n Aufrichtigkeit f.
sing vt vi singen.
Singapore n Singapur n.
singer n Sänger(in) m(f).
single adj einzig; Einzel-.
singular adj (gr) Singular-; merkwürdig.
sinister adj böse; unheimlich.
sink n Spülbecken n:—vt versenken:
—vi sinken.
sinner n Sünder(in) m(f).
sister n Schwester f.
sister-in-law n Schwägerin f.
sit vi sitzen; tagen:—~ down vi sich
hinsetzen.
site n Platz m; Baustelle f.
sitting n Sitzung f.
sitting room n Wohnzimmer n.
situation n Lage f.
six num sechs.
sixteen num sechzehn.
sixth adj sechste(r, s).
sixty num sechzig.
size n Größe f; Umfang m.
skate n Schlittschuh m; Rochen m:—vi
Schlittschuh laufen.
skating n Eislauf m.
skating rink n Eisbahn f.
skeleton n Skelett n.
sketch n Skizze f:—vt skizzieren.
ski n Schi m:—vi Schi laufen.
skid n Schleudern n:—vi schleudern.
skier n Schiläufer(in) m(f).
skiing n Schilaufen n.
skilful adj geschickt.
skill n Können n.
skin n Haut f; Schale f.
skirt n Rock m.
skull n Schädel m.
sky n Himmel m.
skyscraper n Wolkenkratzer m.

slab n Platte f.
slack adj locker; nachlässig.
slam vt vi zuschlagen.
slander n Verleumdung f:—vt verleumden.
slate n Schiefer m; Dachziegel:—vt
verreißen.
slaughter n Schlachten n:—vt schlachten.
Slav adj slawisch.
slave n Sklave m, Sklavin f.
slavery n Sklaverei f.
sledge n Schlitten m.
sleep n Schlaf m:—vi schlafen.
sleeper n Schläfer m; Schlafwagen m.
sleepless adj schlaflos.
sleepwalker n Schlafwandler(in) m(f).
sleepy adj schläfrig.
sleet n Schneeregen m.
sleeve n Ärmel m.
slice n Scheibe f.
slide n Rutschbahn f; Diapositiv n:—vt
schieben:—vi gleiten, rutschen.
slight adj zierlich; geringfügig; gering.
slightly adv etwas, ein bißchen.
slim adj schlank; dünn:—vi eine
Schlankheitskur machen.
slip n Flüchtigkeitsfehler m; Zettel m:—
vi ausrutschen; gleiten.
slipper n Hausschuh m.
slogan n Schlagwort n; Werbespruch m.
slope n Neigung f; Abhang m:—vi ~
down sich senken:—~ up ansteigen.
slow adj langsam.
slug n Nachtschnecke f.
slum n Elendsquartier n.
sly adj schlau.
smack n Klaps m:—vt einen Klaps geben + dat.
small adj klein.
smart adj elegant, schick.
smash n Zusammenstoß m:—vt zerschmettern:—vi zersplittern.

smell n Geruch m; Geruchssinn m:—vt vi riechen.

smile n Lächeln n:—vi lächeln.

smith n Schmied m.

smoke n Rauch m:—vt vi rauchen.

smoker n Raucher(in) m(f).

smooth adj glatt.

smug adj selbstgefällig.

smuggle vt schmuggeln.

smuggler n Schmuggler m.

snack n Imbiß m.

snag n Haken m.

snail n Schnecke m.

snake n Schlange f.

snap n Schnappen n:—adj schnell:— vt zerbrechen:—vi brechen.

snatch vt schnappen.

sneeze vi niesen.

sniff vt schnuppern:—vi schnüffeln.

snip n Schnippel m:—vt schnippeln.

snore vi schnarchen.

snow n Schnee m:—vi schneien.

snowball n Schneeball m.

snowdrop n Schneeglöckchen n.

snowman n Schneemann m.

snub vt schroff abfertigen:—n Verweis m.

so adv so; auch; so viele; also.

soak vt durchnassen:—vi weichen.

soap n Seife f.

soar vi aufsteigen.

sob n Schluchzen n:—vi schluchzen.

sober adj nüchtern.

soccer n Fußball m.

sociable adj gesellig.

social adj sozial.

socialism n Sozialismus m.

socialist n Socialist(in) m(f).

society n Gesellschaft f.

sociology n Soziologie f.

sock n Socke f.

socket n Steckdose f.

sod n Rasenstück n.

soda n Soda f.

sodium n Natrium n.

sofa n Sofa n.

soft adj weich; leise.

soften vt weich machen:—vi weich werden.

softness n Weichheit f.

software n Software f.

soil n Erde f:—vt beschmutzen.

solar adj Sonnen-.

soldier n Soldat m.

sole n Sohle f; Seezunge f:—adj alleinig, Allein-.

solicitor n Rechtsanwalt m, Rechtsanwältin f.

solid adj fest; massiv; solide.

solidarity n Solidarität f.

solitary adj einsam.

solitude n Einsamkeit f.

solo n Solo n.

solution n Lösung f.

solve vt lösen.

some adj pn einige; etwas.

somehow adv irgendwie.

someone pn jemand; acc jemand(en); dat jemandem.

something pn etwas.

sometimes adv manchmal.

somewhat adv etwas.

somewhere adv irgendwo; irgendwohin.

son n Sohn m.

song n Lied n.

son-in-law n Schwiegersohn m.

soon adv bald.

soot n Ruß m.

soothe vt beruhigen; lindern.

sophisticated adj kultiviert.

sordid adj erbärmlich.

sore adj schmerzend; wund.

sorrow n Kummer m, Leid n.

sorry adj traurig, erbärmlich:—~! Entschuldigung!

sort n Art f; Sorte f:—vt sortieren; sichten, in Ordnung bringen.

soul n Seele f; (mus) Soul m.

sound adj gesund; sicher:—n Geräusch n, Laut m:—vt erschallen lassen; abhorchen:—vi schallen, tönen; klingen.

soup n Suppe f.

sour adj sauer.

source n Quelle f.

south n Süden m.

South Africa n Südafrika n.

South African adj südafrikanisch:—n Südafrikaner(in) m(f).

South America n Südamerika n.

South American adj südamerikanisch:—n Südamerikaner(in) m(f).

southeast n Südosten m.

southern adj südlich, Süd-.

South Pole n Südpol m.

southwest n Südwesten m.

souvenir n Souvenir n.

sow n Sau f:—vt säen.

soya bean n Sojabohne f.

space n Raum m; Platz m.

spacecraft n Raumfahrzeug n.

spacious adj geräumig.

spade n Spaten m; Pik n:—**king of ~s** Pik-König m.

Spain n Spanien n.

span n Spanne f:—vt umspannen, überspannen.

Spaniard n Spanier(in) m(f).

Spanish adj spanisch:—n Spanisch n.

spare adj Ersatz-:—vt verschonen; ersparen.

spark n Funken m.

sparkle n Funkeln n:—vi funkeln.

spark plug n Zündkerze f.

sparrow n Spatz m.

sparse adj spärlich.

speak vt vi sprechen.

speaker n Sprecher(in) m(f).

spear n Speer m:—vt aufspießen.

special adj besondere(r, s).

speciality n Spezialität f.

specific adj spezifisch.

specimen n Probe f.

speck n Fleckchen n.

spectacle n Schauspiel n.

spectator n Zuschauer(in) m(f).

spectre n Geist m, Gespenst n.

speculate vi spekulieren.

speculation n Nachdenken n; Grübeln n; Spekulation f.

speech n Rede f, Sprache f; Reden n, Sprechen n.

speed n Geschwindigkeit f, Eile f:—vi eilen, schnell fahren.

speedy adj schnell, rasch.

spell n Weile f; Zauber m:—vt buchstabieren.

spend vt verwenden; ausgeben; verbringen; verbrauchen.

sperm n Sperma n.

sphere n Kugel f, Sphäre f; Bereich m.

spherical adj kugelförmig, sphärisch.

spice n Gewürz n:—vt würzen.

spider n Spinne f.

spill vt verschütten:—vi sich ergießen.

spin vt spinnen; herumwirbeln.

spinach n Spinat m.

spine n Rückgrat n.

spinster n unverheiratete Frau f.

spiral n Spirale f.

spire n Turm m.

spirit n Geist m; Stimmung f; Alkohol m:—**~s** npl Spirituosen pl.

spirited adj beherzt.

spit n Bratspieß m; Spucke f:—vi spucken.

spite n Gehässigkeit f:—**in ~ of** trotz.

splash n Spritzer m:—vt bespritzen: —vi spritzen.

splendid adj glänzend.

splendour n Pracht f.

split n Spalte f; Trennung f:—vt spalten:—vi reißen.

spoil *vt* verderben; verwöhnen.

spokesman *n* Sprecher *m*.

spokeswoman *n* Sprecherin *f*.

sponge *n* Schwamm *m*:—*vt* abwaschen.

sponsor *n* Sponsor *m*:—*vt* fördern.

spontaneous *adj* spontan.

spoon *n* Löffel *m*.

sport *n* Sport *m*.

sportsman *n* Sportler *m*.

sportswear *n* Sportkleidung *f*.

sportswoman *n* Sportlerin *f*.

spot *n* Punkt *m*; Fleck *m*; Stelle *f*:—*vt* erspähen.

spotless *adj* fleckenlos.

spotlight *n* Scheinwerferlicht *n*.

spotted *adj* gefleckt.

spouse *n* Gatte *m*, Gattin *f*.

spray *n* Gischt *f*, Spray *m/n*; Sprühdose *f*:—*vi* sprühen:—*vt* zerstäuben, spritzen.

spread *n* Verbreitung *f*:—*vt* ausbreiten; verbreiten:—*vi* sich ausbreiten.

spring *n* Sprung *m*; Feder *f*; Frühling *m*:—*vi* springen.

sprinkle *vt* streuen; sprenkeln.

sprout *vi* sprießen:—~**s** *npl* Rosenkohl *m*.

spur *n* Sporn *m*; Ansporn *m*:—*vt* anspornen.

spy *n* Spion(in) *m(f)*:—*vi* spionieren.

squander *vt* verschwenden.

square *n* Quadrat *n*; Platz *m*:—*adj* viereckig.

squash *n* Squash *n*:—*vt* zerquetschen.

squawk *vi* kreischen.

squeak *vi* quieksen; quietschen.

squeeze *vt* pressen, drücken.

squid *n* Tintenfisch *m*.

squint *vi* schielen.

squirrel *n* Eichhörnchen *n*.

stab *n* Stich *m*:—*vt* erstechen.

stabilize *vt* stabilisieren:—*vi* sich stabilisieren.

stable *n* Stall *m*:—*adj* stabil.

stack *n* Stapel *m*:—*vt* stapeln.

stadium *n* Stadion *n*.

staff *n* Stab *m*; Personal *n*.

stag *n* Hirsch *m*.

stage *n* Bühne *f*; Etappe *f*; Stufe *m*:—*vt* aufführen.

stagger *vi* wanken, taumeln.

stagnant *adj* stagnierend.

stain *n* Fleck *m*:—*vt* beflecken.

stair *n* Stufe *f*.

staircase *n* Treppenhaus *n*, Treppe *f*.

stale *adj* alt; altbacken.

stalk *n* Stengel *m*, Stiel *m*.

stammer *n* Stottern *n*:—*vt vi* stottern.

stamp *n* Briefmarke *f*; Stempel *m*:—*vi* stampfen:—*vt* stempeln.

stand *vi* stehen.

standard *n* Norm *f*; Fahne *f*:—*adj* Normal-.

staple *n* Heftklamme *f*:—*adj* Haupt-, Grund-:—*vt* klammern.

stapler *n* Heftmaschine *f*.

star *n* Stern *m*; Star *m*.

stare *vi*:—~ **at** starren auf, anstarren:—*n* starrer Blick *m*.

starling *n* Star *m*.

start *n* Anfang *m*; Start *m*:—*vt* in Gang setzen; anlassen:—*vi* anfangen; aufbrechen; starten.

startle *vt* erschrecken.

startling *adj* erschreckend.

state *n* Zustand *m*; Staat *m*:—*vt* erklären.

statement *n* Aussage *f*.

static *n* Reibungselektrizität *f*.

station *n* Bahnhof *m*.

stationary *adj* stillstehend.

stationery *n* Schreibwaren *pl*.

statistics *n* Statistik *f*.

statue *n* Statue *f*.

stay *n* Aufenthalt *m*:—*vi* bleiben; wohnen.

steady *adj* fest, stabil.

steak *n* Steak *n*; Filet *n*.

steal *vt vi* stehlen.

steam *n* Dampf *m*:—*vi* dämpfen.

steamer *n* Dämpfer *m*.

steel *n* Stahl *m*:—*adj* Stahl-.

steep *adj* steil.

steeple *n* Kirchturm *m*.

steer *vt vi* steuern; lenken.

steering *n* Steuerung *f*.

steering wheel *n* Lenkrad, Steuerrad *n*.

step *n* Schritt *m*; Stufe *f*:—*vi* treten, schreiten.

stepbrother *n* Stiefbruder *m*.

stepdaughter *n* Stieftochter *f*.

stepfather *n* Stiefvater *m*.

stepmother *n* Stiefmutter *f*.

stepsister *n* Stiefschwester *f*.

stepson *n* Stiefsohn *m*.

stereo *n* Stereoanlage *f*.

sterile *adj* steril; unfruchtbar.

stern *adj* streng:—*n* Heck *n*.

stew *n* Eintopf *m*.

steward(ess) *n* Steward(eß) *m*(*f*).

stick *n* Stock *m*; Stück *n*:—*vt* stechen, stecken; kleben.

sticky *adj* klebrig.

stiff *adj* steif; dick; stark.

stiffen *vt vi* versteifen.

still *adj* still:—*adv* (immer) noch; immerhin.

stimulate *vt* anregen, stimulieren.

stimulus *n* Anregung *f*.

sting *n* Stich *m*:—*vt vi* stechen.

stingy *adj* geizig.

stink *n* Gestank *m*:—*vi* stinken.

stir *n* Bewegung *f*; Ruhren *n*:—*vt* rühren:—*vi* sich rühren.

stitch *n* Stich *m*; (*med*) Faden *m*:—*vt* nähen.

stock *n* Vorrat *m*; Lager *n*; Vieh *n*; Grundkapital *n*:—*vt* führen.

stockbroker *n* Börsenmakler *m*.

stock exchange *n* Börse *f*.

stocking *n* Strumpf *m*.

stomach *n* Bauch *m*; Magen *m*.

stone *n* Stein *m*.

stony *adj* steinig.

stool *n* Hocker *m*.

stop *n* Halt *m*; Haltestelle *f*; Punkt *m*: —*vt* anhalten:—*vi* aufhören; stehenbleiben; bleiben.

store *n* Vorrat *m*; Lager *n*; Warenhaus *n*, Kaufhaus *n*:—*vt* lagern.

stork *n* Storch *m*.

storm *n* Sturm *m*:—*vt vi* stürmen.

stormy *adj* stürmisch.

story *n* Geschichte *f*; Märchen *n*.

stout *adj* tapfer; beleibt:—*n* Starkbier *n*.

stove *n* Herd *m*; Ofen *m*.

straight *adj* gerade; offen; pur:—*adv* direkt, geradewegs.

straightaway *adv* sofort.

straighten *vt* gerade machen.

strain *n* Belastung *f*:—*vt* überanstrengen; anspannen:—*vi* sich anstrengen.

strange *adj* fremd; seltsam.

stranger *n* Fremde(r) *f*(*m*).

strangle *vt* erwürgen.

strap *n* Riemen *m*; Träger *m*:—*vt* festschnallen.

strategic *adj* strategisch.

strategy *n* Strategie *f*.

straw *n* Stroh *n*; Strohhalm *m*.

strawberry *n* Erdbeere *f*.

stray *vi* herumstreunen:—*adj* verirrt; zufällig.

stream *n* Bach *m*; Strom *m*:—*vi* strömen.

street *n* Straße *f*.

strength *n* Stärke *f*; Kraft *f*.

strengthen *vt* verstärken.

stress *n* Druck *m*; Streß *m*; (*gr*) Betonung *f*:—*vt* betonen.

stretch *n* Strecke *f*:—*vt* ausdehnen, strecken:—*vi* sich strecken.

stretcher *n* Tragbahre *f*.

strict *adj* streng; genau.

stride *n* langer Schritt *m*:—*vi* schreiten.

strike n Streik m; Schlag m:—vt schlagen:—vi streiken.

striker n Streikende(r) f(m).

string n Schnur f; Saite f.

strip n Streifen m:—vt abstreifen, abziehen; ausziehen:—vi sich ausziehen.

stripe n Streifen m.

stroke n Schlag m; Stoß m; (med) Schlaganfall m; Streicheln n:—vt streicheln.

stroll n Spaziergang m:—vi schlendern.

strong adj stark; fest.

structure n Struktur f; Aufbau m.

struggle n Kampf m:—vi kämpfen.

stubborn adj hartnäckig.

student n Student(in) m(f):—adj Studenten-.

studio n Studio n; Atelier n.

study n Studium n; Studie f:—vt vi studieren.

stuff n Zeug n:—vt stopfen; füllen; ausstopfen.

stumble vi stolpern.

stun vt betäuben.

stunt n Kunststück n, Trick m.

stupid adj dumm.

stupidity n Dummheit f.

sturdy adj robust, kräftig.

stutter vi stottern.

sty n Schweinestall m.

style n Stil m; Mode f.

subject n Untertan m; Thema n; Fach n; (gr) Subjekt n:—be ~ to unterworfen sein + dat.

subjective adj subjektiv.

submarine n Unterseeboot n, U-Boot n.

submit vt behaupten; unterbreiten:—vi sich ergeben.

subscriber n Abonnent m.

subscription n Abonnement n.

subsequent adj später, folgend.

subsidiary adj Neben-:—n Tochtergesellschaft f.

subsidy n Subvention f.

substance n Substanz f.

substantial adj wesentlich; fest, kräftig.

substitute n Ersatz m:—vt ersetzen.

substitution n Ersetzung f.

subtle adj fein.

subtract vt abziehen.

suburb n Vorort m.

succeed vi erfolgreich sein, Erfolg haben; gelingen:—vt (nach)folgen + dat.

success n Erfolg m.

successful adj erfolgreich.

such adj solche(r, s).

suck vt saugen.

suction n Saugkraft f.

sudden(ly) adj (adv) plötzlich.

sue vt verklagen

suffer vt vi leiden.

suffering n Leiden n.

suffice vi genügen.

sufficient adj ausreichend.

sugar n Zucker m.

suggest vt vorschlagen.

suggestion n Vorschlag m.

suicide n Selbstmord m:—commit ~ Selbstmord begehen.

suit n Anzug m; Farbe f:—vt passen + dat.

suitable adj passend, geeignet.

suitcase n Koffer m.

suite n Zimmerflucht f; Einrichtung f; (mus) Suite f.

sulk vi schmollen.

sulphur n Schwefel m.

sum n Summe f; Betrag m; Rechenaufgabe f:—~ up vt vi zusammenfassen.

summary n Zusammenfassung f.

summer n Sommer m.

summit n Gipfel m.

sun n Sonne m.

sunbathe vi sich sonnen.

sunburn n Sonnenbrand m.

Sunday n Sonntag m.

sunflower n Sonnenblume f.
sunglasses npl Sonnenbrille f.
sunlight n Sonnenlicht n.
sunny adj sonnig.
sunrise n Sonnenaufgang m.
sunset n Sonnenuntergang m.
sunshade n Sonnenschirm m.
sunshine n Sonnenschein m.
sunstroke n Hitzschlag m.
super adj prima, klasse.
superior adj überlegen:—n Vorgesetzte(r) f(m).
superiority n Überlegenheit f.
supermarket n Supermarkt m.
supernatural n übernatürlich.
superpower n Weltmacht f.
supersonic adj Überschall-.
superstition n Aberglaube m.
superstitious adj abergläubisch.
supervise vt beaufsichtigen.
supervision n Aufsicht f.
supplement n Ergänzung f.
supplementary adj ergänzend.
supplier n Lieferant m.
supply vt liefern:—n Vorrat m; Lieferung f.
support n Unterstützung f:—vt stützen; unterstützen.
supporter n Aufhänger(in) m(f).
suppose vt vi annehmen.
suppress vt unterdrücken.
suppression n Unterdrückung f.
sure adj sicher, gewiß.
surface n Oberfläche f.
surgeon n Chirurg(in) m(f).
surgery n Chirurgie f.
surgical adj chirurgisch.
surname n Zuname m.
surpass vt übertreffen.
surplus n Überschuß m:—adj überschüssig.
surprise n Überraschung f:—vt überreaschen.

surprising adj überraschend.
surrender n Kapitulation f:—vi sich ergeben.
surround vt umgeben.
survey n Übersicht f:—vt überblicken; vermessen.
survival n Überleben n.
survive vt vi überleben.
survivor n Überlebende(r) f(m).
suspect n Verdächtige(r) f(m):—adj verdachtig:—vt verdächtigen.
suspend vt verschieben; aufhängen; suspendieren.
suspense n Spannung f.
suspension n Federung f; Suspendierung f.
suspicion n Verdacht m.
suspicious adj verdachtig.
sustain vt aufrechterhalten; bestätigen.
swallow n Schwalbe f; Schluck m:—vt schlucken.
swan n Schwan m.
swastika n Hakenkreuz n.
sway vi schwanken; schaukeln, sich wiegen:—vt schwenken.
swear vi schwören; fluchen.
sweat n Schweiß m:—vi schwitzen.
sweater n Pullover m.
Swede n Schwede m, Schwedin f.
Sweden n Schweden n.
Swedish adj schwedisch:—n Schwedisch n.
sweep n Schornsteinfeger m:—vt fegen, kehren:—vi rauschen.
sweet n Nachtisch m; Bonbon n:—adj süß.
sweeten vt süßen.
sweetness n Süße f.
swell n Seegang n:—vt vermehren:—vi schwellen.
swift n Mauersegler m:—adj geschwind, schnell, rasch.
swim vt vi schwimmen.

swimming n Schwimmen n.
swimming pool n Schwimmenbecken n.
swimsuit n Badeanzug m.
swine n Schwein n.
swing n Schaukel f; Schwung n:—vt vi schwingen.
Swiss adj Schweizer, schweizerisch:—n Schweizer(in) m(f).
switch n Schalter m; Wechsel m:—vt schalten; wechseln:—~ off vt ausschalten:—~ on vt einschalten.
Switzerland n Schweiz f.
sword n Schwert n.
sycamore n Bergahorn m.

syllable n Silbe f.
syllabus n Lehrplan m.
symbol n Symbol n.
symbolic adj symbolisch.
symmetry n Symmetrie f.
sympathetic adj mitfühlend.
sympathize vi mitfühlen.
sympathy n Mitleid n, Mitgefühl n; Beileid n.
symphony n Sinfonie f.
symptom n Sympton n.
synagogue n Synagoge f.
synonym n Synonym n.
system n System n.

T

table n Tisch m.
tablecloth n Tischtuch n.
tablet n Tablette f; Täfelchen n.
table tennis n Tischtennis n.
tact n Takt m.
tactful adj taktvoll.
tactical adj taktisch.
tactless adj taktlos.
tactics npl Taktik f.
tag n Schild n, Anhänger m.
tail n Schwanz m:—vt folgen +dat.
tailor n Schneider m.
take vt nehmen.
takeover n Übernahme f.
tale n Geschichte f, Erzählung f.
talent n Talent n.
talk n Gespräch n; Gerede n; Vortrag m:—vi sprechen, reden.
tall adj groß; hoch.
tame adj zahm.
tan n Sonnenbräune f:—vt bräunen:—vi braun werden.
tangible adj greifbar.

tank n Tank m; Panzer m.
tap n Hahn m; Klopfen n:—vt klopfen.
tape n Band n:—vt aufnehmen.
tapestry n Wandteppich m.
tar n Teer m.
target n Ziel n.
tariff n Tarif m.
tart n Torte f.
task n Aufgabe f.
taste n Geschmack m; Geschmackssinn m; Vorliebe f:—vt vi schmecken.
taunt vt verhöhnen.
Taurus n (astrol) Stier m.
taut adj straff.
tax n Steuer f:—vt besteuern.
taxation n Besteuerung f.
tax-free adj steuerfrei.
taxi n Taxi n:—vi rollen.
taxpayer n Steuerzahler m.
tea n Tee m.
teach vt vi lehren, unterrichten.
teacher n Lehrer(in) m(f).
teacup n Teetasse f.

team *n* Team *n*; Mannschaft *f*.
teapot *n* Teekanne *f*.
tear *n* Träne *f*; Riß *m*:—*vt vi* zerreißen.
tease *vt* necken.
teaspoon *n* Teelöffel *m*.
technical *adj* technisch; Fach-.
technician *n* Techniker *m*.
technique *n* Technik *f*.
technological *adj* technologisch.
technology *n* Technologie *f*.
teddy (bear) *n* Teddybär *m*.
teenage *adj* Teenager-, jugendlich.
teenager *n* Teenager *m*, Jugendliche(r) *f(m)*.
teething troubles *npl* Kinderkrankheiten *fpl*.
telecommunications *npl* Fernmeldewesen *n*.
telephone *n* Telefon *n*.
telephone call *n* Telefongespräch *n*.
telephone directory *n* Telefonbuch *n*.
telephone number *n* Telefonnummer *m*.
telescope *n* Teleskop *n*.
television *n* Fernsehen *n*.
television set *n* Fernseher *m*.
tell *vt* erzählen; sagen; erkennen; wissen.
temper *n* Temperament *n*:—*vt* mildern.
temperament *n* Temperament *n*.
temperature *n* Temperatur *f*.
temple *n* Tempel *m*; Schläfe *f*.
temporary *adj* vorläufig; provisorisch.
tempt *vt* verleiten; locken.
temptation *n* Versuchung *f*.
tempting *adj* verlockend.
ten *num* zehn.
tenant *n* Mieter *m*; Pächter *m*.
tend *vt* sich kümmern um.
tendency *n* Tendenz *f*.
tender *adj* zart; zärtlich:—*n* Kostenanschlag *m*:—*vt* (an)bieten.
tenderness *n* Zartheit *f*; Zärtlichkeit *f*.
tennis *n* Tennis *n*.
tennis court *n* Tennisplatz *m*.

tennis player *n* Tennisspieler(in) *m(f)*.
tenor *n* Tenor *m*.
tense *adj* angespannt:—*n* Zeitform *f*.
tension *n* Spannung *f*.
tent *n* Zelt *n*.
tenth *adj* zehnte(r, s).
term *n* Zeitraum *m*; Frist *f*; Bedingung *f*; Ausdruck *m*.
terminal *adj* Schluß-; unheilbar:—*n* Endstation *f*; Terminal *m*.
terminate *vt* beenden:—*vi* enden, aufhören.
terminus *n* Endstation *f*.
terrible *adj* schrecklich.
terrific *adj* fantastisch.
terrify *vt* erschrecken.
territory *n* Gebiet *n*.
terror *n* Schrecken *m*; Terror *m*.
terrorize *vt* terrorisieren.
terrorism *n* Terrorismus *m*.
terrorist *n* Terrorist(in) *m(f)*.
test *n* Probe *f*; Prüfung *f*:—*vt* prüfen.
testicle *n* Hoden *m*.
testify *vi* aussagen.
testimony *n* Zeugenaussage *f*.
text *n* Text *m*.
texture *n* Beschaffenheit *f*.
than *prep* als.
thank *vt* danken +*dat*.
thankful *adj* dankbar.
thankless *adj* undankbar.
thanks *npl* danke.
that *pn* das; jene(r, s):—*rel pn* der, die, das:—*conj* daß:—**so ~** so daß.
the *art* der, die, das.
theatre *n* Theater *n*.
theft *n* Diebstahl *m*.
their *poss adj* ihr(e):—**~s** *poss pn* ihre(r, s).
them *pn acc* sie, *dat* ihnen.
theme *n* Thema *n*.
themselves *pn* sich; selbst.
then *adv* dann; danach:—**now and ~** dann und wann.

theology n Theologie f.
theoretical adj theoretisch.
theory n Theorie f.
there adv da, dort; dahin, dorthin.
therefore adv also.
thermometer n Thermometer n.
these pn adj diese.
they pn sie; man.
thick adj dick; dumm.
thickness n Dicke f; Dichte f.
thief n Dieb(in) m(f).
thigh n Oberschenkel m.
thimble n Fingerhut m.
thin adj dünn, mager.
thing n Ding n; Sache f.
think vt vi denken.
third adj dritte(r, s).
thirst n Durst f.
thirsty adj durstig:—**be ~** Durst haben.
thirteen num dreizehn.
thirty num dreißig.
this adj diese(r, s):—pn dies, das.
thistle n Distel f.
thorn n Dorn m.
thorough adj gründlich.
those pl pxn die (da), jene:—adj die, jene.
though conj obwohl:—adv trotzdem.
thought n Gedanke m; Denken n.
thoughtful adj gedankenvoll, nachdenklich.
thousand num tausend.
thread n Faden m, Garn n.
threat n Dröhung f.
threaten vt bedrohen:—vi drohen.
three num drei.
threshold n Schwelle f.
thrive vi gedeihen.
throat n Hals m, Kehle f.
through prep durch.
throughout prep überall in +dat; während:—adv überall.
throw vt werfen.
thrush n Drossel f.

thumb n Daumen m.
thunder n Donner m.
thunderstorm n Gewitter n.
Thursday n Donnertag m.
thus adv so; somit, also.
thyme n Thymian m.
tick vi ticken.
ticket n Fahrkarte f; Eintrittskarte f.
ticket office n Kasse f.
tickle vt kitzeln.
ticklish adj kitzlig.
tide n Gezeiten pl.
tidy adj ordentlich.
tie n Krawatte f, Schlips m; Unentschieden n:—vt binden:—vi unentschieden spielen.
tier n Rang m.
tiger n Tiger m.
tight adj eng, knapp; gedrängt; fest: — adv fest.
tighten vt anziehen, anspannen:—vi sich spannen.
tights npl Strümpfhose f.
tigress n Tigerin f.
tile n Dachziegel m; Fliese f.
till n Kasse f:—vt bestellen:—prep conj bis.
tilt vt kippen, neigen:—vi sich neigen.
timber n Holz n; Baumbestand m.
time n Zeit f; Mal n; (mus) Takt m.
timid adj ängstlich, schüchtern.
tin n Blech n; Dose f.
tiny adj winzig.
tip n Spitze f; Trinkgeld n; Wink m, Tip m:—vt kippen; antippen; ein Trinkgeld geben.
tire vt vi ermüden, müde machen/werden.
tireless adj unermüdlich.
tiring adj ermüdend.
tissue n Gewebe n; Papiertaschentuch n.
title n Titel m.
to prep zu, nach; bis; vor; für.
toad n Kröte m.

toadstool n Giftpilz n.
toast n Toast m; Trinkspruch m:—vt trinken auf +acc; toasten.
toaster n Toaster m.
tobacco n Tabak m.
tobacconist n Tabakhändler m.
tobacconist's n Tabakladen m.
toboggan n Schlitten m.
today adv heute; heutzutage.
toe n Zehe f; Spitze f.
together adv zusammen; gleichzeitig.
toil n harte Arbeit f; Plackerei f:—vi sich abmühen, sich plagen.
toilet n Toilette f:—adj Toiletten-.
toilet paper n Toilettenpapier n.
token n Zeichen n; Gutschein m.
Tokyo n Tokio n.
tolerable adj erträglich; leidlich.
tolerance n Toleranz f.
tolerant adj tolerant.
tolerate vt dulden; ertragen.
toll n Gebühr f:—vi läuten.
tomato n Tomate f.
tomb n Grab(mal) n.
tombstone n Grabstein m.
tomcat n Kater m.
tomorrow adv morgen.
ton n Tonne f.
tone n Ton m:—~ **down** vt mäßigen.
tongue n Zunge f.
tonight adv heute abend.
tonsil n Mandel f.
too adv auch.
tool n Werkzeug n.
tooth n Zahn m.
toothache n Zahnschmerzen mpl.
toothbrush n Zahnbürste f.
toothpaste n Zahnpasta f.
top n Spitze f; Gipfel m; Wipfel m; Kreisel m:—adj oberste(r, s).
topic n Thema n.
topical adj aktuell.
torch n Taschenlampe f.

torment n Qual f:—vt quälen.
tortoise n Schildkröte f.
torture n Folter f:—vt foltern.
toss vt schleudern.
total n Gesamtheit f:—adj Gesamt-, total.
totalitarian adj totalitär.
touch n Berührung f; Tastsinn m:—vt berühren; leicht anstoßen; rühren.
tough adj zäh; schwierig.
tour n Tour f.
tourism n Tourismus m.
tourist n Tourist(in) m(f).
tourist office n Verkehrsamt n.
tournament n Tournier n.
tow vt schleppen.
towards prep gegen; nach.
towel n Handtuch n.
tower n Turm m.
town n Stadt f.
town hall n Rathaus n.
toy n Spielzeug n.
trace n Spur f:—vt nachziehen, durchpausen, aufspüren.
track n Spur f, Weg m; Gleis n:—vt verfolgen.
tractor n Traktor m.
trade n Handel m, Gewerbe f:—vi handeln.
trade fair n Messe f.
trade mark n Warenzeichen n.
trader n Händler m.
tradesman n Händler m.
trade union n Gewerkschaft f.
tradition n Tradition f, Brauch m.
traditional adj traditionell.
traffic n Handel m, Verkehr m.
traffic lights npl Ampel f.
tragedy n Tragödie f.
tragic adj tragisch.
trail n Spur f; Pfad m, Weg m:—vt verfolgen; folgen +dat:—vi schleifen.
train n Zug m; Schleppe f; Folge f:—vt ausbilden; abrichten:—vi trainieren.

trainee n Lehrling m.
trainer n Trainer m; Ausbilder m.
traitor n Verräter m.
tramp n Landstreicher m:—vi stampfen.
tranquil adj ruhig, friedlich.
tranquillizer n Beruhigungsmittel n.
transfer n Übertragung f; Umzug m; Transfer m:—vt verlegen; versetzen; übertragen; überweisen.
transit n Durchgang m.
translate vt übersetzen.
translation n Übersetzung f.
translator n Übersetzer(in) m(f).
transmission n Übertragung f.
transmit vt übertragen.
transparent adj durchsichtig.
transport n Transport m:—vt transportieren.
trap n Falle f:—vt in einer Falle locken.
travel n Reisen n:—vi reisen.
travel agency n Reisebüro n.
traveller n Reisende(r) f(m).
tray n Tablett n.
treacherous adj verräterisch.
treachery n Verrat m.
tread n Schritt m, Tritt m:—vi treten.
treason n Verrat m.
treasure n Schatz m:—vt schätzen.
treat n besonderer Freude f:—vt behandeln; spendieren.
treatment n Behandlung f.
treaty n Vertrag m.
treble adj dreifach:—vt verdreifachen.
tree n Baum m.
tremble vi zittern; beben.
tremendous adj gewaltig, kolossal; prima.
tremor n Zittern n; Beben n.
trench n Graben m; (mil) Schützengraben m.
trend n Tendenz f.
trendy adj modisch.
trial n Prozeß m; Versuch m, Probe f.

triangle n Dreieck n; (mus) Triangel f.
triangular adj dreieckig.
tribal adj Stammes-.
tribe n Stamm m.
tribute n Zeichen n der Hochachtung.
trick n Trick m; Stich m:—vt überlisten, beschwindeln.
trigger n Drücker m.
trim adj gepflegt; schlank.
Trinity n Dreieinigkeit f.
trip n (kurze) Reise f; Ausflug m; Stolpern n:—vi trippeln; stolpern.
triple adj dreifach.
tripod n Stativ n.
triumph n Triumph m:—vi triumphieren.
triumphant adj triumphierend.
trolley n Handwagen m.
trombone n Posaune f.
trophy n Trophäe f.
tropical adj tropisch.
trot n Trott m:—vi trotten.
trouble n Ärger m; Sorge f; Mühe f; Unruhen pl:—vt stören.
trough n Trog m; Rinne f, Kanal m.
trousers npl Hose f.
trout n Forelle f.
truck n Lastwagen m; offener Güterwagen m.
true adj wahr; echt; treu.
truffle n Trüffel f/m.
trump n Trumpf m.
trumpet n Trompete f.
trunk n Stamm m; Rumpf m; Truhe f; Rüssel m.
trust n Vertrauen n; Treuhandvermögen n:—vt vertrauen.
trustworthy adj vertrauenswürdig.
truth n Wahrheit f.
truthful adj ehrlich.
try n Versuch m:—vt versuchen; probieren.
T-shirt n T-Shirt n.
tub n Wanne f.

tube *n* Röhre *f*, Rohr *n*; Tube *f*.
Tuesday *n* Dienstag *m*.
tug *n* Schleppendampfer *m*:—*vt vi* schleppen.
tuition *n* Unterricht *m*.
tulip *n* Tulpe *f*.
tumble *n* Sturz *m*:—*vi* fallen, stürzen.
tummy *n* Bauch *m*.
tuna *n* Thunfisch *m*.
tune *n* Melodie *f*:—*vt* (*mus*) stimmen.
tunnel *n* Tunnel *m*.
Turk *n* Türke *m*, Türkin *f*.
Turkey *n* Türkei *f*.
turkey *n* Puter *m*, Truthahn *m*.
Turkish *adj* türkisch:—*n* Türkisch *n*.
turmoil *n* Aufruhr *m*; Tumult *m*.
turn *n* Umdrehung *f*; Nummer *f*; Schock *m*:—*vi* drehen; umdrehen, wenden; umblättern.
turnip *n* Steckrübe *f*.

turnover *n* Umsatz *m*.
turntable *n* Plattenteller *m*.
turtle *n* Schildkröte *f*.
tusk *n* Stoßzahn *m*.
tutor *n* Privatlehrer *m*; Tutor *m*.
twelfth *adj* zwölfte(r, s).
twelve *num* zwölf.
twentieth *adj* zwanzigste(r, s).
twenty *num* zwanzig.
twice *adv* zweimal.
twin *n* Zwilling *m*.
twist *n* Drehung *f*:—*vt* drehen; verdrehen:—*vi* sich drehen.
two *num* zwei.
type *n* Typ *m*; Art *f*; Type *f*:—*vt vi* machineschreiben, tippen.
typewriter *n* Schreibmaschine *f*.
typical *adj* typisch.
typist *n* Maschinenschreiber(in) *m(f)*.
tyre *n* Reifen *m*.

U

ugly *adj* häßlich; böse, schlimm.
ulcer *n* Geschwür *n*.
ultimate *adj* äußerste(r, s), endgültig.
umbrella *n* Schirm *m*.
umpire *n* Schiedsrichter *m*.
umpteenth *num* zig:—**for the ~ time** zum X-ten Mal.
unanimous *adj* einmütig; einstimmig.
unauthorized *adj* unbefugt.
unavoidable *adj* unvermeidlich.
unbearable *adj* unerträglich.
unbelievable *adj* unglaublich.
uncanny *adj* unheimlich.
uncertain *adj* unsicher; ungewiß.
uncertainty *n* Ungewißheit *f*.
uncivilized *adj* unzivilisiert.
uncle *n* Onkel m.

uncomfortable *adj* unbequem, ungemütlich.
uncommon *adj* ungewöhnlich.
uncompromising *adj* kompromißlos, unnachgiebig.
unconditional *adj* bedingungslos.
unconscious *adj* bewußtlos; unbeabsichtigt.
unconventional *adj* unkonventionell.
uncover *vt* aufdecken.
under *prep* under:—*adv* darunter.
underestimate *vt* unterschätzen.
undergo *vt* durch machen; sich unterziehen + *dat*.
underground *adj* Untergrund-.
underline *vt* unterstreichen; betonen.
undermine *vt* untergraben.

underneath *adv* darunter:—*prep* unter.

undershirt *n* Unterhemd *n*.

understand *vt vi* verstehen.

understandable *adj* verständlich.

understanding *n* Verständnis *n*:—*adj* verständnisvoll.

understatement *n* Untertreibung *f*.

undertake *vt* unternehmen:—*vi* ~ **to do sth** sich verpflichten, etw zu tun.

undertaking *n* Unternehmen *n*; Verpflichtung *f*.

underwater *adj* Unterwasser-:—*adv* unter Wasser.

underwear *n* Unterwäsche *f*.

underworld *n* Unterwelt *f*.

underwriter *n* Assekurant *m*.

undo *vt* öffnen, aufmachen.

undress *vt* ausziehen:—*vi* sich ausziehen.

unemployed *adj* arbeitslos.

unemployment *n* Arbeitslosigkeit *f*.

uneven *adj* uneben; ungleichmäßig.

unexpected *adj* unerwartet.

unfair *adj* ungerecht, unfair.

unfaithful *adj* untreu.

unfashionable *adj* nicht in Mode.

unfasten *vt* öffnen, aufmachen.

unfavourable *adj* ungünstig.

unfinished *adj* unvollendet.

unfit *adj* ungeeignet; nicht fit.

unfold *vt* entfalten; auseinanderfalten:—*vi* sich entfalten.

unforgettable *adj* unvergeßlich.

unfortunate *adj* unglücklich, bedauerlich.

unfortunately *adv* leider.

unfriendly *adj* unfreundlich.

ungrateful *adj* undankbar.

unhappy *adj* unglücklich.

uniform *n* Uniform *f*:—*adj* einheitlich.

unify *vt* vereinigen.

unintentional *adj* unabsichtlich.

union *n* Vereinigung *f*; Bund *m*, Union *f*; Gewerkschaft *f*.

unique *adj* einzig(artig).

unit *n* Einheit *f*.

unite *vt* vereinigen:—*vi* sich vereinigen.

United Kingdom *n* Vereinigtes Königreich *n*.

United Nations (Organization) *n* Vereinte Nationen *fpl*.

United States (of America) *npl* Vereinigte Staaten *mpl* (von Amerika).

unity *n* Einheit *f*; Einigkeit *f*.

universal *adj* allgemein.

universe *n* Weltall *n*.

university *n* Universität *f*.

unknown *adj* unbekannt.

unless *conj* es sei denn.

unlike *adj* verschieden.

unlikely *adj* unwahrscheinlich.

unlimited *adj* unbegrenzt, unbeschränkt.

unload *vt* entladen.

unlock *vt* aufschließen.

unlucky *adj* unglücklich, unglückbringend.

unmarried *adj* unverheiratet.

unnatural *adj* unnatürlich.

unnecessary *adj* unnötig.

unpack *vt* auspacken.

unpleasant *adj* unangenehm.

unpredictable *adj* unvorhersehbar; unberechenbar.

unreal *adj* unwirklich.

unrealistic *adj* unrealistisch.

unreasonable *adj* unvernünftig; übertrieben.

unrelated *adj* ohne Beziehung; nicht verwandt.

unreliable *adj* unzuverlässig.

unrest *n* Unruhe *f*; Unruhen *fpl*.

unsafe *adj* nicht sicher.

unsavoury *adj* widerwärtig.

unscrew *vt* aufschrauben.

unskilled *adj* ungelernt.

unstable *adj* instabil.

unsteady *adj* unsicher; unregelmäßig.

unsuccessful *adj* erfolglos.
unsuitable *adj* unpassend.
unsure *adj* unsicher.
untidy *adj* unordentlich.
untie *vt* aufschnüren.
until *prep conj* bis:—~ **now** bis jetzt.
unusual *adj* ungewöhnlich.
unwind *vt* abwickeln:—*vi* sich entspannen.
unwise *adj* unklug.
up *adv* oben.
update *vt* auf den neuesten Stand bringen.
upheaval *n* Umbruch *m*.
uphill *adj* ansteigend; mühsam:—*adv* bergauf.
uphold *vt* unterstützen.
upholstery *n* Polster *n*; Polsterung *f*.
upkeep *n* Instandhaltung *f*.
upon *prep* auf.
upper-class *adj* vornehm.
upright *adj* aufrecht.
uprising *n* Aufstand *m*.

uproar *n* Aufruhr *m*.
uproot *vt* ausreißen.
upstairs *adv* (nach) oben.
upwards *adv* aufwärts.
urban *adj* städtisch, Stadt-.
urge *n* Drang *m*:—*vt* ~ **somebody to do something** jdn (dazu) drängen, etw zu tun.
urgency *n* Dringlichkeit *f*.
urgent *adj* dringend.
us *pn* uns.
usage *n* Gebrauch *m*.
use *n* Gebrauch *m*; Zweck *m*:—*vt* gebrauchen.
used *adj* Gebrauch-.
useful *adj* nützlich.
useless *adj* nützlos, unnütz.
user *n* Benutzer *m*.
usual *adj* gewöhnlich, üblich:—**as** ~ wie üblich.
usually *adv* gewöhnlich.
utter *vt* äußern, aussprechen.
utterance *n* Äußerung *f*.

V

vacancy *n* offene Stelle *f*; freies Zimmer.
vacant *adj* leer, frei.
vacate *vt* aufgeben, räumen.
vaccinate *vt* impfen.
vaccination *n* Schutzimpfung *f*.
vaccine *n* Impfstoff *m*.
vacuum *n* Vakuum *n*.
vagina *n* Scheide *f*.
vague *adj* vag(e), unklar.
vain *adj* vergeblich, eitel.
valid *adj* gültig.
valley *n* Tal *n*.
valuable *adj* wertvoll.
valuation *n* Bewertung *f*.

value *n* Wert *m*:—*vt* schätzen.
value-added tax Mehrwertsteuer *f*.
valve *n* Ventil *n*; Hahn *m*; Klappe *f*.
van *n* Lieferwagen *m*.
vanish *vi* verschwinden.
vanity *n* Eitelkeit *f*.
vapour *n* Dampf *m*.
variable *adj* veränderlich, wechselhaft.
variation *n* Schwankung *f*.
varied *adj* verschiedenartig.
variety *n* Abwechslung *f*.
various *adj* verschieden.
varnish *n* Lack *m*:—*vt* lackieren.
vary *vt* abändern; *vi* schwanken.

vase *n* Vase *f*.

vast *adj* riesig.

vat *n* Bottich *f*, Faß *n*.

veal *n* Kalbfleisch *n*.

vegetable *n* Gemüse *n*.

vegetarian *adj* vegetarisch:—*n* Vegetarier(in) *m(f)*.

vehicle *n* Fahrzeug *n*.

veil *n* Schleier *m*.

vein *n* Vene *f*.

velvet *n* Samt *m*.

vendor *n* Verkäufer *m*.

ventilation *n* Lüftung *f*.

verb *n* Verb *n*.

verbal *adj* verbal, mündlich, wörtlich.

verdict *n* Urteil *n*.

verify *vt* überprüfen.

versatile *adj* vielseitig.

verse *n* Strophe *f*; Vers *m*.

version *n* Fassung *f*.

versus *prep* gegen.

vertical *adj* senkrecht, vertikal.

vertigo *n* Schwindel *m*.

very *adv* sehr.

vest *n* Unterhemd *n*.

vet *n* Tierarzt *m*.

veterinary *adj* tierärztlich.

veto *n* Veto *n*:—*vt* verbieten; durch ein Veto zurückweisen.

via *prep* über.

viable *adj* lebensfähig; durchführbar.

vibrate *vi* vibrieren, schwingen, beben.

vibration *n* Vibration *f*, Schwingung *f*.

vicar *n* Pfarrer *m*.

vicarage Pfarrhaus *n*.

vice *n* Laster *n*; Schraubstock *m*.

vice versa *adv* umgekehrt.

vicinity *n* Nähe *f*.

vicious *adj* bösartig, gemein.

victim *n* Opfer *n*.

victor *n* Sieger *m*.

victorious *adj* siegreich.

victory *n* Sieg *m*.

video recorder *n* Videorecorder *m*.

vie *vi* wetteifern.

Vienna *n* Wien *n*.

view *n* Besichtigung *f*; Aussicht *f*; Ansicht *m*:—*vt* ansehen; betrachten.

vigil *n* Wache *f*.

vigilance *n* Wachsamkeit *f*.

vigilant *adj* wachsam.

vigorous *adj* energisch.

vigour *n* Energie *f*, Vitalität *f*.

villa *n* Villa *f*.

village *n* Dorf *n*.

vine *n* Weinstock *m*.

vinegar *n* Essig *m*.

vineyard *n* Weinberg *m*; Weingarten *m*.

vintage *n* Weinlese *f*.

viola *n* Bratsche *f*.

violate *vt* verletzen; übertreten.

violation *n* Verletzung *f*; Übertretung *f*.

violence *n* Gewalt *f*.

violent *adj* gewaltsam.

violet *n* (*bot*) Veilchen *n*.

violin *n* Violine *f*, Geige *f*.

violinist *n* Geiger *m*, Geigerin *f*.

violoncello *n* Cello *n*.

virgin *n* Jungfrau *f*:—*adj* jungfräulich.

virginity *n* Jungfräulichkeit *f*.

Virgo *n* (*astrol*) Jungfrau *f*.

virtual *adj* eigentlich, praktisch.

virtue *n* Tugend *f*.

virtuous *adj* tugendhaft.

virus *n* Virus *m*.

visa *n* Visum *n*.

viscous *adj* zähflüssig.

visibility *n* Sichtbarkeit *f*.

visible *adj* sichtbar.

vision *n* Sehkraft *f*; Vision *f*.

visit *vt* besuchen:—*n* Besuch *m*.

visitor *n* Besucher *m*, Gast *m*.

visual *adj* visuell.

vital *adj* lebenswichtig, vital.

vitality *n* Vitalität *f*.

vitamin *n* Vitamin *n*.

vivid *adj* hell, leuchtend.
vocabulary *n* Wortschatz *m*.
vocal *adj* Stimm-, Gesang-.
vocation *n* Berufung *f*; Begabung *f*; Beruf *m*.
vodka *n* Wodka *m*.
voice *n* Stimme *f*.
void *adj* leer:—*n* Leere *f*.
volatile *adj* flüchtig, überschäumend.
volcanic *adj* vulkanisch.
volcano *n* Vulkan *m*.
volt *n* Volt *n*.
voltage *n* Spannung *f*.
volume *n* Band *m*; Volumen *n*; Lautstärke *f*.

voluntary *adj* freiwillig.
volunteer *n* Freiwillige(r) *f(m)*.
vomit *vt* erbrechen; *vi* sich übergehen.
voracious *adj* gierig.
vote *n* Abstimmung *f*, Stimme *f*:—*vt vi* wählen.
voter *n* Wähler *m*.
voucher *n* Gutschein *m*.
vow *n* Gelübde *f*:—*vt* geloben.
vowel *n* Vokal *m*.
voyage *n* Seereise *f*.
vulgar *adj* vulgar, ordinär.
vulnerable *adj* verletzbar, anfällig.
vulture *n* Geier *m*.

W

wage *n* Lohn *m*.
wag(g)on *n* Fuhrwerk *n*; Wagen *m*; Waggon *m*.
waist *n* Taille *f*.
waistcoat *n* Weste *f*.
wait *n* Wartezeit *f*:—*vi* warten.
waiter *n* Kellner *m*.
waiting room *n* Wartezimmer *n*.
waitress *n* Kellnerin *f*.
waive *vt* verzichten auf.
wake *vt* wecken:—*vt* aufwachen:—*n* Totenwache *f*; Kienwasser *n*.
waken *vt* aufwecken.
Wales *n* Wales *n*.
walk *n* Spaziergang *m*; Gang *m*; Weg *m*:—*vi* gehen; spazierengehen; wandern.
wall *n* Wand *f*; Mauer *f*.
wallet *n* Brieftasche *f*.
wallflower *n* Goldlack *m*.
wallpaper *n* Tapete *f*.
walnut *n* Walnuß *f*.
walrus *n* Walroß *n*.

waltz *n* Walzer *m*:—*vi* Walzer tanzen.
wand *n* Zauberstab *m*.
wander *vi* (herum)wandern.
want *v aux vt* wollen.
war *n* Krieg *m*.
wardrobe *n* Kleiderschrank *m*.
warehouse *n* Lagerhaus *n*.
warm *adj* warm:—*vt vi* wärmen.
warmth *n* Wärme *f*.
warn *vt* warnen.
warning *n* Warnung *f*.
warrant *n* Haftbefehl *m*.
warranty *n* Garantie *f*.
warrior *n* Krieger *m*.
Warsaw *n* Warschau *n*.
wash *n* Wäsche *f*:—*vt vi* waschen.
wasp *n* Wespe *f*.
wastage *n* Verlust *m*.
waste *n* Verschwendung *f*; Abfall *m*: —*vt* verschwenden; vergeuden.
watch *n* Wache *f*; Uhr *f*:—*vt* ansehen; beobachten:—*vi* zusehen.

water n Wasser n.
watercolour n Aquarell n.
waterfall n Wasserfall m.
watermelon n Wassermelone f.
watertight adj wasserdicht.
watt n Watt n.
wave n Welle f; Winken n:—vi winken.
wavelength n Wellenlänge f.
wax n Wachs n.
way n Weg m; Art und Weise f; Richtung f.
we pn wir.
weak adj schwach.
weakness n Schwäche f.
wealth n Reichtum m.
wealthy adj reich.
weapon n Waffe f.
wear vt tragen; haben; abnutzen:—vi halten; (sich) verschleißen.
weasel n Wiesel n.
weather n Wetter n.
weave vt weben.
weaver n Weber(in) m(f).
web n Netz n; Schwimmhaut f.
wed vt heiraten.
wedding n Hochzeit f.
Wednesday n Mittwoch m.
weed n Unkraut f.
week n Woche f.
weekend n Wochenende n.
weekly adj wochentlich.
weep vi weinen.
weeping willow n Trauerweide f.
weigh vt vi wiegen.
weight n Gewicht n.
welcome n Willkommen n:—vt begrüßen.
weld vt schweißen.
welder n Schweißer(in) m(f).
well n Brünnen m; Quelle f.—adj gesund:—adv gut:—**as ~** auch.
well-known adj bekannt.
Welsh adj walisisch:—n Walisisch n.
Welshman n Waliser m.

Welshwoman n Waliserin f.
west n Westen m.
western adj westlich, West-.
wet adj naß.
whale n Wal m.
what adj welche(r, s); was für ein(e):—pn was:—excl wie, was.
whatever pn was (immer auch).
wheat n Weizen m.
wheel n Rad n.
wheelbarrow n Schubkarren m.
wheelchair n Rollstuhl m.
when adv wann:—conj wenn; als.
whenever adv wann (auch) immer; jedesmal wenn:—conj wenn.
where adv wo; wohin:—~ **from** woher.
wherever adv wo (immer).
whether conj ob.
which adj pn welche(r, s); wer; rel pn der, die, das; was.
while conj während.
whip n Peitsche f:—vt peitschen.
whipped cream n Schlagsahne f.
whirlwind n Wirbelwind m.
whiskers npl Barthaare pl.
whisky n Whisky m.
whisper n Flüstern n:—vt vi flüstern.
whistle n Pfeife f:—vt vi pfeifen.
white adj weiß.
whiting n Weißfisch m.
Whitsun n Pfingsten n.
who pn nom wer, acc wen, dat wem: — rel pn der/die/das.
whoever pn wer/wen/wem auch immer.
whole adj ganz:—n Ganze(s) n.
wholemeal adj Vollkorn-.
wholesale n Großhandel m:—adj Großhandels-.
whom pn acc wen, dat wem:—rel pn acc den/die/das, dat dem/der/dem.
whore n Hure f.
why adv conj warum, weshalb.
wicked adj böse.

wide adj breit; weit.
widen vt erweitern.
widespread adj weitverbreitet.
widow n Witwe f.
widowed adj verwitwet.
widower n Witwer m.
width n Breite f, Weite f.
wife n Frau f, Ehefrau f, Gattin f.
wig n Perücke f.
wild adj wild; heftig; verrückt.
wilderness n Wildnis f, Wüste f.
wildlife n Tierwelt f.
will v aux werden:—vt wollen:—Wille f, Testament n.
willing adj gewillt, bereit.
willow n Weide f.
willpower n Willenskraft f.
wilt vi welken.
win n Sieg m:—vt vi gewinnen.
wince n Zusammenzucken n:—vi zusammenzucken.
winch n Winde f.
wind n Wind m:—vt winden; wickeln:—vi sich winden:—~ up vt aufziehen.
windfall n unverhoffte(r) Glücksfall m.
windmill n Windmühle f.
window n Fenster n.
windpipe n Luftrohre f.
windscreen n Windschutzscheibe f.
wine n Wein m.
wing n Flügel m.
wink n Zwinkern n:—vi zwinkern, blinzeln.
winner n Gewinner m; Sieger m.
winter n Winter m.
wipe vt wischen.
wire n Draht m.
wisdom n Weisheit f.
wise adj weise.
wish n Wunsch m:—vt wünschen.
witch n Hexe f.
witchcraft n Hexerei f.
with prep mit.

withdraw vt zurückziehen; zurücknehmen:—vi sich zurückziehen.
withdrawal n Zurückziehung f; Zurücknahme f.
within prep innerhalb:—adv innen.
without prep ohne.
withstand vt aushalten, widerstehen.
witness n Zeuge m, Zeugin f:—vt beglaubigen.
witty adj witzig, geistreich.
wizard n Zauberer m.
wobble vi wackeln, schwanken.
woe n Leid n, Kummer m.
wolf n Wolf m:—**she** ~ Wölfin f.
woman n Frau f.
womb n Gebärmutter f.
wonder n Wunder m, Erstaunen n:—vi sich wundern.
wonderful adj wunderbar.
woo vt den Hof machen, umwerben.
wood n Wald m; Holz n.
wooded adj bewaldet.
wooden adj hölzern.
woodpecker n Specht m.
woodworm n Holzwurm m.
wool n Wolle f.
woollen adj Woll-.
word n Word n.
work n Arbeit f; Werk n:—vi arbeiten.
worker n Arbeiter(in) m(f).
world n Welt f.
worldwide adj weltweit.
worm n Wurm m.
worried adj besorgt, beunruhigt.
worry n Sorge f:—vt beunruhigen:—vi sich sorgen.
worrying adj beunruhigend.
worse adj schlechtere(r, s), schlimmere (r, s).
worship vt anbeten.
worst adj schlimmste(r, s), schlechteste(r, s).
worth n Wert m.

worthless *adj* wertlos.
wound *n* Wunde *f*:—*vt* verwunden.
wrap *vt* entwickeln.
wrath *n* Zorn *m*.
wreath *n* Kranz *m*.
wreck *n* Wrack *n*; Ruine *f*:—*vt* zerstören.
wren *n* Zaunkönig *m*.
wrestle *vi* ringen.
wrestler *n* Ringer(in) *m(f)*.
wretched *adj* elend; verflixt.
wrist *n* Handgelenk *n*.

writ *n* gerichtlicher Befehl *m*.
write *vt vi* schreiben.
writer *n* Schriftsteller *m*.
writing *n* Schreiben *n*; Schift *f*:—**in ~** schriftlich.
wrong *adj* falsch; unrecht:—*n* Unrecht *n*:—*vt* Unrecht tun.
wrongful *adj* unrechtmäßig.
wrongly *adv* falsch; zu Unrecht.
wry *adj* ironisch.

XYZ

Xmas *n* Weihnachten *fpl*.
X-ray *n* Röntgenstrahl *m*:—*vt* röntgen.
xylophone *n* Xylophon *n*.
yacht *n* Jacht *f*.
yachting *n* Segelsport *m*.
Yank, Yankee *n* Ami *m*.
yard *n* Hof *m*; Yard *n*.
yarn *n* Garn *n*.
yawn *vi* gähnen:—*n* Gähnen *n*.
year *n* Jahr *n*.
yearly *adj* jährlich.
yearn *vi* sehnen.
yeast *n* Hefe *f*.
yell *vt vi* schreien:—*n* Schrei *m*.
yellow *adj* gelb:—*n* Gelb *n*.
yes *adv* ja.
yesterday *adv* gestern:—**the day before ~** vorgestern.
yet *conj* dennoch:—*adv* noch.
yew *n* Eibe *f*.
yield *vt* liefern; abwerfen:—*vi* nachgeben:—*n* Ertrag *m*; Ernte *f*; Zinsertrag *m*.
yoga *n* Joga *n*.
yoghurt *n* Joghurt *m*.
yolk *n* Eidotter *n*, Eigelb *n*.

you *pn* Sie; du, ihr; dich, dir, euch; Ihnen.
young *adj* jung.
your *poss adj* Ihr; dein, euer.
yours *poss pn* Ihre(r, s); deine(r, s), eure(r, s).
youth *n* Jugend *f*.
youthful *adj* jugendlich.
yule *n* Weinachte.
zeal *n* Eifer *m*.
zealous *adj* eifrig.
zebra *n* Zebra *n*.
zenith *n* Zenit *m*; Höhepunkt *m*.
zero *n* Null *f*.
zest *n* Begeisterung *f*.
zigzag *n* Zickzack *m*.
zinc *n* Zink *n*.
zip, zipper *n* Reißverschluß *m*.
zither *n* Zither *f*.
zodiac *n* Tierkreis *m*.
zone *n* Zone *f*.
zoo *n* Zoo *m*.
zoological *adj* zoologisch.
zoologist *n* Zoologe *m*, Zoologin *f*.
zoology *n* Zoologie *f*.
zoom lens *n* Zoom(objektiv) *n*.